The Internet

THE MISSING MANUAL

*The book that
should have been
in the box*®

The Internet

THE MISSING MANUAL

David Pogue and J.D. Biersdorfer

POGUE PRESS™
O'REILLY®

Beijing • Cambridge • Farnham • Köln • Paris • Sebastopol • Taipei • Tokyo

The Internet: The Missing Manual

by David Pogue and J.D. Biersdorfer

Published by O'Reilly Media, Inc., 1005 Gravenstein Highway North, Sebastopol, CA 95472.

O'Reilly books may be purchased for educational, business, or sales promotional use. Online editions are also available for most titles (*safari.oreilly.com*). For more information, contact our corporate/institutional sales department: (800) 998-9938 or *corporate@oreilly.com*.

Printing History:

July 2006:   First Edition.

RepKover. This book uses RepKover,™ a durable and flexible lay-flat binding.

ISBN: 0-596-52742-X
[M]

Table of Contents

Part Four: Entertainment and Media

Part Five: Communicating with Others

The Missing Credits

About the Authors

David Pogue is the weekly computer columnist for the *New York Times*, an Emmy-winning correspondent for *CBS News Sunday Morning*, and the creator of the Missing Manual series. He's the author or co-author of 38 books, including 17 in this series and 6 in the "For Dummies" line (including Macs, Magic, Opera, and Classical Music). In his other life, David is a former Broadway show conductor, a magician, and a pianist. News, photos, and links to his columns and weekly videos await at *www.davidpogue.com*.

He welcomes feedback about his books by email at *david@pogueman.com*.

J.D. Biersdorfer has been writing the Q&A column for the Circuits section of the *New York Times* since 1998. She has covered everything from 17th-century Indian art to the world of female hackers for the newspaper, and has reviewed dozens of books for the *New York Times Book Review*. She has penned articles for the *AIGA Journal of Graphic Design* and *Rolling Stone,* and has contributed essays about the collision of art and technology to several graphic-design books published by Allworth Press. She studied Theater & Drama at Indiana University and now splits her time between New York City and Pennsylvania. She spends her spare moments playing the banjo and watching BBC World News. Email: *jd.biersdorfer@gmail.com*.

About the Creative Team

Nan Barber (editor) has worked with the Missing Manual series since its inception—long enough to remember booting up her computer from a floppy disk. Email: *nanbarber@oreilly.com*.

Peter Meyers (editor) works as an editor at O'Reilly Media on the Missing Manual series. He lives with his wife in New York City. Email: *peter.meyers@gmail.com*.

Dawn Mann (copy editor) has been with O'Reilly for over three years and is currently an editorial assistant. When not working, she likes rock climbing, playing soccer, and generally getting into trouble. Email: *dawn@oreilly.com*.

Adam Goldstein (technical reviewer) is the teenage founder of GoldfishSoft, a software company specializing in cool programs for Mac OS X. He has worked on several books in the Missing Manual series, including titles on AppleScript (as author) and switching to the Mac (as co-author). In his spare time, Adam attends MIT. Email: *mail@goldfishsoft.com*. Web: *www.goldfishsoft.com*.

Rose Cassano (cover illustration) has worked as an independent designer and illustrator for 20 years. Assignments have ranged from the nonprofit sector to corporate clientele. She lives in beautiful Southern Oregon, grateful for the miracles of modern technology that make working there a reality. Email: *cassano@highstream.net*. Web: *www.rosecassano.com*.

The Missing Manual Series

Missing Manuals are witty, superbly written guides to computer products that don't come with printed manuals (which is just about all of them). Each book features a handcrafted index and RepKover, a detached-spine binding that lets the book lie perfectly flat without the assistance of weights or cinder blocks.

Recent and upcoming titles include:

Access for Starters: The Missing Manual by Kate Chase and Scott Palmer

AppleScript: The Missing Manual by Adam Goldstein

AppleWorks 6: The Missing Manual by Jim Elferdink and David Reynolds

CSS: The Missing Manual by David Sawyer McFarland

Creating Web Sites: The Missing Manual by Matthew MacDonald

Digital Photography: The Missing Manual by Chris Grover and Barbara Brundage

Dreamweaver 8: The Missing Manual by David Sawyer McFarland

eBay: The Missing Manual by Nancy Conner

Excel: The Missing Manual by Matthew MacDonald

Excel for Starters: The Missing Manual by Matthew MacDonald

FileMaker Pro 8: The Missing Manual by Geoff Coffey and Susan Prosser

Flash 8: The Missing Manual by Emily Moore

FrontPage 2003: The Missing Manual by Jessica Mantaro

GarageBand 2: The Missing Manual by David Pogue

Google: The Missing Manual, Second Edition by Sarah Milstein, J.D. Biersdorfer, and Matthew MacDonald

Home Networking: The Missing Manual by Scott Lowe

iLife '05: The Missing Manual by David Pogue

iMovie 6 & iDVD: The Missing Manual by David Pogue

iPhoto 6: The Missing Manual by David Pogue

iPod & iTunes: The Missing Manual, Fourth Edition by J.D. Biersdorfer

iWork '05: The Missing Manual by Jim Elferdink

Mac OS X Power Hound, Panther Edition by Rob Griffiths

Mac OS X: The Missing Manual, Tiger Edition by David Pogue

Office 2004 for Macintosh: The Missing Manual by Mark H. Walker and Franklin Tessler

PCs: The Missing Manual by Andy Rathbone

Photoshop Elements 4: The Missing Manual by Barbara Brundage

QuickBooks 2006: The Missing Manual by Bonnie Biafore

Quicken for Starters: The Missing Manual by Bonnie Biafore

Switching to the Mac: The Missing Manual, Tiger Edition by David Pogue and Adam Goldstein

Windows 2000 Pro: The Missing Manual by Sharon Crawford

Windows XP Power Hound by Preston Gralla

Windows XP for Starters: The Missing Manual by David Pogue

Windows XP Home Edition: The Missing Manual, Second Edition by David Pogue

Windows XP Pro: The Missing Manual, Second Edition by David Pogue, Craig Zacker, and Linda Zacker

Introduction

You think *you* feel overwhelmed by the march of technology? Then how'd you like to be the lady who, one day in the mid-90s, entered a computer store, handed the salesman a blank floppy disk, and asked him if she could please have a copy of the Internet?

The funny thing is, in the mid-90s, you practically *could* fit the Internet on a floppy. It was a novelty then, a toy for computer scientists and power nerds. People didn't have Web addresses on their business cards, didn't buy stuff electronically, didn't have PTA meetings about keeping their kids safe online.

Nowadays, the Internet is a different story.

Physically, the Internet is a *very* long series of wires (with wireless gaps here and there) that eventually connects everyone's computer to everyone else's.

Culturally, though, it's as important a communications system as the telephone—maybe more important. It's a critical piece of every business's business. It gives a global voice to anyone with something to say—for free. It's changing the way we use and do just about everything: relationships, politics, religion, war, radio, TV and movies, news, communications…. In fact, it might be easier to make a list of things that *haven't* been changed by the Internet.

Unfortunately, the Internet is also a playground for the latest generation of electronic pickpockets, scam artists, and hate-mongers.

And the Internet isn't finished growing up, either. Every year there are new developments.

For example, in 2004, you might have said that the two most important Internet technologies were email and the World Wide Web. Today, you'd have to mention stuff like RSS newsfeeds, free phone calls, podcasts, and blogs. (If any of these terms are unfamiliar, well, you're reading the right book.)

About This Book

The thing about the Internet, though, is that nobody runs it. Oh, certain government and university bodies are there to fine-tune the technical protocols, but nobody owns the Internet; nobody's in charge. There's no 800 number to call for help. (Can't you just see it? "Thank you for calling The Internet. Please hold; your call is very important to us.")

And goodness knows there's no user manual for it.

So how are you supposed to figure out how to get online? And how are you supposed to know what to do once you're there?

The answers Internet veterans give you aren't very reassuring. "Oh, you'll figure it out," they say. "Just keep clicking around till you find the good stuff."

But your time is too important for that. And so, ladies and gentlemen, here it is, right in your hands: a user's guide to the Internet.

This book is designed to answer all of the critical questions you might have about the Net, including:

- **How do I get on the Internet?** (Hint: *Not* by taking a blank disk to the computer store.)

  All kinds of gadgets can connect to the Internet these days: cellphones, settop TV boxes, pocket music players, and so on. But what *most* people connect to the Internet is a *computer,* and that's what this book is all about. In Chapter 1, you can find out about the three most attractive ways to connect your Macintosh or Windows PC to the Internet—and how to do it yourself.

- **What do I do once I'm online?** The Internet isn't any one product or service; remember, it's just a network of connections between computers. Specialized software programs can communicate over this digital pipeline in all kinds of interesting ways. This book covers them all.

For example, you've probably heard of email—the electronic version of postal mail. The World Wide Web is also deservedly famous (billions upon billions of "pages" displaying text and pictures that serve as ads, brochures, discussion groups, information flyers, and so on). But some of the up-and-coming technologies are even more intriguing. Young people use *chat* programs daily—like a typed version of CB radio—to carry on conversations, send pictures and music back and forth, and so on.

Other specialized programs let you make free "phone calls" across the Internet, computer to computer, using a microphone and speakers—and if you have a fast Internet connection, you can make *video* calls with these programs. Then there are *blogs* (Web logs, or daily opinion journals) to read. And podcasts (amateur radio and TV shows) to listen to or watch. All of this, by the way, is free.

• **What's out there?** Any 10-year-old next-door neighbor can get your computer hooked up to the Internet. But the meat of this book—its real value—is its tour of the Web. This is the information it takes *years* to pick up on your own—years of trial and error, painful experience, and barking up wrong trees.

Here, in one tidy atlas of the Web, is a summary of the very best ways to find stuff on the Web; do research; shop; manage stocks and finances; make travel reservations; play games and place bets; find and buy music, movies, and TV; post digital photos (or look at other people's); find love on the world's biggest personal-ad matchmaking services; and much more.

• **How do I get represented?** For years, the Internet generally worked like a big newspaper or TV station. The people who knew what they were doing *created* the stuff online; the rest of us peons just *looked* at it.

That's all changing. Why shouldn't *you* create a Web site, blog, or podcast, just like the ones created by the big boys? Or, rather, *not* like theirs—but better, funnier, more personal? This book show you how to use the new generation of incredibly easy-to-use software designed for just these reasons.

• **How do I avoid the nasty stuff?** The Internet isn't just an amazing channel for ordinary, law-abiding citizens. It's also the best thing to happen to scam artists since the invention of innocence.

Spammers fill your email inbox with junk mail, some of it fraudulent. Virus writers, driven by a rotten soul and a perverse desire to get noticed by the world, write software that's deliberately designed to gum up the works of your PC. Spyware authors disguise their evil programs to trick you into downloading them. Phishing scammers try to make you believe that your bank, eBay, PayPal, or some other important institution needs you to re-input your account information—and direct you to what turns out to be a phony Web site that sends this information right back to the scammer. Here and there, you even hear about pedophiles who hang out in your kids' chat rooms and try to lure them into personal meetings.

All of this unpleasantness saps the Internet of a lot of its joy. Still, just being aware of the tricks that the baddies might try to play on you is the most important step in avoiding them; at this point, you can still outsmart most of these traps just by not stepping into them.

Chapter 21 is dedicated to what you need to do to stay safe. And throughout the book you'll find tips and advice on how to keep your guard up. The ground rules are: (a) If it seems to good to be true, it probably is. (b) Don't open file attachments sent to you by email from people you don't know. (c) Don't ever respond to a special offer sent to you by email. (d) Banks, eBay, and similar outfits will never email you to ask for your account information.

The Internet: The Missing Manual is designed to accommodate readers at every technical level. If you're just getting into this whole Internet thing, great; you'll find that the introductory material at the beginning of each discussion will help you along from square one.

But even if you're already online and comfortable with the Net, you'll find useful tips and tricks, not to mention a world of wisdom in the capsule summaries of the Internet's most useful Web sites.

The primary discussions are written for advanced-beginner or intermediate computer users. But if you're a first-timer, miniature sidebar articles called "Up to Speed" provide the introductory information you need to understand the topic at hand. If you're more advanced, on the other hand, keep your eye out for similar shaded boxes titled "Power Users' Clinic." They offer more technical tips, tricks, and shortcuts for the experienced Internet fan.

About → These → Arrows

Throughout this book, and throughout the Missing Manual series, you'll find sentences like this one: "Open the System folder → Libraries → Fonts folder." That's shorthand for a much longer instruction that directs you to open three nested folders in sequence, like this: "On your hard drive, you'll find a folder called System. Open that. Inside the System folder window is a folder called Libraries; double-click it to open it. Inside *that* folder is yet another one called Fonts. Double-click to open it, too."

Similarly, this kind of arrow shorthand helps to simplify the business of choosing commands in menus, as shown in Figure I-1.

Figure I-1:
In this book, arrow notations help to simplify folder and menu instructions. For example, "Choose Start → All Programs → Accessories → Notepad" is a more compact way of saying, "Click the Start button. When the Start menu opens, click All Programs; without clicking, now slide to the right onto the Accessories submenu; in that submenu, click Notepad," as shown here.

About MissingManuals.com

To get the most out of this book, visit *www.missingmanuals.com*. Click the "Missing CD-ROM" link to reveal a neat, organized, chapter-by-chapter list of the shareware and freeware mentioned in this book.

The Web site also offers corrections and updates to the book (to see them, click the book's title, then click "View/Submit Errata"). In fact, you're invited and encouraged to submit such corrections and updates yourself. In an effort to keep the book as up-to-date and accurate as possible, each time we print more copies of this book, we'll make any confirmed corrections you've suggested. We'll also note such changes on the Web site, so that you can mark important corrections into your own copy of the book, if you like.

In the meantime, we'd love to hear your suggestions for new books in the Missing Manual line. There's a place for that on the Web site, too, as well as a place to sign up for free email notification of new titles in the series.

MEA CULPA

The Fine Print

In a certain way, attempting to write a user's guide for the Internet is a futile gesture. The printed page doesn't change—but the Internet itself changes, in thousands of ways, *every second of every day*.

The information in this book was up-to-date the day the ink hit the paper. But Web sites go in and out of business more often than New York City restaurants. Policies change. Business models and pricing offers change.

This is all a polite way of saying, "Hey—we did our best." If you discover that one of this book's write-ups has become obsolete or dated, please let us know. Visit *www.missingmanuals.com*, click this book's title, and then click the "View/Submit Errata" link.

If you take the trouble to send us the nature of the update, we'll make sure the rest of the world knows about it (on the same Errata page). And we'll also be able to update the prose for the next printing.

Thanks in advance!

The Very Basics

To use this book, and indeed to use a computer, you need to know some basics. This book assumes that you're familiar with a few terms and concepts:

- **Clicking.** This book gives you three kinds of instructions that require you to use the mouse that's attached to your computer. To *click* means to point the arrow cursor at something on the screen and then—without moving the cursor at all—press and release the clicker button on the mouse (or your laptop trackpad). If your mouse or trackpad has two buttons, the "clicker button" is the *left* button.

  To *double-click,* of course, means to click twice in rapid succession, again without moving the cursor at all. And to *drag* means to move the cursor while holding down the button.

  When you're told to *Ctrl+click* something, you click while pressing the Ctrl key (on the bottom row of the keyboard). Such related procedures as *Shift+clicking* and *Alt+clicking* work the same way—just click while pressing the corresponding key at the bottom of your keyboard.

- **Shortcut menus.** One of the most important features of Windows and Mac OS X isn't on the screen—it's under your hand. As noted above, you use the left mouse button to click buttons, highlight text, and drag things around on the screen.

When you click the right button, however, a *shortcut menu* appears onscreen, like the ones shown in Figure I-2. (On a Macintosh with only one mouse or trackpad button, you "right-click" something by holding down the Control key as you click.)

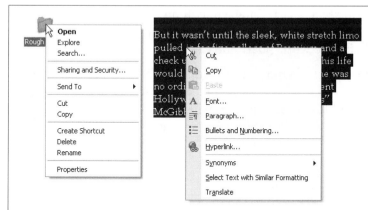

Figure I-2:
Shortcut menus (sometimes called contextual menus) often list commands that aren't in the menus at the top of the window. Here, for example, are the commands that appear when you right-click a folder (left) and some highlighted text in a word processor (right). Once the shortcut menu has appeared, left-click the command you want.

Get into the habit of right-clicking things on the Internet—email messages, Web-page photos, text in an article, and so on. The commands that appear on the shortcut menu will make you much more productive and lead you to discover handy functions you never knew existed.

- **Menus.** The *menus* are the words at the top of your window or screen: File, Edit, and so on. Click one to make a list of commands appear, as though they're written on a window shade you've just pulled down.

- **Keyboard shortcuts.** If you're typing along in a burst of creative energy, it's sometimes disruptive to have to take your hand off the keyboard, grab the mouse, and then use a menu (for example, to use the Bold command). That's why many experienced computer fans prefer to trigger menu commands by pressing certain combinations on the keyboard. For example, in most word processors, you can press Ctrl+B to produce a **boldface** word (on the Macintosh, it's ⌘-B). When you read an instruction like "press Ctrl+B," start by pressing the Ctrl key, then, while it's down, type the letter B, and finally release both keys.

- **Icons.** The colorful inch-tall pictures that appear in your various desktop folders are the graphic symbols that represent each program, disk, and document on your computer. If you click an icon one time, it darkens; you've just *highlighted* or *selected* it, in readiness to manipulate it by using, for example, a menu command.

If you've mastered this much information, you have all the technical background you need to enjoy *The Internet: The Missing Manual*.

Safari® Enabled

 When you see a Safari® Enabled icon on the cover of your favorite technology book, that means the book is available online through the O'Reilly Network Safari Bookshelf.

Safari offers a solution that's better than e-books. It's a virtual library that lets you easily search thousands of top tech books, cut and paste code samples, download chapters, and find quick answers when you need the most accurate, current information. Try it for free at *http://safari.oreilly.com*.

Part One:
Getting Online

1

Getting Online

The Internet, as you may have heard, is a parallel universe. It's a travel agency, bank teller, music store, video player, radio station, and newspaper wire service, not to mention a bulletin board, chat room, post office, and global chess tournament. Or at least the Internet can be all that stuff if you can *connect* to it. That can be the tricky part.

The basic components you need for Internet fun include:

- **Internet service.** Lots of stuff on the Internet's free, but getting *to* the Internet usually isn't. In fact, you have to sign up for an account with somebody—your cable TV company, phone company, or an outfit like America Online—to get your computer connected.

- **Equipment.** Your computer may already have what it takes to get you online: a modem (if you want to get online via phone lines), an Ethernet jack (to connect by network wire), or a wireless card (to connect wirelessly). Details in a moment.

- **Internet software.** If you're going to send email and browse the World Wide Web, you need special programs to do so. Luckily, your computer came with these programs already on the hard drive.

This chapter explains each of these elements in more detail.

This chapter also describes each of the three primary methods people use to get their computers connected to the Internet these days, in this order:

- **Broadband connections.** These are high-speed, extremely satisfying connections that are growing in popularity—but they're fairly expensive.

- **Dial-up connections.** Your computer can also connect to the Internet by dialing out over ordinary phone lines. It's slow, but cheap.

- **Wireless connections.** Pure heaven. Might even be free, if you're in the right place.

UP TO SPEED

The Most Essential Piece of Gear

You'll need some equipment to get to the Internet, of course; you've probably heard of *modems, cable modems,* and *DSL.*

But before you can even consider getting yourself that sort or gear, you need a *computer.*

Computers are a lot cheaper than they used to be; you can buy a new laptop these days for around $500. In general, the newer the computer, the easier it's probably going to be to get it connected to the Internet. That's because fresh new operating systems like Windows XP and Mac OS X have built-in helper software designed to quickly guide your computer online.

But what if you already have a perfectly good four- or five-year-old model that works just fine for word processing or playing solitaire?

Truth is, an old Mac or PC may not let you see all that the Web has to offer.

That's because Apple and Microsoft stop updating their software when they move on to newer versions. So Web browsers—and the software that lets them display video, animations, and other visual goodies—may be out-of-date and incapable of showing you everything that's online.

If you have an older computer that has enough memory and hard drive space to meet the system requirements of Windows XP or Mac OS X, though, you can upgrade the old box with a new system and still see the best of the Web without buying a whole new machine.

Broadband Connections (Fast)

A *broadband connection* delivers songs, videos, and digital photos to your computer in minutes instead of hours. We're talking at least *20 times* faster than a dial-up modem. Complex Web pages that take almost a minute to appear in your browser with a standard modem will pop up almost immediately with a cable modem or DSL.

And that's not the only reason about half of all Internetters have signed up for broadband service. Here are some of the other perks:

- **No dialing.** These connection methods hook you up to the Internet permanently, full time, so that you don't waste time connecting or disconnecting—ever. You're *always* online. There's no 40-second wait while your modem screeches and dials.

- **No weekends lost to setup.** You can set up the equipment yourself to save a few bucks. But most people take the easy road: they allow a representative from the phone company or cable company to come to their home or office to install the modem and configure the Mac or PC to use it.

- **Possible savings.** Cable modems and DSL services cost $30 to $40 a month. If you, a dial-up customer, have been paying for two phone lines just so you can talk and be online at the same time, you'll actually save money with broadband because you can cancel the second phone line.

Broadband connections usually come in the form of a *cable modem* or *DSL box* (digital subscriber line). (In some remote areas, you can also get broadband *satellite* service. But this method is slow, expensive, and rare in residential areas.)

As the name suggests, a cable modem (Figure 1-1) uses your cable-TV company's network of wires to pipe data into your house, right alongside Comedy Central and HBO. DSL, on the other hand, uses your existing *telephone* lines to carry its signal. You usually sign up for DSL service through your phone company.

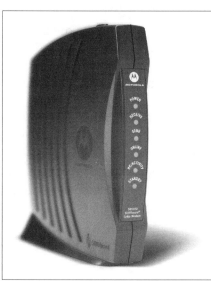

Figure 1-1:
External broadband modems, like this Motorola model for cable Internet service, connect to the back of the computer with an Ethernet or USB cord. Most modems also need their own power supply, so pick a spot within reach of an electrical outlet. Some broadband modems can even connect to your computer wirelessly, but ask your Internet provider about the system requirements.

Note: Cable modems are often slightly more expensive—and slightly faster—than DSL.

Broadband connections generally require a computer with an *Ethernet jack*. It looks like a telephone jack, but slightly fatter. This jack's an indication that your computer contains a *network card,* used for creating a wired connection to a home network, office network, cable modem, or DSL box. Most computers sold since about 2001 have such a jack.

Tip: Your computer may even have *both* a modem jack (described later in this chapter) *and* an Ethernet jack. The two jacks look very similar and accept the same sort of plastic plug on the end of the connecting cord, but the network jack is slightly wider. Using a flashlight, magnifying glass, and small child—if necessary—look for tiny identifying icons on each jack; a tiny telephone handset icon denotes the modem jack.

If your computer doesn't have a network card, you can add one, as an internal card that you install inside; a metal, credit card-size card that fits into a laptop card slot; or an external box that dangles from the computer's USB connector.

The Broadband Setup

If you've ordered cable-modem or DSL service, a technician may come to your house to do all the necessary wiring and configuration for you. All you have to do is be home to let the technician in.

In some cases, however—especially if you already have cable TV or phone service—you may be offered a self-installation kit. As thanks for doing the cable person's job, a tasty discount is usually part of this arrangement.

If you opt for the self-installation route, your kit probably contains the modem itself, a software CD, an Ethernet or USB cable to connect to your computer, a splitter box (Figure 1-2, top) to divide your incoming cable line into two, and paperwork containing account names, numbers, and passwords.

Note: If you've opted for a DSL box, your kit may also include several plastic DSL filters. You're supposed to attach them to all your active phone lines *except* the one the computer's using. (DSL works by maximizing the amount of data that your regular old copper phone wires can carry, but doing so makes the line noisier than a teenage girls' slumber party. The filters you attach to your telephone, fax machine, or other working phone lines screen out the data noise and let you use the phone to order pizza, even as you're downloading a big video file from the Web.)

To your
cable modem   To your TV

To the cable
port in the wall

To the phone
jack in the wall

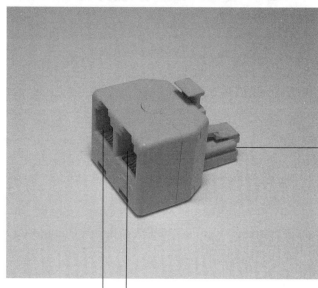

To your PC's
modem   To your telephone

Figure 1-2:
One-eyed jacks are fine for cards, but splitters like these convert one cable or telephone connection into two so you can share your cable or phone line with your computer. You can buy either of these for a few dollars at places like Radio Shack or computer stores.

Top: Screw the coaxial cable from the wall into the single end of this connector. Then screw a cable to each of the two other connectors; one goes back into the TV or cable box and the other goes into your cable modem.

Bottom: Snap this splitter into a phone jack in the wall. Plug in your dial-up modem line or DSL cable into one open jack. If you have DSL, plug in a DSL filter to the other jack, and then plug your phone into the end of the filter.

The company's setup instructions will probably direct you to unscrew the round coaxial cable that runs from the wall to the back of the cable box and attach the splitter. Then you use the additional cable provided to connect one side of the splitter to the cable box, and the other side to the back of the cable modem. Use the Ethernet or USB cable to connect the cable modem to the computer's network (Ethernet) or USB port. Figure 1-3 maps the typical setup.

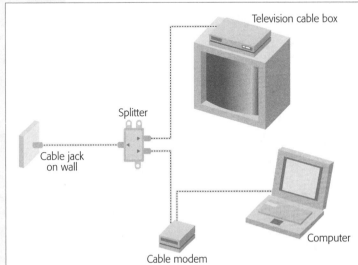

Television cable box

Splitter

Cable jack on wall

Cable modem

Computer

Figure 1-3:
Your TV and your PC can share the single cable coming out of your wall, thanks to a splitter box provided with most do-it-yourself cable-modem installation kits. As shown here, you just need to attach the splitter box to the cable coming out of the wall jack, which converts a single cable jack into two. Then use the coaxial cable provided in your modem kit to connect the cable modem to one side of the splitter; connect the television cable box to the splitter using another cable. When it's all connected properly, you can surf the Web while you watch the Discovery Channel.

Tip: You can plug the cable modem straight into the computer. That's all you need if you only have *one* computer. But if there's more than one computer in the house, consider buying an inexpensive box called a *router*. If you plug the cable modem (and all computers) into *that,* they can all share the broadband connection for a single price. See page 17 for more on sharing strategies if you've got multiple computers.

After everything's all plugged in, the wrapup steps differ slightly depending on whether you're using Windows or a Macintosh.

Wrapping up the Windows setup

Dig the CD out of the box, put it in your computer, and run the setup program on it. You'll be asked to plug in the account information from the cable or DSL company: your new account name, password, and so on. Your provider should also supply the settings and information you need to set up your new email address; see page 267 for instructions on how to configure an email account.

CDs that come with broadband kits are designed to take your hand and walk you through the setup process. If you've got a fistful of account settings, user names, and passwords from your provider—and no fear of your computer's control panels—you can also manually plug in your new connection settings. Choose Start → Control Panel → Network Connections and then choose "Create a new connection." Click "Connect to the Internet" and then click Next.

On the next screen, click the button for "Set up my connection manually." Click Next again.

The next box presents you with two choices for a broadband connection: one that requires a user name and password and one that's always on. In most cases these days, you use the "always on" option, but check the papers from your ISP.

If your connection is always on, click Next to finish up. If your ISP requires a name and password to use your connection (some DSL providers do), the next few screens walk you through typing in the user name and password.

Wrapping up the Mac OS X setup

Once the cable modem or DSL box is connected to your Mac's Ethernet jack, you should be able to get online immediately; no software installation is generally necessary.

The beauty of cable modems and DSL service is that they offer a geeky but wonderful feature called *DHCP*, which means, "I'll configure all the network settings for you." Open your Web browser and enjoy.

Sharing a Broadband Connection

You're paying good money each month for that speedy broadband connection. If you have more than one computer around the house in need of Internet access, you can share your DSL or cable connection with the other, less fortunate machines. You do this by setting up a *home network*.

A home network is like your own personal Internet: All the computers in your house can share files, use the same printer, and divide up the high-speed Internet connection so everyone in the house can surf on their own Macs or PCs.

To create a basic home network, you need to buy an inexpensive, compact metal or plastic box called a *router*. It offers one jack for your broadband modem and several others for network cables from all your computers. Once you plug in the modem and network cables between the router and each computer, the router divides your modem's pipeline among the connected computers so they can all be online at once.

Manual Mac Settings

If, for some reason, you're not able to surf the Web or check email the first time you try, it's remotely conceivable that your broadband modem *doesn't* offer DHCP. In that case, you may have to fiddle with the Network pane of System Preferences, preferably with a customer-support rep from your broadband provider on the phone.

On the Network pane, from the Show pop-up menu, choose either AirPort or Built-in Ethernet, depending on how your Mac's connected to the broadband modem. Now you see something like what's shown in Figure 1-4.

The next step is to make a selection from the Configure pop-up menu. Only your service provider can tell you exactly which settings to use, but you'll probably be asked to choose Manually. That is, your cable or phone company will tell you precisely which *IP address* (Internet address) to type in here. The bad news: You'll also have to fill in all the other boxes here—Subnet Mask, Router, and so on—with cryptic numbers separated by periods.

That's all the setup you'll have to worry about—click Apply Now. If your settings are correct, you're online, now and forever. You never have to worry about connecting or disconnecting.

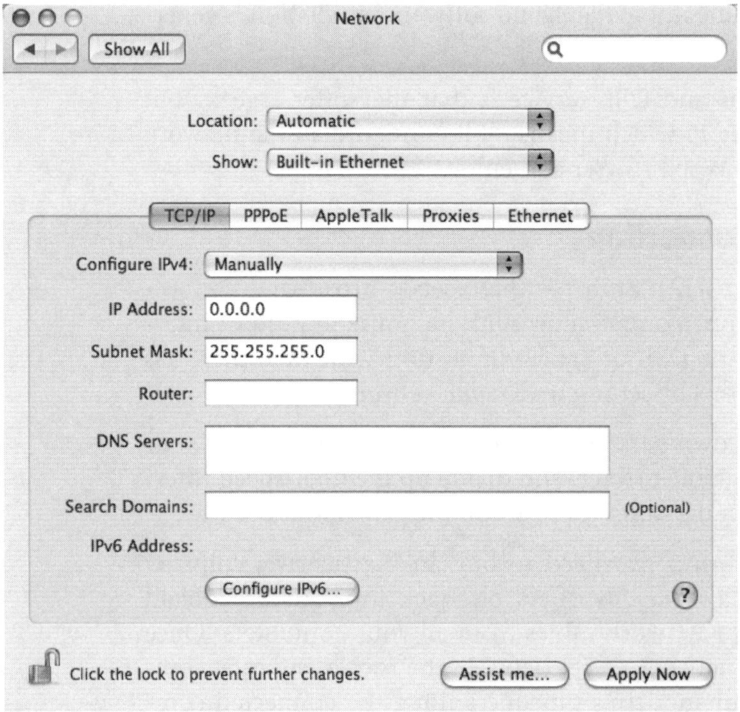

Figure 1-4:
Some broadband modems and ISPs require that you type specific settings into the Mac's Network configuration box in order to get online with your new broadband service. To get to this box, choose ¢ → System Preferences → Network. In the Show menu, select either Built-in Ethernet (for a wired connection to your modem) or AirPort (for a wireless connection). If your ISP's this persnickety about the settings you use, odds are you need to select Manually from the Configure menu and then type in the numbers and other information they gave you when you signed up—or that their tech team gave you when you called to complain that you couldn't get online.

Note: You can also opt for a *wireless* router, which lets you share the broadband computer with all the *wireless* computers in your house. See page 19.

Powerline networking, where your house's existing electrical system is converted into a discreet home network, is another way to get your computers connected without having to string the house with Ethernet cables.

For an in-depth look at setting up your own home network, check out *Home Networking: The Missing Manual,* which shows you how to make a wired, wireless, or mixed network out of PCs, Macs, or Macs and PCs.

Dial-Up Connections (Slow)

The least expensive way to get online is to use a *narrowband* or *dial-up* connection, in which your computer's modem calls your Internet provider's modem over the telephone line. You actually connect a piece of phone wire between your computer and the wall jack.

Sending Internet information over a phone wire is slow (for the geeks scoring at home, the top theoretical speed is about 53 kilobits per second). In today's Internet world of video, audio, and animated, glittering Web pages, this type of connection can be excruciatingly time consuming. You may lapse into a catatonic state waiting for a video clip to play in your Web browser.

On the bright side, a dial-up connection is inexpensive, doesn't require a lot of special hardware, and works just about anywhere you can find a phone. If you're just using the connection for email messages and light Web browsing, it's often perfectly fine.

Two kinds of dial-up services await you:

• **Online services.** Services like America Online, Earthlink, PeoplePC, and Microsoft's MSN are handy if you travel a lot because these national services offer local dial-up numbers just about everywhere in the country. (That is, your laptop can make a local, inexpensive call from your hotel room or friend's house.)

  These services are often easier to set up than standard Internet service providers (described next) because the starter CD walks you through the setup process.

  To go online, open the related program (the AOL program, for example) from your Start menu. Type in your password and click the Sign On button that appears on the Welcome screen. If you use the Mac OS X edition of

AOL's software, open the program by choosing Applications → AOL. Type in your password and click the Sign On button.

After a minute or so, during which your computer's modem connects with AOL's, you see AOL's dashboard of menus and graphics (Figure 1-5), with icons to click for checking mail or browsing the Web. Some services (AOL and MSN, for example) even offer specialized Web pages and other goodies just for subscribers; others provide free anti-virus and security software to their members.

Figure 1-5:
When you log on to AOL, you land on its Welcome screen. On this page, you can quickly see the top news stories of the day, the current weather conditions, and a link to the latest sports scores. This onscreen dashboard also gives you icons to click your way into other corners of the service—like your AOL mailbox or the company's online music and video offerings. As you can see, your eyeballs also get pelted with a few advertisements here and there for good measure.

Note: Along with its traditional dial-up plans, America Online now offers broadband service for Windows. Even if you sign up for and install the dial-up software, you can always upgrade to the broadband plan online at *http://discover.aol.com/aolhighspeed.adp* or by calling 800-392-5180.

- **Standard Internet Service Providers (ISPs).** If you just want to get on the Net and aren't afraid of rolling up your sleeves and setting up your computer's communications software yourself, a traditional *Internet service provider* (ISP) company can get you online for a few bucks less than most online services. You don't have to install some space-hogging proprietary program, either; you can use any email program or Web browser you like.

The following pages apply primarily to people who've signed up for this kind of standard ISP service.

Two Calls at Once

This is a note to people who have chosen the economical path to the Internet: a dial-up service.

When you computer connects to the Internet, it ties up the phone line just as effectively as a family member yakking away: When your computer's online, nobody else can use the phone.

Consider, therefore, how you plan to connect your modem to the phone jack of your house. Here are your choices:

Share a single line with the modem. At a store like Radio Shack, you can buy a *splitter,* a little Y-shaped plastic thing that makes your wall phone jack split into two identical phone jacks. You can plug your phone into one, and your computer into the other. This arrangement lets you talk on the telephone whenever you *aren't* using the modem and vice versa.

Install a second phone line. Giving your computer a phone line unto itself has a number of benefits. For example, your main family phone number's no longer tied up every time your Mac or PC goes online. In fact, you can talk to a human on one line while you're modeming on the other.

The drawback is that this option's expensive. If you're paying for dial-up Internet service *and* a second phone line, you can probably afford to pay for broadband service.

Meet the Modem

Modem is short for *m*odulator-*dem*odulator, a bit of circuitry that sends and receives information over telephone lines. Almost every computer made in the last 10 years has a modem built right inside. (If you see what looks like a standard phone jack on the back or side panel of your computer, that's it.)

If your computer has a built-in modem jack, all you have to do is connect it to a phone jack in the wall (or, if you're in a hotel room, to the Data jack that usually appears on the side of the hotel room's phone). Use a standard phone cord, just like the one that connects your phone to the wall jack.

In the unlikely event that your computer doesn't have a modem, you may have to buy an external one that connects to your computer's USB jack. In that case, install the software that came with it as a first step; the modem won't work without it. You may have to plug the modem into a power outlet, too.

Note: *Almost* every computer sold in the last 10 years has a built-in modem. Weirdly, the exception is the very latest Apple laptops, which lack one. Apple evidently believes that all of its enlightened customers stay exclusively at hotels that offer wireless Internet service. If you want to connect one of these MacBook or MacBook Pro laptops to the Internet through a dial-up connection, you'll have to buy Apple's $50 external USB modem. Fortunately, there's no software setup or power cord involved.

Finding an ISP

You can find Internet service providers in the phonebook, computer-magazine ads, and, of course, online. Here are some key factors to consider when shopping for an ISP:

- **What do other people think of the service?** Ask friends what they use and how they like it. If you can get onto the Internet somehow (from a friend's computer or at the library, for example), read the reviews at *www.broadbandreports.com* or *www.theispguide.com*. (And see page 51 if you've never used a Web address before and don't know what the previous sentence means.)

- **How much is it really going to cost per month?** Some companies offer special deals for the first few months of service—but then the real rate kicks in. (Hint: It's never *lower* than the teaser rate.) Furthermore, some require you to buy your own modem and other equipment. Find out all the costs ahead of time to prevent unpleasant surprises later.

- **Can you get to your email from anywhere?** Are there local phone numbers you can use all over the country?

- **How's the company's technical support?** If you're up in the middle of the night trying to get your Internet connection to work, having a company with 24/7 tech help can be a real comfort.

Once you've narrowed down a service provider, make sure it's compatible with your computer hardware and software. The truth is, virtually every broadband and dial-up service should work identically with Macintosh and Windows. Not all ISPs are equipped to answer questions about both kinds of computers, though, so if you're a Mac fan, ask before you sign up.

Setting Up a Dial-Up Connection (Windows)

Windows XP lets you set up the software side of your Internet connection before you've actually picked an ISP. In fact, it even offers to help you *find* an

ISP. Of course, its offerings include only Microsoft services or partners—but hey, what did you expect?

If your Internet service provider supplied a setup CD, pop it into your computer's drive and click your way through the setup screens until you arrive on the Internet. Be prepared to whip out your credit card and punch in some numbers as part of the process. The company will keep your card on file and you'll see a charge pop up on your credit card bill once a month.

The New Connection Wizard

If you didn't get a setup CD from your ISP, you can use the Windows XP New Connection Wizard (Figure 1-6).

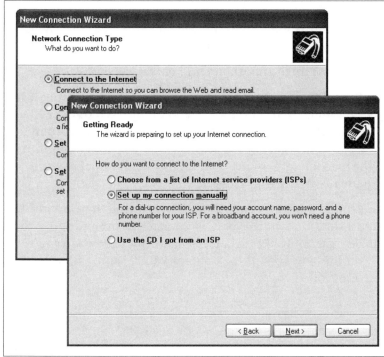

Figure 1-6:
Top: The New Connection Wizard in Windows XP is determined to get you on the Internet no matter what service provider you've decided to use.

Bottom: In fact, you don't even need to have selected an ISP since the wizard can find one for you from its own list—that's just how determined it is to get you on the Internet. But if you've already made your decision and have a sheet of settings from your new ISP, select the "Set up my connection manually" option.

Note: This section describes setting up an Internet connection with Windows XP. If you're still using an older version of Windows, choose Start → Programs → Accessories → Communications → Internet Connection Wizard, or Start → Programs → Online Services to find the wizards to lead you to the online Wonderland.

It may sound like a magical dating guru for lonely single people, but the Windows XP New Connection Wizard is designed to get you on the Internet by asking you a series of questions about your computer and software. (As for actual dating sites, see Chapter 17.)

To open this wizard, choose Start → All Programs → Accessories → Communications → New Connection Wizard. Make sure that your computer is plugged into a phone jack.

Click Next, "Connect to the Internet", Next, "Set up my Internet connection manually", and Next. Then click "Connect using a dial-up modem", and then Next.

On the following several screens, you'll be asked to type in a few pieces of information that only your ISP can provide: the local phone number that connects your PC to the Internet, your user name, and your password. (You can call your ISP for this information, or consult the literature delivered by postal mail when you signed up for a dial-up account.)

You'll also be offered these three important checkboxes:

- **Use this account name and password when anyone connects to the Internet from this computer.** This option refers to the Windows XP *user accounts* feature, in which various people who share the same computer keep their worlds of information and settings separate by signing in each time they use the machine. It's asking you, "Is this the Internet account you want this PC to use no matter who's logged in?"

- **Make this the default Internet connection.** Some people have more than one way to access the Internet. Maybe you connect your laptop to a cable modem when you're at home but dial out using the modem when you're on the road. Turn on this checkbox if the account you're setting up is the one you want to use most often.

Tip: You can always change your mind. In the Network Connections window (Figure 1-7), right-click a connection icon and choose "Set as Default Connection" from the shortcut menu. On the other hand, if you're a laptop-toting traveler, you might want to specify a different connection in each city you visit. In that case, right-click the default icon (shown by the checkmark at right in Figure 1-7) and choose "Cancel as Default Connection" from the shortcut menu. This way, your laptop will never dial automatically, using some hopelessly irrelevant access number for the city you're in.

- **Turn on Internet connection firewall for this connection.** Windows XP offers a certain degree of protection from incoming hacker attacks in the form of a personal firewall (see page 414). Turn this off only if you've equipped your PC with other firewall software (or if you have a *router*, as described on page 17).

When it's all over, you'll find that you've given birth to a *connection icon*, as shown at right in Figure 1-7. Once you've correctly typed in all the necessary information, you should be ready to surf.

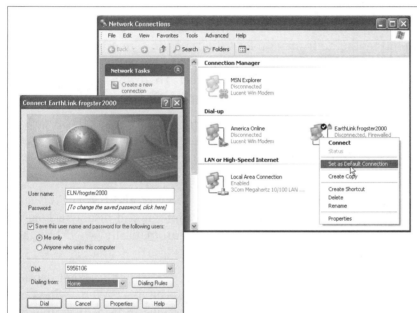

Figure 1-7:
Right: This particularly well-endowed individual has four different ways to get to the Internet. The New Connection Wizard created two of them—the ones represented by the MSN Explorer and EarthLink icons. One of the many ways to go online is to double-click either of these icons.

Left: Double-clicking one of these icons produces this dialog box, where you can click Dial to go online. (Turning on "Save password" eliminates the need to type your password each time—in general, a great idea.)

Tip: If you carry a laptop from city to city—each of which requires a different local Internet number—you might want to create more than one connection icon by plugging in a different local access number each time. (Alternatively, just create one connection icon—and then, in the Network Connections window, right-click it and choose Create Copy.) Another helpful hint: Name each of these connections after the appropriate location ("EarthLink Cleveland," "EarthLink Stamford," and so on), so you'll remember which one to use for which city.

Wading through all these dialog boxes sets up *almost* everything—but not your email account. Skip over to Chapter 14 for the details on that. If you want to check out the Web right away, though, you only have to flip to the next chapter.

Actually going online

When your PC dials, it opens up a connection to the Internet; this may take a minute or so as your modem dials the right phone number, issues its high-pitched squeals of welcome, and so on. But aside from tying up the phone line, your PC doesn't actually *do* anything until you launch an Internet program, such as an email program or a Web browser. By itself, making your PC dial the Internet's no more useful than dialing a phone number and then not saying anything.

Therefore, using the Internet is generally a two-step procedure: First, open the connection; second, open a program.

People who bill by the hour may prefer to initiate the connection manually— for example, by double-clicking the connection's icon in the Network Connections window (Figure 1-7, right). The Connect To dialog box appears, as shown at left in that figure. Just press Enter, or click Dial, to go online.

Fortunately, Windows offers an automated method that saves you several steps: You can make the dialing/connecting process begin automatically whenever you launch an Internet program. That way, you're saved the trouble of fussing with the connection icon every time you want to go online.

To turn on this feature, just open your Web browser and try to Web surf. When the PC discovers that it's not, in fact, online, it will display a Dial-up Connection dialog box. Turn on the "Connect automatically" checkbox, and then click Connect.

From now on, whenever you use a program that requires an Internet connection, your PC dials automatically. (For example, specifying a Web address in a window's Address bar, clicking the Send and Receive button in your email program, clicking a link in the Windows Help system, and so on.)

The Notification Area icon

While you're connected to your ISP, Windows XP puts an icon in the notification area (Figure 1-8, top), reminding you that you're online. You can watch the icon light up as data zooms back and forth across the connection. And if you point to it without clicking, you'll see a yellow tooltip showing your speed and how much data has been transmitted. (If this little taskbar icon isn't visible, take a moment to turn it back on, as directed in Figure 1-8. You'll find it to be an important administrative center for going online and offline.)

Figure 1-8:
Top: To make the notification area icon appear, right-click the icon for your connection (Figure 1-7). From the shortcut menu, choose Properties.

Bottom: At the bottom of the General tab, you'll see the key feature, "Show icon in notification area when connected." Turn on this option, and then click OK.

Disconnecting

The trouble with a standard dial-up Internet connection is that, unless you intervene, it will never hang up. It will continue to tie up your phone line until the other family members hunt it down, hours later, furious and brandishing wire cutters.

Therefore, it's worth taking a moment to configure your system so that it won't stay online forever.

When you're finished using the Internet, end the phone call by performing one of the following steps:

- Right-click the little connection icon on your taskbar. Choose Disconnect from the shortcut menu (Figure 1-9, top).

- Double-click the little connection icon on the taskbar. Click the Disconnect button in the Status dialog box that appears (Figure 1-9, bottom), or press Alt+D.

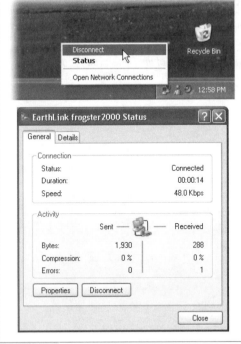

Figure 1-9:
Top: The quickest way to hang up is to use the notification-area icon. Right-click it and choose Disconnect from the shortcut menu that appears.

Bottom: You can also double-click the icon to view statistics on your session so far, and to produce a Disconnect button for hanging up.

- Right-click the connection icon in your Network Connections window. Choose Disconnect from the shortcut menu.

You can also set up your PC to hang up the phone *automatically* several minutes after your last activity online.

To find the necessary controls, right-click your connection icon (page 25); from the shortcut menu, choose Properties. In the resulting dialog box, click the Options tab. Near the middle of the box, you'll see a drop-down list called "Idle time before hanging up." You can set it to 1 minute, 10 minutes, 2 hours, or whatever.

Setting Up a Dial-Up Connection (Macintosh)

If your Mac uses AOL, EarthLink, or another online service, you've probably already enjoyed the step-by-step setup software that prepares your Mac for its online adventures. Happy surfing!

If you have a traditional ISP, though, you must plug a series of settings into the Network pane of System Preferences. You'll need to get this information directly from your ISP by consulting either its Web page, the little instruction sheets that came with your account, or a help desk agent on the phone.

The PPP tab

Start by opening → System Preferences and clicking the Network icon. You're shown the view pictured in Figure 1-10: a *Network Status* screen that summarizes the various ways your Mac can connect to the Internet or an office network, and how each connection is doing.

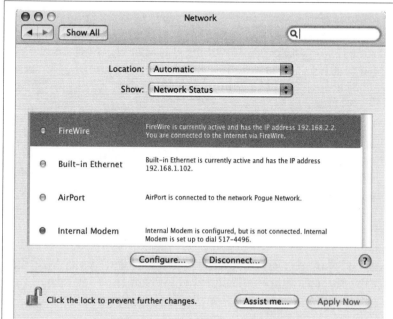

Figure 1-10:
Mac OS X's Network Status screen shows you how each of your network connections are doing at the moment (the status messages actually change as circumstances change). To adjust the network settings for a connection, double-click its "row."

From the Show pop-up menu, choose Internal Modem. (Or just double-click the Internal Modem "row" of the status screen.) You should see the PPP tab, where you fill in the blanks like this:

• **Service Provider.** Type in the name of your ISP (*EarthLink*, for example).

• **Account Name.** This is your account name, as assigned by the ISP. If you're *BillG@earthlink.net*, for example, type *BillG* here.

• **Password.** Specify your ISP account password here. Turn on "Save password" if you'd rather not retype it every time you connect.

• **Telephone Number.** This is the local access number that your modem's supposed to dial to connect to your ISP.

Tip: If you need your Mac to dial a 9 or an 8 for an outside line (as you would from within a hotel), or *70 to turn off call waiting, add it to the beginning of the phone number followed by a comma. The comma means "pause for two seconds." You can also put the comma to good use when typing in the dialing sequence for a calling card number.

- **Alternate Number.** This blank lets you type in a number to dial if the first one's busy.

- **PPP Options.** Click this button to bring up a special Options dialog box. Here, for example, you can specify how long the Mac waits before hanging up the phone line after your last online activity, and how many times the Mac should redial if the ISP's phone number is busy.

Tip: In the Session Options, one checkbox you'll almost certainly want to turn on is "Connect automatically when needed." It makes your Mac dial the Internet automatically whenever you check your email or open your Web browser. (Otherwise, you'd have to establish the Internet call manually, using the Internet Connect program described on page 30. Only then could you check your email or open your Web browser.)

Going online

If you've turned on "Connect automatically when needed," your Mac dials and connects to the Internet automatically whenever an Internet-related program tries to connect (a Web browser or email program, for example).

If you didn't turn on that option, you can make your Mac dial the Internet in one of two ways:

- **Using Internet Connect.** This little program is in your Applications folder. The main item of interest here is the Connect button, which makes the Mac dial the Internet. Once Internet Connect indicates you're online, open your Web browser, email program, or other Internet software and get surfing.

  If you're smart, however, you'll turn on the "Show modem status on menu bar" checkbox. It adds a tiny telephone icon—the Modem Status menulet—to the upper-right corner of your screen, which lets you completely bypass Internet Connect the next time you want to go online (Figure 1-11).

- **Using the menu-bar icon.** Just click the Modem Status menulet and choose Connect from the pop-up menu. Your Mac dials without even blocking your desktop picture with a window.

Figure 1-11:
Going online automatically (by launching an Internet program) is by far the most convenient method, but you can also go online on command, in one of these two ways.

Top: The quick way to dial or hang up is to use this menulet (which doesn't appear until you turn on "Show modem status on menu bar" in Internet Connect or on the Network pane's PPP screen).

Bottom: You can also go online (or disconnect) the long way—using the Internet Connect program in your Applications folder.

Disconnecting

The Mac automatically drops the phone line 15 minutes after your last activity online (or whatever interval you specified in the PPP Options dialog box).

Of course, if other people in your household are screaming for you to get off the line so that they can make a call, you can also disconnect manually. Either choose Disconnect from the Modem Status menulet (Figure 1-11) or click Disconnect in the Internet Connect window (Figure 1-10).

Wireless Connections (Awesome)

For years, getting onto the Internet meant plugging into it—that is, literally connecting a wire to your computer that, if you could crawl inside and follow it through all the walls, ceilings, pipes, and relay stations of the world, would eventually lead you to the Internet.

Nowadays, however, an increasing number of people get online without connecting any wires at all. *Wireless hot spots,* also known as WiFi or AirPort networks, are invisible pools of Internet signal, 300 feet across, that let wireless-equipped computers get onto the Internet at high speed. Travelers with wireless-ready laptops connect to the Internet via these wireless hot spots in airports, coffee shops, hotel lobbies, and just about anywhere else they have work to do or time to kill.

Usually, you have to pay a fee to use one of these public hot spots. But if you live in an apartment building or other tightly spaced housing, an even better option may await you. You may be able to hop onto the Internet using someone *else's* wireless signal. Sometimes the signal bleeds into your home without the owner's knowledge, in which case—you very lucky person—you may be able to get online *free,* at least until the owner catches on. More often, though, someone in the building makes his signal available deliberately, collecting, say, $5 a month from each person who shares it.

If you're such a lucky neighbor, then it's *not* true that you need an ISP to get onto the Internet. Your *neighbor* has an ISP account, which he's sharing with you. In that case, you're getting online not via an ISP, but through a VSN—a Very Shrewd Neighbor.

WiFi at Home

But WiFi networks are also very useful at home. If your cable modem or DSL box is in an inconvenient area of the house, and you don't feel like snaking 50 feet of ugly network cable from the den to the bedroom, setting up a *wireless network* to share your broadband connection is just the ticket.

Setting up a wireless hot spot in your home is easy, at least compared with other networking tasks. Remember how you'd ordinarily connect your cable modem or DSL box directly to your computer? For a wireless network, you connect it instead to a $40 box called a *wireless router,* which then beams the network signal over radio waves to the entire house (or at least to the nearest 150 feet of it, even through walls). Any computer with *wireless networking* circuitry can join this type of network; in fact, they can all surf simultaneously.

Note: Most laptops sold these days have a built-in wireless card inside, but you can easily add one to an older laptop. Wireless network adapters are also available in different forms for desktop computers as well. *Home Networking: The Missing Manual* covers creating and configuring a wireless network in detail.

How to Join a Hot Spot

When you first turn on your wireless laptop in the vicinity of a wireless network—whether at home or in some public place—Windows XP and Mac OS X usually bring it to your attention. A dialog box asks if you want to join it. (Figure 1-12 shows this situation in Windows.)

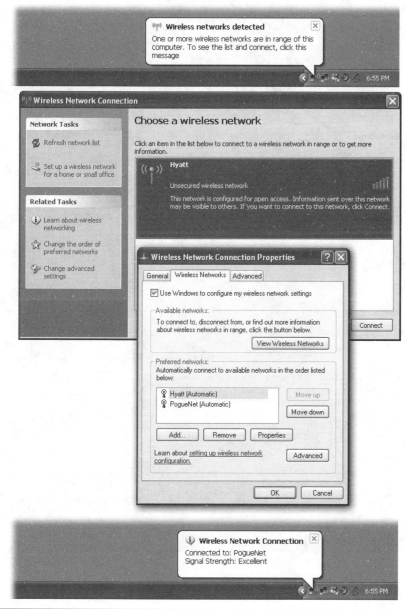

Figure 1-12:

Top: You're wandering with your WiFi laptop. Suddenly, fortune smiles: this system-tray balloon appears. You've found a hot spot! You click the balloon.

Second from top: You get to read about the network you've found. To get online, click the network's name and then click Connect. (This message is warning you that hackers with network-sniffing software could, in theory, intercept your wireless transmissions—always a concern with public wireless networks.) If a yellow padlock appears, you can't use the network without a password.

Third from top: In your Network Places window, getting Properties on a wireless connection produces this box. By rearranging the networks' names, you tell Windows which ones you want to connect to first, in the delightful event that more than one hot spot is available at once.

Bottom: The next time you wander into a hot spot you've connected to before, XP connects automatically—no muss, no dialog boxes.

Trouble in WiFi Land

Maybe you *know* there's a wireless network in the air, but no message is popping up on your screen. Or maybe the message *does* pop up, but it won't let you by without a password. Or maybe no password's necessary, but you still can't actually do anything on the Internet.

Here's your guidebook to the obstacles that may stand between you and wireless Internet heaven.

Possibility 1. Sometimes the dialog box just doesn't pop up, even though the hot spot is otherwise perfectly available.

In Windows XP, choose Start → Connect To. If you don't see any networks listed, right-click the Wireless Connection icon in the Network Connections window and choose View Available Wireless Networks from the shortcut menu.

On a Mac, click the AirPort icon on the Mac's menu bar to see a list of wireless networks in the area.

Possibility 2. At many conferences, libraries, hotel lobbies, and schools, just clicking Connect or OK in the "a wireless network is available" dialog box is all it takes to get online.

At commercial hot spots, though—the ones you have to pay for—you can't just open your email program to start communicating. Instead, you must first open your Web browser and log in at the welcome page.

At Starbucks, Kinko's, and many airports, that welcome page bears the T-Mobile logo; at many hotels and other airports, it's a Wayport page. Either way, this is where you're supposed to plug in your credit card number (or, if you have an existing account, sign in).

Only then can you use your Web browser, email program, chat software, and other functions that require your laptop to be online.

Possibility 3. Occasionally, your laptop will detect and connect to a wireless network, but you won't be able to pull up a Web page or send email. That's probably because you've found a network that's intended for internal use, not public. Someone has deliberately turned off the feature that can connect outsiders to the Internet.

Possibility 4. These days, many hot spots—either free or commercial—offer admission only with a password. (You'll know because a password box will appear on your screen.)

Sometimes you just have to ask the person behind the counter what the password is. Sometimes you get it when you pay, for example, a hotel desk clerk for access.

Possibility 5. If your laptop sees the hot spot but can't get you to the Internet, the wireless router may not be configured correctly. Try to find whoever's in charge (like the hotel desk clerk) to hit the Reset button on the access point or router, which may do the trick.

If the hot spot is free and unprotected by a password, just click OK or Connect; you're online. Check your email, browse the Web, and do other Internet-based tasks.

If the hot spot, like those in airports and hotels, requires payment up front, clicking OK or Connect doesn't actually get you onto the real Internet. Instead, you're now supposed to open your Web browser, where you'll find a demand for your credit card number. Prices vary, but $8 for 24 hours worth of access isn't unusual. You can't proceed to the wider Web or check your email until you first plug in a credit card number and sign up for a plan (that is, you pay for 15 minutes, an hour, or a day of service).

Note: Public networks are not private places. It's theoretically possible for a hacker seated nearby, using special *packet sniffing* software, to intercept text that you're sending by email or writing in a chat room. (Transactions on Web pages, however, are safe as long as you see a tiny padlock icon in the corner of the Web browser window.) Chapter 21 has plenty of information on how to keep yourself safe online at home and in the hotspot.

Software

The last piece of the Getting Online puzzle is the software. But here's the good news: Your computer probably has the essentials already installed: an email program, Web browser, and text-chat program, for example. And once you have those, getting anything else you need is a snap.

If you have a PC, check your Start menu for Outlook Express and Internet Explorer, the free email and Web programs Microsoft has included with every copy of Windows it's made in the past 10 years. If you're a Macintosh sort of person, open Mac OS X's Applications folder to see your free Apple Mail and Safari browser programs there waiting for you.

The rest of this book covers each software type in detail. But for your appetite-whetting pleasure, here's a summary of the key, free Internet software pieces and what kinds of happiness they'll bring you.

Web Browsers

A *Web browser* program is your window to the World Wide Web: the Internet's vast collection of documents, pictures, videos, games, music, and other elements of the human experience. A browser lets you do just what it says: browse from page to page by pointing and clicking with your mouse.

As mentioned in the previous section, your computer has a Web browser already installed on it. Chapter 2 explains the alternatives, and it also explains *how* to use this browser thing to get around the Web.

Email Programs

An *email program* is like a cross between a word processor and an electronic postal worker. It lets you exchange typed messages with people around the world.

It also lets you store, sort, and save all the messages other people have sent to you. This means you can keep track of ongoing correspondences, file away electronic receipts of items you've purchased online, or collect all of the annoying junk mail that finds its way to your digital mailbox—and it *will*—and erase it all at once.

As you now know, your computer has a basic email program on it already. Chapter 14 describes how to use it—and why you might want to consider alternative programs, including Web-based mail programs that let you check your messages from any computer in the world.

Instant Messaging Programs

Humorist Dave Barry once described the Internet as "CB radio, but with more typing"—and using an instant messaging program certainly makes you feel that way. Instead of sending off an email message and waiting for your pal to reply, an *instant messaging* (IM) program, also called a chat program, lets you conduct real-time, typed conversations with the person on the other end. You get instant feedback ("Where should we go to dinner tonight?"), and you save money on long-distance phone calls.

Many instant messaging programs also let you transfer files directly to the other person, make free audio and video calls, and chat with several people at once (helpful for party planning or remote family meetings).

You may already have an IM program on your computer, too. Windows XP comes with Windows Messenger, and Mac OS X comes with iChat. Chapter 15 has details on how to use them.

Security Software

You've probably heard the stories in the paper about people getting ripped off on the Internet, getting infected by viruses, or having their computers taken over by evildoers. This sort of thing *can* happen. But you can take precautions so that the bad side of the Internet doesn't infringe upon all the good you can do with it.

Another piece of software you may want to consider—alas, one that probably did *not* come free on your computer—is an Internet security suite that protects you and your computer from Internet evils like viruses, worms, hackers, crackers, phishers, pharmers, and identity thieves. (For more, see Chapter 21.)

Viruses and spyware are generally Windows-only treats. Some of the online scams, though, are equally dangerous to Mac fans. Chapter 21 explains what all of these sinister-sounding creatures are, and how to keep yourself safe with software.

POWER USERS' CLINIC

Shareware and the Kindness of Strangers

Once you make your way online, you'll find that the Web isn't just a huge store of news, audio, video, photos, and other cool stuff, it's also a giant treasure chest of inexpensive software called *shareware.* These programs include video games, currency converters, mini-databases that let you catalog every CD in your collection, and an infinite variety of other programs.

Programmers have a long tradition of creating these inexpensive, homemade programs for the greater good (and sometimes to show off their superior skills)—and then releasing them to the public and requesting a small fee in exchange.

Most shareware programs work on the free-trial system: The free version has built-in restrictions that hinder some features, or it stops working after about 30 days. If you send the requested amount of money to the programmer, you unlock the full, unrestricted version.

Other shareware works on the honor system: If you like a program, you return the favor by kicking him or her a requested donation.

And then there's software that the creator doesn't want *any* money for, called *freeware.*

To find useful shareware, visit a shareware vault like Download.com (*www.download.com*), the bovinely divine Tucows site (*www.tucows.com*), or VersionTracker (*www.versiontracker.com*). You'll find the shareware organized by category, like "Audio & Video" or "Business," but you can also use key words to search most archives for programs that match your terms, like "calculator."

Advanced Connection Tricks (Windows)

Because so many people consider the Internet such an important PC feature, Windows XP lets you fine-tune its dialing, modem, and Internet settings to within an inch of their lives. You should consider this section optional—or power-user—reading.

To adjust the settings for your modem's dialing patterns, choose Start → Control Panel. Click the "Show Classic view" link, and then double-click "Phone and Modem Options". The resulting dialog box (Figure 1-13, left) consists of three major tabs (Dialing Rules, Modems, and Advanced), each serving important functions.

Dialing Rules Tab

The Dialing Rules tab (Figure 1-13, left) is made for travelers. As you move from place to place, you may wind up in locations that have very different dialing requirements. The area code may change, not to mention the requirement to dial 9 for an outside line, the availability of touch-tone dialing, and so on.

To set up the dialing rules for your current location, click its name and then click the Edit button. The New Location box appears (Figure 1-13, right), bristling with enough controls to make your modem sing, dance, and stand on its head.

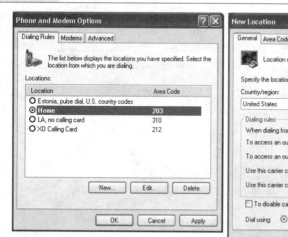 

Figure 1-13:
Left: This dialog box has two priorities: To establish rules for dialing out, and to define as many different sets of rules for dialing as you need. If you're setting up dialing properties for a desktop computer, you won't need to change these settings after the first successful call.

Right: Setting up a new dialing rule.

General tab

Here are the guidelines for filling out this dialog box:

- **Location name, Country/region, Area code.** These boxes inform Windows where you're presently located. When your modem dials another city or country, Windows XP will know when to dial a 1 (and a country or area code, when necessary) before dialing.

- **To access an outside line for local/long-distance calls.** In many offices and hotels, you must dial a number (usually 8 or 9) to get an outside line. If you enter numbers into these text boxes, Windows will dial them before the regularly scheduled Internet number.

- **Use this carrier code to make long-distance/international calls.** These options specify the codes that you have to dial, even before the area code, when dialing internationally. For example, in the United States, the long distance carrier code is 1. For international calls, the carrier code consists of the digits you dial before the country code—to make international calls from the United States, for example, the carrier code is 011.

- **To disable call waiting.** If you have call waiting, that little beep that announces an incoming call can scramble your Internet connection. Fortunately, Windows XP is delighted to automatically disable call waiting whenever you use the modem. Turn on this checkbox; from the drop-down list to its right, choose from the list of the common call waiting disabling key sequences (*70, 70#, and 1170). (If you don't know which sequence works for your local phone company, check the front of your phone book.)

  When the modem disconnects from the Internet after your online session, call waiting automatically returns to the phone line.

- **Tone or pulse dialing.** Specify whether your telephone service is touch-tone (push-button) or pulse (as on old-fashioned rotary-dial phones).

Area Code Rules tab

It used to be easy to dial the telephone in America. For local calls, you dialed a seven-digit number. Calls to other area codes started with 1 and then the area code.

Not anymore. Many metropolitan areas now utilize *10-digit dialing*—an insidious system that requires you to dial the full area code even for your next-door neighbor. Worse, some cities have several *different* area codes—not all of which require a 1-plus-area-code dialing pattern. To confuse things further, in some cases, you dial *only* the area code plus the seven-digit number.

To clue your modem in to the vagaries of your own area's area code practices, click the Area Code Rules tab. From there, set up the dialing sequences for certain locations by clicking the New button to open the New Area Code Rule dialog box. The resulting options let you specify the area code and three-digit prefixes. Click OK to return to the New Location dialog box.

Calling Card tab

If you, the shrewd traveler, feel that there's a better use for your money than paying most of it to your hotel's $3-per-minute long-distance scheme, this dialog box is for you. It lets you train your modem to bill its calls to a calling card (Figure 1-14).

> **Note:** Creating a calling card profile doesn't mean you *must* use it every time you use your modem. In fact, you can choose whether or not to use the calling card each time you dial out.

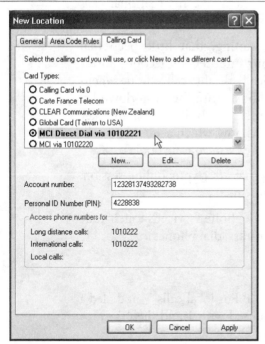

Figure 1-14:
Windows XP already knows about the dialing requirements for most major calling cards. When you choose one from the Card Types list box at top, Windows XP automatically fills in the fields at the bottom with the correct information. On the remote chance you can't find your own card, just type in the necessary dialing codes manually.

If your calling card isn't listed, you can create a setup for it yourself, which Windows then adds to the list. Armed with the instructions from your calling card company, click the New button. In the resulting dialog box, specify the card name, account number, PIN, and so on.

By clicking the Long Distance tab in the New Calling Card dialog box, you can specify the steps needed to use the card for long distance. For instance, you may need to dial a number and then wait for a tone that confirms that the number has been accepted. In this dialog box, you can specify the number of seconds you want Windows to wait. (You can set up the same kinds of rules for international and local calls by clicking the appropriate tabs.)

Once you've set up a calling card, it becomes part of one of these dialing rules. Now when you want to go online, you'll be able to bill your modem calls to your calling card on a case-by-case basis.

To do so, start by double-clicking your connection icon (Figure 1-7). When the dialog box appears, use the "Dialing from" drop-down list to choose the name of the dialing-rule setup that contains your calling card configuration. Now click Dial to start your call.

Modems Tab

All the preceding discussion concerns only the first of the three tabs in the "Phone and Modem Options" program. The second tab, called Modems, is simply a list of the modems currently connected to your PC. (Most people not in Oprah's tax bracket, of course, see only one modem listed here.)

Double-clicking the name of your modem opens its Properties dialog box, which bursts with technical parameters for your modem. In general, you'll need to visit these dialog boxes only when troubleshooting, following the instructions of some telecommunications geek from your modem company. Two of them, however, are more generally useful:

• **Change the speaker volume.** The modern modem may have revolutionized computer communications, but the squealing sounds it makes could wake the dead—or, worse, the spouse. To turn the speaker off, so that you no longer hear the shrieks every time you dial, click the Modem tab, and then drag the Speaker volume slider to Off.

Tip: The slider affects the speaker volume only while it's dialing and making a connection to another computer. After the connection's established, the speaker *always* goes silent, so you don't have to listen to all the squawking noises that indicate data transmission.

• **Wait for dial tone before dialing.** This checkbox is normally turned on. If you travel abroad with your laptop, however, you may experience trouble connecting if the foreign country's dial tone doesn't sound the same as it does back home. Turning off this checkbox often solves the problem.

Advanced Tab

These controls, too, are extremely advanced options that you'll never need to adjust except in times of intense troubleshooting.

Advanced Connection Tricks (Mac OS X)

The Mac has its own assortment of Internet connection stunts, especially for the laptop crowd.

Switching Locations

If you travel with a laptop, you know the drill. You're constantly opening up System Preferences → Network so that you can switch between Internet settings: Ethernet at the office, dial-up at home. Or maybe you simply visit the branch office from time to time, and you're getting tired of having to change the local access number for your ISP each time you leave home (and return home again).

The simple solution is the → Location submenu. As Figure 1-15 illustrates, all you have to do is tell it where you are. Mac OS X handles the details of switching to the correct Internet connection and phone number.

Creating a New Location

To create a *location,* which is nothing more than a set of memorized settings, open System Preferences, click Network, and choose New Location from the Location pop-up menu. You'll be asked to provide a name for your new location, such as *Chicago Office* or *Dining Room Floor.*

When you click OK, you return to the Network panel, which is now blank. Take this opportunity to set up the kind of Internet connection you use at the corresponding location, just as described on the first pages of this chapter. If you travel regularly, in fact, you can use Location Manager to build a long list of locations, each of which "knows" the local phone number for your Internet access company (because you've entered it on the PPP tab).

A key part of making a new location is putting the various Internet connection types (Ethernet, AirPort, Modem, Bluetooth) into the correct order. Your connections will be slightly quicker if you give the modem priority in your Hotel setup, the AirPort connection priority in your Starbucks setup, and so on.

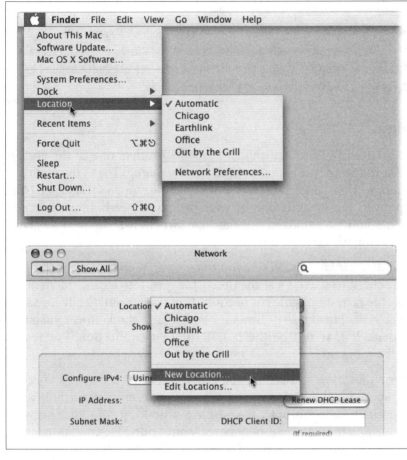

Figure 1-15:
The Location feature lets you switch from one "location" to another just by choosing its name—either from the menu (top) or from this pop-up menu in System Preferences (bottom). The Automatic location just means "the standard, default one you originally set up." (Don't be fooled: Despite its name, Automatic isn't the only location that offers multihoming, which is described later in this chapter.)

In fact, if you use nothing but a cable modem when you're at home, you may want to create a location in which *only* the Ethernet connection is active. Conversely, if your laptop uses nothing but its dial-up modem when on the road, your location could include *nothing* but the modem connection. You'll save a few seconds each time you try to go online because your Mac won't bother hunting for an Internet connection that doesn't exist (see the upcoming section "Multihoming").

Making the Switch

Once you've set up your various locations, you can switch among them using either the Location pop-up menu (in System Preferences → Network) or the → Location submenu, as shown in Figure 1-15. As soon as you do so, your Mac is automatically set to dial the new phone number or to connect using the different method.

Tip: If you have a laptop, create a connection called Offline. From the Show pop-up menu, choose Network Port Configurations; turn off *all* the connection methods you see in the list. When you're finished, you've got yourself a setting that will *never* attempt to go online. This setup will save you the occasional interruption of a program that tries to dial but takes three minutes to discover you're on Flight 800 to Miami and have no phone line available.

Multihoming

Speaking of different ways to get online, Mac OS X offers one of the coolest features known to Internet-loving humanity: *multihoming.* That's the ability to maintain *multiple simultaneous* network connections open—Ethernet, Air-Port, dial-up, even FireWire. If one of your programs needs Internet access and the first method isn't hooked up, the Mac switches to the next available connection—automatically.

This feature's ideal for laptops. When you open your Web browser, your laptop might first check to see if it's at the office, plugged into a cable modem via the Ethernet—the fastest possible connection. If not, it automatically looks for an AirPort network. Finally, if it draws a blank there, the laptop reluctantly dials the modem. It may not be the fastest Internet connection, but it's all you've got at the moment.

In short, for each location you create, you can specify which network connections the Mac should look for, and in which order. You can even turn off some connections entirely. For example, if you have a desktop Mac that's always connected to a cable modem, you may never want your Mac to dial using its built-in modem. In that case, you could turn off the modem entirely.

Here's how to go about using this multihoming feature:

1. **Open System Preferences. Click the Network icon.**

   The Network Status screen (Figure 1-10) brings home the point of multi-homing: you can have more than one network connection operating at once.

   Make sure the appropriate location is selected in the Location pop-up menu.

2. **From the Show pop-up menu, choose Network Port Configurations.**

   Now you see the display shown in Figure 1-16. It lists all the different ways your Mac knows how to get online, or onto an office network.

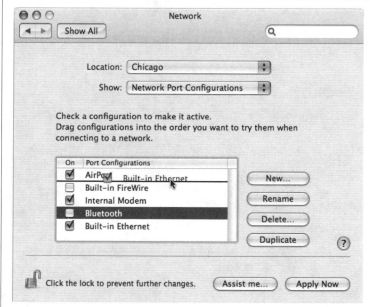

Figure 1-16:
The key to multihoming is sliding the network connection methods' names up or down (and turning off the ones you don't intend to use in this location). You can also rename the different configurations by double-clicking them.

3. **Drag the items up and down in the list into priority order.**

If you have a wired broadband connection, for example, you might want to drag Built-in Ethernet to the top of the list, since that's almost always the fastest way to get online.

At this point, you can also *turn off* any connections you don't want your Mac to use when it's in this location—the internal modem, for example.

4. **Click Apply Now.**

Your Mac will now be able to switch connections even in real time, during a single Internet session. If lightning takes out your cable modem in the middle of your Web surfing, your Mac will seamlessly switch to your dial-up modem, for example, to keep your session alive.

Surfing the Web

No doubt about it: the Web has transformed the world. From its humble beginnings as an information-sharing system for scientists and academics, the Web has rapidly developed since the early 1990s into a complex collection of sites and services that have changed the way people interact with each other.

It's safe to say the World Wide Web has something for *everybody*. It's a massive reference library, photo archive, software center, radio station, television network, music store, movie distribution system, and repository of such giddy weirdness as a page of dancing hamsters or a live video camera transmitting pictures of corn growing in Iowa. This chapter shows you how to set up your own personal window into this world: your Web browser.

Your First Web Page

Start up your computer, get on the Internet, and open up your Web browser program, like so:

- If you're a Windows person, open your Start menu and click the name of your Web browser. Unless you've installed an alternative browser like Firefox or Netscape, that probably means Internet Explorer because that's what comes with every version of Windows since the last century.

- If you're a Macintosh maven, open your Applications folder and double-click Safari, Apple's own Web-browsing software. If your Mac's really old, you may find the Mac version of Internet Explorer or Netscape on your computer instead of—or in addition to—Safari.

• If you use America Online or a similar service, open the software bearing its name; it has a Web browser built in.

Tip: Even though AOL offers a built-in browser, you don't have to use it. If you prefer Internet Explorer, Firefox, Safari, or some other browser, try this: First connect to the Internet using the custom AOL software. Then, once you're on and you hear the cheery voice say "Welcome!", you can open up Internet Explorer, Firefox, or any browser you like to use *on top of* AOL's browser.

The first Web page you see is probably one chosen by Apple, Microsoft, AOL, or whoever provided your browser software. It doesn't matter, because you can easily jump to a new page or change your browser's startup page to be one of your *own* choosing (page 62).

No matter what the Web page, you're bound to see some *hyperlinks*. Hyperlinks—or links for short—are typically sprinkled throughout the text of a Web page as words or phrases that stand out against the regular text, because they're a different color, they're underlined, or both. Clicking a link immediately takes you to another Web page containing information about the words in the link you just clicked. Links are what make the Web *the Web*: They connect pages to other pages, weaving them all together over the Internet.

For example, on a movie review page, you may see the lead actor's name as a link. If you click it, your browser takes you to a page containing a biography of the actor and a list of previous film appearances. On portal sites like MSN (page 54), just about every word on the page may be a link to something else. On news sites (page 97) that display a list of headlines, the headlines themselves are usually hyperlinks that take you right to the page containing the text of the story.

Pictures (usually little ones), labeled buttons, bars, and icons can be links, too. Clicking one whisks you away to another page or section of the Web site. These graphics are basically tarted-up hyperlinks.

Tip: Clicking a photo on a Web page often gives you a larger version of the picture in a new browser window—or takes you to the page containing the story the photo accompanies.

Parts of a Web Browser

Now that you've got a Web page up on your screen, it's a good time to learn how to use the browser's buttons and menus to go where you want to go (and do what you want to do). Figure 2-1 shows a sample. Although the look and design may vary slightly, most Web browsers have similar controls.

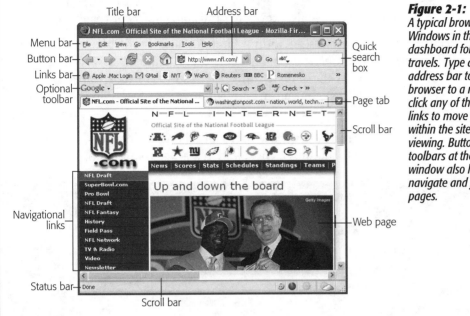

Title bar   Address bar

Menu bar
Button bar
Links bar
Optional
toolbar

Quick
search
box

Navigational
links

Page tab

Scroll bar

Web page

Status bar

Scroll bar

Figure 2-1:
A typical browser, Firefox for Windows in this case, is your dashboard for your Web travels. Type a URL into the address bar to beam your browser to a new site, or click any of the onscreen links to move to other pages within the site you're viewing. Buttons and toolbars at the top of the window also help you navigate and jump to new pages.

- **Title bar.** This strip of text at the very top of the browser window tells you the name or title of the Web page you're looking at, like "BBC NEWS | News Front Page" or "Slate Magazine." When you click the title bar, you can drag the browser window around on your screen if you want to move it.

- **Button bar.** There's a row of buttons along the top that lets you do things like navigate through sites you're visiting, reload a fresh version of the present Web page (which is helpful, say, if you're stuck at work with no TV and are desperately checking the baseball game's score), print the current Web page, or see a list of all the sites you've recently visited. Typical buttons include Back, Forward, Stop, and Reload.

- **Address bar.** Every Web page has its own address, which starts with *http://* and is shown at the top of the browser.

  You can type a new Web page address into this box and then press Enter to go to a new Web page. A Web address is known by the nerds as a URL.

  And where do you get good Web addresses? From friends, articles, television, and so on. Look for *http://* or *www* at the beginning of the address.

- **Quick Search box.** To find specific information on the Web, you usually have to search for it, and a built-in search box lets you type in keywords right there, without having to stop and go to a search engine site (page 71).

- **Links bar.** Most browsers let you store quick links to your favorite sites right on the toolbar. It's also known as the *bookmarks bar* (page 53).

- **Tabs.** Modern browsers, including Firefox, Safari, and Internet Explorer 7, offer a neat trick: *tabbed browsing.* This useful feature lets you keep several Web sites open on the screen simultaneously—not in a hopeless mess of overlapping windows, but all in one window. File folder-like index tabs at the top of the window keep them straight.

With these basic features, your browser can take you all around the Web and back home again with a point, a click, and just a wee bit of typing.

UP TO SPEED

Power Users' Web: Tabs

You can't possibly imagine the feelings of power and indomitability that come from using *tabbed browsing.* If you have any aspirations whatsoever of becoming a power user, this feature's well worth exploring.

Tabbed browsing is a way to keep a bunch of Web pages open simultaneously—in a single, neat window. Turning on tabbed browsing unlocks a whole raft of browser shortcuts and tricks.

For example, you can control when clicking a link takes you to that linked page in your *current* window and when it opens the linked page in a new *tab.* The secret: Press the Ctrl key (⌘ on the Mac) when you want a new tab.

To close a tab, click its little X (close) button, or press Ctrl+W (⌘-W on the Mac).

You can also control whether a new tab appears in *front* of the other tabs you've opened or *behind* them. (Having new tabs appear in back is great when you're working your way down, say, a list of Google search results, and earmarking the most promising links this way for review later.)

The secret: In Internet Explorer, add the Alt key (that is, Ctrl+Alt+click a link) to open a new tab in front. In Safari, add the Shift key to open the tab in *back* (that is, Shift-⌘-click a link). All browsers offer a Preferences or Options dialog box, too, that lets you set these preferences permanently, so you don't have to remember the keystrokes.

Moving to Another Page

Once you're done looking at your first Web page, it's time to move on to something more interesting. As described below, you have several ways of getting to your next page.

By address

Like houses in a city, every Web page has its own address so people can find it. As noted above, Web page addresses have their own official nerd name: *Uniform Resource Locators*, or URLs. You see URLs displayed on everything from the sides of soda cans to highway billboards. They're recognized as a shorthand way to say, "visit our Web site for more information."

To get to a Web page using its address:

1. **Open your Web browser program and click in the address bar (page 49).**

   To save time and mousing energy, you may also want to learn the keyboard shortcut for highlighting the address bar. For example, in Internet Explorer and Firefox for Windows, it's Alt+D. In Safari for the Macintosh, it's ⌘-L.

2. **Type in the URL.**

   That *http://www.missingmanuals.com* sure is a good one!

Tip: Most browsers can save you typing by filling in the *http://www.* and the *.com* parts for you. You can get to sites by just typing in the domain name, like *cnn* or *yahoo*. (In Internet Explorer, you get this effect by pressing Ctrl+Enter, rather than the Enter key alone, after entering the address.) In fact, this book generally leaves off the *http://* part in many of the Web sites listed, just because it's a given.

UP TO SPEED

URL Breakdown

A standard Web address, like *http://www.dilbert.com,* is composed of distinct parts. Over time, you'll come to recognize them and cherish them as friends.

The first part of an address, for example, is *http://*. That HTTP business stands for *HyperText Transfer Protocol*, which is a sort of computer language (a Web standard) that describes to your Web browser how a page is supposed to look.

The *www* section of the address stands for World Wide Web. It used to be a very common part of a URL because it let you know you were going to a Web site, but many sites don't even use it anymore. In fact, you can see URLs like *http://images.google.com* that go to a specific part of a site.

The last part of the address, *dilbert.com*, is the *domain name* (the overarching site name, often the company's name), which the Web site's owner must register with a company (called a "registrar") that's certified to catalog Web site domain names and add new ones to a centralized Internet database.

3. **Press the Enter or Return key on the keyboard.**

Your Web browser should pause a minute as it redirects itself to the new address and then unfurls the new page in your browser window.

Tip: You can also cut and paste URLs into your browser's window to save yourself some typing.

By link

As mentioned on page 48, Web pages are usually full of links, either in the form of colored (usually blue), underlined words in a page's text, or clickable buttons, bars, and icons on the page. Headlines in bold or photographs also usually take you to a new page.

By button

Those Back and Forward browser buttons mentioned on page 49 can also take you around the Web. Click the Back button to cycle back page by page from all the sites you previously viewed, and click the Forward button to go the other way. You need to have done a bit of surfing already for these buttons to work—your browser needs pages to go back or forward *to*—and neither button works on your first page of the day because you haven't been to any other pages yet.

Tip: Keyboard shortcut nuts should note that you can "click" the back button by pressing the Backspace (Delete) key in most browsers. Add the Shift key to go forward again.

By history

Web browsers can remember a list of the sites you've recently visited in the past few days in a place called the browser *history*, and it's often sorted by the day you visited the page. Click the site or page name in the history file to return to that page. Different browsers put the history menu or button in different places, so you may have to look around for it (see page 63 for tips on how to add it as a button). In Microsoft Internet Explorer 7, it's a small drop-down menu triangle by the Forward button. Safari has its own History menu, and in Firefox, the history list is in the Go menu.

Tip: On most Web browsers for Windows, you can call up your history file by pressing Ctrl+H on the keyboard. Press ⌘-Shift-H to get your History with Firefox for the Mac.

Bookmarks: Getting Back to Where You've Been

The history list can get you back to sites you previously visited, but it remembers only the last few dozen sites.

When you find a Web page you might like to visit again, a better way to bookmark it for future visiting is, well, to *bookmark it.* Thereafter, the *next* time you want to visit that page, you're spared having to remember *http://www.hothollywoodhairstyles.com* or whatever; you can just choose the page's name from your Bookmarks or Favorites menu (Figure 2-2).

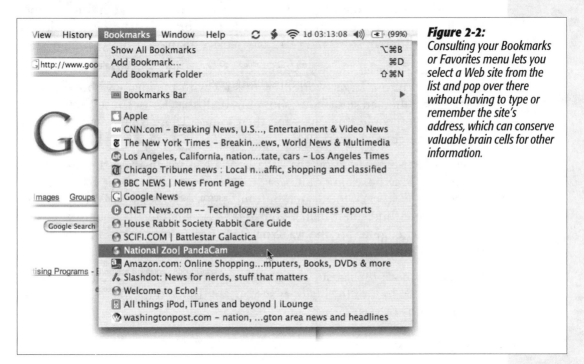

Figure 2-2:
Consulting your Bookmarks or Favorites menu lets you select a Web site from the list and pop over there without having to type or remember the site's address, which can conserve valuable brain cells for other information.

Adding bookmarks

To bookmark a page or site that's currently up on your computer screen, go to the Bookmarks or Favorites menu and choose the relevant command: "Add Bookmark," "Add Page to Favorites," "Bookmark this page," or whatever. Most Windows browsers also let you right-click on a page and choose the add bookmark command from the shortcut menu; in Internet Explorer 7, you can just click the big yellow plus sign (+) at the top of the browser window.

Once you start saving a lot of bookmarks, though, the list can get as unwieldy as an old overstuffed paper address book with Post-Its and business cards constantly slipping out. If you want some tips for tidying up and organizing your Bookmarks/Favorites list, stroll over to page 64.

Portals: Dashboards of the Web

As you may have gathered from this chapter already, the Web is *huge*. Filled with sites devoted to news, stocks, sports, games, movies, real estate, television, and more, it's hard to decide where to go first. It's like having a shopping list with dozens of things you need to buy, but every item is for sale in a completely different store and you have to drive all over town to get it all.

This is where a *portal* site comes in handy. As the name suggests, a portal site is an entryway into a larger world. Or, to stick with the analogy above, a good portal site is like an enormous shopping mall that houses just about all the stores that you could think of—and then some. (There isn't, however, a Corn Dog Hut franchise in *this* mall.)

A *search box* somewhere on the page is one feature all these portals have in common. These boxes are quite easy to use: Type in keywords related to the subject you seek, click the Search button, and wait to see what Web pages the search engine thinks best match your query. As Chapter 3 explains in greater detail, search engines are the way you find specific information in the Web's massive sprawl.

Portals are more than just search engines, though. This section gives you a guided tour of four of the big ones so you can decide if they'll be useful to you in your online travels.

Google

Google is the Web's card catalog, the closest thing it's got to a master directory. Hundreds of millions of people a day use this simple, streamlined search box to find what they're looking for online.

Google started out as a Web-search company created by two Stanford University students. Although it's officially been around only since 1998, Google didn't take long to explode in popularity to become the Web's dominant search site.

With a well-stocked arsenal of ambition, skill, and venture capital money to fuel its projects, Google soon became much more than a search box—to see what lies behind that clean white façade, go to *www.google.com* and click the

More link. Google's vast suite of software, services, and online tools fills the page. Many of these features like Google Maps, Earth, Froogle, Groups, News, Images, and oh, yes, *Search*, are discussed in various chapters of this book.

But to turn this page into a portal that lists what you consider the most useful sites, hit the browser's Back button and click the Personalized Home link at the top of the main Google page. With the personalization tools that appear on the left side of the screen, you can knock yourself out cluttering up Google's nice clean interface by adding the local weather forecast, stock market updates, the *Washington Post*, *Forbes* magazine, and sports and news headlines from major outlets like ESPN. And if you don't have enough news tidbits on your page to keep your brain burning, you can also add Quote of the Day and Word of the Day sections to your page.

If you sign up for a free Google account, the company will store your personalized page's settings on its servers so you can see it on other computers. And no matter how much stuff you slather on your personal Google page, the tidy blocks of links on the clean white background still make the page look neater and less chaotic than most other portal sites.

Yahoo

Yahoo, too, was founded (in 1994) by two Ph.D. students at Stanford University in California (perhaps the school should change its mascot from the Cardinal to the Fighting Search Engines).

Yahoo was one of the early pioneers out on the Web frontier and has become a major destination for many an online traveler. Although it was first known as a search engine and directory site for finding things on the Web, Yahoo has boomed into an integrated network of software and services, with its own free e-mail accounts and instant messaging software, plus online merchants, news services, personal ad directory, and much more.

The Yahoo home page, located at *www.yahoo.com*, is a jumble of links, icons, and images, plus a few flickering Web advertisements stuck in the middle of it all. In fact, it has a certain mall-like hyperactivity of many things trying to get your attention all at once. But, if you need a diving board to leap into the deep end of the Web, Yahoo has plenty of spring to it.

Links on the main page lead the way to pages with all kinds of information, including Hollywood gossip, the current weather forecast for your town, financial news, movie listings, sports updates, and even your daily horoscope. The link to Yahoo Maps lets you type in an address and get a map showing its location, plus driving directions to get there. There's even a section of the site especially for children. Dubbed "Yahooligans," the kids' table at the Yahoo feast offers games, jokes, and research links for history papers about the Teapot Dome scandal and other boring homework assignments.

To use some of Yahoo's "services," which include its free Web-based email (page 263), online calendars, and discussion groups, you need to sign up for a Yahoo account. Don't worry—it's free, but you may find yourself getting a lot of mail and "special offers" from the company and its partners. Once you sign up, you can customize your Yahoo home page more to your liking, like having your own local weather and news displayed.

Note: MSN and AOL are both subscription-based online services, but you can use their portal pages for free.

MSN

Microsoft's MSN portal page, found at *www.msn.com*, is also crammed with features and links, many of which compete with Yahoo's services. Buttons for Microsoft's free Hotmail email accounts and its MSN Messenger instant message program (Chapter 15) invite you to click and sign up, and headlines from its MSNBC cable television and Web site dominate the news section. Other Microsoft properties, like *Slate* magazine and the Encarta reference collection also have prominent spots on the MSN portal page.

Topics are arranged neatly in groups according to categories like News & Sports, Living & Finances, and Entertainment. Its handy Look It Up reference section with links to pages containing maps, telephone listings, and city guides can make finding your way around town easier.

MSN also invites you to create your own free account and craft your own My MSN version of the page. Once you sign up, you can see your Hotmail inbox, local listings, news, weather, and other personalized content all in one convenient place. And, if you decide that you're a better designer than the MSN folks, you can change the page's layout, color, and theme.

AOL

America Online, one of the first major online services to jump on the Internet bandwagon and lasso millions of customers in the 1990s, also maintains its own Web portal at *www.aol.com*. America Online customers who already have an account with the company can use the portal to check their AOL mail from whatever computer they happen to be using.

Craigslist: The Bizarre Bazaar

Combining classified advertising and an online community of people around the world looking for jobs, love, and used furniture, Craigslist (*www.craigslist.org*) is a simple, no-frills, no-design Web site used by 10 million people a month. The site grew out of an Internet mailing list started in 1995 by software engineer Craig Newmark, the man who put the *Craig* in Craigslist.

Since it began, Craigslist has bloomed into a worldwide marketplace and trading post that has put a dent in many a newspaper's classified-ads department. That's because people can post their ads and messages for *free* on Craigslist (except for the job listings in San Francisco, Los Angeles, and New York). This non-commercial attitude harkens back to a more innocent, socially oriented time in the Internet's history when people were willing to help other people without charge.

Most major cities around the world have their own specialized areas on Craigslist, so if you're looking for a one-bedroom flat for a summer in Edinburgh, you can click the link for Edinburgh on the main

Craigslist page and then browse through all the listings around the Scottish capital. Each ad listed on the site has an e-mail address to use for contacting the person posting the item, service, or personal plea for a boyfriend or girlfriend.

Placing an ad on Craigslist is simple—just click the link for the city you live in on the main page, and then click the "Post to Classifieds" link to get started filling out your ad. When you're going through the ad-posting steps, you can also choose to use an anonymous address provided by the site so that your real email address isn't out there in the open.

Auto parts, music lessons, and college basketball tickets are among the thousands of items hawked on the site every day, and Craigslist also hosts a number of discussion forums where people can post messages on various topics. It's a relatively uncensored space with a fair share of explicit posts, though, and the fact that it doesn't cost anything makes Craigslist an attractive space for people to gather—taste, decorum, or sanity *not* required.

A block of links called the AOL Directory provide a gateway to the site's popular topics and services, like its Diet & Fitness, Food & Home, and Research & Learn pages, plus all the usual city guides, sports news, and financial information you've come to expect from a portal site.

There are also links to the popular MapQuest mapping-and-driving directions site and the Love@AOL personal ads area. Thanks to AOL's membership in the Time Warner entertainment empire, its corporate partnerships, and its own deep well of content, the site hosts a large collection of video clips from film and television, links to streaming music from XM Satellite Radio, and plenty of news stories and photos.

Tip: If you want a blast from the past, AOL may be the place for you. With its In2TV feature, the company has freed hundreds of old sitcoms, adventure shows, and Westerns from the vaults of time and made them available for anyone to watch on the Web for free. Chapter 12 has details on how you can relive the glory days of *F-Troop* and *Maverick*.

And, if you like the portal page enough and are tempted by some of the members-only services, you can find a link to download AOL's own software and sign up for a full-fledged America Online account. You can also download the free AOL Instant Messenger (AIM) software for your Windows or Macintosh computer here, too. (See Chapter 15 for more about instant messaging.)

Tip: Many portal sites also have alternate versions in Spanish that you can switch to just by clicking an Español link or button on the English version of the page. For AOL's Spanish edition, go to *http://latino.aol.com*.

Browser Choices

If you have a Windows-based computer, a copy of Microsoft's Internet Explorer Web browser is already on your hard drive. Likewise, if you've got yourself a Macintosh machine running the Mac OS X operating system, Apple's Safari browser is right there in your Applications folder.

These built-in browsers get you tooling around the Web with a minimum of fuss, but someday you may find yourself wanting, well, *more*. More security and flexibility in the case of Internet Explorer, or more sites that work with your browser in the case of Safari, which still encounters some Mac-browser bias here and there from certain Web sites that only display their pages properly for Windows browsers.

Lucky for you, there are plenty of other Web browsers to choose from. If you think you want to surf with new software, you merely have to point your current browser to the right download page, snag a copy of the new program, and install it on your computer. This section gives you a look at some of the other Web browsers worth a look.

Firefox

Free, fast, and fun to customize, the Firefox browser has only been out since 2005 but has already been adopted by more than 10 million people—many of whom were rattled by Internet Explorer's vulnerably to malicious tampering.

So what makes Firefox so great? For one thing, it can do just about everything Internet Explorer can do, and then adds these chocolate sprinkles on top:

- **Cross-platform.** Firefox is available, in nearly identical versions, for both Windows and Macintosh.

- **Better security.** Internet Explorer allows the use of little bits of code called ActiveX controls to run Web-based games and other interactive features, but Firefox doesn't. So when rogue programs or spyware (Chapter 21) try to install themselves on your machine through your Web browser, Firefox slams the door shut. After a flurry of IE-related security incidents, some experts even advised people who use Windows to ditch Explorer altogether and run with Firefox.

- **Pop-up blocking.** Pop-ups—pesky extra windows that multiply all over your screen on behalf of an advertiser or worse—make browsing more aggravating than it should be, but Firefox blocks them from even opening. (The latest versions of Internet Explorer can block pop-ups as well. Safari also wields a pop-up shield.)

- **Tabbed browsing.** The ability to have multiple Web pages open in the same window—with each one sporting a folder-like tab at the top for easy clicking back and forth—isn't as unique to Firefox as it once was now that Safari and Internet Explorer 7 have jumped on the tabbed browsing bandwagon. But Firefox still makes elegant use of this time-saving innovation and keeps your desktop free of extra browser windows.

- **RSS.** With blogs, news sites, and even technical support pages constantly updating themselves, Firefox's use of *RSS feeds* (page 111) makes it much easier to keep up with all the latest headlines each time your favorite sites add new information. Subscribing to a site is as effortless as clicking a button.

- **Extensions.** Firefox is a spawn of the Mozilla Foundation, an *open source* (volunteer) software group dedicated to sharing code among programmers and building a better, sturdier product than companies that keep their code closed to public view. And with so many people contributing to Firefox's development, it's only natural that really fun add-ons called extensions would develop alongside the browser. Adding a few extensions to your Firefox browser can make it do really cool things, like flash the current temperature, control your MP3 jukebox program from the browser window, or zoom in on images; check out the Extensions list at *https://addons.mozilla. org/firefox.*

- **Find box.** When you search within a Web page for a specific word or phrase, Firefox gives you a convenient Find box down at the bottom of the browser window that doesn't block your view of the page you're searching.

- **Search shortcuts.** You don't even need to jump to a search engine page to search the Web with Firefox. The browser has a search box embedded right in its toolbar with shortcuts to many different sites including Google, Amazon, and eBay.

But while other browsers have added similar features, Firefox still continues to make great strides in Web surfing. On the downside, some sites just won't display properly or even work right if you try to view them with Firefox. But back to the upside: Firefox can import your bookmarks, passwords, cookies, and other information from Internet Explorer, Safari, and older versions of Netscape, so switching browsers is easy.

Getting and setting up Firefox

If you want to join the millions of people on Team Firefox, point your current browser to *www.getfirefox.com* and download a free copy for yourself. It works with Windows 98 or later and Mac OS X 10.2 and beyond.

Once the installer file downloads to your computer, double-click the file to install the program. As part of the setup process, Firefox asks if you'd like to import information from another browser. If you say yes and tell it which one you use, the program snags all your bookmarks and Web-site passwords, plus Internet connection settings and the data that lets Internet Explorer and other browsers automatically fill in your name and address on Web forms.

After you install the program, you can find it on your Windows machine at Start → All Programs → Mozilla Firefox or as a desktop shortcut. If you choose to make it your default browser during the installation process, the Firefox icon replaces Internet Explorer's at the top corner of the Start menu. Mac folks can find the Firefox icon nestled inside their Applications folder, where it can easily be dragged onto the Mac OS X Dock for easy access.

Netscape

Once the King of Browsers, thanks to its fast start out of the gate in the early 1990s when the Web was still young, Netscape found itself dethroned and booted to the royal curb by Internet Explorer before the turn of the century. It's still around in versions for Windows and Macintosh systems and can be downloaded from the Browser link at *www.netscape.com* (a not-so-bad portal page in its own right). The Mac edition inevitably lags a version behind the

Windows browser, though, which often annoys Mac people enough to ignore Netscape and use something else.

The latest version of Netscape for Windows includes spyware-stopping security, support for RSS feeds (page 111), pop-up blocking, tabbed browsing, and many of the features becoming standard on most modern-era browsers. Installing Netscape is basically the same procedure as the Firefox installation described earlier: Download the installer program from the Netscape site, double-click the downloaded file to install the browser, and follow the onscreen instructions for configuring the software.

Opera

Bursting onstage from a Norwegian laboratory comes Opera, a versatile alternative browser with versions for Windows and Macintosh at *www.opera.com*. Not content to just stay on the desktop, Opera's also the browser of choice on a number of cellphones and the Nintendo DS handheld gaming console.

The browser's Web site boasts of its page-loading speed, plus its tightly woven programming code and excellent security record. Other features include the usual tabbed browsing, pop-up blocking, and integrated quick search bar.

Tip: For people still using Mac OS 9 systems and unable to surf with Safari or Firefox, both Netscape and Opera have older versions of their browsers available on their sites that still work with OS 9. For those wondering whatever happened to Internet Explorer for the Mac, Microsoft stopped supporting it and removed the program from its Web site at the end of 2005.

Top Tips for Setting Up Your Browser

Since your browser speeds you around the Web and all its sites, it's only natural that you'd want to customize it for a more comfortable ride. Instead of sheepskin seat covers, a big stereo system, and fuzzy dice hanging from the rearview mirror, you can make your Web vehicle fit your needs by choosing your own home page, rearranging your program's onscreen buttons and controls, organizing your bookmarks, and adding on helpful browser toolbars that save time and mouse clicks.

Choose your own home page

Every time you sign on to the Web, your browser starts by showing you the same darned page—probably one foisted on you by Apple, Microsoft, or Firefox.

One of your first acts, therefore, should be to change this startup page to a more desirable starting point. For example, you may prefer *www.dilbert.com*, which is a daily comic strip; *www.google.com*, the Web search expert; *www. nytimes.com* for the day's headlines; or even your own home page, if you have one. Thereafter, you can instantly return to your startup page by clicking the little icon shaped like a house in your browser's toolbar.

To change it, you need to go into your browser's Home Page settings (a sample of which is shown in Figure 2-3). Here's where to find them in the most common browsers:

- **Internet Explorer.** Choose Tools → Internet Options → General
- **Safari.** Choose Safari → Preferences → General
- **Firefox (Windows).** Choose Tools → Options → General
- **Firefox (Mac).** Choose Firefox → Preferences → General

Figure 2-3:
In the settings or preferences box for your browser program, add the URL you'd really like to call Home.

In the box under Home Page, you can type or paste the URL of your preferred starter site. If you happen to have your browser parked on the very page you want to use, just click the "Use Current Page" button in the box. Once you've typed, pasted, or clicked, click OK to close your settings box. Your new home page is set.

Most other browsers keep this setting in a similar place within the program. Check under the Tools menu in a Windows browser or in the program's Preferences area on a Mac.

Tip: Internet Explorer 7 lets you have multiple home pages that all open in separate tabs when you start the browser. Choose Tools → Internet Options → General, and hit the Enter key after you add each URL in the Home Page box so each address is on its own line. If you regularly visit the same handful of pages, this multitab tool is a real timesaver.

Customize your button and toolbars

Your browser's button and toolbars are like your dashboard controls that help you navigate your way around the Web, and they're easy to adjust. For Internet Explorer and Firefox for Windows, right-clicking in the toolbar area of the browser brings up a Customize option on the shortcut menu (Figure 2-4). Control-clicking the Safari or Firefox toolbar area on the Mac brings up the same menu.

Figure 2-4:
Top: Right-click (or Control-click for you single-button Mac folks) in the toolbar area of your browser to get the Customize menu option Toolbar.

Bottom: In the Customize box, you can pick and choose the toolbar buttons for your browser to make it better suit your point-and-click needs.

Once you get the Customize Toolbar box (Figure 2-4, bottom) on screen, you can drag and drop new buttons (say, History, Copy, Paste, or Print) onto your toolbar, drag buttons you never use out of your sight, and add vertical separator lines to group your buttons into sections. You can often adjust the size of the icons on your toolbars and even add whole new toolbars.

The View menu of most browsers also has options to add to your browser window, like a Status bar that shows the progress of a loading page. You can also open vertical panes along the side of the browser window to display your History file or bookmarks.

If you decide you want to return to the browser window as you first found it, use the Restore Defaults option to go back in time and put the browser back to the way it was.

Note: In versions of Safari before 2.0, you customize the browser buttons by selecting items listed on the View menu.

Set up and organize your bookmarks

Imagine vertically stacking every book you own in a large, unalphabetized pile and then trying to find a particular title in a couple of seconds. If you don't have very many books, this isn't difficult, but the higher the pile, the longer it's going to take to find what you want. Bookshelves that let you divide up your library by topic or title are one way to get that pile of books organized, and most Web browsers include features that let you similarly get your bookmarks in a sensible order.

Just about every browser has an Organize Favorites, Show All Bookmarks, or Manage Bookmarks option under its Favorites or Bookmarks menu. Selecting this menu item opens a window where you can see all your bookmarks or favorites in a list, as shown in Figure 2-5. In this window, you can drag the titles of Web pages higher or lower on the list so they appear that way in your Bookmarks/Favorites menu. You can also click and delete the bookmarks of sites you no longer wish to visit.

- **Folders.** Want to have all your bookmarks on a certain topic grouped together in the list? Just make a new folder in your bookmark manager window and drag in the desired site titles so they all appear in the same section of your list. For example, if you constantly check out news on your hometown pro football team and want to find all the right bookmarks for it, make a new folder, call it "Cleveland Browns," and drag in your bookmarks for the team's official Web site (*www.clevelandbrowns.com*, but you knew that already), plus the *Sports Illustrated*, ESPN, NFL, and *Cleveland Plain Dealer* Web sites.

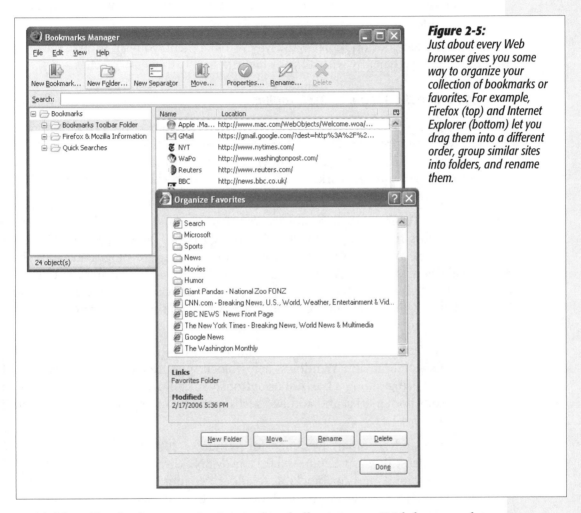

Figure 2-5:
Just about every Web browser gives you some way to organize your collection of bookmarks or favorites. For example, Firefox (top) and Internet Explorer (bottom) let you drag them into a different order, group similar sites into folders, and rename them.

• **Dividers.** For further organization and eyeball ease, most Web browsers let you add horizontal separator lines between certain groupings of bookmarks in a list.

• **Sorting.** If you're not super-fussy about topical organization, you can make the browser sort your list alphabetically, based on the Web page's title. Look for a Sort By Name option in the menus or when you right-click on the list.

• **Links or Bookmarks bar.** Many modern browsers let you sport a horizontal clickable list of your absolute, all-time favorite bookmarks right on a "bookmarks bar" area of the browser window so you don't even have to pull down a menu to get to the site. One easy way to add a bookmark to this area is to simply drag the address out of the Address bar and drop it on the Bookmarks bar (flip back to Figure 2-1 for a reminder of where both these bars are).

Once you get your bookmarks the way you like them, you can browse the Web much more efficiently with all your favorite sites within easy reach.

Add a Google, Yahoo, or MSN toolbar

And when your browser doesn't give you enough toolbars on its own, you can always add more. Specialty toolbars from Google, Yahoo, and MSN add their own search boxes and a number of enhancements to the browsing experience, but not every toolbar works with every browser, so check the system requirements carefully before downloading.

- **Google Toolbar.** Available for Internet Explorer and Firefox (both Mac and Windows flavors) and shown back in Figure 2-1, the Google Toolbar lets you share Web pages you like by email, text message, or blog. You can highlight your search terms in bright yellow on the pages you find, automatically fill in and check your spelling in Web forms, and even translate English words into different languages when you wave the mouse cursor over them. (*http://toolbar.google.com*)

- **Yahoo Toolbar.** The Yahoo bar, which works with Internet Explorer and Firefox for Mac and Windows, helps block spyware from infiltrating your PC and brings along a box full of buttons you can click to check your email, see your bookmarks, and add RSS feeds with one mouse tap. (*http://toolbar.yahoo.com*)

- **MSN Search Toolbar.** Designed for Windows 2000 and XP systems running at least Internet Explorer 5.0.1, the MSN Search Toolbar brings tabbed browsing and pop-up blocking to older versions on Microsoft's flagship browser. (An earlier version of the toolbar is available for Windows 98 systems.) The latest version of the toolbar also includes a feature to automatically fill in Web forms and Window Desktop Search, which lets you search for files and documents stored on your PC's hard drive. (*http://toolbar.msn.com*)

Once you've got your browser custom-fitted to your liking, you're ready to zoom around the Web in style. But before you get too far from your home page, remember that the Web's not always the safest place to travel. Check out Chapter 21 for the lowdown on how to stay safe when you're online.

Note: Sometimes add-on toolbars can cause bad browser behavior like constant crashing. If you install one and your browser immediately heads south every time you try to launch it, odds are you have a bit of a software war in progress. To uninstall the toolbar, choose Start → Control Panel → Add/Remove Programs, select the toolbar from the list of programs, and click the Change/Remove button to yank that thing out of there.

UP TO SPEED

Essential Software for Your Software

Once you get a Web browser, you may need to install a handful of little helper programs to see all the different kinds of files and documents available on the Web. These helper programs are usually called *plug-ins* because they plug right into your existing Web browser, giving it additional powers.

When you start your Web-surfing adventures, you may even get warning messages from some Web sites telling you that you need a particular plug-in to properly view the site. Here are some of the more common plug-ins and what they plug you in to. (You can also find links to these plug-ins on this book's "Missing CD" page: *www.missingmanuals.com*.)

Adobe Reader. The Adobe Reader plug-in lets you view and print files in the Portable Document Format (PDF). PDF files have become the lingua franca of the Web, as they preserve the original look of a printed document, down to the typefaces, pictures, colors and other elements. Click the button for Adobe Reader at *www.adobe.com* to get yourself a copy of the free program.

Flash. Web pages that have graphics, pictures, or animations all bouncing around onscreen often use Adobe's Flash Player plug-in. If you don't see anything bouncing or get a message about not having the plug-in, you need to download and install the latest version of Flash Player. Don't worry, the plug-in is free, as is its sister software, Shockwave Player, which is used by a lot of online games. You can get both of these by clicking on the links for them at *www.adobe.com*.

RealPlayer. Many news-oriented Web sites (see Chapter 5 for information about finding your favorite news spots online) that offer digital video clips use the RealPlayer software from RealNetworks to create these Web-sized videos. To watch any of them, you need the RealPlayer plug-in installed on your system. Real will try to sell you a monthly service and fancy player software for a price, but look for the free version at *www.real.com*.

QuickTime. Apple's video-playing program shows up everywhere from iPods to home video productions; most big-budget movie trailers are also made with QuickTime. If you have a Mac, you already have this plug-in. If you use a PC you can download the free plug-in at *www.apple.com/quicktime*. Either way, you can watch dozens of upcoming movie trailers at *www.apple.com/trailers*.

Part Two:
Finding Information

2

How to Search the Web

Ever walk into a used bookstore? You know, the kind that has thousands of books jammed ceiling-high? The book you want is probably in there somewhere—but good luck finding it. The Web's a little bit like that jumbled bookstore—times a billion.

Enter the *search engine*. As mentioned back on page 54, a search engine is a site that seeks out Web pages, using the words you type in as clues (like *1960 best actress Oscar* or *weather New Jersey*).

This chapter takes a look at the Web's major search engines and explains how searching the Web is more than just typing in a couple of terms into Google and sifting through the first few entries on the results page. Finding gold, after all, goes a lot quicker when you know where to mine it. This chapter saves you the trouble of panning through 10 acres of dirt looking for the good stuff.

You'll also find tips on looking for information effectively, so you can find what you want and still have some time left over…to go read a book.

UP TO SPEED

How Search Engines Work

Most search engines learn what's on the Web by sending out automated programs called *spiders* or *crawlers* (searching the *Web,* get it?) to scan the Internet for pages that have been created or changed since the spider's last spin around the Web. When it finds fresh material, the spider program adds the page to its *index,* a huge catalog of all the sites it's seen.

Search Basics

Using a search engine is pretty simple. For example, if you want to learn how to give haircuts to poodles in Pensacola, you can click in the search box at Google.com (for example), type in *dog grooming schools in Pensacola*, and hit Enter (or click Search).

The search engine's software jumps head-first into its index of the billions of Web pages it's catalogued, and then presents you with a ranked list of all the pages that it thinks best match your keywords. This *search results* page (Figure 3-1) contains brief descriptions of each site that matches your search, along with a link to click so you can go see the whole page yourself.

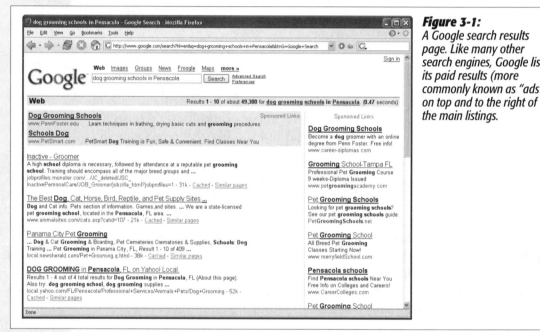

Figure 3-1:
A Google search results page. Like many other search engines, Google lists its paid results (more commonly known as "ads") on top and to the right of the main listings.

Many search engines have become household names, and the next three sections describe the major dogs in the search race: Google, Yahoo, and MSN.

Searching with Google

Unless you're fresh off the shuttle from Alpha Centauri, you've probably heard of Google (*www.google.com*). Google made its mark in the late 1990s by doing one thing really, really well: teasing relevant search results from the morass of information on the Web. It got so popular—it's by far the most widely used search engine—it became a pop-culture verb ("He gave me his business card at the party, and I went home and Googled him").

Beyond Googling

Google may look simple when you first behold its home page. But, man, is it tippy and tricky. You could write a whole book about it, in fact (like *Google: The Missing Manual*).

Here, though, are a few favorite tricks:

- Phrase your question in the form of an answer. So instead of typing, *What is the average per capita income of Greece?*, you might get better results by typing, *Average per capita income of Greece is*.

- You can also use Google as a global White Pages and Yellow Pages. Search for *home depot cleveland, oh* and Google instantly produces the address and phone number of the Cleveland Home Depot. This works with names (*robert jones las vegas, nv*) as well as businesses.

- To track your packages, type in a FedEx or UPS package number (just the digits); when you click Search, Google offers a link to its tracking information.

- Google is a calculator, too. Type in an equation (*32+2345*3-234=*) and click Search to see the answer.

- Put Google to work as a units of measurement converter. Type *inches in a mile*, for example, or *teaspoons in a quart*. Click Search to see the answer.

- Type in *AAPL* or *MSFT*, for example, to see a link to the current Apple or Microsoft stock price, graphs, financial news, and so on.

- Type in an area code, like *415*, to see a link to a map of the area.

- Type in a UPC bar code number, such as *036000250015*, to see a description of the product you've just "scanned in."

- Type in a flight number like *American 152* or *VS 03* for a link to a map of that flight's progress in the air. Or type in the tail number you see on an airplane for the full registration form for that plane.

- Type in a VIN (vehicle identification number, which is etched onto a plate, usually on the door frame), like *JH4NA1157MT001832*, to find out the car's year, make, and model.

- Poke around the Services & Tools link on the Google.com home page and you'll find some of the other lesser-known Google features. For example, there's Froogle (product search), News, Groups (Internet discussion boards), Google Catalogs (hundreds of scanned-in product catalogs), Images (find graphics and photos from other people's Web sites), Blogger (publish your own online journal), Google language translation, Google Answers (pay a couple of bucks to have a professional researcher find the answers for you), and much more.

You may never leave Google.com again.

Basic Search

You're using the Internet to save time, right? So don't waste time by typing more than necessary or missing out on the timesaving features your chosen search engine offers. In addition to the tips in the box on page 76, here's how Google can make searching more productive and efficient:

- **Try "I'm Feeling Lucky."** This button offers more than a cute Clint Eastwood quote. Clicking it skips the whole results list and takes you straight to Google's #1-ranked page for the words you typed. Google's ranking system is its claim to fame, so this button gets it right a surprising amount of the time. For example, if you want to check out the academic offerings at Tulane University, type *tulane* and hit your Lucky button to arrive at the school's home page.

- **Don't stress over spelling.** When you type in the search box, your spelling doesn't have to be perfect. Just take your best guess. Google's smart enough to figure it out and even offer to link you to the correctly spelled results ("Did you mean: *schwarzenegger*").

- **Word variations count, too.** Google uses a technology called *stemming* that looks at the basic part of your search term and can find pages with similar terms as well. If you're looking for *swimming*, you'll probably get pages with *swim* and *swimmer* as well. If you're not getting the results you want, though, try typing in the word variations yourself, especially for more obscure words.

- **Skip the conjunction junction.** Older search systems make you use *and* between words to find pages that include all of them. Google automatically searches for all words you type, but ignores commonplace words like *and, the, where, how,* and so on. The site also ignores single letters and numbers. Should you need to include one of these babies in your search, preface it with a plus sign (+): *george +h +w bush, +the donald,* and so on.

Note: Google and most other search engines make their money by displaying ads on your results page. For example, a Honda dealer can pay for a sponsored link whenever somebody searches for *motorcycle*. But don't worry—no one's tricking you into clicking an ad. Sponsored links are clearly labeled and separated from your *real* results, at the top or side of the page.

Advanced Search

If you can't find satisfactory results with Google's basic page, click the Advanced Search link. As shown in Figure 3-2, filling out the Advanced Search form lets you narrow your query and target very specific pages in your results.

You can search for German-language pages about Nietzsche that have been written since last year, for example.

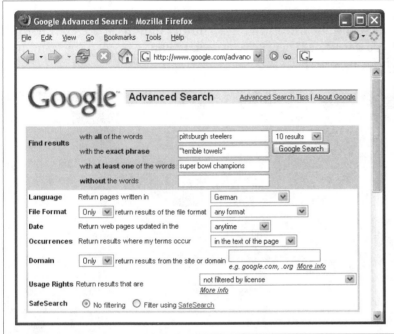

Figure 3-2:
The more information you supply on Google's Advanced Search page, the narrower your search results will be. The form goes on much longer than shown here, giving you plenty of ways to whittle down your results with precision.

The Advanced Search page works with several common *search operators*—shortcut symbols that let you narrow the focus of your search terms. Here are a few Google search tricks to try:

- **Synonym search.** You can broaden your results to include the synonyms for a search term by typing a tilde (~) in front of the word. Say you're looking for good ol' bluegrass fiddle information but don't want to miss important information that may be hiding on hoity-toity violin sites. Type *~fiddle,* and Google rounds up sites about both fiddles and violins (maybe even a mandolin or two).

- **OR search.** Computers are binary little things by their very nature, and you can choose *this* or *that* as part of your results by typing a big capital OR between your search terms. If you want pages about dachshunds *or* beagles in your puppy research, type *dachshunds OR beagles.* It's like two searches in one.

- **Numrange search.** Searching for pages that include a specific range of numbers is a big help when you're zeroing in on a price, doing some history research, or brushing up on your sports stats. All you need is a couple of dots (..) between your dates. If you want to review Larry Bird's Boston Celtics career during the 1980s, type *larry bird 1980..1989*.

- **Domain search.** You can also search for results within a specific Web site by typing your keywords in front of the word *site:*, followed by the site you want to scour. Want the lowdown on dormitory options at the University of Chicago? Type *dorms site:www.uchicago.edu* to eliminate all other campuses from your housing search.

Things Every Searcher Should Know

Schools don't offer Web Searching 101. After all, you just type stuff into a box and click Search, right? Well, some search box techniques are so obvious *once you know them* that nobody talks about them. So, in case you were asleep the day the world was talking about things like exact-phrase searches, this box is your free cheat sheet. (And, by the way, *nobody* clicks Search anymore. Just hit Enter.)

Don't bother with capital letters. Search engines read every word you type as lowercase, so save your strength.

Use quotation marks to find exact phrases. Unless you specify otherwise, search engines look for pages containing *all* the words you put in the box, in any order. If you type in *ruler of the Queen's Navy*, you'll likely find Web pages that combine those great twin passions: office supplies and military recruitment.

But if you put quotation marks around the phrase, you get only pages containing those words in that sequence. This trick's great for finding song lyrics when you can't remember the exact title. For example, *"ruler of the Queen's Navy"* finds pages about Gilbert and Sullivan.

Use straightforward search terms. To paraphrase Einstein, "As simple as possible, but no simpler." If you're searching for Thai restaurants in London's Soho district, then *london soho thai restaurant* gets much better results than something long and redundant, like *london england soho neighborhood with moderately priced thai food places*. And if you have specifics, use 'em. If you know you want *Depression glass,* search for those words instead of the more general *old bowls*.

Use the minus sign (–) to eliminate unwanted results. Most search engines let you use a minus sign to subtract information you *don't* want to see. For example, say you're searching for hotels in New York's Soho neighborhood. Typing *hotel soho new york –london* eliminates listings of accommodations in England. On the flip side, most search engines recognize the plus sign (+) in front of a word as an indicator that you want to see only pages containing that word.

Your favorite search site may have its own tips and tricks for maximizing your results. Look for a Help or Services link on the main page that leads you to a guide for using the site to its fullest potential.

Searching with Yahoo

As one of the Web's first, and still most popular, portals (page 54), Yahoo is an information empire unto itself. It offers online auctions, personal ads, travel service, TV listings, and more, as you'll find throughout this book. Oh yeah, and a search engine.

Yahoo's search box was digging up reliable results long before Google entered the fray. Shortly after Google's appearance, though, Yahoo gave its search engine its own page (*http://search.yahoo.com*). (Apparently, the company suddenly felt compelled to offer an alternative to the notorious sensory overload of its portal page.)

Yahoo's search page (Figure 3-3) greets you with a search box right in the middle of the screen. In the row of links along the top of the search box, you can scoot over to special search departments, including:

• The Yahoo Directory (page 82)

• Images (page 234)

• News (page 99)

• Maps (page 88)

• People (page 86)

Figure 3-3:
Like most search sites, Yahoo follows Google's lead in placing its search box front and center, with links to other categories clearly arranged above. It also manages to squeeze in a few links to news stories and the closing market prices (in case you're wondering what's going on in the world while you search the Web).

Tip: The More link to the right of these listings reveals links to Yahoo's Preferences (similar to Google's preferences, as described earlier) and other new and cool features. There's a toolbar to make Yahoo's search box, People search, Job search, and so on, a part of your browser window.

Every self-respecting search engine has its own way of helping your search along. Google's got the "I'm Feeling Lucky" button, and Yahoo has "Also try". If others in the Yahoo universe have conducted searches similar to yours, you get links to these related searches at the very top of your results page. If you search for *flutes*, for example, Yahoo suggests that you also try *wedding flutes* and *native american flutes.* If one of those other searches sounds closer to what you're looking for, click it.

Attention shoppers: If you're online to buy, Yahoo's your search engine. Like a personal shopper on steroids, Yahoo Shopping has connections to thousands of online merchants, manufacturers, and auction houses. It knows where to find stuff and who has the best prices. If anyone's selling something you've typed in Yahoo's search box, you'll see a shortcut at the top of your results list: *Flutes on Yahoo! Shopping,* for example. Clicking this link reveals a ready-made comparison-shopping list, complete with pictures, prices, descriptions, and links to the seller's page.

Advanced Search

Yahoo's Advanced Search form lets you fine-tune your information request with many of the same features as Google's (page 74). For example, you can narrow your search to specific Web domains like *.gov* (federal- and state-run sites) or *.edu* (colleges and universities).

The Advanced Search page also gives you the option to include subscription-only sites and databases like Lexis-Nexis, *Consumer Reports*, and *The Wall Street Journal* that you may have access to. (If you're curious what kind of info you get when you pay Lexis-Nexis, Factiva, and other database sites, see the next chapter.)

Note: There's a SafeSearch feature on Yahoo's Advanced Search page, but it applies only to that one search. To block pornographic sites permanently, do so in Preferences (click the More link on Yahoo's Search home page).

404 Page Not Found

There's nothing worse than plugging in some Web site's address and being greeted with nothing but the stupidly worded message, "404 Page Not Found".

This cryptic (and frustrating) message simply means your Web browser can't get to a page. Perhaps a computer has crashed or a Web designer has deleted or rearranged pages. The Web is ever changing, so your browser displays this message to let you know that it didn't find the page where it expected. If only you could turn back the clock to when the page was there.

Actually, you can. If you found the missing Web site by using Google or another search page, look for the word Cached underneath the link.

Most search engines memorize, or *cache,* snapshots of the Web at regular intervals. If you click the word Cached on the search results page, you get to see what the page looked like the last time Google looked it over. The cached version of the page may be out of date, but if you just need basic facts, the old page may help. As a bonus, your search terms are usually highlighted on the page.

Searching with MSN

Microsoft has its own version of pretty much everything, and a search engine is no exception. To use MSN Search, steer your browser to *http://search.msn.com.* As on Google and Yahoo, you can search the site's index of Web pages, images, and news sites by clicking the appropriate category, typing your terms, and hitting Enter.

As shown in Figure 3-4, though, MSN Search has a drop-down menu with these (and other) category options right next to the Search button. If your query's related to shopping, music, stocks, movies, or whatever, you can save yourself a few clicks by choosing from the menu first. For example, if you type in a film title and use MSN Search's Find Movies option, you get a page full of background information on the movie, plus images and cast bios from the production.

Although Apple has claim to the slogan "Think different," Microsoft does have its own way of doing things. For example, instead of an Advanced Search option, you get a page called Search Builder. To create a complex query, you must construct it in stages by typing words and then clicking the "Add to Search" button.

Figure 3-4:
With the menu on the end of the MSN Search box, you can search a specific source or focus on a particular angle of your keywords. If you have or want to install the MSN Search bar (page 66), you can include the files on your hard drive in your search by selecting the Desktop option just above the search box.

There's also a stack of options on the left side of the page, like Site/Domain, Country/Region, and Language that you can use to sharpen your aim for pages from specific areas. The Search Builder on the whole isn't as intuitive as Google or Yahoo's Advanced Search option. In fact, it's clunkier than a '74 Volkswagen microbus trying to maneuver in a crowded supermarket parking lot.

Instead of a Preferences page, MSN Search has a Settings page where you can turn on the SafeSearch anti-naughty-page filter and adjust the number of results per page. Just click the Settings link on the MSN Search home page.

One MSN Search feature is especially good as a homework helper: Microsoft's Encarta reference database. This is the same Encarta encyclopedia you can buy on DVD (or 30 dust-collecting hardback volumes). Until the company decides to charge for it, you can use the Encarta link on the MSN Search page for two free hours of access to the online version. (The two-hour deal is a limited offer, not available worldwide, and good *only* for a total of two hours.) It's a great place to look up facts, statistics, and other information you look for in an encyclopedia.

Alternative Search Engines

The Big Three search engines got that way by helping most people find what they need on the Web most of the time. Remember, though, all a search engine does is round up information on the Web and serve it up on your screen. Creative programmers are finding different and better ways of doing that all the time. Depending on what you're looking for, you may find that a lesser-known search site—like one of the following—works even better:

- **Vivísimo.** The Vivísimo (*http://vivisimo.com*) site takes a different approach to rounding up search results. It organizes them into *clusters,* groups of similar types of documents. This technique can save time for academic or technical research, presenting results in batches of scientific or scholarly articles. The search box on the main page lets you cluster-hunt through a batch of preselected sites like eBay or the BBC's news site. The company also has a more consumer-friendly search site called Clusty (*http://clusty.com*) that makes it easy to search blogs (page 109) and wikis (page 93).

- **Dogpile.** Why limit yourself to using one search engine at a time when one site harnesses the searching power of several engines at once? Dogpile (*www.dogpile.com*) does just that, using the Google-Yahoo-MSN Search trinity. It also draws upon Ask.com (described next). Dogpile makes it easy to go straight to the type of information you're looking for. It offers easy access to Yellow and White Pages directories, for example. The Favorite Fetches section lets you choose from standard searches for things like song lyric sites and Blue Book values for used cars.

- **Ask.com.** The Web site formerly known as AskJeeves.com has a whole new look, name, and reputation after a complete overhaul in 2006 (during which the spiffy cartoon butler mascot got the sack). Now at *www.ask.com*, the site's especially great for looking up famous people. Type in the baseball player *johnny damon,* for example, and you get a photo, a biographical excerpt, and links to his official Major League Baseball stats page—all on the top part of the page. A vertical tower of options along the right side of the results page lets you narrow your search to get a more detailed biography—or broaden it to get general information about his two main teams, the Boston Red Sox and the New York Yankees. Fetching maps, flags, and background data, Ask.com is superb for looking up places as well as people. For the homework crowd, there's also a link to the safe version for children (called Ask for Kids) right on the main page.

• **AltaVista.** Meaning "a view from above," AltaVista (*www.altavista.com*) was the first site to index the Internet in 1995 and remained one of the dominant search engines in the early days of the Web. With its Babel Fish technology, it was the first search engine to offer language translation for Web pages. Although it's no longer on top of the search engine heap, AltaVista clings to its tradition of developing new ways to search.

POWER USERS' CLINIC

Take the Shortcut

Need to find really simple information like what's playing at the local movie house or what weather you're in for this weekend? Most search sites recognize shortcut words like *movies* or *weather,* and, when you add your Zip code to the mix, give you results for your area. Most sites also let you use *define* in front of a word to get the definition (type *define pulchritudinous,* for example) or *map* in front of a city name (*map Chicago*) to get some cartographic goodness onscreen.

Most major sites now have a Local Search feature. Look for a link to it on the search engine's main page. To do a local search, type your Zip code as well as your keywords, like so: *private detectives 90210.* The result's a list of businesses, plus a map showing their locations in the surrounding area.

Directories at Your Service

Search engines are fantastically good at finding exactly what you're looking for—*if* you know exactly what you're looking for.

Another approach is to window-shop—to browse. For this purpose, the Internet offers you *Web directories:* massive online catalogs that are edited, sorted, and organized by humans, for humans.

Instead of searching for specific terms, you browse by category. It's a slower process because you have to click your way down, subtopic by subtopic. But you can bask in the security that some person, somewhere, actually visited the sites and made sure they're relevant to the topic you're researching.

On the downside, handcrafted directories can never be as up to date as the ones that automated Web spiders generate on the fly, because it takes humans more time to sift through mountains of data and notice things like broken page links.

The three big directories are run by Google (*http://directory.google.com*), Yahoo (*http://dir.yahoo.com*), and the Open Directory Project (*http://dmoz. org*). Each starts out with a page of general topics, like Arts, Computers, Recreation, Science, and so forth. To start exploring, just choose a broad category to delve into.

Suppose you want to learn more about organic chemistry, but don't have a specific area of interest within that yet. Click the Science link on the directory's main page. (Figure 3-5 shows the Open Directory Project.) The next page lists all sorts of areas that fall under the heading of Science, like astronomy, biology, and chemistry.

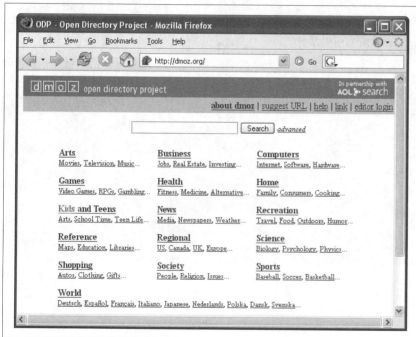

Figure 3-5:
From the Open Directory's main page, start by choosing the general topic you're interested in. Keep clicking deeper and deeper into the directory until you find the precise aspect of the subject that interests you.

Click the Chemistry link, and the next page shows you links to information about dozens of aspects of chemistry, including academic departments, conferences, and software. Next on the list are the many different types of chemistry, including Organic. Numbers in parentheses beside each link tell you how many links to further information there are if you click here. Click the Organic link, and several subtopics having to do with organic chemistry appear. Pick the one you want and click again.

Let Your Phone Do the Browsing

Most cellphones sold today have some sort of Web-browsing capability. To use it, you must sign up for your wireless carrier's data plan along with your monthly voice minutes. Also, unless your phone has a built-in keyboard—like a Treo, Sidekick, or BlackBerry—it may take some fancy fingerwork to tap out Web addresses on your keypad.

If you have a favorite search page, find out whether it plays nice with your carrier and phone. All of the big search sites have some sort of mobile phone offering. For example, Google's is at *http://mobile.google.com*, Yahoo's is at *http://mobile.yahoo.com/search*, and MSN's awaits at *http://mobile.msn.com*.

Google and Yahoo offer a Short Message Service, or *SMS,* search that lets you send queries about local businesses as mini-emails. Try it the next time you're in a tight spot (like your guests are coming in 30 minutes, Rascal has cream on his nose, and you need 12 more cannoli *pronto*).

It works like this. On your cellphone, create a new, outgoing text (SMS) message. (You may have to cuddle up with its instruction book to learn how.)

Address the message to 46645 for Google or 92466 for Yahoo. (Guess what those codes' alphabetic equivalents are?)

Then, in the body of the message, type your Zip code or city and a shortcut word like *weather* or *movies*—or *cannoli.* (See the box on page 73 for more on search shortcuts.) A few seconds later, the site rings you back with a text message containing the address of the nearest bakery.

Google's SMS service also lets you ask general questions. So if you draw a blank just before that big English test, you can ask Google SMS "Who wrote *Moby Dick*?" and with luck "Herman Melville" arrives before it's time to turn off your phone.

Searching by Information Type

By now, you know how to conduct basic and advanced Web searches with the major search engines (and if you don't, read the previous chapter). But even advanced queries and precise keywords can't always help you find what you need to know. Suppose you need directions from your mother-in-law's house to the nearest Motel 6. Or a copy of Form 8283 to fill out for your tax preparation package. Or who's hiring people with a Master's in zoology.

For quests like these, start your search at a site that specializes in that type of information. This chapter's a compendium of sites that help you find people, businesses, maps, careers, health and government information, and more.

White Pages, Yellow Pages

When you're at your computer, the Web can be faster than a telephone book. Plus, you can search the entire country, not just the area in the book the phone company dumps on your porch once a year.

To look someone up in an online directory, you need to know at least the person's last name, plus any other information you can supply, like first name, city, and state. For very common surnames, this additional information gets you more accurate results.

Here are the most popular people-finder sites:

• **Switchboard.com.** Billing itself as Your Digital Directory, Switchboard.com (*www.switchboard.com*) lets you search for phone numbers and addresses.

You can also do a *reverse lookup* on the address if you know the phone number, look up area codes, and get maps and directions between two addresses.

Tip: Some sites let you remove your own entry from their listings. If seeing yourself listed in one of these sites gives you the creeps, look for a "phone book removal" link.

• **Yahoo People Search.** This site (*http://people.yahoo.com*) helps you try to find a person's email address, as well as the usual phone number and postal address. Since no one's invented a completely comprehensive or accurate email directory yet, though, don't count on getting an up-to-date, working email address this way. But at least it's a start.

• **Google.** Along with all the other tricks up its sleeve, Google has its own phone book. You can get to it right from the regular search box at *www.google.com*. Simply type the person's name (and city and state if you know them)—for example, *douglas smith 10024* or *timothy ettlinger chagrin falls, oh*—and hit Enter. Google lists all matching names on your results page, complete with links to maps of the address.

If you know the phone number but not the address, you can also do a reverse lookup: type the full phone number with area code into the box and click Search to get the address listing.

• **WhoWhere.** Powered by Verizon's SuperPages directory, WhoWhere (*http://whowhere.lycos.com*) offers searchable White Pages, reverse lookup, and its own email address directory.

Note: When you go digging for people on some of these sites, you may see offers to sell you all kinds of data on the person, from criminal background checks to high school information. Most of this data's freely available in public records, so selling it online is crass capitalism. Not to mention disturbingly Orwellian.

Driving Directions

It's easy enough to find the address of an individual or business on the Web, but you may also need help finding your way there. Most mapping sites are easy to use: Type a street address, and the site shows you a map pinpointing its location. Most maps let you zoom in for a closer look or zoom out to orient yourself in the surrounding area. You can even print the map out to take with you or email it to someone.

Tracking Down Businesses

What if I want to find the address and phone number for a store, hotel, restaurant, or company? Is there a "yellow pages" version of the online phone book?

Yup. In fact, it's at *www.yellowpages.com*. Also, most of the online phone directories, notably Switchboard.com (page 85), also let you look up businesses by name or category.

Another option is the Local Search feature offered on most major search sites. Google, Yahoo, and MSN, for example, offer links to local listings on their main pages. Using Local Search, you can quickly pinpoint addresses in a certain area, or even find amenities and businesses in an unfamiliar town.

For example, say you're on an away-game trip, looking for a good pizza joint near Wrigley Field. Hop onto Google Local, type *pizza wrigley field Chicago*, and hit Search. Google brings back a list of pizza restaurants in the area, complete with addresses, phone numbers, and locations marked on a map.

Finally, the mapping sites listed on page 87 also help you find businesses by area. Instead of entering a street address, you can search for hotels, restaurants, airports, and so on.

If you need to not only find an address, but also *get there* from your current location, most sites also give you driving directions between the two points. Just type in the address you're starting from and the one where you want to end up. The site lists your turn-by-turn instructions and draws your route on a map.

Map sites aren't always 100-percent accurate; among other things, most don't account for current road construction, detours, rush hour, flash floods, or other factors that may cause you to vary your route. Still, their directions should get you there eventually and are almost always better than stopping 54 times to ask directions.

With that in mind, here's where to find maps on the Web:

• **Google Maps.** Google's maps section (*http://maps.google.com*) serves up easy-to-read street maps, clearly indicating the location of your entered address. Google also offers unique hybrid maps that overlay markers like state and city boundaries over satellite photographs. (See the Tip on page 89.)

• **Yahoo Maps.** Gunning to keep tabs on current road conditions, Yahoo now adds live traffic updates (Figure 4-1) to its maps. Standard maps and driving directions are also on the menu at *http://maps.yahoo.com*.

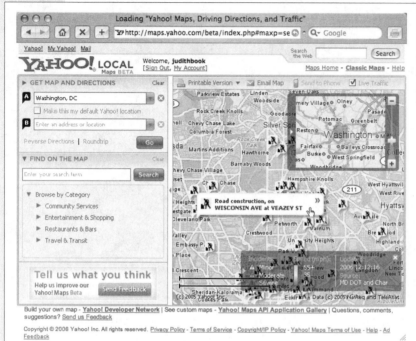

Figure 4-1:
Yahoo's new live traffic feature factors in traffic delays and construction hazards along the way, so you'll know what to expect before you head out.

• **MapQuest.** Owned by America Online, *www.mapquest.com* was one of the first sites to deliver street maps and driving directions to your desktop computer—and it's continuing to innovate. MapQuest's mobile features for phones and personal organizers let you find places (including your own current location) on compatible wireless phones. They also sell a personal navigation device for your car that gives directions and displays real-time satellite-generated maps.

• **MapBlast.** Part of the MSN Empire, MapBlast lets you specify maps in miles or kilometers, the shortest route or the quickest one, and has links to traffic maps as well. Microsoft's in the process of changing the site, at *www.mapblast.com*, into a new service called Windows Live Local with more interactive features for Windows folks.

Tip: Want to feel like Superman swooping high above the Earth? Google and Microsoft have been diligently working on interactive mapping services that combine satellite and aerial photography. To see the world from your desktop, check out Google Earth (*http://earth.google.com*) or Microsoft's Virtual Earth (*http://local.live.com*), which works for Windows computers and Macs running the Firefox browser.

Health and Medicine

There's a wealth of online information about medical conditions and all aspects of health and fitness. Healthcare sites can provide quick answers to your questions and support your at-home efforts to stay in tip-top shape.

These sites are especially good for getting background information before or after you see a doctor. (As disclaimers on all these sites tell you, never use information you read on the Web as your sole source in diagnosing a medical condition or prescribing treatment.)

For general healthcare information on the Web, you can explore one of these sites:

- **WebMD.** WebMD (*www.webmd.com*) is one of the most comprehensive health-related sites. Here, you can research symptoms, read the latest medical news, and submit your own questions to experts. There's also a section of message boards and blogs where regular WebMD visitors exchange everything from advice to recipes.

- **MedicineNet.** Run by a healthcare publishing company, *www.medicinenet.com* is known for its plain-English articles on a wide range of medical topics. Sections devoted to describing various procedures, guides to symptoms and illnesses, and a dictionary of medical terms are laid out for easy browsing.

- **Mayo Clinic.** The world-famous Mayo Clinic has its own Web site (*www.mayoclinic.com*) with sections dispensing information about diseases and medical conditions, drugs and herbal supplements, and various treatments. There's also a section called Healthy Living with medical advice on just that.

Tip: While you're waiting on hold to ask your health insurance company a question, you could be finding the answer even faster online. Oxford, Medicare, Blue Cross/Blue Shield, and other providers let you look up specific information about your plan, find a doctor or specialist, and see your coverage options online. Look for a URL on your member card or statement.

Job Hunting

For centuries, the local newspaper's Help Wanted section had a monopoly on the job listings market. And, in fact, your local newspaper's *electronic* classified ad section is still a good place to start. On sites like the *Boston Globe*'s BostonWorks.com and the *Seattle Times*' NWjobs.com, you'll find the latest job listings and get much less ink on your fingers.

Scores of job hunters post their résumés on one of the huge sites devoted solely to job searching. Most career sites let you browse and search through job postings by field, salary, and geographical area. Many offer career advice, too.

Note: These sites let you post your résumé in hopes that a prospective employer may browse through the listings. You're more likely to get an email from a recruiter (a.k.a. headhunter) than from someone who's actually doing the hiring. Still, recruiters can and do have connections to employers with active job openings.

- **CareerJournal.com.** This site (*www.careerjournal.com*) from the folks at *The Wall Street Journal* caters to executives. If you're looking to move up in the business world, this site tells you what's out there and how to go about getting it.

- **Monster.com.** If you're not happy in your present employment, the site's name may remind you of your boss. Monster (Figure 4-2) offers more than just an electronic job board where you can scan listings and post your résumé. It (*www.monster.com*) has loads of career advice, self-assessment tests, and articles. It also has a community section full of tips and stories from people in the same boat.

- **HotJobs.** This site (*http://hotjobs.yahoo.com*) is the career-counselor corner of Yahoo world, with a searchable database of jobs around the country. It also has a Career Tools section where you can calculate how high a salary you need to ask for, find out what to expect in an interview, and so on.

- **CareerBuilder.** Like a dating site, CareeerBuilder (*www.careerbuilder.com*) offers to match you with the jobs you're best suited to do—or you can browse the listings yourself in search of new horizons. The site lets you search for jobs by company or industry and provides links to career fairs around the country and articles dispensing job-hunting advice.

- **Craigslist.** Much more low-key than the big job-focused sites, the Craigslist (*www.craigslist.org*) jobs section posts jobs in all kinds of fields in hundreds of cities. Because it's mostly free to post ads (except for employers posting

Help Wanted ads in New York, Los Angeles, and San Francisco), it's a great place to find and fill part-time jobs, like tutoring. It's also popular among nonprofit companies that can't afford to place ads in newspapers. (See page 57 for background on this little list that grew into an Internet anchor.)

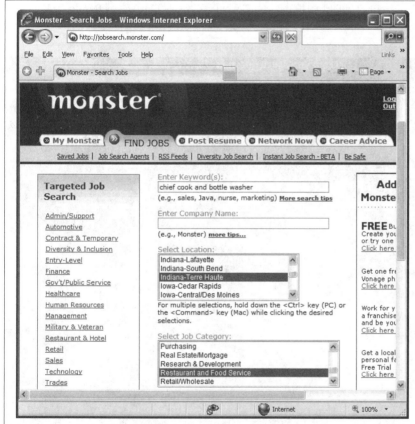

Figure 4-2:
Monster's job-search page lets you look for work in your desired city and field. In addition to its huge database of jobs, the site has career advice and other features to help you with your job search.

Getting the Facts

Quick—what movie won the Oscar for Best Picture in 1942? If you need fast facts to finish your homework, settle a bet, or bone up on game-show trivia, the Web is quicker than a trip to the library and cheaper than a bookstore spree.

You may be able to pull up the bit of information you need in a standard Web search. But when accuracy counts, you want a resource you can trust—like an encyclopedia. The Web contains many electronic encyclopedias for your reference needs, although some of the name-brand stalwarts like Encyclopædia Britannica charge a subscription fee to see every article available on the site.

Tip: If you're researching a topic very thoroughly and deeply, you may need to access published articles from thousands of sources. Services like Lexis-Nexis maintain databases of every newspaper and magazine article published in the last several decades, although you'll pay dearly for access to this miraculous storehouse of text. See the box below.

Information for a Price

Many of these database and encyclopedia sites want me to sign up for a paid subscription. Is it worth it?

It depends on what you need the research for and how fast you need it. Reference sites designed for students and home users aren't horribly expensive, and most offer monthly payment plans or free trial periods. One of these may be just long enough to get the information you need.

Professional research databases, which contain millions of published articles from magazines and newspapers, court opinions, and legal briefs, can save you a ton of time. They can also cost hundreds of dollars a month, depending on how you use the service. These expensive databases are designed for business professionals who need accurate business, financial, and trend information—and whose companies foot the bill to download articles and reports. On the other hand, although it's primarily a subscription-based service, Lexis-Nexis (*www.lexisnexis.com*) also offers an à la carte plan that lets you purchase individual articles for as little as $3.

Services like Hoovers (*www.hoovers.com*), which compiles reports on companies and growth, and the trend-tracking research firm NPD Group (*www.npd.com*), offer data of interest to sales and marketing folks. They may be too specialized and expensive for the casual searcher who isn't planning a corporate takeover or a dot-com startup company. (If you're just looking for stock and financial information for your own trading purposes, flip ahead to Chapter 9.)

By the way, *Mrs. Miniver* won Best Picture in 1942. If you answered *Casablanca* (which won in '43), you need a better online encyclopedia, like one of the following:

• **Encylopedia.com.** With 57,000 articles from the Columbia Encyclopedia, this free site (*www.encyclopedia.com*) often adds links to maps and newspapers to its entries so you can read other sources on the topic. Some material is subscription-only, but there's a free trial period—so in a pinch, you can sign up, get the goods, and skedaddle. If you decide you like the service, however, subscriptions cost about $20 a month or $100 annually.

- **Reference.com.** On the site that also brings you Dictionary.com and Thesaurus.com, you can find brief articles culled from other encyclopedias around the Web (*www.reference.com*). (See page 94–95 for more on the dictionary and thesaurus options.)

- **CIA World Factbook.** The free CIA World Factbook (*www.cia.gov/cia/ publications/factbook*) is great for looking up geographical information and population statistics. It also displays maps and the flags of the world.

- **Wikipedia.** Wikipedia (*www.wikipedia.org*) is a collaborative, grassroots encyclopedia. Anyone who reads it can also add to it or edit it, quickly and easily (Figure 4-3). (The "wiki" part of the site's name means "quick" or "fast" in Hawaiian.) As a result, Wikipedia is brilliant, unusually helpful, and occasionally incorrect. Although Wikipedia's creators made provisions for correcting or deleting erroneous information, it's best to verify the facts on another site.

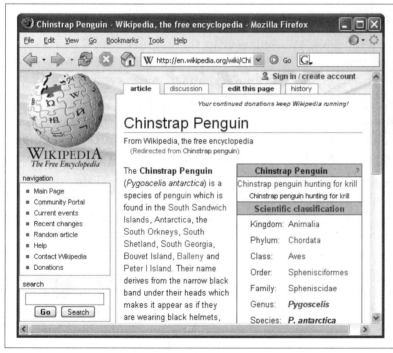

Figure 4-3:
Anyone can edit articles in the Wikipedia by clicking the "edit this page" link—which makes for some very interesting articles indeed. Wikipedia is available in dozens of different languages, and the English version now boasts more than a million articles.

• **Encarta.** Microsoft's digital reference work, usually sold as a DVD aimed at students, is also online at *http://encarta.msn.com*. Some articles are free, but you have to pay to get the good stuff ($5 per month or $30 per year).

• **Encyclopædia Britannica.** This famed collection, founded in Scotland in 1768, is still an authoritative reference in the Internet age (*www.britannica.com*). Non-members can search and browse brief articles and summaries, but paying members enjoy unlimited, ad-free access to the entire collection and qualify for discounts in Store Britannica. Fees are about $12 per month or $70 per year.

Tip: In addition to these encyclopedias, you can sometimes find answers to trivia stumpers on *www.funtrivia.com*. If you can't find your answer online, try asking an expert directly. Google (*http://answers.google.com*) offers professional researchers who scurry off and dig up answers for you for a fee that you propose. Yahoo (*http://answers.yahoo.com*) offers a different spin: You can post a few questions to the Yahoo community at no charge, but use up your free allotment of "points" by doing so. When you run out, you can earn points back by answering other people's questions.

Word Definitions

What with email, blogging, and online chat, the Internet has created a resurgence of written communication. With more typing, however, comes more room for embarrassing errors in spelling, grammar, and vocabulary.

The spell checkers built into many programs are handy, but they can't tell you whether you're using a word correctly or help you find the right word in the first place. If you need quick access to a dictionary or thesaurus while composing a memo, report, or letter, consider sites like these:

• **Dictionary.com.** A dictionary that gathers definitions from other dictionaries and presents them all on the same page, Dictionary.com saves you a lot of thumbing through heavy, paper-based resources. Although peppered with advertisements, the site includes free guides to grammar, usage, and style (*http://dictionary.reference.com*).

• **Onelook.com.** A search engine that specializes in finding words, OneLook (*www.onelook.com*) boasts five million different words in its index, collected from 900 different dictionaries around the Web. The site also features a Word of the Day. In a reverse lookup feature, you type in a description of something and OneLook tries to supply the word you're grasping for.

The Internet: The Missing Manual

• **Thesaurus.com.** If you want to avoid using the same words all the time, this site (*http://thesaurus.reference.com*) gives your vocabulary an instant boost. Like Roget's on steroids, Thesaurus.com brings back a whole screenful of alternatives.

Tip: If you want to improve your vocabulary while entertaining your eyes, try the Thinkmap Visual Thesaurus at *www.visualthesaurus.com*. When you look up a word, Visual Thesaurus displays synonyms or other terms commonly associated with the original word. Built-in audio files even pronounce the words for you. The site lets you explore 145,000 English terms (and 115,00 different meanings) for $3 a month or $20 a year.

UP TO SPEED

Getting Information from Uncle Sam

Wouldn't it be great if you could find all Federal facts, forms, and answers in one place—without standing in line for hours under unflattering fluorescent lights?

You can. Just visit *www.firstgov.gov*, the U.S. Government's Official Web portal. At FirstGov, you can download a passport renewal form, apply for government jobs, get student aid, or even write a letter to your Congressperson.

In addition to links to all kinds of forms and Web-based services, FirstGov has its own reference center. There you can look up U.S. laws and read historical documents (in case you wake up at 3 a.m. wondering what the Articles of Confederation have to say). There's also a section of data and statistics with current census results, crime rates, and other surveys of American life.

You can also browse official government photo collections. Hankering for some new desktop wallpaper? How about an Air Force fighter jet, perhaps, or an undersea scene from the Smithsonian?

News and Blogs

If you're obsessed with the news, the Web is the place for you. No longer tied to newspaper publishing schedules or TV broadcast times, news on the Web melds the best attributes of print and broadcast journalism. You get (usually) thoughtful written analysis, combined with the immediacy of TV and radio; articles often appear on your screen within minutes of filing.

Furthermore, news-oriented Web sites deliver more than just text and pictures. Many sites include audio and video clips to enhance the main story. And you're not stuck reading them at your desktop computer: Almost all news sites now let you receive updates via handheld computer, cellphone, or email.

This chapter takes a look at the most popular mainstream sites for international and local news, sports, weather, and entertainment. But since news can pop up anywhere on the Web, these pages also give you the lowdown on the *blogosphere*—a kind of real-time, free-form, virtual op-ed page.

News Sites

In recent years, Web portals like Google and Yahoo have entered the news biz. Their sites let you peruse headlines from hundreds of news organizations at once. Broadcasters like the BBC and CNN have also created Web sites, making text versions of their stories—along with photos, audio, and video—available online. This section takes you on a tour of the major news Web sites so you'll know where to go for that blast of fresh news.

Google News

Google News (*http://news.google.com*) is a computer-generated page of news headlines culled from over 4,500 English-language news sites. It tracks the latest developments in world and national affairs, business, sports, science and technology, entertainment, and health. The page automatically updates itself every 15 minutes, so you see new headlines every time you go back.

Unlike Google's minimalist home page, Google News is positively bustling with headline links, story summaries, and pictures. The page is laid out on a two-column grid for easy reading, like a newspaper page. When you see a story you want to read in full, click the link to go to the full article.

As shown in Figure 5-1, a vertical navigation bar along the left side lets you jump to a page with all the top stories for each Google News category, which can be convenient if you want to skip the world-in-crisis stuff in the international section and go straight to Sports to check who went where on NFL Draft Day. Links at the bottom of each category's page let you show more or fewer articles in that area.

Figure 5-1:
The Google News page brings the world to your screen in tiny bite-size chunks. There's a search box at the top the page so you can hunt for stories on topics you don't see on the main page. Just click the Search News button instead of "Search the Web."

You can also edit the categories even further, make and add your own areas, and arrange the page to suit your fancy. To do so, click the "Personalize this page" link, which you can see at right in Figure 5-1. To save your customized version and see it on any computer you use, you must create a free Google Account. (Look for a sign-in link at the very top of the page.)

You can take Google News with you in other ways, too. You can sign up for any of these services from links on the main Google News page:

- **Google Mobile.** If you've got a data plan and a Web browser on your cellphone, you can cruise Google News on the go. Just tap out *google.com* on your phone's browser and click the News button. You can see all the hot headlines and even search for news by topic.

- **News Alerts.** On the left side of the Google News main page, click News Alerts to reveal a form that lets you specify topics you're interested in (like raw-food diets or Manchester United, for example). Once you supply your email address, the site sends you regular messages with links to the latest stories on your chosen subjects.

- **News feeds.** As explained in detail on page 111, a news feed is a summary of updates collected in a special browser window or news-reader program. With a news feed, you don't have to keep going back to the original Web site to check for new articles. When you subscribe to the feed of a Google News section (like Business or Sports), you can get notified every time a new story appears, with a link to go read the text in full.

Tip: The other hardcore newsie sites described on the following pages offer similar features. Look for links to mobile, alerts, or feed features usually at the page's top, bottom, or left column.

Yahoo News

Yahoo News (*http://news.yahoo.com*) is like a coffee table full of newspapers from around the world that you can browse at your leisure—and you don't even have to recycle them when you're finished.

Neatly laid out in tabbed sections are links to comics (Figure 5-2), weather, and photos of the day. Tabs at the top let you browse the latest developments in international, national, and local news. Yahoo News lets you view audio and video clips of newsworthy events from sources like the Associated Press, ABC News, and CNN.

Figure 5-2:
You don't need a newspaper subscription to keep up with the daily doings of Dilbert and the gang. Yahoo News has dozens of comics to choose from. Another popular section of the site is the Odd News area, which collects stories of bizarre events from around the globe.

Yahoo News is loaded with features that help you find your way around. For example, some stories contain highlighted words or names. Click once to open a floating window containing the top search results for the highlighted word.

You don't even need to click the main page's headlines to learn more about a story. In most browsers, you can simply point to the link without clicking to see background information in a floating box.

Like Google News, discussed earlier, if you sign up for a free account, Yahoo News lets you personalize the page and offers email alerts and news feeds. The site can even send the alerts to your cellphone or ping you with an instant message from Yahoo Messenger. (Chapter 15 discusses instant messaging.)

BBC News

The British Broadcasting Corporation has been in the news business since 1922, back when *wireless* meant the radio. Commonly known as the BBC—or if you happen to be English, the *Beeb*—it has one of the Web's best sites for pure, high-quality news. Check it out at *http://news.bbc.co.uk*.

Note: That URL may look a bit odd if you're used to *.com* or *.org*. Being British and all, the BBC is in the United Kingdom, where most sites have domain names ending in *.co.uk* to specify the country of origin.

As you can tell from a glance at the main page (Figure 5-3), the BBC News site takes a truly global view of the day's news. Under the main section of breaking news, the site carves up its subsections not by topic like Business or Entertainment, but by geographic region like Americas, Asia-Pacific, and Europe. You can even choose to read the site in one of several different languages on the Languages page.

Figure 5-3:
The BBC News site is densely packed with information from around the world. The site also taps into the BBC's extensive multimedia resources, with links to streaming audio and video clips from its far-flung correspondents.

Tip: If you have a dial-up connection, you may prefer the Low Graphics edition of the BBC News site. It lightens the load by shrinking images to postage-stamp size and displaying the stories as simple bits of text.

Clickable tabs at the top of the BBC News page take you to other sections of the BBC's Web site, including its TV and radio programs in the UK. Its Sport section has thorough coverage of cricket, squash, rugby, and football (that's the British translation of what Americans call *soccer*).

As with the other major news sites, you can sign up for email news alerts and BBC News on your cellphone or wireless handheld organizer if you just can't bear to be away from this steady information pipeline pumping world events into your Web browser.

CNN.com

The companion Web site to the Cable News Network, CNN.com, keeps you in the loop when you can't be glued to the TV set. At *www.cnn.com*, the latest headlines span the top of the page, along with links to free CNN video clips and streaming radio news.

For the CNN groupie, there are also links to of the channel's current programming. The site encourages viewer feedback on CNN's television shows with links to its message boards. The site isn't a complete mirror of the TV version, though. There's original content like technology columns and health news.

CNN is part of the Time Warner media conglomerate, so it links to stories on the company's other sites (*Sports Illustrated*, *Time*, and *Money*). If you want a different perspective on the news, click the World link to see CNN.com's International edition with its overview of the world at large.

Tip: As with the Google and Yahoo news sites, you can sign up for email news alerts and newsletters. You can also subscribe to news feeds (page 111) and podcasts (page 205) of CNN material.

Online Newspapers

The world's major print newspapers have also launched online editions that you can browse for free. Many ask you to fill out a free registration form so the site can harvest a little demographic data for its advertisers. Other newspapers try to make a few bucks by charging for online articles, either by monthly subscription or per article. For example, a number of newspapers let you read breaking news for free, but make you pay for archived articles more than, say, a week old.

Tip: News sites like Google and Yahoo News frequently link to articles on newspaper sites. If you hit a for-pay site, use your Back button and try another link. You can usually find the same article for free from another paper's site.

NYTimes.com

The venerable *New York Times*—once nicknamed The Old Gray Lady—hit the Internet in 1996 with a burst of color. Still residing at *www.nytimes.com*, it's expanded in all sorts of directions, including podcasts, video and audio clips, and multimedia slideshows.

The *Times* is known for its deep international reporting, but its coverage of the cultural issues that are centered in New York City (mainly theater, opera, dance, art, and books), is also vast and wide. The online edition often includes many features not found in the print edition, like audio interviews between reporter and subject.

A special upper tier of the site called TimesSelect, which requires a $50 annual paid subscription (or free if you get home delivery of the actual paper), contains some members-only material. Certain columnists, for example, appear only in TimesSelect, and searching the *Times*'s archives going back decades is free. But most of what's in the paper version of the *New York Times* is free on the Web for a week after publication.

Unlike the paper version, which only comes out once a day, the Web edition of the *Times* is updated constantly throughout the day—every 10 minutes or so—and you can sign up for daily email alerts and updates. Readers can participate in discussion forums, send messages to reporters, and email links or text from stories to friends.

WSJ.com

De facto required reading in the business or financial world, *The Wall Street Journal* lives on the Web at *www.wsj.com*. The WSJ Web site is just as brisk and informative as the print edition, with a meaty diet of corporate news, market coverage, and technology forecasts. Unfortunately for those on a budget, you need a subscription to read even today's articles. (If you don't get the print version dumped on your doorstep, you can get a Web-only subscription for about $10 a month.)

On the other hand, you can browse a handful of free articles each day on the WSJ.com home page. A quick glance at the *Journal*'s headlines should clue you in to what's going on. You can always toddle off to a free news site for further reading.

Your Local Paper

Thousands of local newpapers are on the Web, and they're often the best place to look for news about your own community. If you already subscribe to your hometown paper, check its front or editorial page for its Web address.

If you don't subscribe or want to read your local news from far away, several sites list most daily, weekly, campus, and alternative newspapers around the country. Try looking up your favorite paper at News Voyager (*www. newspaperlinks.com*), Online Newspapers (*www.onlinenewspapers.com*), or the Newspapers section on the American Journalism Review's Web site at *www. ajr.org*.

Tip: If you don't like the Webified version of a newspaper and wish you could read the print edition without waiting three days for it to arrive, check out *www.newsstand.com*. The company sells subscriptions to electronic editions of many major publications. These PDF files you download to your computer are exact copies of how the paper or magazine appeared in print—ads and all. And you don't get showered with perfume strips and subscription card inserts.

Sports, Weather, and Entertainment

General news sites do a great job covering issues that affect the big picture—current events, stock market trends, and politics. But sooner or later everybody needs a break from the hard news. Check out the professional hockey scores, peek at the latest Hollywood gossip, or look up the local forecast so you can decide whether to pack an umbrella.

Sports

To keep up with the sporting life in all forms, you have plenty of choices. Most print publications like *Sports Illustrated* (*www.si.com*) and *Sporting News* (*www.sportingnews.com*) have overstuffed Web sites, as do the major sports television networks like EPSN (*http://espn.go.com*) and FOX Sports (*http:// msn.foxsports.com*).

Looking for a place to commiserate with fellow fans? The Sports Fan site (*www.sportsfan.com*) provides group therapy and verbal sparring matches between fans. If you just want to wallow in All Things Sport, slip on over to The Sports Network (*www.sportsnetwork.com*), where jock-themed movies, books, and tech products are reviewed alongside a near-complete listing of scores, TV schedules, and news briefs on a huge variety of sporting events.

Of course, if you're obsessed with one sport above all others, go straight to the source. Most individual sports and leagues have their own official sites. In addition to bringing you the latest stats, scores, and schedules, official sites also have links to each team's site. You may also find player biographies and fan forums where you can post messages and banter with other fans. You can find things to buy, like tickets, team jerseys, and souvenirs.

Here are the sites for popular American major league sports:

- The National Football League (*www.nfl.com*)
- Major League Baseball (*www.mlb.com*)
- The National Basketball Association (*www.nba.com*)
- The Women's National Basketball Association (*www.wnba.com*)
- The National Hockey League (*www.nhl.com*)
- Major League Soccer (*www.mlsnet.com*)
- The Professional Golfer's Association (*www.pga.com*)
- The Ladies Professional Golf Association (*www.lpga.com*)
- NASCAR (*www.nascar.com*)
- Indy Racing League (*www.indyracing.com*)

If international sport is more to your liking, here's your list:

- Fédération International de Football Association (*www.fifa.com*)
- English Football (*www.thefa.com*)
- The Canadian Football League (*www.cfl.ca*)
- Rugby Union (*www.irb.com*)
- Rugby League (*www.rleague.com*)
- The Olympics (*www.olympic.org*)

And if you don't like any of those sports, basic Webs searches should bring you links to sites that cover sports like gymnastics, figure skating, archery, and more. Even the National Duckpin Bowling Congress has a Web site (*www.ndbc.org*).

Tip: If college sports are your thing, visit the school's Web site for all the sports it participates in.

Weather

Sites devoted to meteorological observation take on special importance during the more volatile times of the year, like winter in the Northeast and hurricane season in the South. Whether your weather interest lies in browsing for official government data and charts or just getting the weekend forecast up at the ski lodge, there are plenty of good sites to check.

- **National Weather Service.** You can get your national and local forecasts, read official weather bulletins, check the radar, and see more maps than in a Rand McNally store by visiting the U.S. government's official weather page (*www.weather.gov*). It's also a good place to learn about aviation and marine conditions, and what to do when a storm's headed your way.

- **National Oceanic & Atmospheric Administration.** NOAA also runs the National Weather Service, but its main site (*www.noaa.gov*) focuses on global climate and marine matters. It has links to satellite pictures, nautical and navigational charts, plus in-depth coverage of coastal and environmental issues.

Tip: If you live in a coastal region or other area prone to hurricanes and Nor'easter storms, consider bookmarking the National Hurricane Center's home page at *www.nhc.noaa.gov*. It may help you keep one step ahead of Mother Nature when she's in a bad mood.

- **Weather.com.** The Web site of TV's Weather Channel (*www.weather.com*) is just as informative as the cable network, but it lets you find out more about your area's weather patterns without waiting around for the "Local on the 8s." You can click to view the 10-Day Forecast, the Weekend Forecast, and traffic reports. There are also special sections devoted to home and garden, business travel, and ski and golf outlooks.

- **AccuWeather.** A regular presence on most local TV news programs, "the world's best-known commercial weather service" has its own home on the Web. The site, at *http://home.accuweather.com*, is full of weather news, trivia, video, gadgets, and even weather blogs for the true weather junkie.

- **Hurricane Hunters.** At *www.hurricanehunters.com*, this site details the exploits and history of the Air Force Reserve's 53rd Weather Reconnaissance Squadron. From Keesler Air Force Base in Biloxi, Mississippi, its mission since 1944 has been to fly into active hurricanes and take pictures. The site's an intriguing blend of past and present hurricane lore.

Entertainment

Web sites devoted to entertainment come in two flavors. First, there are Web sites about the entertainment world, including celebrity sightings, industry news, and vicious, delicious Hollywood gossip. Then there are sites that help you find ways to entertain *yourself* by listing upcoming events in film, theater, and so on.

Most portal and news sites (page 97) have hearty helpings of news from the entertainment universe. If you want to dig deeper, though, try sites like these:

- **E! Online.** If the cable television channel doesn't saturate you with enough Hollywood news, you can find even more on the E! Web site (*www.eonline. com*). The Gossip section is your ticket to guilty pleasure.

- **Variety.** Like showbiz's answer to *The Wall Street Journal*, *Variety* is its industry's must-read rag. Also like the WSJ, *Variety* charges a subscription fee for the online edition. Still, if you have a deep interest in the movies, television, music, and other players in the entertainment business, it's worth checking out at *www.variety.com*.

- **Hollywood Reporter.** Another entertainment industry standard, the *Hollywood Reporter* lets you read more of its content than other show-biz online rags before demanding a subscription fee (*www.hollywoodreporter.com*).

- **Rolling Stone.** The groovy rock and roll magazine that floated out of San Francisco in the '60s now sports a companion Web site at *www.rollingstone. com*. The site combines coverage of current music, movies, and politics with columns, blogs, podcasts, and audio and video samples.

- **Entertainment Weekly.** The magazine may come out weekly, but its Web site, at *www.ew.com*, is updated daily with news and opinions spanning the world of pop culture.

If you don't care what celebrities are wearing, but want to know if there are any good Broadway musicals headed your way, the following sites are up your alley:

- **Citysearch.** One of the first and most thorough of the city-guide sites, Citysearch (Figure 5-4) covers about 40 major U.S. cities at *www.citysearch.com*. It lists local events, shops, spas, restaurants, nightlife, and other leisure activities around town.

Figure 5-4:
If you live in a major U.S. city, there's probably a Citysearch site that tells you everything to do in town, from concerts and movies to hot new restaurants. You can also find directions and reviews. (The next chapter has even more sites to find reviews written by regular people.)

- **AOL CityGuide.** You can find America Online's own city guides in its desktop program or by pointing a Web browser to *http://cityguide.aol.com*. Either way, you'll find plenty of entertainment opportunities. And after you choose something from the copious listings, you can buy tickets for many events right there.

- **Movies.com.** This start-to-finish site lets you do everything from read about movies in development to buy tickets for final releases. Movies.com (*http://movies.go.com*) also includes trailers, gossip, and DVD previews.

- **The Internet Movie Database.** If you want to know what's playing or who's in it, check out the IMDb at *www.imdb.com*. (There's more information on this essential site on page 116.)

- **FilmFestivals.** If indie films are more to your liking, check out the FilmFestivals site, which turns the lens on new and upcoming filmmakers (*www.filmfestivals.com*).

- **American Theater Web.** With a database of 3,000 theaters around the country, the American Theater Web (*www.americantheaterweb.com*) provides information on upcoming productions on local and regional stages.

- **Broadway.com.** A combination news/travel/ticket broker, *www.broadway.com* puts a spotlight on the New York and London stages with detailed descriptions of the shows currently playing.

- **Music.com.** At *www.music.com*, the focus is on contemporary music and video. The Tickets link leads to a long list of schedules and tickets for major music, sports, and theatrical events.

Tip: Remember, if you need directions to a concert or festival, you can always look up the venue's address on one of the mapping sites mentioned on page 87.

Blogs

If you want your news fast, furious, and highly opinionated, a *Web log* or *blog* may be just the thing to spice up your day. A blog is an online diary or journal posted on the Web for all to see.

There are millions of blogs peppered around the Internet, turning it into the world's largest populist press. While many of them are deeply personal sites that read like someone's diary (*"Today I took my pet chinchilla, Wee Fergus, to the vet…"*), other blogs aim higher.

Tip: Anyone with Internet access, a little software, and something to say can set up a blog—including you. Chapter 19 has all the details.

A few of these blogs have risen to media prominence, even making a little money and getting a modicum of respect from established news organizations with much bigger budgets and staff payrolls. The vast majority of blogs, however, don't get much readership beyond the immediate family and friends of their publisher.

Bloggers are free from the usual editorial constraints of responsibility, impartiality, and fact checking. In fact, some can be downright biased and mean—which can make them maddening or a lot of fun, depending on your point of view. If you like super-snarky snipes from the worlds of publishing and entertainment, for example, visit Gawker (*www.gawker.com*), which consistently offers sarcastic dispatches on everything from celebrity sightings around New York to gossip leaked from the inner offices of glossy magazines.

Like your politics on the right side of the aisle? Try Little Green Footballs at *www.littlegreenfootballs.com/weblog* for conservative commentary. If you're more of a lefty, try Talking Points Memo (*www.talkingpointsmemo.com*), which provides in-depth observations on current events from a more liberal perspective. The blog-search sites described in the next section tell you how to find all kinds of blogs to suit your interests.

One thing about blogs: They're generally not censored or bound by the same fairness rules as established news organizations. If a blog seems especially cranky or spewing a lot of venom, it's not you being too sensitive—it's probably just a really cranky, venomous blog. There are a lot of them out there, especially those that focus on politics or technology.

The more politically driven bloggers often take joy in critiquing, slamming, and supplementing the work of their brethren in the print and broadcast worlds—the *MSM* (mainstream media), as bloggers derisively term them. (Most bloggers also link to their original source material that inspired the post, like, say, a mainstream media story about a politician falling off a Segway or a celebrity who named her baby Apple.)

During the 2004 Democratic and Republican Conventions, it was clear that the voices from the blogosphere had taken their place alongside those of the MSM. Blogs have gotten so much buzz that even mainstream media stalwarts like the *New York Times* and *The Washington Post* now have their own blogs on the company Web sites. These officially sanctioned blogs allow reporters and editors to write in a more casual style and explore topics in a more informal way than on the news pages. If your favorite online news-source has its own blog, odds are there's a link to it right on the home page.

Using Blog-Search Sites

Like Web pages, there are too many blogs online to get through in any reasonable amount of time. Also like Web pages, you can find search engines to help you zero in on blogs that touch on topics you're interested in. Get your keywords ready and point your browser to any of the sites below to start your Blog Quest:

- **eTalkingHead.** Conservative, liberal, moderate, libertarian, independent—name the viewpoint and there's a blog leaning that way. If you're stumped about where to start, visit eTalking Head's directory of political blogs at *http://directory.etalkinghead.com*, which groups them by persuasion and provides links to those listed.

- **Technorati.** Here it is: the Google of blogs. You can see what people are blogging about, either by category or by typing in a search term (*www. technorati.com*).

- **Blogwise.** The site's design has all the visual pizzazz of a phone book, but BlogWise (*www.blogwise.com*) has a huge catalog of blogs to sample.

- **Google Blog Search.** If there's a way to search something, leave it to Google to find it. Type your keywords at *http://blogsearch.google.com*, and Google runs out and brings you every blog it can find that's mentioned them. You can save a Google Blog search results page just like a regular bookmark (page 53) and return to it whenever you want to see if any new blogs have popped up on your chosen topic. Click any of the Subscribe links on the left side of the results page, and Google Blog Search lets you subscribe to feeds (described in the next section) that alert you to new blogs without you having to go look for them.

One more thing about bloggers: They love to share and link to each other. So, if you find one particular blog you like to read, check the site for links to blogs of a similar vein. When it redesigned its Web site in early 2006, the *New York Times* even added a page that shows which of its articles bloggers are linking to the most. Click the "Most Popular" tab at *www.nytimes.com* to see what *Times* stories are creating the most buzz in the blogosphere.

Feeds: Having the News Come to You

If you've slogged through this much of this chapter, you're clearly getting the idea that there's a lot to read on the Web. Way, way too much, actually. Who on earth would have the time to go clicking around to even a fraction of a fraction of a fraction of the world's 20 billion Web pages?

Nobody. That's why the ranks of the truly time-efficient have dreamed up a way for the best Web sites to *send* their information to *you*, through a recent invention called a *news feed* or *RSS feed*.

If you use the latest version of Internet Explorer, Firefox, or Safari, you can sign up for a Web site's feed right in your browser—for free (and, gloriously, ad-free). When you've stumbled onto a Web site that offers a feed, a special icon appears at the top of your browser window to let you know (Figure 5-5). Just click it to subscribe to the feed.

Most mainstream news sites now offer RSS feeds to keep you up to date on current events. Many blogs offer feeds as well and subscribing to a feed alerts you whenever your favorite blogger has summoned the energy to make another post.

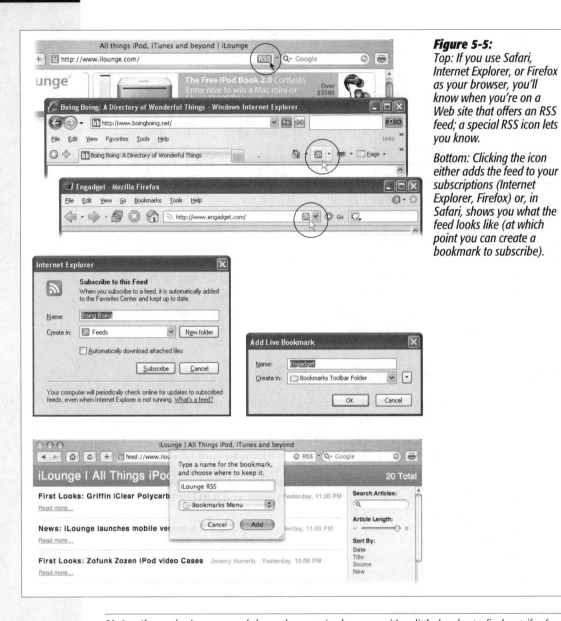

Figure 5-5:
*Top: If you use Safari,
Internet Explorer, or Firefox
as your browser, you'll
know when you're on a
Web site that offers an RSS
feed; a special RSS icon lets
you know.*

*Bottom: Clicking the icon
either adds the feed to your
subscriptions (Internet
Explorer, Firefox) or, in
Safari, shows you what the
feed looks like (at which
point you can create a
bookmark to subscribe).*

Note: If you *don't* use one of those three major browsers, it's a little harder to find out if a favorite Web site offers a feed. You have to look for and click a button (usually orange and rectangular)
that says RSS, Atom, or XML. *RSS* stands for Really Simple Syndication (or Rich Site Summary,
according to some people); *Atom* is a news-feed format popular with bloggers; and *XML* stands for
Extensible Markup Language, which is the technology that makes news feeds possible. None of this
will be on the test.

As shown in Figure 5-6, you can tell the browser how often to check for updates to your subscribed sites, and when there are new articles, the program usually displays a number indicating how many new articles there are.

Tip: Versions 6 and earlier of Internet Explorer don't handle feeds. In that case, shareware like TinyRSS (*www.codeproject.com/jscript/TinyRSS.asp*) can display the news updates in your browser window.

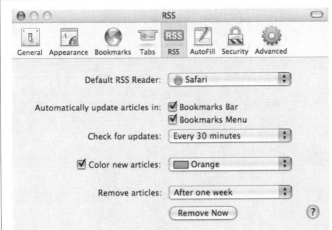

Figure 5-6:
If your Web browser can collect news feeds for you, you can tell it how often to check for updates in the program's settings. Here, in the preferences box for Safari, the browser checks every half hour for new news and displays the number of unread articles in both the Bookmarks bar and the Bookmarks menu.

Reading RSS feeds right in your browser is extremely convenient—a natural idea. But real RSS hounds find that they get more power and more features using a standalone, dedicated *feed reader* or *news aggregator* program instead.

Inexpensive feed readers for Windows include Newz Crawler (*www.newzcrawler.com*), FeedDemon (*www.feeddemon.com*), or the free Awasu program (*www.awasu.com*). Popular Mac OS X readers include NetNewsWire (*http://ranchero.com/netnewswire*) and NewsMac (*www.thinkmac.co.uk*).

Dedicated feed readers like these aren't quite as convenient as the one built into your Web browser. To subscribe to a feed, for example, you generally have to drag or paste the URL for the feed into the reader program. Once you get your feeds set up, however, all your tasty snack-bites of news are right there waiting for you.

Reviews and Ratings

In the olden days (1990 or so), film, food, music, and literary critics had the stage (or the page) to themselves. A negative review from the *New York Times* theater critic could close a Broadway show overnight. There wasn't much room—or any forum—for dissenting opinions, let alone a critical mass of them.

The Web changes all that. Some of the most insightful and useful critiques online are on ratings and reviews sites where regular folks say what they think.

This simple twist changes everything because now you, as a potential customer of that movie/restaurant/band/book, can read the accumulated comments of *hundreds* of people. There will always be oddballs who rip apart *Gone with the Wind* or declare *Catwoman* to be the century's greatest artistic achievement. But because the laymen's reviews are all in one place, you'll be able to see what *most* people think—and you'll be able to ignore the freaks at the fringes.

This chapter shows you where to find reliable reviewers online—and how to find your own voice.

Note: If you take the opportunity to submit your review of a movie, book, product, or whatever in a public forum, be sure to follow the site's posting guidelines. Above all, remember that millions of people may read anything you say online.

Movies

Alfred Hitchcock once said, "A good film is when the price of a dinner, the theatre admission, and the babysitter were worth it." Your standards may be a little higher, especially when the price of a movie ticket can exceed $10. While every news and entertainment site includes movie reviews of some sort these days, you'll probably find more trenchant observations and informed options on Web sites that specialize in the cinema.

The Internet Movie Database

Known around the Net as IMDb (from its URL at *www.imdb.com*), this site claims to be the earth's largest movie-related database—and so far, no one's found a bigger one. IMDb has facts and figures on every movie ever made, including cast lists and biographies, trailers, production information, and trivia.

Best of all, IMDb is the intergalactic headquarters for viewer comments. Read them before you see a movie that's still in theaters, or before you rent a DVD, to make sure you're not about to spend two hours watching dreck. (Hard though it may be to believe, there is such a thing as a movie that critics have loved but the moviegoing public didn't.)

If you register, you can post your own movie reviews and converse with other film buffs on IMDb's discussion boards. The site helpfully links to articles about current movies in other publications, including *Time*, *Newsweek*, and *The Onion*'s A.V. Club.

DVDs and TV have their own little corners of the IMDb, too.

Rotten Tomatoes

The site, at *www.rottentomatoes.com*, takes its name from a time when audiences really did hurl festering produce on stage to express their displeasure.

Rotten Tomatoes rounds up reactions from major print and broadcast film critics, then calculates and averages an overall percentage rating in its "Tomatometer" (Figure 6-1). The site also provides credits lists, trailers, production photos, and discussion forums. Links for each film let you buy tickets, posters, soundtracks, and other memorabilia.

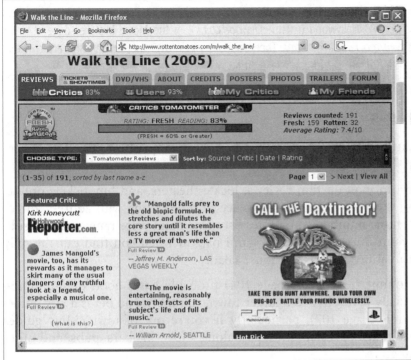

Figure 6-1:
The "Tomatometer" rating at www.rottentomatoes. com gives you an idea of how well major critics and publications liked a film. New video game and DVD releases get tomatoes thrown at them, too. A 60-percent or better rating means generally positive ("fresh") reviews. Below that, you're in "rotten" territory.

Ain't It Cool News

Ain't It Cool News (*www.aintitcool.com*) was started by movie maven Harry Knowles in the mid-1990s, but it quickly became a popular hangout for fan-boys and film lovers (especially comic-book movies and anime). The site's claim to fame is a mix of snarky reviews, hype, and gossipy tidbits leaked from sets and screenings. With its big cartoony headline type, the site also previews and reviews TV shows and DVD releases. Live discussion forums and message boards add to the chattering mass of opinions.

Film Threat

Film Threat started out in 1985 as a printed magazine with a focus on independent, cult, alternative, and underground movies. The magazine is no longer published, but the Web site, *www.filmthreat.com*, caters to fans of movies that *aren't* Hollywood blockbusters. The site links to stories and interviews about indie films. And after you read Film Threat's take on a flick, you can post your own review at the site's Back Talk section.

Tip: Love to catch continuity errors and other movie goofs? Join the eagle-eyed crew at Nitpickers (*www.nitpickers.com*), Wallywood (*www.wallywood.co.uk*), or the Movie Mistakes page at *www. ebaumsworld.com/moviemistakes.html*. Then you can giggle over the fact that the actor in that multimillion dollar Roman epic forgot to take off his wristwatch.

Restaurants

After "What movie should we see?", the followup question often is, "Where shall we eat?"

Just as you can look up film reviews, locate theaters, and buy tickets online, you can use the Web to find a nice place to dine. Along with address, directions, and phone numbers, most sites list menus and price ranges. As a result, you won't faint into your fancy origami napkin when you find out the only thing you can afford there is the house salad.

Your local online newspaper (page 104) probably has a good online dining guide, especially if you live in a larger town. Another good bet is a city guide, like Citysearch (page 107), particularly if you're out of town. Most guides cover a wide range of restaurant types, along with wine bars, pubs, and other nightlife hangouts.

Several excellent restaurant review sites have also popped up in recent years. In addition to letting you search for a place to chow down by cuisine, location, or price, most restaurant sites allow diners to post their opinions of the food and service.

Restaurant Row

With information on more than 170,000 restaurants in 13,000 cities worldwide, it's safe to say you'll find *somewhere* to eat on Restaurant Row (*www. restaurantrow.com*). You can look up an eatery by name or do a Zip code search to find nearby restaurants. If you register, you can even make your dinner reservations through the site (member price plans, like wine lists, vary). The Reviews section lets you read others' comments and add your own. You also get photos, directions, and—best of all—a digitized copy of the restaurant's actual menu, so you can start planning what you want to order (see Figure 6-2).

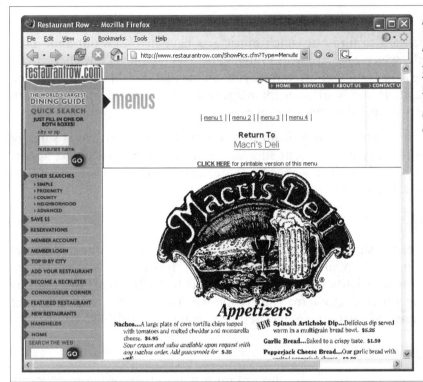

Figure 6-2:
The View Menu feature on RestaurantRow.com gives you an advance peek at the selections and prices before you even leave the house. (The View Menu button is on the main listing page for most restaurants.)

DineSite

Part restaurant guide, part electronic magazine on the art of eating, DineSite (*http://dinesite.com*) offers a studied view of the local food scene in 12,000 cities. You can search by style of food, location, or price. Eateries are also catalogued under Business or Romance, in case you're hoping to get lucky at work or play. The site provides maps, menus, and reviews for each restaurant, and lets diners post comments. (In fact, if you fancy yourself a food writer or photographer, DineSite welcomes you to contact them about contributing your talents.)

Restaurant.com

Virtual tours of dining rooms, special offers, and gift certificates make Restaurant.com (*www.restaurant.com*) a good place to visit before heading out to eat. After you browse the menu, you can read the chef's biography or email the manager if you have further questions. The site often has special deals and discounts with other food companies, like cookies from Mrs. Field's or live crustacean deliveries from LobsterGram.

Music

When you want to find out which music acts have new CDs out and, more importantly, which ones are worth buying, reviews are only a few clicks away. Music magazines and their accompanying online editions, like *www.vibe.com*, *www.rollingstone.com*, and *www.spinmagazine.com*, are good places to start, but you're not limited to mainstream rags.

Online music resources range from industry publications that cover some of everything to feisty independent sites that focus on indie music and upstart new bands. Or, if you love a specific genre, chances are there's a site just as devoted to it. Read on.

Billboard

Billboard, trade magazine for the recording business, has an online edition at *www.billboard.com*. While you're checking an interactive version of the famous Billboard Charts (the pop-song and CD bestseller lists), you can buy the CD—or a new ringtone for your cellphone. You can also read reviews of recent albums and catch up on the latest news from the music biz.

Music Critic

Covering newly released albums in most musical genres, *www.music-critic.com* proudly claims to have "reviews by the people, for the people." Refreshingly, Music Critic's reviewers don't pull any punches when they find a recording not quite up to snuff. The site invites "the people" to submit reviews, as well.

Pitchfork

Online music mag *Pitchfork* lives up to its claim as the "home of the gratuitously in-depth record review." The site, at *www.pitchforkmedia.com*, specializes in detailed analysis of newly released rock and pop albums, plus free song downloads and feature articles. If you seek new sounds, *Pitchfork* is a great place to find up-and-coming artists.

Music Sites by Genre

If you're a classical music buff or jazz aficionado, you know where to find the special radio stations, music stores, and concert halls devoted to your particular preference. So don't waste time scrolling past Beyoncé and Green Day; go straight to a Web site that speaks your musical language.

HipHop DX

Centered in the realm of hip-hop and rap, HipHopDX (*www.hiphopdx.com*) hosts reviews, news, and lists of upcoming releases. You'll also find audio tracks, video clips, and playlist ideas (in the Mixtape section). The Community area holds message boards, contests, and RSS feeds (page 111).

Gramophone

The austere classical-music publication that's been reviewing recordings since 1923 has its online residence at *www.gramophone.co.uk*. You can browse the site's archive of recommendations for the best versions of popular works. An Editor's Choice section lists the 10 best classical recordings of the month. Feature articles on the state of classical music today, a section devoted to upcoming concerts and tours, and discussion forums round out the site.

Classics Today

With daily updates and tons of reviews in its searchable archive, Classics Today (*www.classicstoday.com*) makes old music feel new again. The site reviews live concerts as well as classical recordings on new high-fidelity formats like Super Audio CD, DVD, and so on.

Jazz Review

Critiques of jazz CDs, concerts, and books are just some of the fare at Jazz Review (*www.jazzreview.com*). The site also offers columns, interviews, and photos. The site's discussion forums range from listening guides and polls to musician-oriented boards where performers can trade tips and all that...er, jazz. (There's also a monthly email newsletter if you still can't get enough.)

Country Stars Online

Long-form reviews of new albums, an indie-artist spotlight, and a bustling news section keep country music fans in the know at *www.countrystarsonline. com*. CSO hosts links to official artist Web sites and lovingly created fan monuments, so you never have to look far to find more information about your favorite country band or singer.

World Music Central

Whether you like lilting Celtic melodies, tingly Asian string music, pulsating African drums, or any other tradition from the global jukebox, World Music Central (*www.worldmusiccentral.org*) has some news—and reviews—for you.

The site invites submissions of album, concert, and book reviews, and its World Music Forum hosts discussions on everything from upcoming festivals to finding traditional folk instruments.

Ask MetaCritic

Browsing the Web for the latest buzz on albums, DVDs, books, movies, and video games is fun, but time doesn't always allow for it. When you're splurging on a gift (even if it's for yourself), sometimes you just want a general thumbs-up or thumbs-down from the critics. Before you plunk down your hard-earned cash, point your browser to *www.metacritic.com*.

MetaCritic collects reviews from various mainstream publications and comes up with an overall score. To make things easy, a color-coded label appears next to each item reviewed: green for *good;* yellow for *yuh-huh, whatever;* and red for *run for the hills, as far away from this thing as you can get*.

The site may even settle your family's next remote-control tug-of-war: MetaCritic reviews TV shows, too.

Books

Books for sale on the Web aren't hard to find—and neither are reviews of them. If you waste your money on a dog of a book these days, it's your own darned fault.

Amazon and B&N

The two biggest online bookstores are, of course, Amazon (*www.amazon.com*) and Barnes & Noble (*www.barnesandnoble.com*). These companies list, for each book, all the usual details like price, page count, author name, and publisher's praise for its own book.

Far more valuable, though, are the reader reviews: writeups from people who have already read the books and have come to warn you away (or confirm your good taste).

You should know that not every review is impartial. The reviews may be padded by entries from the author's friends (or enemies), and even from paid reviewers. Fortunately, if there's a reasonable quantity of reviews, the good and bad books still float to the top or sink to the bottom.

The New York Times Book Review

The *New York Times* has published a Books section for more than a century, and its Best Seller List is still the measure of literary success. Some people used to subscribe to the paper just for the Sunday Book Review—but now you don't have to. You can read all current book reviews (both Sunday and daily) at *www.nytimes.com/books* with a free registration. On the Books section of the site, you can read all fiction, nonfiction, and children's book reviews and search all reviews published since 1996. The site also posts the entire first chapters of many currently reviewed books and hosts an online book club.

The New York Review of Books

The New York Review of Books—not to be confused with the *New York Times* Book Review—celebrates the art of the long-form review. A good percentage of them are available online for free at *www.nybooks.com*. (Twenty bucks gets you a year's worth of access to all the *New York Review*'s articles, if you're a subscriber to the print publication; everyone else pays $66.) Its scholarly essays touch upon issues affecting contemporary society, including the present state of politics and culture.

Tip: If the publishing industry fascinates you, visit Moby Lives for the latest headlines from the book biz (*www.mobylives.com*). This literary blog also has a regular podcast of current author interviews.

Consumer Electronics

Consumer electronics covers a lot of territory, from tiny handheld organizers to giant plasma televisions. Sites that review these products are usually organized by category. You pick your type of gadget (digital camera, wireless speakers), manufacturer (Sony, Philips), and price range (under $300, say) to winnow through the selection. When you get to an individual product page, you see the full technical specifications and requirements.

Along with the site's professional opinion, you may also see comments from people who own and use the device you're considering. So if everyone says that shiny new photo printer's a dud, you can cross it off your list.

CNET

If it's got a circuit board, code, screen, woofer, tweeter, or buttons to push, the electronic media company CNET Networks has probably written about it (*http://reviews.cnet.com*). Products are reviewed by technical experts and rated on a scale of 1 to 10, but readers are encouraged to chime in with their own comments. The site has several gadget-themed blogs, discussion forums, short video reports, and buying guide pages to help you make shopping decisions. It also lists price ranges at various stores.

Dontbuyjunk

Dontbuyjunk (*www.dontbuyjunk.com*) fuses the results of consumer ratings and professional reviews of computers, cameras, and audio-video equipment. It sums up the overall consensus in a "TotalRank" rating for each device. As shown in Figure 6-3, you can narrow your product search by price or whatever attributes are most important to you. When you're shopping for a television, for example, you may value picture quality the most—or user-friendly controls.

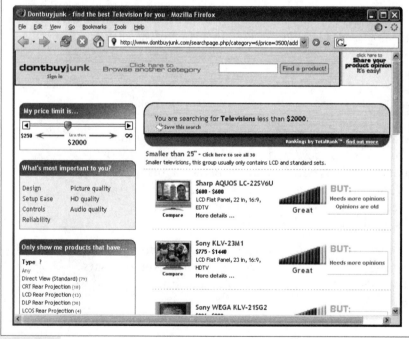

Figure 6-3:
The Dontbuyjunk site lets you compare products by price. Move the price slider on the left side of the page to instantly weed out products out of your budget. The site also lets you sort results according to other criteria, like how other people like the design or how easy the thing is to set up once you get it home.

Consumer Search

You can read reviews for just about every category of consumer electronics at Consumer Search (*www.consumersearch.com*). This ambitious site offers reports and rating for all sorts of other items as well, including tractors and teeth-whiteners. The site gathers product rankings from reviews it finds all over the Web.

Epinions

People who have an opinion on everything (you know the type) have found a home on the Web at *www.epinions.com*. Professional reviewers and regular consumers have put thousands of products and services under the Epinions microscope, and the sentiment is rarely lukewarm. It's up to you to decide. As well as providing a forum for picks and pans, Epinions maintains links to online stores that stock the items in question. Simply click to purchase if you're an efficient (or impulse) buyer.

WORD TO THE WISE

News for Nerds

In real life, there's no easy way to silence some idiot who's monopolizing a conversation, even if everyone else present is silently wishing he'd shut his pie hole. Online, though, it's another story.

Slashdot (*http://slashdot.org*) is an intense, free-wheeling discussion site for uninhibited, sometimes over-the-top geeks, nerds, and programmers. It pioneered the use of using ratings to rank *people*. If you contribute a comment that's smart, concise, and interesting, the other members rank you highly; your "stock" goes up, and you gain more powers on the bulletin board. If everyone else consistently finds your postings to be off-point or self-important, your rankings sink, and fewer people read your comments.

Every Slashdotter therefore has an incentive to keep the discussion on point, and—if you're into things like operating systems and programming—this makes for some truly intriguing reading.

Digg (*www.digg.com*) does something similar with technology *reporting*. It's a massive list of headlines from all over the Web, ranked by Digg readers in real time. The point, of course, is to save you time; the highest-ranked tech-news stories are, of course, the most interesting ones. They've been pre-screened for you by a staff of hundreds or thousands of strangers

---

Cars

A car is probably the most expensive thing you'll ever buy (after a house); doing some Web research before you buy is practically mandatory these days. Besides, if you're going to whiz down the highway at 60 miles an hour in 3,000 pounds of steel, rubber, and plastic, safety should be a concern. And with gas prices persistently shooting skyward, you have to research mileage as well.

Well-known automotive magazines like *Motor Trend* and *Car and Driver* have posted their Buying Guide sections online (*www.motortrend.com* and *www.caranddriver.com*). These sites let you assemble your desired make and model from pop-up menus and then show you the technical specifications: curb weight, seating capacity, fuel economy, and so on. You can also price out a model with your own personal options. Or, if you're in the market for a used car, these sites offer used listings and reviews as well.

Here are some other rest stops on the road to automotive reviews and ratings:

Cars.com

Large portions of Cars.com (*www.cars.com*) are devoted to Research and Shopping Advice. You can read helpful articles like "Things to Consider When Choosing a Pickup Truck" and peruse lists such as "Best & Worst Gas Mileage." Payment calculators and links to nearby dealers await when you're ready to make a decision. And if you're looking to *sell* your car, Cars.com lets you place an online ad for as little as $25.

Kelley Blue Book

The infamous Blue Book started out as a small printed list passed around among California car dealers in the 1920s. It's a list of car prices that's become the definitive national reference for deciding the worth of a used car—an essential resource when buying or selling one. In convenient World Wide Web form (*www.kbb.com*), Kelley Blue Book has blossomed into an inviting place to read up on cars old and new. The site includes reviews, ratings, and yes, the Blue Book values.

Car Talk

The NPR radio show where Tom and Ray banter about cars, ex-wives, and life in general has its own Web site at *www.cartalk.com*. You can read the results of Tom and Ray's test drives (Figure 6-4), and their thoughts on new models. If you have a specific automotive question, take it to the message boards or the instant Q-and-A system.

Figure 6-4:
You learn a lot about cars when you spend a few decades fixing them, and Tom and Ray love sharing their wisdom. You can also hear an audio stream of the latest episode of Car Talk in case you missed it.

The Family Car

The Family Car (*www.familycar.com*) may not be your best bet if you're looking for a zippy little two-seater. But the site has a trunk-full of articles on car care, shopping advice, driving safety, highway tips, and other roadworthy stuff. Active user forums provide a place to share and care.

Part Three: Shopping, Travel, and Finance

3

Shopping

The Internet may be a nearly instantaneous communications channel that transcends geopolitical borders and turns the earth into a truly global village. But let's not forget that it also lets you buy a Swiss Colony beef log at 3:00 a.m. from *www.swisscolony.com* and have it shipped by Second Day Air to arrive in time for your brother's birthday. Such is the power of the Web when it comes to finding stuff you really need to buy.

Sales of merchandise online have been steadily climbing since the late 1990s, when the Web gained traction as an online emporium. Some research analysts predict online sales will surpass $300 billion a year by 2010, which is a heck of a lotta beef logs.

But as you've probably heard, shopping online does come with security risks. And finding things on the Web that you want to buy can be tricky. The good news is that you can take steps to protect yourself when you're shopping, and you can employ a few techniques for finding stuff efficiently.

If you're new to the concept and practices of online shopping, or if you just want to know where to find stuff and how to *safely* handle the transaction online, this chapter will help you fill up your cart.

How to Shop Online

Online shopping's a lot like regular shopping, except you can do it in your pajamas (without risking being stared at). The online shopping experience is pretty universal, give or take some quirks and variations in Web sites' designs.

When you go to an online store, you can search or browse for products displayed or listed on the site. When you click the link for a cable-knit sweater, a ferret cage, or whatever you're looking to buy, you get a full product description on screen.

Here's the typical online shopping routine once you find the item you want to get:

1. **Select your merchandise.**

   When you landed on a product's page, you find out more about it (price, material, physical dimensions, all that) and have the chance to select a size, color, or style.

2. **Click the Buy or "Add to Shopping Cart" button.**

   You've just placed your selection into a virtual shopping cart, which, like a real-life shopping cart, holds everything you intend to buy until you hit the checkout lane. Online, the shopping cart is just a Web page that memorizes each item you've chosen so far; it lets you go browse for more things to buy without worrying that the Web site will forget what you've already picked out.

3. **Proceed to checkout.**

   Once you've added enough stuff to your cart, look for a link that says something like "Proceed to Checkout."

4. **Enter your shipping, billing, and credit card information.**

   This part makes some people nervous. After all, you're typing personal and account information into a Web form. What if some hacker sees it and swipes it and runs up a huge bill at *FerrariOnlineAutoSales.com*?

   Fortunately, any good shopping Web site comes with built-in high-security measures that scramble (encrypt) any text you send from your computer, so thieves can't read it while it's in transit across the Internet.

   Such sites are called *secure* sites or servers. Two signs let you know when you're on a secure site. First, the URL in your browser's address bar changes from *http://* to *https://* (the extra *s* stands for secure). Second, a tiny padlock appears in your browser window (Figure 7-1). Depending on your browser setup, the padlock icon may appear at the bottom of the screen rather than the top.

   If you *don't* see the secure address or padlock, don't shop there. See the box on page 142 for more information.

Figure 7-1:
That extra s in the http:// part of
the Web address and the icon
of a padlock both tell you that
you're on a site that's secure for
financial transactions to travel
between your computer and the
Web store.

5. **Finalize the transaction and get your receipt.**

Once you submit your credit card billing and shipping information, the site processes the transaction just like the clerk at Macy's who swipes your MasterCard at the register. In a few seconds, you should see a receipt, complete with order number and purchase summary. You can print this out for your records. (Most shopping sites send you an email copy, too.)

Tip: On the Macintosh, don't bother wasting paper and ink by printing out the final "This is your receipt" page. Instead, choose File → Print and, from the PDF pop-up button, choose Save PDF to Web Receipts folder. Safari saves it as a PDF file into a tidy little folder (in your Home → Documents folder) called Web Receipts, so you'll know where to look for it (and where you can find it easily using the Mac's Spotlight feature). Nice touch!

Then, just wait for your order to arrive. Some online shops send you another message when they've actually loaded your item onto the UPS truck or dropped it off at FedEx, and give you a tracking number so you can monitor your package's progress and get a delivery date.

Now that you know what to expect, it's time to get to the fun part of this chapter: the stores.

The Top Shopping Sites

There are plenty of places to shop online, from little niche sites selling everything from specialty mustards to hand-crafted lutes, but if you want an all-around shopping workout, consider the giant Web emporiums that sell a little bit of everything. These sites have a huge selection of merchandise that can keep you wandering the virtual aisles for days.

Amazon

What started in 1995 as a little Web-order book company shipping out of a Seattle garage has morphed into a worldwide Web mega-mega-megastore that sells everything but the kitchen sink. (Correction: It sells everything *including* kitchen sinks, and some very nice models at that.)

Now with nine million square feet of warehouse and order-processing space in 21 locations around the globe, Amazon's determined to sell you *something* and get it to you quickly.

You start your Amazon trip at *www.amazon.com*. Upon landing, you notice dozens of links, pop-up menus, and navigation bars pointing you to different corners of the store: Apparel & Accessories, Gourmet Food, Electronics, Musical Instruments, Automotive, and oh, yes, *Books* are among the more than 30 product categories (Figure 7-2).

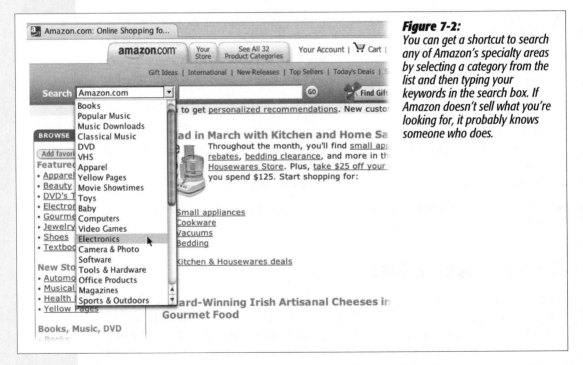

Figure 7-2:
You can get a shortcut to search any of Amazon's specialty areas by selecting a category from the list and then typing your keywords in the search box. If Amazon doesn't sell what you're looking for, it probably knows someone who does.

If you're looking for something in particular, say like a snow cone maker or Richmond Lattimore's translation of *The Iliad of Homer*, you can use the search box at the top of the page to type in your keywords (*snow cone maker* or *richmond lattimore*, in this case) and wait for Amazon to round up all the matching products on a search results page. When you've clicked through the links and found the very thing you're looking for, click the "Add to Shopping Cart" button on the product's page.

Among e-commerce sites, mighty Amazon is tops for ease of use and the sheer number of goods and services. Some of these include:

- **Customer reviews.** As described on page 122, Amazon's known for its customer reviews, which can be helpful when you're trying to decide whether to buy a product. After all, when you're standing in a store, you can't usually ask a bunch of experienced customers whether they liked the product you're considering.

- **Partnerships with other e-commerce sites.** Thanks to Amazon's deals with other merchants, you can order a box of pears from Harry & David or a mid-season jacket from Lands' End right on the Amazon site.

  The left side of the main Amazon.com page lists some of the featured partner stores, but you can also click the See All 32 Product Categories tab at the top of the main page. A full menu of product groups pops up; click the category for the store you're hunting, like Gourmet Food for those Harry & David pears.

- **Gift certificates.** You can give someone an Amazon shopping spree with gift certificates you can buy and send by email. To get started with your electronic gifting, scroll down the main Amazon page to the Special Features section on the left and click the link for Gift Certificates.

- **Address book.** If you regularly send gifts to certain friends and family members, you can store their addresses in your account (see the next section) and select them for shipping with one click. Thanks to this feature and the optional gift-wrap service, holiday shopping just got a lot less stressful.

- **Wish lists.** You can let others know what you really want for your birthday, wedding, or graduation day by creating an Amazon Wish List. (Click Your Lists at the top of the Amazon page and select Wish List.)

  You can choose to make your wishes known to anyone who searches Amazon for your name or email address, share it with only selected friends, or keep it to yourself so you can remember how you wanted to spend your next paycheck.

- **"Search Inside" books.** If you miss the sensation of standing in a regular bookstore and flipping through the first few pages to see if it's something you want to buy, explore the Search Inside feature (available only on books bearing the Search Inside logo).

When you click the book's cover illustration, you get to see the book's cover, table of contents, index, flap copy, back, and a few inside pages. The Search Inside logo even means that you can search the entire book for specific phrases; Amazon shows you a list of page excerpts containing your search terms. When you click a result, you can see an image of the entire page—a great way to find out whether the book covers a certain topic.

• **1-Click Shopping.** If you turn on Amazon's 1-Click Shopping preference in your account settings, you can, thereafter, instantly purchase and send a product to you (or anyone already in your Amazon address book) anytime you click the "Buy now with 1-Click" button.

• **New and used merchandise to buy and sell.** This part is awesome: You can be one of Amazon's partner stores, too. Click the Sell Your Stuff link near the top of the main Amazon page to get started.

The Books category, in particular, is a great place to unload all those books you've accumulated but would rather turn into cash. Click "I have a used copy to sell" on any book's page.

(Why would Amazon help you sell your used books, thereby depriving itself of selling *new* books to the same customers? Because you do the packaging and shipping; Amazon's happy to sit back and get a cut of your sale for doing absolutely nothing.)

There's plenty more to see (and buy, of course) on Amazon.com, and the best way to see it all is to just let your cursor wander through its pages.

Your Amazon account

When you check out of the Amazon store for the very first time, the site walks you through setting up your *Amazon account,* which is where Amazon keeps your billing information, shipping address, order history, and other data about you. The email address you provide is your account name.

Note: If you're genuinely paranoid about supplying your credit card number to a company online—even though the number is encrypted—you can also order by phone. Amazon's number appears on the checkout page.

Once you set up your Amazon account, you can view and edit it by clicking Your Account at the top of the page. This is also where you can cancel orders, return items, track your pending packages—all the things you'd do in a Customer Service counter at a regular store after standing in line with other cranky people.

When you set up your Amazon account, the site places a cookie (page 410) on your machine, so the next time you go back to buy more stuff, you're greeted by name at the top of the page. If you use a shared or public computer, you can give Amazon amnesia and return it to its anonymous state by going to the top of the page to the area marked "(If you're not [Your Name], click here.)"

Note: When Amazon recognizes you, it presents selections of merchandise it thinks you might buy on its main page. It bases its guesses on your previous purchases on the site, hoping to snag your interest. For example, if you bought one Miles Davis album on an earlier visit, you may be presented with other recordings from the Miles Davis catalog, books about Miles Davis, DVDs featuring filmed performances by Miles Davis, and so on. It's sort of like being stalked by a warehouse. Amazon also uses your purchase history to send product suggestions by email, say if you bought a movie on DVD two years before, you might get a message from the company offering to sell you the film's sequel when the later film is released on DVD. If you don't like getting the messages, you can tell Amazon to stop pestering you. Log into your account on the site, and then click "Updating Subscriptions and Communications Preferences." The page that comes up gives you choices for limiting the email Amazon sends you.

---

eBay

eBay (*www.ebay.com*) is the world's largest auction house; at this moment, literally millions of items are up for auction to the public. Not only can you find cultural artifacts you forgot even existed—like a vintage Fireball XL-5 lunchbox in perfect condition—you can also buy new clothes, vintage cars, palettes of industrial tubing, Broadway tickets, and, of course, kitchen sinks.

The genius behind eBay is that *eBay* doesn't sell things; instead, the site just facilitates the auctioning and sale of stuff *by* ordinary people *to* ordinary people. Any person or business can—and does—sell whatever they own that isn't nailed to the floor.

Note: There's a whole art to finding, buying, and selling stuff on eBay. If you want a detailed course, including tips for getting stuff at the lowest possible prices, check out *eBay: The Missing Manual*. In addition, eBay's own extensive Help system (linked from the top of every page on the site) includes lots of forums where you can read and post questions and answers.

On eBay, most items are up for auction. There's a starting price and a limited time during which you can submit bids (say, a week). The highest bid takes the prize.

To look for something to buy, you can either search or browse the category links. Either way, you wind up with listings of items for sale. Click one to get a page of information supplied by the seller—which almost always includes a photo—and the option to bid on the item. (If you don't want to pussyfoot around with auctions, many sellers give you a link to Buy It Now, which lets you pay a set price to circumvent the auction and acquire the treasure in one fell swoop.)

On an item page, most sellers include details about the item, plus shipping and payment information. In addition, in the corner of every item page is information about the seller, including a *Feedback* rating, which comes from other eBayers.

People who use eBay regularly take Feedback very, very seriously. After all, you're buying something from total strangers; the only basis you have for trusting them is the accumulated experiences of people who've already bought stuff from them. For more information about the Feedback system, check out *http://pages.ebay.com/help/feedback/index.html*.

Note: Anyone can search and browse eBay. To bid, buy, or sell stuff on eBay, though, you have to register and set up an eBay account. Registration's simple, and you can do it by clicking the Register link at the top of most eBay pages.

Bidding and buying items

Each item up for auction on eBay has a *starting bid*, which is the minimum amount of money the seller is willing to accept.

Fortunately, you're not obligated to sit there by your computer the whole week of the auction, your cursor hovering over the Bid button just to make sure somebody else doesn't outbid you. Turns out eBay can do the bidding automatically while you're not even online, up to a maximum that you specify in advance. As the auction progresses, eBay incrementally edges up your bid, in an effort to top other bidders who are doing the same thing.

When you click the Place Bid button, you get a form where you type in the maximum amount you want to pay for the item. If, for example, you're considering an old set of Legos that has a starting bid of $15, but you want it so much that you'll go up to $25 just to get your hot little hands on it, type in $25 as your bid. The weird thing is, you might pay *less than* $25 and still win the auction.

This system, called *proxy bidding,* means that, depending on the other bidders' maximum prices, you could get the item for slightly more than the starting price. Or you might get it for your maximum amount. Or you might not win at all if someone outbids you. If you're winning or if you've been outbid, eBay sends you an email with your status.

If you've never bid on anything before in your life and the whole thing makes you nervous, visit eBay's help section for interactive tutorials. You can even place a few practice bids to get your confidence up, as shown in Figure 7-3.

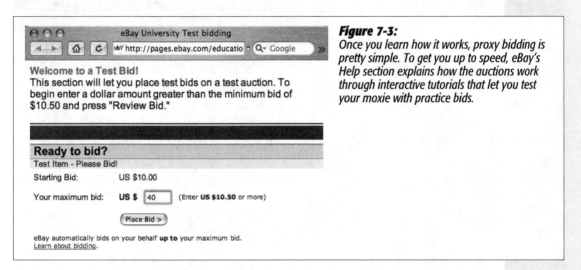

Figure 7-3:
Once you learn how it works, proxy bidding is pretty simple. To get you up to speed, eBay's Help section explains how the auctions work through interactive tutorials that let you test your moxie with practice bids.

When you're trying to decide on a maximum bid for an item, bear in mind that prices don't include shipping costs. Most sellers post shipping costs on the item's page or, if you provide your Zip code, the seller will give you an estimate. (Use the "Ask seller a question" link in the upper-right corner of the item page.)

If you have any questions about the item or the shipping costs, ask *before* you start the bidding process. Once you place a bid, by eBay rules, you've just entered into a contract with the person selling the item, and you're bound to buy the item if you win the auction.

When you win an action, eBay informs you via email that it's time to pay. The email directs you to your My eBay page, which is where you pay for winning auctions, leave feedback for sellers, track multiple auctions you're involved in, bookmark your favorite categories to make it easier to check for new items, and adjust your account settings.

You can pay for most eBay purchases by credit card, and many sellers use the PayPal service for safe online payments (see the box below).

If you get into an argument with a seller or buyer on eBay, you can track and manage problems in the My eBay Dispute Console area (which sounds like the place cantankerous crew members on the Starship Enterprise had to go for misbehaving). The site's Buyer Protection program helps guard against rip-offs; if you get burned by a seller, eBay will reimburse you up to $175.

POWER SHOPPERS' CLINIC

You've Got a Friend in PayPal

With all this shopping and auctioneering going on, there's a lot of money flying around the Internet. PayPal helps keep it straightforward by letting individuals transfer money to each other. PayPal is a division of eBay, and it's popular among the auction site's denizens.

You sign up for a free account at *www.paypal.com*, supplying a user name, password, and a bank account/credit card/debit card number that you want to use as your source of funds. To prove that you're not some hacker somewhere, hiding behind phony account numbers, PayPal makes a couple of teeny test deposits into your account. You're supposed to write back and tell them how much they were, proving that you're legit.

When you send money to someone via PayPal, the site taps your money source for the bucks; the payment credits show up in the other people's PayPal accounts.

Because PayPal is a popular international banking system with more than 96 million accounts, it's also a huge target for scams, frauds, and other criminal activity. One popular phishing scheme (page 412), for example, works like this: You get an email message, purportedly from PayPal's security team, telling you your account is outdated/compromised/inactive. It encourages you to click the link provided in the message and fill in your personal details on the site.

While the link may look like it's going to PayPal's site, it's actually fake, and it sends you to a *forged* PayPal Web page. Someone behind that page gleefully collects all your personal credit card, bank account, and personal identification numbers to use for his own shopping sprees.

If you think there's *actually* something wrong with your PayPal account, don't click any email link. Instead, fire up your browser, go directly to *www.paypal.com*, and log in there. Click the Contact Us link at the bottom of the page for customer service options, including a phone number to call.

On the flip side, if you win an auction but refuse to pay, you get a Non-Paying Buyer label slapped on your account. You get warned twice about that, but three strikes and you're booted off eBay.

If you find your house is filling up with all the cool stuff you've found on eBay, you know where you can sell off older junk to make room to buy more.

Craigslist

With its sheer size, Craigslist (*www.craigslist.org*) is another good place to shop for goods and services online. Craigslist itself doesn't sell items; instead, it gives neighbors a place to post listings about stuff they're selling. Like the classified advertising it emulates, many of the items for sale on the site are used and often very affordable. If you need a small table for the kitchen in your very first apartment and have barely any money to spend, see what folks are selling via Craigslist. (In case you missed it earlier in the book, there's a whole box about how to use Craigslist back on page 57.)

Craigslist is known as a good way to connect with other people in your area, and the site has a homegrown feel. There's a search box right on the main page and you can browse by subject, too. If you find something you want, click the link on the listing to email the seller. Once you make contact, it's just like buying an item from the newspaper classified where you negotiate and interact with humans.

Note: Craigslist has local versions all over the world. So be sure to click the name of your city (or the city nearest to you) to get posts and listings in your area. You don't want to get your heart set on a large, hard-to-mail oak desk from a seller in California if you live in New Jersey.

Of course, there's always room for fraud. But Craigslist is scrupulous about kicking out people who are known scammers and those who use the site to post warnings about frauds and scams. Craigslist also offers this additional advice:

• Non-local deals involving shipping, escrow accounts, wire transfers, or cashier checks are usually fraudulent.

• There are no such things as "Craigslist payment systems," "Craigslist buyer protection," or "Craigslist seller certification."

• Don't give out personal information or credit card numbers to sellers.

When Not to Give Your Credit Card Info

As you've heard, fraud, scams, and rip-offs abound on the Internet.

Now, there's not really much cause for paranoia. The following paragraphs will help you avoid having your credit card number intercepted. But even if that happens, you won't be left with ghastly bills and a ruined credit rating. Under the U.S. Fair Credit Billing Act, your liability for lost or stolen credit cards is limited to $50—and if it was just the credit card number that got swiped (and not the actual card), you don't have to pay anything *at all*. More information on consumer protection and anti-fraud measures is available at *www.ftc.gov*.

Still, having to change your credit card number is a hassle, and you may as well make life as difficult as possible for the Internet thieves. So here's some advice along those lines.

A common scam is *phishing* (page 412). That's when people send you fake emails *pretending* to be from PayPal, eBay, America Online, your bank, your financial service company, or any other institution that deals with money. These messages clog your inbox, hoping you'll be duped into following the links provided and handing over credit card numbers and other personal data.

These types of messages look authentic, appear to have Web links going to the right place, and sound sincere. But be very, very careful. Graphics and bank logos are easy to swipe from legitimate Web sites, and URLs are simple enough to disguise.

Besides, even if the bank did have your email address on file, it wouldn't start off the message with "Dear Washington Mutual Customer." (You'd better believe that they *know* your name—and everything else about you.) *Never* give your credit card number or any account information to anybody that sends you an email message like that.

Also, never give your credit card number to Web sites unless you went directly there yourself (by typing the address into your Web browser) to buy something and you trust the store. As mentioned in Step 4 on page 132, check to make sure the Web site is using secure encryption on the page where you type in your credit card number.

Do *not* type in your credit card number at a Web page whose address begins with *http://*. (It should say *https://* instead, meaning that your information is scrambled before being sent.)

And *never* send your credit card information, Social Security number, bank account numbers, or other personal data by email. That's like writing the information on the back of a postcard and mailing it for anyone to see; your email passes through a lot of different computers on its way to its destination.

Finding Good Deals

For many dedicated practitioners of the Shopping Arts, the thrill isn't just in the hunt of tracking down the very thing you were looking for, but in getting an extremely good price to boot. Happily, a number of Web sites are dedicated to rounding up prices from *hundreds* of competing online stores. You find the best deal, and click the link to go make a victorious purchase.

Froogle

Froogle, by Google, is a search service that specifically searches Web pages listing products for sale (*http://www.froogle.com*). When you type terms into Froogle's search box, say *left-handed mandolin* or *suede moccasins*, Froogle looks at its vast database of Web stores and finds product pages selling objects that match your search terms. Many online merchants submit their pages to Froogle directly for inclusion in the index.

On your results page, Froogle lists all the things it found for you (Figure 7-4), complete with photos, a list of online stores selling the item, and a range of prices on these sites. Click Compare Prices to see what each individual store is charging; Froogle displays the list for you, complete with ratings other shoppers have given the sites.

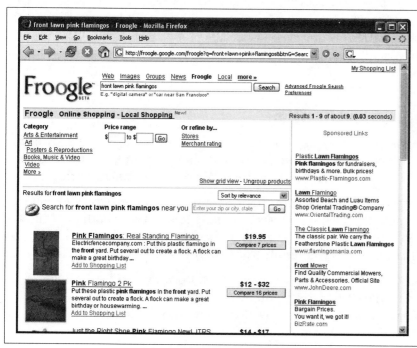

Figure 7-4:
No matter how tacky, if it's out there and it's for sale, Froogle can probably find it for you. The listings on the left are your search results, while the listings under Sponsored Links are ads. The Compare Prices button lets you see what the various merchants are charging for the item.

Tip: If you're settling in for an afternoon of online shopping with Froogle, the site's Shopping List feature can come in handy. You need to set up a free Google account (page 99), if you don't already have one from a Gmail or Google Groups account. You can set one up from the prompt when you click the "Add to Shopping List" link on the page next to the item you want to add. Once you have your Google Account, the site stores the links and product descriptions for the items you add to your Shopping List. If you don't have the time or money right then to follow through with the purchase, the items on the Shopping List are still listed to remind you the next time you log back in.

You can also use Froogle to find products in physical stores near where you live—handy if the product isn't sold online or if you want to inspect it in person before buying. After you type in your product search on the main Froogle page, click the link for Local Shopping at the top of the results page and type in your Zip code or your city and state to have Froogle narrow down your product results to those from sellers in your area.

Tip: If you love that something-for-nothing feeling you get from racking up frequent-flier miles and converting them to free flights or an escape from coach class, check out any of the shopping-rewards sites around the Web. Ebates (*www.ebates.com*), for example, slips you a rebate check every few months when you buy goods from the company's partners—which includes Apple Computer, Wine.com, The Home Depot, and Sears. Another site, MyPoints (*www.mypoints.com*), gives you "points" for filling out a shopping profile, taking surveys, reading email offers, and buying stuff from MyPoints partner sites, which include Neiman Marcus, Ann Taylor, and Best Buy. When you score enough points, you can convert them into gift cards, movie tickets, and even…frequent flier miles.

Shopping.com and DealTime

Shopping.com (*www.shopping.com*), a serious price-comparison site, owns the similar DealTime (*www.dealtime.com*)—and Shopping.com, in turn, is owned by eBay (page 137). Sometimes, the World Wide Web is a small world.

But no matter who owns whom, both Shopping.com and DealTime aim to bring you results for whatever you're searching for, and they both look and act the same. Stop by either home page, type what you want in the search box, and marvel as the site brings you results from hundreds of stores around the Web.

Your results page (Figure 7-5 shows a sample) gives you a list of items, with photos and manufacturer descriptions. For each brand or model of your item listed, the page tells you how many stores have it, the range of prices offered from those stores, and invites you to compare the prices and features. You can sort the results page based on price or rating, and links at the top help you narrow down your search by maximum price, manufacturer, or technical specifications.

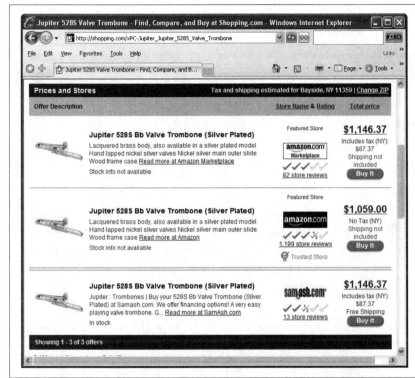

Figure 7-5:
Shopping.com shows you every place it's found your item and politely adds in the sales tax so you get an idea of what you'll actually be paying.

Clicking the Compare Prices button takes you to a new page where each merchant is listed, along with the asking price. A nice touch from both Shopping. com and DealTime: Click the Enter ZIP link on the page, type in your postal code, and the site calculates your total price for the item, including state sales tax (if any) and shipping fees to that location.

Both sites also have features that let you look at the specifications of similar products side by side, so for digital cameras, you can see how each one stacks up in terms of lens length, resolution, zoom ability, and so on. To compare the features, turn on the checkbox on the left side of different items in the list and click the Compare button to get the features charts for each selected model all lined up in a row.

If you're not searching for anything special, you can also use the category links and tabs on each home page to wander deeper and deeper into the site from product to product. Of the two, Shopping.com has a member registration program where you can sign up to get newsletters about the site and have the privilege of posting your opinions. On Shopping.com, you can also click to save items you're considering for purchase to a shopping list, similar to Froogle's shopping list feature.

WORKAROUND WORKSHOP

How Not to Be Gamed by the System

Price-comparison sites like Shopping.com can save you *huge* amounts of money, especially on electronics.

Unfortunately, many consumers reflexively order from the lowest bidder. Some of the online stores, well aware of how much business gets generated by rock-bottom prices, have begun playing nasty games. They post ridiculously low prices—but then pull sleazy tactics to make up the difference.

For example, after you order, they'll call to say that your camera doesn't come with a power adapter; would you like to buy one for $50 more? Or when they talk you into ordering accessories with your purchase (another standard practice), they'll send you ill-fitting, no-name brands.

Once again, your best weapons against these tactics are the battle scars of other people. Each online store listed on sites like Shopping.com bears a rating—an average grade provided by thousands of people who've come before you. That grade and the customer comments let you know whether tricks are being played to get the price so low.

What you really want to find, therefore, isn't the lowest price available. It's the lowest price *from a highly rated store*.

That's the purpose of the Smart Buy logo on Shopping.com. It's usually a good indicator that your transaction will go smoothly.

Believe it or not, some of the online stores are now trying to game *this* system, too. After you buy something, you'll get an email message offering you a $30 savings coupon if you'll post a good review on Shopping.com or PriceGrabber.com. They're basically buying votes.

That's a good argument for sticking with a store once you've had a good experience there. You may be paying a few bucks more than the lowest possible price, but that's a small price to pay for headache insurance.

Shopping for Big-Ticket Items

Shopping for stuff like books, CDs, clothing, food, electronics, and other stuff is pretty easy. But what if you have a larger purchase in mind, like a car or a house? Although these aren't exactly point-click-ship items, you can still use the Web to search and see what's out there, indicate your interest in a vehicle or property, and get on track to make a purchase if everything works out for both buyer and seller.

Cars

The automotive sites on page 126 are great places to research and look for new cars. Used cars, which are vast and plentiful, are also for sale on the Web, from listings in your local newspaper's online edition (page 104) to sites like eBay (page 137) and Craigslist (page 141).

Your local car dealer's Web site can show you the latest models if you're mulling a new vehicle, and many of the automotive review-and-ratings sites like Cars.com maintain national databases of used cars that you can browse. There are also sites mainly devoted to the buying and selling of used vehicles, like these:

- **CarMax.** Imagine a used car lot with 20,000 cars, trucks, and vans all parked out front, and you get some idea of CarMax's inventory. The company has 67 stores around the country; you can search their inventory at *www.carmax. com.* You can search for specific makes and models, set your price limit, and narrow down your search to the CarMax retail location closet to you.

  The site gives detailed descriptions and photos of each vehicle for sale, along with other factors that can influence your purchasing decision, like total mileage.

- **AutoTrader** (*www.autotrader.com*) has a huge database of new, used, and manufacturer-certified vehicles You can search for your preferred price range, make, and model in your area. Many used cars listed are on dealer's lots and have a wealth of information about each one. If you want to know the full background of the car—like how many previous owners it's had or if it's been in any major accidents—you can click the link to read the Carfax vehicle history report right there on its page.

- **Edmunds'** used car listings are provided by the aforementioned AutoTrader site, but Edmunds (*www.edmunds.com*) is a great source for background research on the whole car-buying process. It's got tips and advice for buyers, links to reviews, and its Inside Line Webzine covers new models, road tests, and other worthy car news.

Real Estate

The Web can help you do a lot of valuable research when it comes to buying property, too. Real estate sites offer search engines, interior and exterior color photos, and links to email the broker. They're a great way to scope out listings without having to pick up those smudgy catalogs in the supermarket or wait for the weekend paper.

Realtor.com

Realtor.com (*www.realtor.com*) lets you browse two million properties in America's major cities, including both houses for sale and rental properties. You can specify the number of bedrooms and bathrooms you're looking for in your Dream House.

Many listings include a "virtual tour"—a 360-degree view of the property that you can manipulate right in your Web browser (Figure 7-6). Other links let you check out the schools in the area, get background information on the location, and—if things work out—find a moving company.

Figure 7-6:
Virtual tours, which let you manipulate pictures to see things from many angles, give you a much clearer picture of a property and its surrounding grounds than still photos do.

RealEstate.com

RealEstate.com (*www.realestate.com*) aims to be a total source of information for buying or selling a home. It has an extensive setup questionnaire that gathers information on where you want to live, what kind of house you want, and how much you can afford to pay for it. Once it gets your information, it hooks you up with a realtor and listings in your preferred area. And since it's owned by the LendingTree loan site, it also offers to point you in the direction of a mortgage.

Century 21

This international realtor's site at *www.century21.com* lets you search its index of properties. It offers tools like a First Time Home Buyer's Guide and a mortgage calculator. If you register with the site, you can save property searches, see the company's reports on local sales trends, and read exclusive content.

Tip: Want to get a sense of what your friends and neighbors paid for their places? Check out *RealEstateABC.com* and *Zillow.com*, both of which provide historical purchase prices, current value estimates, and other real-estate-buying goodies.

Planning Trips

If you think shopping in general got easier when the World Wide Web arrived, wait until you see what it's done for the travel industry. Those days of relying on a travel agent, waiting in the airline's reservation line for them to check available flights, or even trying to decipher routes in thick, impenetrable time-tables are long gone. A good travel Web site lets you look up dozens of flights at once, compare prices from different airlines, and even pick out your seat on the plane.

Many sites also guide you through booking the hotel reservations and rental cars for your trip. You can also book luxury vacations, cruises, spa trips, and other getaways—and often save money doing so over the Internet. So if you're planning your next vacation or merely dreaming about it in the distant future, buckle up and take a spin through this chapter to see *where* to go when you want to go.

Booking Tickets and Reservations

People plan trips in different ways. Some spend weeks doing meticulous research on the area's attractions, and then schedule events right down to the nanosecond. Other travelers just wake up one Friday, decide to skip work and start the weekend early, and buy a ticket to the cheapest interesting destination—allotting an hour to pack and get to the airport.

What to Do When Some Planes Don't Play

Mega-travel sites like Expedia and Travelocity make it very convenient to buy plane tickets. As great as some of the bargains are, however, they don't include the fares of all airlines. Some of them, notably Jet Blue, Southwest, and regional carriers, don't make their routes and tickets available to the travel sites.

The bottom line: If you use the mega-travel sites, you may be missing deals that you weren't even aware of.

Of course, you can always check fares and book tickets on an airline's own Web site—if you know it services your city. You may even save a few bucks buying directly from the airline, since mega-travel sites like Orbitz, Travelocity, and Expedia usually tack a $5 "processing fee" onto your purchase. If you have no idea where to start, though, you don't have to click around tediously until you find something cheaper than what Orbitz is offering.

That's because there's such a thing as a *meta*-travel site. This is a supersearch site that rises above the fray and searches other travel sites around the Web, *including* individual airline pages and the big travel sites as well. Some of these meta-travel search engines include SideStep (*www.sidestep.com*), Mobissimo (*www.mobissimo.com*), and Kayak (page 156).

You can't buy your tickets directly from one of these search sites. Still, they do all the hard work for you by scanning over 100 other travel sites at once. If you find a flight that fits, you just have to click a link to bop right over there.

Most travel search sites also include hotel and rental car providers, too. Using one of these sites means adding a tiny bit of time to your booking ritual—but what you lose in time, you can more than make up for in money if you score a bargain flight.

No matter how you like to travel, though, there's a Web site that can keep up with you. With the advent of the *e-ticket*—a ticket receipt and boarding pass issued at the airport—you don't even have to wait for an old-fashioned paper ticket to arrive in the mail. You just get to the airport, swipe your credit card through a kiosk at the airline's check-in counter (for I.D. purposes only), and collect the boarding pass that's printed on the spot. Then you show your government-issued ID (like a driver's license or green card) when you check your bags at the counter and go get in line at the metal detectors.

Buying a plane ticket on the Web is simple—specify the airports you want to use, plus the dates and times of travel. You can indicate how many people are traveling together, which airlines you prefer, and what seating class you'd like.

The travel site brings you a page showing all the flights that match your chosen travel dates and times. If you find a flight you like, follow the Web site's instructions for booking the flight. You can usually select your own seat from a seating chart—a clickable map of the actual model of plane you'll be riding. For the flights that still serve food, you can choose meals with special dietary preferences like low-sodium, vegetarian, or meals that conform to religious observations.

Tip: Excited about picking your own seat? First consult the SeatGuru at *www.seatguru.com*, where you can see seating charts and floor plans for just about every type of airplane. SeatGuru color-codes the especially good and bad seats on each plane—which ones are noisy because they're over the engines, which ones have extra legroom—and provides basic information about the aircraft, onboard amenities, and other useful data.

Booking hotel rooms and rental cars works roughly the same way. At hotels, you can specify things like how many beds you want and whether you want a smoking or non-smoking room. Rental car companies let you select things like the vehicle size you need and any necessary infant or child car seats as you book online.

Yahoo, MSN, and AOL (Chapter 2) have their own little travel corners, often with special deals and discounts. But if you don't hang out on portal sites and want to go site-seeing around the Web before you pack the sunscreen, read on.

TripAdvisor

Travel magazines can make just about anyplace sound sophisticated and glamorous, but sometimes you can get more useful advice from people who paid their own money to go there. If you're wondering if that tiny motel in Gettysburg is a dump or want to find out whether a visit to the Biltmore Estate on your upcoming trip to Asheville would be a good way to spend the day, visit the TripAdvisor site at *www.tripadvisor.com*.

With four million reviews from people who had something to say about 200,000 hotels, restaurants, and attractions, you can get unadorned, unbiased advice from the site.

TripAdvisor is more than a message board full of posts and photos praising the food at a Kansas City barbecue joint or complaining about broken air conditioning at the roadside motel in Reno. It offers tools to help you plan your trip, too.

On TripAdvisor, you check out a city's most popular hotels by price, location, and rating, check pricing across a bunch of separate hotel-booking sites at once, and sign up for customized email newsletters bringing you the latest from your chosen destination before you leave. If you're in the early stages of

---

thinking about your next vacation (which for many people starts the day they get back from their last one), spending some time with the TripAdvisor site can let you know what to expect the next time you hit the road.

Tip: Many airline Web sites now include flight-tracker pages that show a flight's current progress on the ground or in the air; you just need to know the airline and flight number to get a map of the plane's location and details of its whereabouts. (Actually, if you have a Mac, press F12 to see a Flight Tracker widget in the Dashboard feature that does the same thing.) This is helpful if you're the one picking up at the airport, because you can see if the flight has been delayed and plan your run to the Arrivals lane accordingly.

Travelocity

Owned by Sabre Holdings, a long-time player in the travel industry that built the first computerized reservations system in the 1960s, the Travelocity Web site at *www.travelocity.com* is one of the best-designed and easiest-to-use travel sites online (Figure 8-1).

Figure 8-1:
Travelocity invites you to find a flight right off the bat with its prominently placed flight-search box. If there's no major airport in your town, the site gives you a list of all the ones nearby. Once you pick an airport, you can see all the fares to your desired destination.

To tempt you further into traveling, the Travelocity home page has an ideas section with articles outlining themed or regional trips.

Travelocity powers a few other sites as well, including AOL Travel and the AARP Passport service, which offers deals and discounts for members of the American Association of Retired People.

Along with flights, hotels, and cars, you can book cruises, train tickets in Europe and Canada, and full vacation packages to near and distant lands—including Disneyland. If you're one of those get-up-and-go types, Travelocity regularly has a number of deals for cheap, last-minute trips for this weekend or next. If you're really on the hunt for a deal, sign up for the site's RSS feed (page 111), which sends out an update to your Web browser or feed reader program if the fares to your favorite places drop by 20 percent or more.

Expedia

Expedia (*www.expedia.com*) is another big all-purpose travel site. (Because it was founded by Microsoft and later spun off into its own company, Expedia is also the booking muscle behind the MSN Travel Service.)

As its name suggests, Expedia's an expedient way to book a flight, hotel, and rental car all at once and potentially save a chunk of money.

Once you sign up, the site remembers your personal info (including frequent travel companions) and stores your trip details in its My Itineraries section. If you fly to the same place on a regular basis, Expedia saves completed reservations in My Itineraries; if you liked the airline route and hotel, you can use the same ones again by clicking the "Repeat trip" button (Figure 8-2, circled) and just changing the dates for your next go-around.

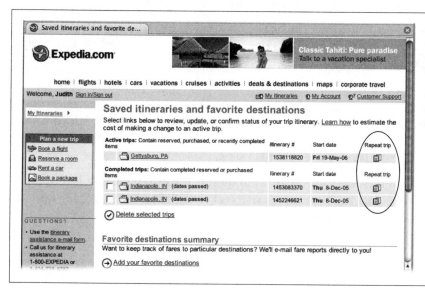

Figure 8-2:
In the My Itineraries section, Expedia remembers where you went so if you want to go there again the exact same way, you have the information you need.

The site offers plenty of packages like ski trips, Caribbean cruises, and romantic getaways; you can easily add special tours and attractions (like Broadway tickets or a tour of Mozart's Salzburg). Expedia also offers a link to maps and driving directions right on its main page, so you don't have to wander off to another URL to see where your hotel is or how to find it.

Tip: Online travel services act as the middlemen between you and the airline, hotelier, and car rental place. It's a good idea to print—or save to your hard drive—all receipts and reservation confirmations. Have these documents available, on paper or on your laptop, in case there's a computer glitch or mix-up at one of your destinations.

Orbitz

The Orbitz site at *www.orbitz.com* was started by several major airlines (American, Continental, Delta, Northwest, and United) who came together to do their own version of a Web-based travel service. The site can find flights on hundreds of airlines, rooms in thousands of hotels, and transportation from a dozen different rental car places.

You can compare several hotels onscreen or search for lodging by specific amenities like a pool or business center. The hotel-search feature lets you pinpoint your hotel by brand or proximity to a tourist attraction.

Orbitz has built part of its reputation on its customer services. For example, if you sign up for the company's Care Alerts, you'll get electronic updates of traffic conditions, weather advisories, and other things to watch out for via email, cellphone, pager, or wireless palmtop.

Orbitz has its own RSS feed (page 111) of daily travel deals for those afflicted with severe wanderlust and has its own package deals for baseball-game trips, Valentine vacations, and other themed getaways.

Kayak

As the box on page 152 makes clear, not every airline shows up on the big Web travel sites. Fortunately, sites like Kayak (*www.kayak.com*) make sure you don't miss any of the possible flights.

Kayak is one of the best travel search engines. It tracks fares across hundreds of different airline sites and other online travel sites. It can quickly find, say, 400 different possibilities for an April trip from Newark to London.

When you get your results, the site tells you which ones are direct and which flights have stops; dragging the sliders on the page (Figure 8-3) lets you narrow down the list of possibilities based on the time of day you'd like to take off or your top ticket price.

Once you find a flight that looks good, click it; Kayak sends you to the site selling the seat so you can buy it there. You can search across multiple hotel sites just as you can with flights, and even compare rental car fees all at once.

Kayak offers trip ideas, email alerts, and RSS feeds (page 111) for hot deals, and a link to specials—both foreign and domestic—for a variety of travel budgets and moods.

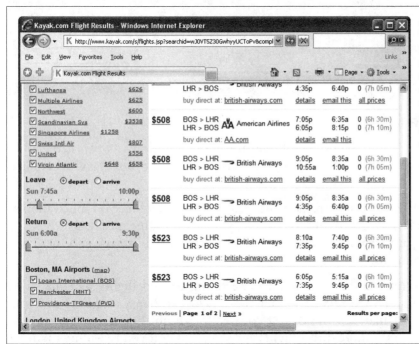

Figure 8-3:
When Kayak paddles back with hundreds of flights that match your query, you can narrow down the results by moving the time sliders for arrival and departure and have the results instantly reconfigure to match the new criteria.

Last-Minute Deals

If you're not fussy about when or where you go, you can find even bigger, better bargains on the Web. Certain discount travel sites specialize in selling off empty airplane seats, unreserved rooms, and unrented cars at the last minute—at rock-bottom prices.

The Art of the Last-Minute Deal

Some Web-travel services sell *nothing* but imminent departures. These fire-sale sites may not give you as many potential destinations as regular electronic travel agents, but spontaneous and savvy shoppers can get some crackin' good bargains.

Some of these time-sensitive agents include Site59 (*www.site59.com*, named for the last minute on the hour), 11thHour (*www.11thhourvacations.com*), and LastMinuteTravel (*www.lastminutetravel.com*). All specialize in deals that have you in the air anywhere from a few *hours* from now to less than two weeks hence.

Most sites sell you package deals, say flight and hotel, or a rental car and hotel if you're not going far. In many cases, you have to buy an e-ticket (page 152) because there's no time to mail paper tickets to you.

The last-minute deal sites let you buy a whole weekend getaway to *somewhere* with a minimum of clicks, getting you on that mini-vacation you deserve that much faster.

Priceline

The original "Name Your Own Price" travel site, Priceline (*www.priceline.com*) can save you up to 40 percent on flights and hotels—if your travel schedule is flexible.

If you need to leave at a precise time, Priceline may not save you much money. But if you're not locked into a schedule, you can get some nice deals when you punch in your airport information, the day you want to travel, and the maximum amount you're willing to pay.

Priceline crunches through its database trying to find flights that match all your criteria. The results may offer more layovers than you'd like, but your bank account may not mind. (Of course, you're not limited to those cheap seats; you can get more direct flights at specific times if you're willing to up the ante.)

Like the other travel sites, Priceline directs you to hotels, cruises, cars, and package deals. Its Pricebreakers deal page specializes in limited-time offers, mostly from big hotels and resorts looking to fill up empty rooms on short notice—a great way to get luxury accommodations at low, low motor-lodge prices.

Hotwire

If Expedia is a name-brand department store full of travel opportunities, then Hotwire is its discount store at the outlet mall. Like Priceline, Hotwire (*www.hotwire.com*) requires some flexibility on your part, but offers up to 60 percent off hotel rooms and 35 percent off air fares. Last-minute flights purchased within 7 days can be up to 50 percent off.

Hotwire finds hotels and flights that match your requests, but doesn't tell you where you're staying or who you're flying until *after* you make your purchase. This setup may be a little suspenseful for some people, but it's what allows Hotwire to find the lowest prices from the hotels and airlines that really want to sell off unused inventory.

If you don't like that idea of flying blind, Hotwire also displays the lowest published price from its partners, too.

Travelzoo

The point of Travelzoo (*www.travelzoo.com*) isn't to book trips; it's to get descriptions of the very best deals of the moment, generated not by a database but by human researchers who hand-pick the goodies. Once you find an appealing offer, you can buy the trip from the site that's actually selling it.

Travelzoo also acts like the other travel discounters described here. When you search for a flight or hotel on the site's Super Search page, Travelzoo presents you with a list of links to other sites selling what you want, like Hotwire, Priceline, or even the airlines themselves.

If you like to travel inexpensively, you may want to sign up for the Travelzoo Top 20 newsletter, which comes to you by email each Wednesday. It rounds up the best travel sales and specials that week so you can make plans before the weekend.

Finance

The previous chapters have described various ways to spend money online, whether on Wonder Woman Pez dispensers from eBay or last-minute weekend trips to Charleston. This chapter's different: It tells you how to manage, save, and *make* money online through online banking, stock trading, and money-management sites.

Tales of hackers, scams, and identity theft may make you nervous about trusting an electronic link to your literal life's savings, but banks and financial companies have been working hard to have the best Internet security out there. Nowadays, most *guarantee* that your account will remain secure.

With such security measures in place, you can pay bills online, spruce up your financial portfolio, file your taxes, and much more, all from the comfort of your own computer. You can even trade stocks or apply for a mortgage wearing your bunny slippers—something you can't do in real life without people whispering behind your back.

Online Banking

Many major American banks—Citibank, JP Morgan Chase, Washington Mutual, and so on—have online banking capabilities. In most cases, all you need to sign up is your ATM/debit card, personal identification number (or PIN, otherwise known as your ATM passcode), and one of your bank account numbers. Check your monthly bank statement for the digits.

Most banks require that you use a relatively modern browser (technically, one that offers 128-bit encryption). If you're using Internet Explorer 5.5 or later on Windows, Safari on the Mac, or Firefox on either Mac or Windows, you should be fine.

Once you sign up online, you can log into your bank's Web site just like you'd log in to eBay, Amazon, or any other password-protected Web site.

Once you're logged in, you can do a number of things with your accounts online, including:

- Check balances and account activity (Figure 9-1)
- Pay bills online (page 163)
- Read your monthly account statements on the Web
- Perform real-time money transfers to your linked accounts
- Perform money transfers to accounts in other banks
- Do international and domestic wire transfers
- Receive banking alerts via email or mobile phone
- See scanned images of cleared checks

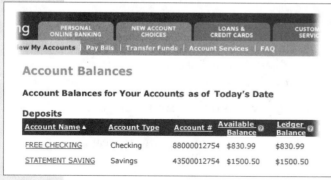

Figure 9-1:
Here at Washington Mutual, you can see exactly how much money is in each of your accounts with a quick trip to the bank's online branch.

The main thing you *can't* do online is deposit physical items like checks and cash into your account; they're a little hard to stuff through an Internet connection, no matter how broad your band is.

But you can do things like check to make sure your paycheck's direct deposit has landed, transfer money between checking and savings accounts, and do a lot of the little things that used to mean, at the very least, hauling yourself to an ATM. Many banks also let you download your financial data to programs like Quicken or Microsoft Money.

Note: If you do your financial business from a Windows computer, keep your computer safe with the suggestions in Chapter 21, especially by installing an Internet security suite and an anti-spyware program. These programs protect your computer from Internet invaders who'd like nothing more than to swipe your secret passwords and account information for their own nefarious purposes.

Paying Bills

Tired of running out of checks, getting paper cuts from return envelopes, or scrounging around for increasingly expensive postal stamps? With online bill payment, you can chuck all that into the shredder and disburse your utilities, services, and other bills with convenient, tree-friendly electronic payments.

What's especially great about paying bills electronically is—actually, there are two great things.

First, you can set up recurring regular payments (like your mortgage or cable TV bill) to go out automatically, so you don't forget. Say goodbye to late fees and service charges.

Second, you can sit down and do your bills all in one session, even though their due dates are scattered throughout the month. You just tell your bank *when* you want each one mailed, essentially postdating all of your payments. The beauty here is that the money stays in your account until the last possible moment, earning interest for you (instead of for the utility, phone, or cable company, which would have happened if you'd paid *early*).

There are three ways to pay bills online:

- Use your own bank's online bill-payment feature.

- Make many payments directly through the recipient's Web site with your credit or debit card or—if you're sure of the biller—by authorizing the company to make a withdrawal from your checking account.

- Use a third-party bill-payment service like CheckFree (*www.checkfree.com*) or PayTrust (*www.paytrust.com*); most of these companies gather up your bills and ping you with email alerts when you've got a payment coming up.

When you pay your bills online, you get an onscreen record of the transaction and can keep track of past and present payments.

With the online record of all your bills, you get the extra benefit of having a running record of your monthly expenditures. This is helpful if you're on a tight budget and want to keep a close watch on your funds. If you do any contract or freelance work where you can deduct certain utilities and services as part of your home office setup, having a electronic record of all your paid bills comes in especially handy during tax-preparation season.

Tip: Online services like America Online and MSN offer bill-payment options, too.

Bill Paying for the Bankless

Most people who've discovered the joys of electronic banking do their bill paying on the bank's Web site. But services like CheckFree can perform the same function. They're online services that don't require you to have an electronic bank account.

Bill-payment services can also eliminate the paper billing statements that fill up your mailbox each month; they can send you *electronic* bills that you manage, approve, and pay online.

CheckFree's bill-payment service lets you receive and pay e-bills online for free, as long as your payees are on its list of 300 common power and utility firms, department stores, and credit card companies; there's a list on the Web site (*www.mycheckfree.com*). Most other bill-paying services charge a small monthly fee.

"But how," you say, "can I pay the babysitter or anybody else not on that list?"

In that case, you have to sign up for the full Check-Free service, which involves a small fee unless your bank has a deal with CheckFree (Bank of America, SunTrust, and Wachovia do, for example). Once you sign up, you can pay people who aren't large corporations by having CheckFree print and mail a regular old-fashioned check to the party needing payment.

Finding Loans Online

Unless you're independently wealthy, life-changing purchases like a house, car, or college education usually require life-changing amounts of money. If you don't have that much cash on hand, you'll need a loan.

If you already bank online, you're probably quite familiar with your bank's electronic offerings; most have links to their "personal lending" services right on their home pages. Because banks *looooove* to lend money to qualified borrowers, their loan pages tend to be incredibly well-designed, with plenty of information and telephone numbers to call if you have questions.

In the case of home loans, banks and other mortgage companies include useful areas where you can see the current lending rates for 30- and 15-year fixed loans, adjustable rate mortgages, and so on. Tools like mortgage calculators

(Figure 9-2) let you type in a property's asking price and instantly calculate what the monthly payment would be with the assorted types of loans and rates.

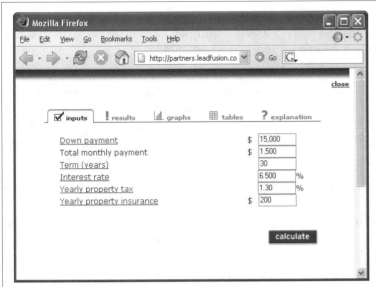

Figure 9-2:
Most online banks and housing lenders have tools like mortgage calculators so you can see how high a monthly payment you can afford when you're shopping for a new home.

Even if you're not an existing customer, you can still check bank Web sites for loan rates and information, and even *apply* for a loan online. All major banks have their own Web sites (find them with Google), and some of the bigger, better-known loan companies include:

- **LendingTree.** After you fill out a form describing the kind of loan you want, LendingTree rounds up offers from up to four different banks, essentially pitting their offers against each other so you can pick the best one. You can apply for mortgages, car loans, student loans, commercial loans, and more. (*www.lendingtree.com*)

- **E-Loan.** Search for the type of loan you need, and save money and paperwork if you find a good one. The site has loan pros on the phone to help with questions, plus tools like payment calculators and free credit reports right on the main page. (*www.e-loan.com*)

Tip: Order a free copy of your credit report online at *www.annualcreditreport.com*. Each of the three main credit rating bureaus are now required by Uncle Sam to give you your report once a year; this is the official site where you put in your request.

- **Countrywide Financial.** You can search and apply for a home loan here or schedule an appointment with a consultant. First-time homebuyers may appreciate the site's informative articles and advice on the whole big adventure. (*http://my.countrywide.com*)

- **Ditech.** You can apply for a new mortgage, refinancing deal, or home-equity loan from this direct-lending company that's part of the General Motors Acceptance Corporation and has deeply annoying TV commercials. (*www.ditech.com*)

- **Sallie Mae.** Sallie Mae focuses on school costs; it's been making higher education a reality for people since 1972. It offers both federal and private student loans on its site. Once a government-sponsored entity, Miss Sallie is now a private company that handles personal and mortgage loans, too. (*www.salliemae.com*)

The U.S. government lends money, too. To see what's available, go to the GovLoans site at *www.govloans.gov*. You can find details on just about every loan the federal government offers, including specialized loans for veterans, farmers, and business owners. Loans covering disaster relief, education, and housing are also listed.

Note: If you value your fiscal health, it's wise to stay away from the many "payday loan" sites around the Web. These companies offer to loan you the bucks you need to make it to your next paycheck—*if* you give them your bank account number so they can withdraw repayment when your check lands. They also charge exorbitant fees (sometimes $30 for every $100 borrowed), which takes a bite out of the account when the loan comes due. Finally, giving your bank account, Social Security number, and other deeply personal data to a Web entity is not a good practice to get into.

Trading Online and Tracking Investments

If you like the sheer thrill and adrenaline of shuffling stocks and making trades the old-fashioned way with phone and broker in tow, you may find the Internet a non-stop rollercoaster of financial fun, too. For one thing, if you don't need a financial advisor to guide you in your buying-and-selling adventures, you can trade stocks online for as little as $7 per deal.

Finding Stock Information

The Web is full of tools that let you research companies you might want to invest in. You can keep tabs on your portfolio, get instant share prices, and keep the current state of major market indicators like the Dow Jones, NASDAQ, and the S&P 500 onscreen all day long.

All of the big portal sites mentioned in Chapter 2—Yahoo, AOL, Google, and MSN—have financial areas where you can go to read up on the day's markets and important news, see charts and stock quotes, and track your investments. For beginning investors, these sites have a big batch of "Investing 101"-type articles and features intended to get you acquainted with the stock market, help you understand mutual funds and bonds, and learn how to develop an investment strategy that suits you.

Tip: If you're not so much a buy-and-hold investor as a buy-and-obsess investor, how'd you like to know how your portfolio is doing at any given moment with the press of one key? The trick is to harness the power of tiny, single-purpose mini-programs called desktop *widgets*. If you have Mac OS X (10.4 or later), press F12 to see the Dashboard—a collection of widgets, one of which is a stock ticker/portfolio summary, updated over the Internet. If you use Windows or an older version of Mac OS X, you can download the free Yahoo Widgets (*http://widgets.yahoo.com*); look for the Yahoo Stock Ticker, Scuttlebutt, or My Stocks programs in the Widget Gallery.

Setting Up an Online Trading Account

To trade stocks and mutual funds online, you need to open an account with a good brokerage firm or financial company.

Tip: As always, *don't* flaunt your passwords over unprotected public wireless networks where someone could snag your data, and *do* get security software for your Windows computer that keeps spyware and other evils at bay; Chapter 21 has details about staying safe.

Trading stocks online is not unlike shopping on the Web or hawking stuff on eBay: Once you open an account with a brokerage site, you can browse what's out there, put together an order, and click a button to make the purchase. (Figure 9-3 shows the form at Smith Barney Access.)

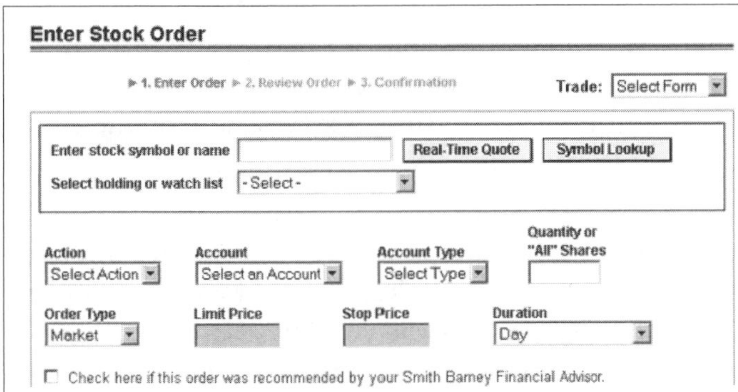

Figure 9-3:
Once you find a stock you like, you can select how many shares you want through your online broker and submit your order.

Obviously, serious players want to do as much research on stocks and market trends as possible; fortunately, most financial-services sites give access to plenty of information on your account page, where you can monitor your holdings, track stocks, place orders and check each order's status, and regularly scan updated news and prices.

If you're new to the whole investment game, you may want to start your career with one of the big, established financial firms. They have thorough, comforting Web sites that explain it all thoroughly, and they provide services like customized research and professional broker advice whenever you need it. These companies include:

- **Charles Schwab.** Well-organized with plenty of market-watching articles and a "New to Investing" section, the Charles Schwab site is a good place to start if you've never done this before. Prices per *trade* (that is, prices to buy or sell shares of one stock) are typically $20 and under, and you can get professional advice for a small fee. (*www.schwab.com*)

- **Merrill Lynch Direct.** Another good site for new investors, Merrill Lynch Direct makes free research reports and analyst commentary available to its account holders. Members get access to the Merrill Lynch Global Investor Network, a daily multimedia presentation of international facts and findings by financial-planning pros, economists, and mutual fund managers. Trades start at around $30 and the company has a collection of mutual funds, bonds, and other investment opportunities. (*www.mldirect.ml.com*)

- **Smith Barney Access.** The online broker's office of the Smith Barney firm is a full-service shop. Once enrolled, you can make investments, view your portfolio, trade stocks and mutual funds, and do company research all on your account page. The service also lets you integrate any other aspect of your financial life where you pay bills and transfer funds, get electronic copies of your monthly statements, and send secure emails to the Smith Barney Financial Advisor who's there to help. (*www.smithbarney.com*)

- **Fidelity.** If mutual funds are your thing, you can find plenty of help and thousands of funds to choose from over at Fidelity's site, where there's free portfolio consultation, round-the-clock customer service, and online equity trades for about $8. (*www.fidelity.com*)

If you're confident in your knowledge of securities, you can save money by using a discount brokerage. The tradeoff: You don't get all that research and investment advice, you'll have less contact with humans, and you may not find some of the luxuries like automatic checking account transfers. Still, the research is plentiful and free on the Web. If you're a hands-on money-saving investor or active trader, you may want to consider a low-cost broker, such as:

- **E*Trade Financial.** E*Trade is a brokerage and banking site that has a service for just about anything you can do with money, from banking to mortgages to stock trading to retirement accounts. It even has free research to browse—and trades cost only about $7 each. (*www.etrade.com*)

- **TD Ameritrade.** You can make your own trades over the Internet for around $11 a toss, or have a human broker assist you for $25. If you plan to stay glued to the market all day, the company's free Streamer Suite displays quotes in real time. (*www.tdameritrade.com*)

- **ScottTrade.** Online trades start at $7, and the site has plenty of free tools to help you get a view of the market, including free research from Dow Jones, Standard & Poor's, and Thomson Financial Research. (*www.scottrade.com*)

Fortunes have risen and fallen on the stock market. But the money-making power of smart investments has proved durable, especially now when company pensions are disappearing and the future viability of Social Security has been called into question. Online trading may be cheap and convenient, but if anything, the Internet has made learning how to invest wisely and take your financial matters into your own hands much easier.

Note: The Internet may be fast, but that real-time stock quote you see on screen isn't a lock on the price you'll get when you place your order. Prices fluctuate constantly; by the time your order gets to the floor, things may have changed.

Doing Your Taxes Online

If you've moved your banking and investing activities to the Internet, it's not much of a leap to move another big money matter into the electronic realm: paying the piper—Uncle Sam—in the annual Filing O' the Taxes. *Electronic* filing, where you submit your return directly to the Internal Revenue Service's computers over the Internet, has been steadily gaining popularity. In fact, Congress wants the IRS to have at least 80 percent of tax returns filed electronically by 2007.

Now, you can't prepare your return directly on the IRS Web site. You have to hire a professional tax preparer or use computer software like TurboTax to upload your finished file.

But even if you still like to do the yearly summation on paper—wearing your green eyeshade while your fingers tap-dance across the calculator—the Web can at least save you a trip to the post office on a quest for obscure forms you might need. And if you have questions on your return as you wade through it, there are plenty of experts around the Net to offer advice—including the Tax Man himself, Mr. Internal Revenue Service, with a government Web site full of answers.

Filing a Federal Tax Return Electronically

Having software help you calculate your taxes saves both time and temper when preparing a return. It can mean more accurate results—the IRS recently estimated than more than 17 percent of tax returns filed on paper contained mistakes like calculations based on the wrong tax tables, basic math errors, and general oversights in submitting some forms and information.

Tip: If, like 70 percent of Americans, you make less than $50,000 a year, you might qualify for free online filing right from the IRS itself. Its Free File program provides online tax preparation and electronic filing from the government's online tax-accounting partner firms. You can find out more about the program, the companies working with the IRS, and its other requirements, at *www.irs. gov/efile*.

A software program like TurboTax or TaxCut guides you through the process, does the math, and automatically checks for errors. Both programs let you upload the information right to the IRS before April 15 rolls around. Even if you don't have the desktop versions of these programs, you can use their online editions to calculate and file your return for a small fee; read on.

Using a tax-preparation service online

To file your taxes electronically with a Web service, you first set up an account.

Thereafter, the site walks you through preparing your return. You'll be asked a series of questions; you should have all your important tax documentation, like your W-2 forms, within reach. Once you complete the process, your finished return's electronically filed over a secure connection right to the IRS. The IRS then runs your electronic return through a programmed set of error checks and validations, right on the spot, to make sure you supplied all the information it needs, and in the right format.

If everything passes muster, the IRS accepts your return, and you can move on with life for another year. If your return flunks a test, the IRS gives you an error code telling you why. The online tax software can tell you how to fix the problem and resubmit your return.

Note: In 38 states and the District of Columbia, you can e-file your *state* tax returns at the same time you send in your Federal return. The IRS passes your state return on to your local tax collectors. You can find out if your state participates in this Federal/State e-file for Taxpayers program by searching at *www.irs.gov* or on this book's "Missing CD" page at *www.missingmanuals.com*.

If it turns out you owe money on your taxes, you can either print out a voucher to send with a check by mail, or you can have the IRS automatically deduct the money from your bank account. If you're one of the fortunate souls getting money *back* from your Dear Uncle Sam, you can have it deposited directly into your bank account in much less time than it takes them to cut you a check and mail it to you.

Here are some popular sites that handle Federal and state tax preparation:

- **H&R Block TaxCut Online.** The online do-it-yourself department of the well-known tax-prep firm's offers services whose prices depend on how complicated your return is. If you're just filing a simple 1040EZ, you can do your Federal return for under $10. If you need extra forms for deductions or other income, though, you need to move up to the more expensive options that can cost up to $100 but include professional advice from an H&R Block tax expert. (*http://taxcut.com*)

- **TurboTax Online.** The Web version of Intuit's desktop taxware (Figure 9-4) also gives you several levels of service for less than $100. If you need to factor in IRA investments, real-estate holdings, and forms like Schedule C, you need one of the more expensive services; but here again, the top-dollar package brings live tax advice with it. There's also a TurboTax solution for people making money by selling things on eBay who need to pony up at tax time. (*www.turbotax.com*)

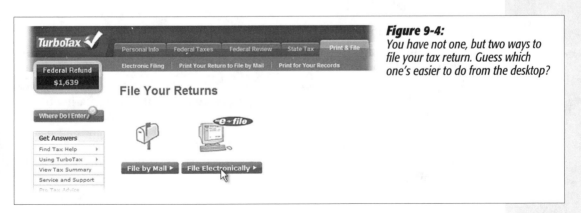

Figure 9-4:
You have not one, but two ways to file your tax return. Guess which one's easier to do from the desktop?

- **TaxBrain.** With secure email and a live-chat feature that lets you type questions and get answers from the tax pros logged onto the site, you're never too far from help at TaxBrain if you get stuck with questions in the middle of your online return. Prices start at around $20 for a federal filing. For additional fees, you can store up to five years' worth of returns on the site or order bound copies. (*www.taxbrain.com*)

Beware of tax-preparation services from companies you've never heard of, or email offers from "accountants" who promise cheap, excellent returns whipped up in no time. You don't want to share your personal information with these people.

Finding Tax Information and Forms Online

For any sort of tax-related question, make the Internal Revenue Service's Web your first stop at *www.irs.gov*. Not only do you get your information straight from the horse's mouth, but the horse also has every tax form you could possibly need available for download.

These downloadable forms come as PDF files (page 67), which you can print out on your own printer; they come out looking exactly like the forms you would get at the post office or H&R Block. If you still do your taxes by hand, this is your one-stop-shopping place for paperwork. The IRS site has useful tools, too, like a calculator for figuring out your withholding and a list of tax-exempt charities you can claim on your return if you made a donation.

The major online services and portal sites mentioned earlier in this book—mainly AOL, MSN, and Yahoo—have tax-preparation advice, plus tax calculators, forms, checklists, glossaries, rates, rules, and more.

Part Four:
Entertainment and Media

4

Games and Gambling

In the old days, people used to play chess through the mail, on the premise that any game's a little more fun when your challenger is far, far away instead of across the coffee table. You'd send off your move, and then wait a few weeks for your opponent to write back so you could make the move on your chessboard. While there was an old-world kind of charm in the arrival of a beautifully illustrated postcard, a single game could take months.

On the Internet, you can play chess with someone halfway around the world in real time. If you get really good, you can make checkmate in less time than it takes to address a postcard. In fact, you can read about chess, chat about chess, and even watch chess right from your computer screen.

But chess is only the tip of the iceberg. This chapter's your guide through the dense forest of games people play online, including:

- **General family games.** Scrabble, solitaire, hearts, backgammon, dominos, and so on.
- **Online bridge and chess.** Complex games with massive online followings.
- **Shoot 'em up games.** Online, the bullets and paintballs are virtual.
- **Multiplayer games.** Dungeons & Dragons meets the Internet.
- **Virtual worlds.** Lead a second life via an online alter ego.
- **Fantasy sports.** Test your management skills fielding a team.
- **Gambling.** Win (or lose) real money in a virtual casino.

Games for the Whole Family

The Web has no shortage of games—or people to play them with. If you can play it with cards or a board, chances are there's an online version: solitaire, hearts, euchre, spades, canasta, Scrabble, mahjong, Sudoku...the list goes on. You usually have a choice of playing by yourself or against other Internet players. Devoted followers of games like chess and bridge can pursue their passion on dozens of Web sites. (You may have to pay a fee to play.)

UP TO SPEED

What You Need to Play Online

You can play most interactive games in your regular Web browser. If the game requires a plug-in like Java or Shockwave (page 67), it asks you to install that additional bit of software before you join the action.

Games written in *Java,* a platform-independent programming language, work on both Windows and Macintosh computers. (If you have trouble playing a Java game—like if you see a picture of a coffee cup instead of the game screen—your Web browser's too old for Java. A software update should fix the problem.) Games that rely on ActiveX, an interactive Windows technology, though, don't work on Macs.

Some sites let you download game programs so you can play when you're not online. These may be free versions, limited trial versions, or—if you're willing to whip out the plastic—the full version.

If you plan to download a lot of free games for Windows, make sure you've got anti-spyware measures in place. Some games are only free because they come bundled with spyware and adware (page 408). You may not know you've installed these troublemakers until your computer grinds to a halt from all the extra programs running in the background.

Where to Find Games Online

If you're looking for a good all-around selection of amusements, try the online arcades of the big portal sites:

- **AOL Games.** America Online's game section (*http://games.aol.com*) offers plenty of name-brand fun, including World Series of Poker, Scrabble Blast, and SpongeBob Collapse. Most games are Java-based, but a few won't work on the Mac. Although you don't need a full AOL account, you must log into the site (with a free membership) to play some of the games.

- **Yahoo Games.** Once you log into *http://games.yahoo.com* with a free Yahoo ID, you can play hundreds of games, join online leagues, chat with other players, post on message boards, and more. Most games are Java-based and work with recent browsers. If you're just learning, or you've forgotten how to play, each game has a Rules link.

- **MSN Games.** Strictly for Internet Explorer on Windows, Microsoft's online game area (*http://zone.msn.com*) has all the classics—checkers, chess, cribbage, dominos, bingo, backgammon, and so on. You'll also find newer games like Zuma, Chuzzle, and Luxor.

Tip: Young fans of the Nickelodeon cable channel can find online games featuring characters from the most popular shows at *www.nick.com* in the Games area.

Online game emporiums are all over the Web. Most work the same way: Sign up for a free registration and then choose from about a hundred games. If you like what you play, look for a subscription plan that gives you faster, more challenging versions for a low monthly fee. Some sites to consider:

- **Miniclip.** With 150 free, inventive online games to choose from, you can release a lot of stress and tension from (or during) your workday at *www.miniclip.com*. Favorites include Puzzle Pirates, RuneScape, and Club Penguin. Although you can *play* most games in a Mac browser, the for-sale versions are Windows-only.

- **Pogo.** A kid-friendly site from game giant Electronic Arts, *www.pogo.com* has free board, card, and word games. After registering with the site, you can chat with other players while you play.

- **ArcadeTown.** With a huge, searchable collection of games for both Windows and Mac, you can easily spend a day at *www.arcadetown.com*. Play the free version of a game online, and, if you like it, check for a downloadable version.

- **Shockwave.** At *www.shockwave.com*, you can play (and review) dozens of solo action games created in Macromedia Shockwave (page 67). On the multiplayer side, there's chess, Sub Hunt, and snooker. Either way, your browser must have the Shockwave plug-in. Subscriptions to Shockwave's GameBlast service, which unlocks 200 online games, start at $5 a month.

Tip: If you're a Macintosh maven, visit Apple's online gaming guide at *www.apple.com/games/gettingstarted/online*. The page lists lots of Apple-flavored games and a whole slew of links to Mac-friendly game companies.

Bridge

To get a taste of this complex card game, you can find free games on many of the sites mentioned previously in this chapter. If you're a serious player, you can join international Web tournaments at all skill levels at OKbridge (*www.okbridge.com*). After a seven-day free trial, membership costs $100 a year.

If that's out of your price range, try the free Java-based JBridge site at *www.jbridge.net*. This site has its own game interface, discussion boards, and other features. To find more places to play online and read the latest bridge news, visit the Great Bridge Links site (*www.greatbridgelinks.com*).

Chess

Chess also has a dedicated online following. One of the biggest online boards is the Internet Chess Club (*www.chessclub.com*), a community of 30,000 dues-paying members. For $50 a year (half-price for students), you can play in tournaments, team games, and unlimited one-on-one matches. Members can also watch live games with grandmaster commentary, take private lessons, and browse the club's database of five million master games.

Or you can go the à la carte route: 100 games for $7.50 at InstantChess (*www.instantchess.com*). This site pairs you with opponents and lets you play in your Web browser, on your cellphone, or by email. You can also watch live games in progress with its ChessViewer page (Figure 10-1).

Figure 10-1:
For many people on the Web (well, at least 57 of them), chess is a spectator sport. On InstantChess' ChessViewer page, you can watch a match in progress any time of day. To go there directly, point your browser to www.chessviewer.com.

Members of the U.S. Chess Federation can play officially scored matches (which can boost their USCF player ranking) online at *www.uschesslive.org*. The site isn't limited to Federation members, though, and anyone can sign up to play for free. For another free option, there's GameKnot (*http://gameknot. com*). Through this site, you can play multiple games that last 10 minutes in real time—or the entire day via email.

Shoot 'Em Up Games

Blasting an annoying smiley face icon with a virtual paintball gun relieves a little tension—and sharpens your reflexes to boot. If you'd like to play the aim game, you can find plenty of sites that offer shoot 'em ups (contracted to just *shmups* in the local gunslinger parlance). For example, there are shmups on Miniclip and ArcadeTown (page 177).

Tip: Java- or Flash-based games you can play in your Web browser, like the ones mentioned in this chapter, are good news if your computer budget is limited. They don't consume massive amounts of system resources like Doom, Quake, and other big ol' hard drive games.

With a blog, downloads, and news, Shoot the Core (*http://shootthecore. moonpod.com*) is a good place to start blowing things out of the air, sea, and ground. The Goriya site (*www.goriya.com*) has many free online games as well, plus freeware and demo versions for download.

To many parents' relief, shooting games don't have to involve a gun. You can find non-violent shooting games that use basketballs or darts at Kaboose's Games section (*http://resources.kaboose.com/games*). Squigly's Playhouse (*www.squiglysplayhouse.com*) also has plenty of games for kids, including the one in Figure 10-2. (Some adults may also enjoy splatting Mr. Smiley with paint after a day of endless meetings.)

Note: Educational games don't have to be boring. Food Force, an animated game from the United Nations World Hunger Programme, sends players on six separate missions to bring food to starving people. You can download it free at *www.food-force.com*. The site also lets players post high scores and participate in contests.

Massive Multiplayer Games

Massive multiplayer online games (MMOs) have let people combine socializing with a little friendly competition for decades. Back in the 1980s, Genie and

Figure 10-2:
If you've had one too many people tell you to "have a nice day," you can get it out of your system with a little Stress Relief Paintball. You can find this Miniclip game at www.miniclip.com and other game sites.

CompuServe hosted early MMOs on their proprietary networks. By the 1990s, the Internet was providing a wide-open forum for anyone who wanted to join the fun.

Of course, you can always play video games like *EverQuest, Ultima Online, Star Wars Galaxies*, and *World of Warcraft* alone at home. But online, you can play against people you've never met, whose moves you can't predict. Hundreds of people are logged in at once to the games' servers. You buy the software at a game store or computer store as usual, and then check the instruction booklet to learn how to take your gaming skills online.

These games tend to evolve into tightly knit online communities where people post messages on Web forums or join mailing lists to discuss the game when they're not playing. We're talking *serious* time drain here.

Tip: To find people to play with, check out GameSpyArcade (*www.gamespyarcade.com*). This site can match you up with players on hundreds of game servers.

In another globe-shrinking bit of technology, many MMO games now let you use voice chat while playing. That's right: You can talk to other members of your platoon, guild, or team over a headset mike. (If the notion of transmitting your voice over the Internet without having to use a telephone intrigues you, be sure to read Chapter 18.)

But you don't have to lay down $50 to buy a game just to massively meet multiple players online. Some free, Web-based role-playing MMOs (also known as MMORPGs) include:

- **Aegis.** A browser-based fantasy realm full of provinces, politicking, and quests for power. (*www.aarcserver.com*)

- **Imperia Online.** A medieval battle strategy game played in real time with swords and horses and the whole bit. (*www.imperiaonline.org*)

- **X-Kings.** A turn-based fantasy game from Italy where workers and soldiers plot against each other to get the gold. (*www.x-kings.com*)

- **Kingdom of Loathing.** Low on fancy graphics (Figure 10-3) but long on woozy, offbeat humor, KoL spoofs the traditions of role-playing adventure games like Dungeons & Dragons. (*www.kingdomofloathing.com*)

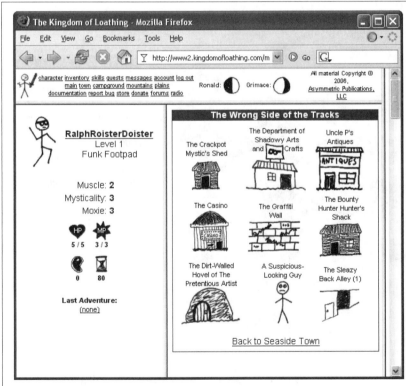

Figure 10-3:
Illustrated with hand-drawn graphics, the Kingdom of Loathing is a refreshing send-up of online adventure games. How can you not love monsters with imaginative names like the Sabre-Tooth Lime and the Ninja Snowmen?

There are hundreds of MMOs scattered about online. Sites like ONRPG.com (*http://onrpg.com*) can help you find the free ones that are worth playing and serious gamers have plenty of Web magazines to browse for game news, previews, demos, hints, and more. Try 1UP (*www.1up.com*), GameSpot (*www.gamespot.com*), or GameSpy (*www.gamespy.com*) for the latest buzz.

Virtual Worlds

Online games are great places to meet new people and work toward a shared goal, like defeating enemy troops or saving the universe. But sometimes you may just want to hang out in a highly visual environment and chat with your friends—*without* having to dodge enemy fire or an alien fleet.

In times like these, a *virtual world* is the place for you. A virtual world is a graphically rendered, simulated setting that can resemble an island, a city, or other location (Figure 10-4).

Figure 10-4:
Whizzing by the Sphinx on a hoverbike with your in-world friends is one of the many ways to relax in There. Adventure quests, paintball games, or just chatting side-by-side with friends (who actually live across the country) are other popular activities.

Virtual spaces for kids tend to be cartoon-like, two-dimensional places (see the box on page 184). Virtual worlds designed for adults typically resemble the more realistic environments found in 3-D video games, crossed with the sleek styling of *The Matrix*. Some worlds encourage their players to build structures and manufacture goods within the realm, which can lead to a full-blown society complete with currency and property.

Life in a Virtual World

You travel through this world in the form of an *avatar*—an onscreen representation of yourself. Dressed as your digital alter ego, you move around and interact with other people's avatars. In some worlds, you can create realistic avatars that closely resemble what you look like in real life; in others, everyone wears a more or less generic-looking figure.

You usually communicate with other people by typing your thoughts; your comrades see them as cartoon speech bubbles that appear over your avatar's head. Depending on the world, you can move your avatar around the space with keyboard commands, menus, or mouse clicks. You can use a variety of built-in gestures like waving, walking, and smiling.

Virtual worlds can accommodate many players at once, often in multiple rooms or areas. Inhabitants interact with each other in real time. Clubs, cliques, guilds, and teams encourage members to form social bonds, which often makes the world more emotionally realistic to those who participate.

Virtual Worlds Online

Once you find your place in a virtual world, it's a great place to escape—and you don't even have to worry about booking a plane ticket. Some worlds charge subscription fees to join; others are free but are tied to commercial products like Coca-Cola or Disney theme parks. Here's a selection:

- **There.** Set in exotic locales including tropical islands and a virtual Egypt, avatars in There (*www.there.com*) can race around the land on hoverbikes or in dune buggies. With a credit card, you can convert cash to Therebucks and buy handcrafted goods and services created by other players, creating a very realistic social experience (Figure 10-4). Basic membership is free, but premium powers such as voice chat cost $9.95.

- **Second Life.** Its creator, Linden Lab, gave this virtual world a beautifully rendered landscape populated by fully customizable avatars. Members of Second Life (*www.secondlife.com*) also get the tools to create interactive objects like houses, clothes, and vehicles, which they can then sell for the local currency, Linden Dollars. Second Life is one of the few adult virtual worlds that work on the Macintosh as well as Windows. Basic membership is free, but if you want to own land in Second Life, you need to pay a monthly fee based on the amount of property.

- **The Sims Online.** Windows owners of the popular desktop computer game can join the online offshoot (at *www.thesimsonline.com*) by paying a monthly fee. Your Sims avatar still has to play by the game's rules of eating, napping, and socializing in order to stay alive and earn Simoleans (the standard Sim monetary unit).

- **Coke Studios.** At *www.mycoke.com*, the ulterior motive is clear: to plaster Coca-Cola ads all over teenagers' screens. But they can have fun trying on avatars and making music mixes to play for their virtual pals.

- **Habbo Hotel.** This world is designed to look like an enormous hotel. Kids ages 13 and up can check in, don an avatar (Habbo), and roam the rooms and halls. Parents can supply a credit card number so their kids can buy additional props like furniture to go in the hotel's rooms (*www.habbo.com*).

JUST FOR KIDS

Virtual Worlds for Real Children

The Internet universe has plenty of digital worlds for kids. Once signed up and logged on, kids can run around and play, chat with their pals next door (or from other countries), or just hang out after school. Here are some worlds for children ages 8 to 14 that work on both Windows and Mac:

- **Whyville.** A virtual world with an emphasis on real learning, Whyville is a browser-based educational space with a focus on science. (*www.whyville.net*)

- **Mokitown.** Sponsored by DaimlerChrysler, this site's name is short for "mobile kids town." Members can don a Moki avatar and learn about traffic safety as they wander around virtual city streets with other Mokis. (*www.mobile-kids.net*)

- **Virtual Magic Kingdom.** This digital recreation of Disney's signature theme parks lets kids sign up and enjoy the attractions without worrying about rain and crowds. (*http://vmk.disney.go.com*)

Most virtual worlds for kids and tweens are at least partially monitored by adult staffers who are on the lookout for bad behavior. But if you're a parent, read the user guide posted on each site for all the rules and details. Make sure kids don't use their full, real names as screen names or reveal any other identifying information online.

Fantasy Sports

Die-hard sports fans are renowned for their hunger for statistics about favorite teams and players. Pair that with the Web's ability to deliver this type of information in a flash, and you've got the phenomenal boom in *fantasy sports*. These games let you create your own dream teams in virtual football, baseball, basketball, and other sports.

Here's how it works: As a team owner in, say, a fantasy baseball league, you "draft" real-life professional players. As the season progresses, each player's actual statistics earn points in the fantasy league. Needless to say, players who have exceptional seasons score a lot of points for their pretend team owners. The team owner with the most points at the end of the season wins the league championship.

Fantasy sports sites have popped up all over the Web in recent decades. If you're a member of AOL, Yahoo, or MSN, you've got them right in your home portal. In your browser's address bar, type *http://fantasysports.* followed by *aol.com*, *yahoo.com*; for MSN, go to *http://msn.foxsports.com/fantasy*. Other fantasy sports hangouts include:

- **ESPN Fantasy Field.** The cable sports network has a huge collection of fantasy sports to choose from (including fantasy bass fishing). There are also news and message boards for virtual team owners. (*http://games.espn.go.com*)

- **Sandbox.** A $5 monthly premium subscription qualifies you for cash prizes, draft guides, news, and injury reports customized for all the players on your team. But Sandbox has a few free games to join as well. (*www.sandbox.com*)

- **CBS SportsLine.** Several fantasy sports are here for the playing with free registration. The newsy site also offers columns and commentary throughout the fantasy season. (*www.sportsline.com/fantasy*)

Tip: For a roundup of fantasy sports news, try Fantasy Sports Central at *www.fantasysportscentral. com*. Here, you can also buy tickets to actual, real-life games.

Gambling

Games of chance have popped up in just about every culture for thousands of years, so it's only natural that they'd find a home on the Internet. Despite the objections of certain politicians, online casinos and poker rooms flourish by the thousands.

Not all of them are honest parlors of friendly play, of course; there's no shortage of dishonest sites looking to take the money and run. The gambling and poker sites mentioned in this section are all large, established operations with good reputations. As for sites not listed here, remember that the Web is filled with sites that give "gambling" a whole new meaning.

Online Poker

Online poker is *huge*. Fueled by TV shows about poker and a general resurgence of interest in this very old card game, the Web-based version has sucked down countless man-years and millions of dollars.

You can find online poker games at several of the sites listed on page 176, but most calculating cardsharps gravitate to one of the secure sites dedicated to playing for money.

Most professional online poker rooms require you to register before you can enter. Some let you play right in your Web browser; others require you to download special software (make sure your computer meets their system requirements before you do).

If you're playing for money, you must add a credit card or bank account number to fork over the cash for bets. Many sites also offer online money-transfer systems like Click2Pay or NETeller that you can use to get money to or from your bank account. This option is a necessity for many people, as U.S. regulations don't permit credit cards to accept money, only to spend it.

Note: Most banks, in an effort to avoid the questionable legality of online gambling, don't allow purchases at online gambling sites. If yours doesn't, you can use a money-transfer system like NETeller instead.

Once you log on, you usually wind up in an onscreen lobby—a general gathering area where you can see what games are available and how many players are already at tables. You can usually pick the style of poker you want to play, say Texas Hold 'Em, Omaha Hi/Lo, or 7-Card Stud. As you browse the tables in the lobby area, you can see the size of the pot for each. Some sites let you play for practice, but most tables are in it for real.

Once you join a game, you usually see a picture of a poker table with other people, cards, and wagers, as shown in Figure 10-5. You get buttons to fold, call, or bet. When you've had enough (or lost enough), you can click to return to the main lobby area. From there, you can join another table, log out, or cash out.

Note: Cheating has always been a problem with card games, and the online version is no different. With cell phones, instant messaging, and other forms of real-time communication, it's possible for two or more players to be in collusion by sharing information and running up bets against unsuspecting parties. Many poker sites analyze betting patterns and table attendance in an effort to catch cheaters, but the possibility still remains. You've been warned.

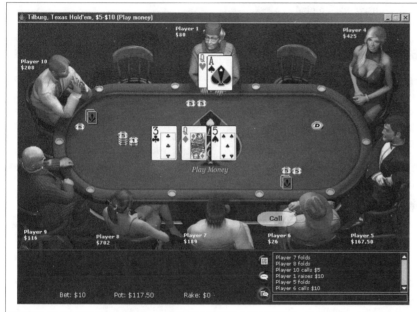

Figure 10-5:
It's not a smoke-filled back room, but a clean and tidy virtual poker table at HollywoodPoker.com. As your cards are dealt, you control your play with onscreen buttons.

Not all of the many poker rooms you find on the Web are legitimate establishments. Before you sign up with a site, search the Internet for reviews to see what other people are saying about it. Here are some good bets:

- **PokerRoom.** Dealing cards since 1999, this poker playhouse has thousands of players logged on at any given time and also supports tournaments and team games. There's also a casino for blackjack, roulette, and other table staples. (*www.pokerroom.com*)

- **Hollywood Poker.** At *www.hollywoodpoker.com*, you'll find a well-ordered Help section, tutorials, poker blogs, tournaments, and forums. It also has a Hollywood page of fame featuring photos of celebrities who've stopped by to play. (But then, they're probably friends with the site's movie-star owners, actors James Woods and Vincent van Patten.)

• **Paradise Poker.** This Windows-only site (*www.paradisepoker.com*) lets you play for free or for money, and you can usually find about 7,000 other poker fanatics online during peak times. (Mac fans disappointed at this site's lack of compatibility can head to *www.pacificpoker.com* instead.)

Note: Most legitimate poker rooms and online casinos accept only players over the age of 18. Although this may be hard to verify in the wilds of cyberspace, the credit card requirement usually stops younger teens from placing bets.

Other Casino Games

If poker isn't your game, you can find other ways to wager money in online casinos. Even if you've never been to Vegas, Reno, or Atlantic City, you can roll the dice, spin the wheel, or get another card onscreen.

Note: Unfortunately for Macintosh fans, many casinos require you to download and install their software—and that software probably works with Windows only. You can find some browser-based, Mac-friendly games at PlanetLuck (*www.planetluck.com*).

• **Bodog Casino.** Bodog is one of the larger, better-known casinos on the Net. It has slots, poker, and table games (*www.bodog.com/casino*). (It works on Macs, too.)

• **SunVegas Casino.** With 200 games to play, you can while away the hours strolling from virtual table to virtual table or testing your luck at the slots (*www.sunvegas.com*).

• **32Red Casino.** A large casino popular in the United Kingdom, 32Red welcomes players from all over to play blackjack, poker, baccarat, and so on, with slots and keno nearby (*www.32red.com*).

Tip: As with the poker sites mentioned above, you should make sure that the online casino you're considering is a legitimate operation that won't fold (and take your wallet with it). For tips on which sites are legit and which might be shady, consult the Casino Meister at *www.casinomeister.com*. This gambling portal also has a lengthy collection of advice for novice players.

Music and Audio

The Internet can deliver a lot of things right to your desktop, from your bank statement to the menu of a restaurant 3,000 miles away. But with the right software, it can also deliver Aretha Franklin's greatest hits, Beethoven's Ninth Symphony, the audio book version of every single Harry Potter novel, and that episode of *All Things Considered* you missed earlier this week when you were at the doctor.

If you have a high-speed broadband connection, you can turn the Internet into the world's biggest jukebox, listening room, and radio station. This chapter tells you how to get an earful no matter what your musical taste.

Digital Audio and the Internet

Recorded music has appeared in a variety of shapes and sizes over the decades, including fragile discs spinning at 78 rpm, vinyl records in colorful sleeves that were artworks in themselves, pocket-size cassette tapes, and CDs that gave all those predecessors a hard shove into the Bargain Bin of History. But no music format ever exploded into the public consciousness as quickly and widely as the bits of computer code known as *MP3 files*.

Using the MP3 format makes it possible to *compress* the digital files that represent songs into files small enough to be uploaded, downloaded, emailed, and stored on hard drives by the hundreds. That feat of smallness set off a sonic boom in the late 1990s that continues to reverberate across the music world.

Of course, the other big technology that made noise in the 1990s was the Internet itself. Even though dial-up modems were still the standard way to connect a computer to the Internet, MP3 files were still small enough that you could download a pop single in just a few minutes, even over a telephone line.

File-sharing services like Napster began to flourish as people realized they could find music for free on the Internet. Young music fans would *rip* their entire CD collections (that is, copy the songs from the CD to the computer) and make them available to download, bypassing the whole buy-the-CD-and-give-royalties-to-the-labels-and-artists thing.

Of course, this wasn't the recording industry's favorite technology. Its lawyers eventually sued most of the original file-trading sites right out of business.

But from the ashes of the litigiously stomped file-swapping sites came the realization that people enjoy the convenience of downloading music off the Internet and might even *pay* for songs. Several recording-industry deals later, online music stores selling songs *legally* began to pop up like Starbucks franchises. The arrival of affordable broadband connections also made it easier and faster to download even more songs.

So you have the music—and you have a method of getting it to your computer. Now you just have to figure out *how* you want to listen to it and *where* to find it.

Listening to Digital Audio

There are two main ways to listen to all of these wonderful things echoing around the Internet: *downloading* or *streaming*.

Downloading Songs

With downloading, you copy a whole audio file from the Internet to your hard drive. It could be from a Web site offering free music files or an online music store like Rhapsody, Yahoo MusicMatch, or the iTunes Music Store. Once you have the file, it lives on your machine. Depending on what type of file it is, you can play it whenever you want on your computer or copy it to a player like an iPod to take with you.

Having your whole music collection on your computer means you never have to get up from your Web browsing to change the CD. There's an important factor to remember, though, with downloaded music: it takes up hard drive space. Depending on how the file was created, a three-minute pop song can take three to five megabytes of disk space, which means that the hard drives of music lovers tend to fill up fast.

When you buy a song to download from an online music store, it's usually copy-protected so that you can't freely distribute it to your friends (and thereby sending the recording industry back to their 1990s hell-hole).

The geeks call this copy protection *digital rights management,* or *DRM.* Most online music stores charge $1 per song, and once you've bought it, you own it and can play it forever. The DRM rules usually go like this:

- You can copy the song onto up to five computers.

- You can burn the song to an unlimited number of blank CDs—however, you can burn no more than seven copies of the *playlist* it's part of. (Playlists are customized song collections that you create.)

- You can copy the song onto an unlimited number of pocket players (like iPods).

Then there are "subscription" music services, in which you pay, say, $15 a month to download *as many songs as you want.* The catch is that if you ever stop paying that monthly fee, it all goes up in smoke; you're left with nothing but memories.

Streaming Audio

Streaming is more like radio: the music is sent from the Internet directly to your speakers. No file ever lands on your hard drive; if you want to hear the song again, you usually have to go back to the place you found it and stream it again. Most Internet radio stations (page 202) send streaming music. Some music-store sites (like RealNetwork's Rhapsody, shown in Figure 11-1) also let you stream songs for free or for a small monthly fee, too.

The problem with streaming music is, of course, that you can't hear the tunes except when you're connected to the Internet. This isn't so good if you want to kick back and play some jazz through your laptop's headphones while you work on that spreadsheet during a flight. And even when you're connected to the Internet, your music stream may stutter and stagger through network congestion, dropping out here and there as online traffic disrupts it.

Then again, you don't have to choose one or the other (downloads or streaming) as your main music source. You can buy songs from an online store to load on your portable player and also have a streaming music service to pipe in fresh tunes as you work at your desk. You may have to use a couple of different programs if you want to do both, but the point is that you're not locked in to choosing one or the other if you want to rock out.

Figure 11-1:
The Rhapsody streaming music player lets you stream songs and sample tunes for free if you register with the site. Streaming music doesn't fill up your hard drive, gives you something to listen to while you work, and can open your ears to new artists you may have missed. There's more on streaming music on page 198.

Online Music Stores

Portable players like iPods drive the success of many Internet music-download stores. After all, you can't take it with you unless you've got something to *take*. Downloading music files to your computer and then transferring them to your iPod, Creative Zen, or any other digital audio player gives you a pocketful of songs on the go; depending on your model, you might have 15,000 tracks on a device the size of an Altoids tin resting comfortably inside your jacket.

The cost of filling up that player (and your computer along with it) averages $1 per song on most download sites, or about $10 to $12 per album. This can add up if you're aiming for a music library of Smithsonian proportions, but it's still slightly cheaper than buying CDs. And you don't wind up with 5,000 flimsy jewel cases that take up precious space and eventually break.

There is such a thing as a *free* online music store (page 197), but the selection may not be as expansive as what you'd find at a more mainstream legal download store. The songs from these sites come in the MP3 format, which isn't copy-protected and can play on just about any portable player or jukebox program. (Music files from pay-to-play music stores are encoded in different formats—copy-protected ones. Apple's iTunes Music Store favors something called the AAC format; rival music stores like Napster and Rhapsody supply songs in something called WMA format.)

The iTunes Music Store

With a catalog containing 2 million songs, 16,000 audio books, 35,000 pod-casts, 3,500 videos, and a whole slew of TV shows, Apple Computer's iTunes Music Store is the Big Kahuna of digital downloads. All of this is designed to work with Apple's various iPods—42 million of which were sold in their first five years, making the iPod the King Kamehameha of music players.

Using the iTunes Music Store is a breeze. All you need is an Internet connection, an Apple account, and a copy of the free iTunes software, available for download at *www.apple.com/itunes*. (It also comes preinstalled on every Mac.)

Broadband connections work best for downloading music because music files are huge and slow to download. You can still download songs over a dial-up connection, but if you go on a huge shopping spree, you may want to start the process just before you go to bed at night and hope that your files have arrived on your hard drive in the morning.

You sign up for an Apple account the first time you go to the iTunes Music Store and supply an account name, password, and billing information, so Apple knows who to charge when you start clicking to buy songs and albums.

Once you install iTunes, you see that it's not just a front door into the iTunes Music Store. It's a whole management system that lets you:

- Rip tracks (that is, copy songs) from your CDs to MP3, AAC, or other file formats

- Add artwork, lyrics, star ratings, and comments to your song files

- Create playlists and play your music collection

- Transfer and manage the music and audio book files on your iPod

- Record CDs from your playlists and make CD album covers

- Display trippy screensavers on your computer monitor as the music plays

- Watch movie trailers, videos, TV shows, and more

And then there's the Music Store part. To get there, make sure you're online. Then click the Music Store icon (Figure 11-2).

Right in the main Store window, iTunes gives you plenty of albums, songs, and audio books to consider; click any link or image and you get the opportunity to read more about it, hear a 30-second preview of the song, and click a button to buy it. Once you click to buy, your song begins to download. After a moment, it lands right in the iTunes window where you can see it, play it, burn it to a CD, or transfer it to your iPod.

Figure 11-2:
Click the Music Store icon on the left side of the iTunes window and the program quickly beams you into Apple's online music-and-video emporium. Click anything in the window and you land on a page with more information on the item and the option to buy it and download it to your computer.

Note: As noted earlier, you can copy iTunes Music Store purchases onto up to four other computers. To make this work, iTunes must be on each Mac or PC, and you need to *authorize* each machine by typing in your iTunes Music Store user name and password the first time you try to play the copied song.

Unless you pay again, you can only download a file from the iTunes Music Store once. You can't download your purchases all over again for free if something bad happens to your computer. For this reason, you should regularly back up your iTunes Music Store purchases (and your entire music collection, for that matter, unless you want to re-rip it all) onto backup drives, CDs, or DVDs, and keep copies in case your hard drive dies a horrible death.

The CD album cover artwork is embedded into every song you download from the iTunes Music Store; it gives you something to look at while the song plays in iTunes or on the iPod screen. Some full-length albums for sale in the Store include bonus videos or digital booklets with liner notes and artwork.

WORD TO THE WISE

The iPod-iTunes Exclusivity Clause

The online music-store economy works like this: Apple's iTunes Music Store has 80 percent of the online music-store business. The Apple iPod music player has 80 percent of the music-player business.

That's not a coincidence.

Turns out the songs you buy from iTunes are copy-protected in such a way that the iPod is the *only* music player that can play them.

Conversely, the iPod plays *only* songs bought from the iTunes Music Store (not counting MP3 files and other non-copy-protected music—we're talking legal music stores here).

Now, iTunes/iPod have generated millions of dollars in sales and become the envy/enemy of the rest of the computer/music industry. Microsoft, therefore, devised a rival song format (called *protected WMA*) and a design for rival pocket players (known as *PlaysForSure*).

There are now many Microsoft-format music stores (Napster, Rhapsody, MSN Music, Yahoo Music, and so on), and even more Microsoft-format pocket players. For the most part, any music you buy from any Microsoft-format music store plays on any Microsoft-format player.

Even so, industry insiders call this business "iTunes and the Seven Dwarves" because all of the Microsoft stores and players put together haven't made a dent in the popularity of the iPod/iTunes duopoly.

But if you remember nothing else from this page, remember this: iPod and iTunes Music Store go only with each other. And the non-iPod players and non-iTunes stores go only with each other.

MusicMatch

MusicMatch, now owned by Yahoo, is another all-purpose jukebox program for managing your audio collection. Although it doesn't have the depth of inventory that iTunes offers, it has more than 900,000 songs in the protected WMA format to download and buy, as well as a streaming music service for $5 a month (page 198). And unlike iTunes, which works on Windows and Mac systems, MusicMatch is a Windows-only program and works only with Windows XP; you can get it at *www.musicmatch.com*.

The latest version with the most features costs about $20, although a free edition allows you to do the essentials like rip tracks from your own CDs, buy new songs in the MusicMatch Music Store, and transfer them all to your portable player. For people who get the paid version, there's also MusicMatch Radio, a set of pre-programmed stations that stream music over your Internet connection instead of the airwaves. There's more on Internet radio on page 202.

Napster, Rhapsody, MusicMatch, Yahoo Music...

The once-outlawed Napster hung up its spurs as an illegal, free, renegade file-sharing service and went legit in 2003, transforming itself into a $10-a-month music rental service for your PC at *www.napster.com*. That is, you can download as many songs as you like for that flat fee, provided you understand that (a) you have to sit at your PC to listen to them, and (b) you lose them all if you ever stop paying. (For $5 more a month, you also have the right to copy them to a non-iPod music player.)

(Rhapsody, MusicMatch, Yahoo Music, and others work similarly.)

As long as you keep paying your monthly dues, you can feast on as many of the site's million-and-a-half songs as you can download or stream. The songs come in Microsoft's protected WMA file format; the Napster software requires Windows 2000 or later.

Note: You can also buy songs outright for $1 each from the Napster Light store, but the company pushes the monthly-fee version heavily.

---

eMusic

If discovering the music of emerging artists on independent record labels gives you chills, there's an online service sure to perk up your ears. It's called eMusic (*www.emusic.com*), and it boasts a catalog of more than a million songs from thousands of indie labels around the world.

Along with the focus on independent music, three other things make eMusic stand out from other online stores. First, it sells its tunes in the unprotected MP3 format, which means you can play those songs on just about any digital audio player out there, iPods included. Without the copyright-protection built into the files, you can also burn those songs to CD as many times as you want and copy them to all your computers for personal use.

Second, eMusic is less expensive than the mainstream music stores with their mainstream price of $1 a song. Instead of charging you per song or album, eMusic sells monthly subscriptions that give you a certain *amount* of songs for one overall price. The basic subscription costs $9.99 a month and gives you 40 downloads, which averages out to 25 cents per tune; other plans for more downloads are available as well.

Once you download eMusic tracks, you can add them to your jukebox program of choice just like any other song. In iTunes, for example, choose File → Add to Library and navigate through your hard drive to the file or folder you want to add the songs to.

The third great thing? Because eMusic is a Web-based service selling its songs in the near-universal MP3 format, it works with Windows *and* Macintosh.

You can sign up for a free eMusic trial on the site's home page. The free trial gives you 25 free downloads to keep forever even if you don't sign up for a full subscription.

Tip: Into music from other cultures? Satisfy your world music jones by paying a visit to the Smithsonian Institution's musical archives (*www.smithsonianglobalsound.org*) where you can download songs from Afghanistan to Zimbabwe. Songs cost around $1.

Places to Find Free Music Downloads

"Free music downloads? Sure, dude," any teenager will tell you. "It's called Kazaa, dude, and all the kids are doing it."

And it's true that song downloads from illegal file-swapping sites like Kazaa outnumber songs that are legitimately purchased by a huge margin. The record industry and its lawyers are working on that problem.

Unfortunately, Kazaa is also a fount of viruses and spyware—nasty Windows programs that piggyback on your song downloads without your knowledge.

There are, fortunately, such things as free, *legal* music downloads—if you know where to look for them:

• **The Internet Archive** is a vast collection of cultural artifacts in convenient digital form. It has more than 78,000 free audio files, 31,000 live concert recordings, plus thousands of movies and text files. In the searchable Audio section, you can find complete Beethoven symphonies recorded by the BBC Philharmonic, Buddhist lectures, lovingly digitized old 78 rpm records, and other sonic samples of human achievement. (*www.archive.org*)

• **Amazon.** Tucked away between the millions of books, movies, and other stuff it sells, the Web's Giant Store of Everything has a small aisle of free music downloads; see Figure 11-3. (*www.amazon.com*)

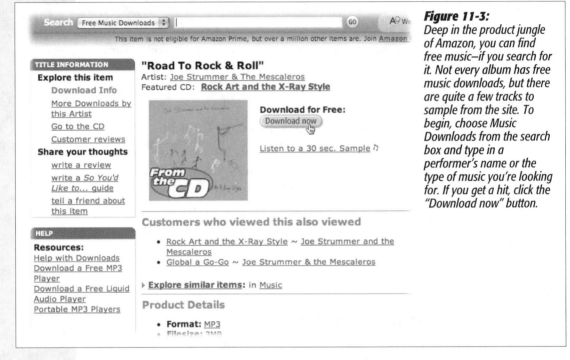

Figure 11-3:
Deep in the product jungle of Amazon, you can find free music—if you search for it. Not every album has free music downloads, but there are quite a few tracks to sample from the site. To begin, choose Music Downloads from the search box and type in a performer's name or the type of music you're looking for. If you get a hit, click the "Download now" button.

• **Download.com.** CNET's music sampler contains 75,000 free, download-able MP3 files in every genre available; it's a great way to hear new music from emerging artists. Music videos and previews of major-label commercial albums are also available. (*http://music.download.com*)

Streaming Music Sites

If hard drive space is tight and you'd like to hear even more music without maxing out your computer, streaming new music is another way to get a little ear candy.

If you have a broadband connection, streaming music is a nice alternative to downloading files. You don't have to worry about file compatibility with your portable music player because you're usually just listening at your computer. You can even buy gadgets like the Squeezebox or the Sonos Music System to pipe the streaming music to speakers all around the house.

Streamed music may also make you more adventurous in your listening habits; because it's all free or included in a monthly subscription fee, you don't have to worry about feeling gypped that the album you paid for and downloaded actually sounded nothing like the preview you heard. You can sample all kinds of new things over the songstream without lifting a wallet.

Many companies like RealNetworks that offer streaming service also have downloads for sale, too. (And programs like iTunes let you stream your own downloaded music, but only to authorized computers on your home network.) Each streaming site has its own rules and regulations, so make sure you know what you're getting when you sign up for a service.

Real Rhapsody

The real business of Rhapsody.com (which is owned by RealNetworks, maker of the RealPlayer program used by many Web sites to stream audio and video clips) is selling downloaded music, as described earlier. You can pay $1 a song, or you can pay $10 or $15 a month for one of those music-rental programs.

But Rhapsody also has a *free* program called Rhapsody 25. After signing up at *www.rhapsody.com*, you can listen to 25 free songs right in your Web browser, as shown back in Figure 11-1. It works in Windows and Mac OS X.

This may seem like a piddling amount—even moderate audiophiles listen to at least 25 songs a day—but the free pass can serve as your listening booth for a little shopping reconnaissance. Like the band but hated their last album enough to make you feel iffy about springing $15 for their new CD? Listen to a few tracks in full on Rhapsody to get a better-informed opinion.

Note: If you decide to sign up for one of Rhapsody's paid music services—and the company dearly hopes you will—its Rhapsody Jukebox software for Windows handles library management chores for organizing downloaded songs, transferring tunes to portables, and burning CDs of purchased music. Unfortunately, to keep your songs playing after you transfer them to an audio player, they must check in with the mother ship—to connect to the Rhapsody Web site via your PC. Otherwise, they expire after a month. This is annoying if you're on a long trip or at camp for the summer with no access to your computer and your music evaporates from your player.

Yahoo Music

Yahoo has everything else, so it makes sense it would have its own music service as well. You find the music in the vast Yahoo universe at *http://music. yahoo.com*. If you already have a Yahoo ID from any of the company's other offerings like Mail or Messenger, you can use the same name and password to log into the music site.

Yahoo Music has a million songs to listen to, as long as you're using Internet Explorer for Windows—no Firefox, no Opera, no Macs.

Once signed in, you can listen to music through Yahoo's LAUNCHcast player, which streams music you select from Yahoo's inventory of preprogrammed genres over your PC's Internet connection. This part of the service is more like Internet radio (page 202), although you can customize your Yahoo station with preferred artists and genres. A commercial-free version of LAUNCHcast that lets you skip songs you don't want to hear costs $4 a month.

For $5 a month (paid annually in advance—and this price may change), Yahoo's own Music Engine player software lets you save any of those million tunes (the service is called Yahoo Music Unlimited). You have to pay extra to burn songs to a CD or transfer them to a player ($1 per song, same as most other online download shops), but at least you can make playlists out of your favorite tunes and record the CDs with the Yahoo software.

Pandora

Musical tastes run far and wide. Some people will listen to anything, from the head-bangiest of heavy metal to a delicate Chopin prelude and everything in between; others tend to have distinctive preferences for certain styles of music, say acoustic folk or Latin salsa. If you find yourself in the latter camp, you may want to investigate Pandora, a streaming music service at *www.pandora.com*.

Pandora is part of the Music Genome Project, a music analysis experiment set up by musicians and technology types to look for specific musical attributes or "genes" that make up certain styles of music. These attributes include melody and harmony styles, rhythm, instrumentation, lyrics, and orchestration. The project's goal is to listen to thousands of artists and bands and attempt to group them "genetically," based on their musical qualities.

What's in it for you? Lots of free streaming songs that give you a chance to listen to singers and groups that have similar qualities to your favorite types of music. You can listen to Pandora's tunes for free if you register and don't mind ads in your browser window, or get the ad-free version for $36 a year.

In order to learn your music tastes so it can find similar artists, Pandora asks you to type in the names of your favorite bands or songs. Based on this info, the site creates a "radio station" for you that plays exclusively songs or bands with similar musical attributes (Figure 11-4).

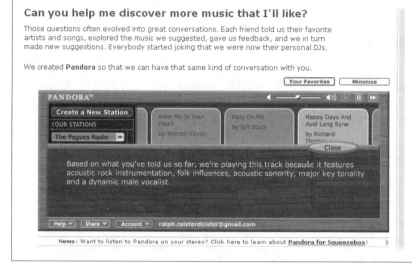

Figure 11-4:
Pandora gives you a detailed explanation of why it picked a song for you, and it may even give you some insight into why you like a particular style or genre of music.

If you like the song, you can click a button to confirm that Pandora is on the right track. If you hate the tune it finds, click your displeasure and Pandora goes back to its library to get another tune. It keeps trying until it finds something you like and refines your personal radio station from there.

You can see the playlist as it progresses as album covers in a horizontal row, complete with song title and artist info. If you like a song, hate a song, or want to know where you can buy it, click the album cover to see a pop-up menu.

You can also have Pandora create a new personal station based on this one song. Say you've created a station of hard-charging Celtic rock and a softer, acoustic track comes on. You can select that track and make a whole new station featuring music of soft acoustic songs. You can have up to 100 different stations of your own on Pandora.

The site can come up with some surprising choices that you probably never would have found on your own. It's sort of like having a pal with a huge music collection that you can sample without having to be over there all day, and anything you actually want to buy is just a click and a credit card transaction away.

Tip: If you want to find music that matches your tastes and people with the same musical interests, take a walk through Last.fm (*www.last.fm*). Once you sign up (free), the site finds music similar to what you already like, and every song you play goes in your musical profile that other Last.fm members can view. You can create your own radio station to play through the site, and blogs, forums, and discussion groups help you find new music—and maybe some new friends—at the same time.

Piping Sound from Computer to Stereo

Odds are the speakers on your computer—especially if it's a laptop—can't match the ones on your home entertainment system. And odds are if you've compiled gigabytes of music files or have access to miles of music streams on your computer, you'd love to have a way to play those songs through your nice big sound system.

Luckily for you, the odds of getting this to happen are really, really good. You can now link the two machines and blast your digital music at top volume in a number of different ways.

An old-fashioned Y-shaped audio cable running between your computer's sound card and an auxiliary jack on the back of your stereo receiver is one way to connect the two, but requires that your computer is somewhere near the stereo.

If you have a home network, you have much more flexibility. For example, the Roku SoundBridge network music player ($150 and up for Mac and PC at *www.rokulabs.com*) has connections for both the computer network and the stereo, and it also works with wireless networks. Plug the Sound-Bridge into the stereo and connect it either wired or wirelessly to your network. Then, when you click

Play in iTunes, MusicMatch, or Windows Media Player, the sound travels over the network to the connected SoundBridge and booms out through the stereo's speakers.

The Squeezebox (*www.slimdevices.com*) performs a similar service. The Sonos Music System ($1,000) is a much higher-end version because it lets you stream the music wirelessly into *multiple* rooms of your house, and because you can start, stop, and control these different streams of music using a handheld color remote control. See *www.sonos. com* for details.

The AirTunes feature of Apple's Airport Express wireless base station lets you stream iTunes music to a stereo as well. (That's almost a secondary feature to its primary purpose: letting you share a cable or DSL connection by turning it into a wireless, WiFi network.) You just plug the AirPort Express ($130 for Mac and PC at *www.apple.com*) into the wall near the stereo system, close enough to run a digital audio cable between the two. Then you select the name of the base station from a pop-up menu on the bottom of the iTunes window and pick the playlist you want to hear. With enough playlists on your computer, you'll never have to hire a DJ for parties again.

Internet Radio

Internet radio stations are just like regular radio stations, except that you "tune in" to them over the Internet instead of the airwaves.

Some stations, like National Public Radio affiliates, broadcast exactly the same shows this way. But since there's no need for a specific radio frequency or broadcasting license from the FCC, there are tons of Internet radio stations that exist *only* online—and some of them are pretty inventive. You can find everything from mystical Scottish melodies to American pop to programming from Japan, the Caribbean, Germany, and other spots around the globe.

Computers with high-speed Internet connections have a smoother streaming experience, but the vast and eclectic mix of musical offerings is well worth checking out—even if you have a dial-up modem. You can listen to Internet radio in several ways:

- **Through the radio feature of a jukebox program like iTunes or Music-Match.** These programs come with dozens of pre-set radio stations in all different musical genres. To listen in, just click a stream in the program's window. Once you've listened to all the stations listed in iTunes, hit the Internet. You can find more radio stations that stream around the Web at sites like *www.shoutcast.com* and play them through iTunes when you click the link to listen.

- **Through your Web browser with audio plug-ins like RealPlayer.** Many broadcast radio stations now offer Web streams of their programming that you can listen to, which is great if you're 5 or 5,000 miles out of the station's signal range. If you don't know if your favorite station has a live stream, try looking it up by city or call sign at the Radio Locator site (*www.radio-locator.com*), which has links to 10,000 radio-station Web pages and 2,500 audio streams. The Radio Tower page (*www.radiotower.com*) and Live-Radio.Net (*www.live-radio.net*) can also help you track down radio streams from around the world.

  Some online radio stations require certain listening software on your end. RealPlayer (Figure 11-5) and Windows Media Player are two of the most common programs for audio streams; you can download free Mac or Windows copies of the players at *www.real.com* and *www.microsoft.com/windowsmedia*.

- **Through software radio players like Yahoo or Mac OS X Widgets.** You can read about widgets—colorful, free, mini-programs—on page 167. You can find widgets that stream the BBC World News or other specific stations in the Gallery at *http://widgets.yahoo.com* or at *www.apple.com/downloads/dashboard*.

- **Through an online service like AOL that has its own online radio stations.** America Online and MSN each have streaming radio stations with tons of tunes right at your fingertips when you're logged into the service. Just look for the Radio icon or link on the screen and stream your heart out.

The best things about Internet radio? Free, infinite variety, infinite geographical reach, and 100 percent static-free.

Figure 11-5:
Free audio programs like RealPlayer let you stream online radio stations from around the world to spice up your workday and give your ears something new to absorb.

WORKAROUND WORKSHOP

Saving Streams

Most broadcasters of streaming music assume that nobody's going to record it. They'll listen to it as it comes across the Internet, but then it's gone forever. That's how, for example, Rhapsody can afford to give everyone on earth 25 free songs every month—it assumes they'll be listened to once but not captured.

In fact, you *can* save music streams to your hard drive, although the practice dances dangerously close to copyright infringement. All you need is a program designed to capture everything coming through your computer's speakers. For Windows, such programs include RipCast (*www.xoteck.com/ripcast*) and Audiolib MP3 Recorder (*www.audiolib.*

com/recorder); for the Mac, RadioLover (*www.bitcartel.com/radiolover*), Audio Hijack (*www.rogueamoeba.com/audiohijack*), and Streamripper X (*http://streamripperx.sourceforge.net*).

If you really love radio, check out Griffin Technology's radio SHARK, a fin-shaped USB attachment that plugs into your computer. It lets you listen and record *traditional* (over-the-air) AM/FM radio broadcasts even when you're not at the computer. You can easily transfer the recorded files to your iPod so you can time shift your favorite shows right into your pocket. The radio SHARK sells for $70 at *www.griffintechnology.com*.

Podcasts

Just as Web logs, or *blogs* (page 109), have given anybody with a computer the power to publish their thoughts on the Web, *podcasting* lets you speak those thoughts out loud—and lets others download and listen to them on their computers or portable music players.

Note: The culturally savvy neologists out there who make up names for things are obviously iPod fans; *podcast* is a pun on "broadcast," but includes an obvious reference to the iPod. But, in fact, podcasts work on just about any digital music player. After all, they're just MP3 files.

Podcasts are basically homemade radio shows. They're usually saved as MP3 files and are free to download from the Web. Anyone can make one—from media pros like former MTV VJ Adam Curry to bloggers who find speaking more fun than typing. And because they're MP3 files, you can play them through audio programs like iTunes or Windows Media Player.

You can find podcasts on a huge variety of topics from agriculture to politics to daily life in Hawaii, all there for your listening pleasure.

Most podcasts are updated regularly, just like daily radio talk shows. Going back to the podcast's home page to look for new installments is a drag, so most people use software designed to snag and download podcasts automatically. This way, you always have the most recent episode. Setting up such a system is called *subscribing* to a podcast.

Podcasts on iTunes

If you've got iTunes 4.9 or later on your PC or Mac, you can use iTunes as your podcast wrangler. The iTunes Music Store lists 35,000 different podcasts, all free. To see them, click the Podcasts icon on the iTunes main page (it's on the left-side Source list), and then click the Podcast Directory link at the bottom of the window.

You're immediately transported into the Podcast section of the Music Store, where you can browse or search by title, topic, or category. Podcasts with talk-show style commentary from all the major news organizations are here, plus shows covering recent developments in computing, entertainment, travel, business, and more.

If you see one you want to hear, click the Subscribe button next to it; iTunes signs you up while downloading the first episode to your computer.

Tip: There's also such a thing as a *video* podcast. It's the same idea, except instead of being an amateur radio show, it's an amateur video. Video podcasts, too, are listed at the iTunes Music Store. You can watch them on your computer, or play them on the small screen of, for example, your video iPod or Sony PSP.

As you can see in Figure 11-6, the Podcasts list is the place to go to find the podcasts you've subscribed to. (Just click the Get button next to a grayed-out past episode to go fetch yourself a copy.)

A blue dot denotes an episode that you haven't listened to yet. If you decide you don't like a podcast, stop future downloads by selecting it in the iTunes window and clicking the Unsubscribe button, also shown in Figure 11-6.

Figure 11-6:
Let iTunes be your window to the world of podcasting. By clicking the Podcasts icon in the iTunes Source list, you can see all the shows you've subscribed to. Along the bottom of the screen, you can cancel your subscription to shows you don't want anymore (click the Unsubscribe button) and gain easy access to your podcast management preferences with the Settings button.

Once you sign up for a podcast or six in iTunes, you can tell the program how you want to handle your shows. Click the Settings button (bottom-right corner) to specify how iTunes should handle your podcasts, like how often to check for new shows and how many episodes to keep around. There's also a button in the box to open the iPod's Podcast preferences. In the resulting box, you can tell iTunes which podcasts you want to regularly copy over to the iPod for your portable listening pleasure.

Tip: If a podcast's page doesn't have a Subscribe button, but gives you an odd-looking URL and a screen full of gibberish instead, you can subscribe to the program by choosing the Add New Feed option in your podcast program and pasting that URL into the box. To add feeds for shows not in the iTunes podcast directory, for example, choose Advanced → Subscribe to Podcast, and paste the subscription URL from the podcast's own Web page in the resulting box to add its feed to your subscription list. Your podcast receiver now knows where to look for new episodes.

Yahoo Podcasts

Well *of course* Yahoo has its own Podcasts directory. (It probably has its own military and a United Nations representative, too.) Point your browser to *http:// podcasts.yahoo.com* to see the collection.

If you just aim to do a little listening at your desk, you don't need anything more than a compatible Web browser on your PC or Mac. Find a show you want to hear and then click the Listen button. A pop-up player opens (Figure 11-7) and streams the show through your speakers.

Figure 11-7:
Yahoo has a full slate of podcasts and a Web-based player to pipe them through your computer. You can find all sorts of things in the Podcasts area of the site, including free Mandarin Chinese lessons.

A button next to each podcast lets you to subscribe to the show, too, as long as you have a Yahoo ID. (You can sign up for one on the spot.) And you need an audio program to play the MP3 file—like iTunes or the Yahoo Music Engine for Windows, mentioned previously in this chapter.

Odeo Podcast Sharing

This audio-sharing site (*www.odeo.com*) does more than let you listen to podcasts—it helps you make your own. You can record your audio using the site's free tools and then upload your efforts to the Odeo podcast directory.

To listen to podcasts, browse Odeo's directory and listen in your browser with the built-in player software. Each podcast has its own "channel" page with links to previous episodes, information about the show's creator, and so on. If you really like a podcast, use the E-Mail button on the right side of the page to spread the word.

With a free Odeo registration, you can subscribe to podcasts and find them waiting in your Inbox page when you log in. Your page has controls that help you Create, Manage, and Browse podcasts. You can also download podcasts and play them in iTunes or any program mentioned in the previous section.

Recording an Odeo podcast

To record your own podcast, you need a microphone connected or built into your computer. To get started, click the Record Audio button in the Create box. Odeo ushers you into its own Web-based recording studio. Use the controls—just like a tape player—to start and stop recording as you speak into the microphone. Once you're satisfied with your recording, a few more clicks add it to your Odeo channel.

Recording a podcast by phone

If you don't have a microphone, don't despair; Odeo even lets you record a podcast *over the telephone*. You can maintain your podcast empire on the road, or simply use Odeo's phone service to post audio messages for friends and loved ones.

To use the Phone Record feature, click its link on your Inbox page. Once you're set up, dial the Odeo Phone Record number anytime: (415) 856-0205. (Yes, this is a long-distance call if you don't live in the Bay Area.)

If you've ever left a message on somebody's voicemail, you'll have no trouble with Odeo's phone-recording feature. Just let the audio menus and voice prompts guide you along. Once you finish recording, Odeo saves your message as an MP3 file. Then you just need to tell your friends and family where to go to hear your dulcet tones echoing out of their Web browsers.

Note: Odeo's great for quick-and-dirty podcasts. But for a more polished effect—with sound effects, music, and other audio bits—check out Chapter 19 for coverage of other podcast creating tools, including GarageBand.

NPR Podcasts

If you're a National Public Radio listener, you can find podcasts of most of the organization's shows—like Morning Edition or World Cafe (Figure 11-8)—at *www.npr.org*. NPR.org offers podcasts of member station programming, too, like WNYC's *Brian Lehrer Show*. Click the orange NPR Podcasts button to get started. You can browse hundreds of shows by title and topic.

You can listen to the podcasts with your Web browser right on the program's home page. Or, you can take the shows with you on your laptop or iPod by clicking the Subscribe button on each podcast's page. If you subscribe, you can play the podcast in iTunes (page 193), Yahoo's Music Engine (page 200), or your podcast receiver software (paste the podcast feed's URL into the program's "Add a Feed" area).

Figure 11-8:
Listen to your favorite NPR shows on your own time—and have them come to you. Just visit the organization's Podcasts page to subscribe.

Podcast Directories

Using iTunes to find and manage your podcast life is the easy way out. It's all built-in, beautifully organized, and easy to transfer to an iPod.

You can also do the whole podcast thing manually, though, bypassing the Apple editors who compile the iTunes podcast list.

For example, you can find hundreds of podcasts listed on *podcast directory* Web pages. For example, check out Podcast Alley (*www.podcastalley. com*) and Indiepodder (*www.ipodder.org*), Adam Curry's great big podcast site.

When it comes to *subscribing* to podcasts, the alternative to iTunes is to use a *podcast receiver* or

aggregator program. It keeps tabs on your subscriptions and automatically downloads new shows when they become available.

The two podcast sites mentioned here list receiver programs. For example, a program like Juice Receiver (free; *http://juicereceiver.sourceforge.net*) handles podcast subscriptions for both Mac and Windows.

(P.S. Because podcasters often submit their work to several distribution sites, you'll see some of the same shows in multiple directories. But don't get complacent: Browsing different podcast sites may still reveal ones you missed on another site.)

Videos, Movies, and TV

History has shown that audio inventions are inevitably followed by corresponding video versions. Radio preceded TV; audio tape was followed by videotape; CDs led to DVDs. No wonder, then, that music files were first to squeeze through the Internet pipeline—and video came later.

After all, downloading even audio files was an exercise in patience back when everyone was still using telephone modems. Waiting eight or nine minutes for a three-megabyte, three-minute pop song to shimmy down the wire was pretty common. But a full movie, hundreds of megabytes big—well, the downloading of such monster files would last longer than some Hollywood marriages.

Broadband changed all that. With super-fast cable or DSL connections, you can get an entire high-resolution movie in a matter of minutes, not months. Movie and video companies have also noticed that people want to watch stuff on their own schedules and on their own devices, like laptops or portable video players.

The ability to watch movies wherever and whenever you want has led to a boom in downloadable video services, peddling everything from full-length movies to free quirky bits of home-cooked funny videos.

This chapter gives you the big picture on the little picture.

Videos and Movies Online

Early Web video of the 1990s was often a fuzzy, grainy affair with jerky movements and not the sharpest of onscreen images. You usually got a few minutes of low-resolution action, but it was exciting at the time because it was new and cool.

Just as the kinetoscope gave way to movie shorts and then to full-length film with sound, color, and Clark Gable, Web video has also come a long way—but in a much shorter time than it took to go from 1902's *A Trip to the Moon* to *Star Wars, Episodes I–VI*.

Tip: If you want to see some examples of absolutely gorgeous Web video, take a peek at Apple's movie trailers page at *www.apple.com/trailers*; you need a broadband connection and the free QuickTime software (version 7 or later; it's preinstalled on Macs).

There are several ways to watch movies, videos, TV shows, music videos, video podcasts, and film shorts online. Some of these methods include:

- Renting a video file from an online store and downloading it to your computer to watch in a certain amount of time before the file goes *poof!* in the night.

- Buying a video file from an online store and downloading it to your computer.

- Streaming video files through your browser or video player software.

- Downloading free video files from the Web.

That last option also includes the underground file-sharing and trading sites like BitTorrent that specialize in the free, mostly illegal swapping of movies and television shows. Of course, the movie industry is already in Full Lawsuit Mode against these services, so no one knows how much longer they'll be around. There are, however, other sites that offer free videos, as described on the next few pages.

The software you need to play video on your computer depends on the Web site in question. RealPlayer and Windows Media Player are two common video browser plug-ins that play online videos (both are free). Both kinds of software can handle copy-protected videos (the only kind you'll find on legal movie-download sites).

Note: The newest versions of RealPlayer and Windows Media Player don't work on the Mac, so Mac fans can't yet thrill to some of the online video rental places. Mac folks, however, *can* buy and download TV shows, music videos, and even some movies from the iTunes Music Store and see non-protected videos in other Web-based video collections.

Downloading Movie Rentals

If you've got a fairly new PC, Windows XP with Internet Explorer, a big chunk of extra hard drive space, and a broadband connection, the days of schlepping down to the corner video store to see if someone's returned that copy of *The Aviator* are over. Now you can do your renting over the Internet. Several companies now offer "rentals" that you pay for and download to watch on your laptop or portable video player; the prices are often even better than renting the scuffed DVD at the video place.

Note: For copyright and licensing reasons, most movie-rental download sites restrict their sales to customers living in the United States.

You may be wondering about how you "rent" a download. Once you've got a copy on your computer, it's not like you can *return* it.

But there's certain coding in the file that disables the whole thing after a certain period of time. It may be after you've had the file for 30 days or after you've watched it once all the way through; but, in some way, the file will be unplayable or will automatically delete itself, *Mission Impossible*–style, when your rental term expires.

Note: Make sure your computer meets the movie-rental site's system requirements. This may require installing or upgrading the required video-player software.

Movielink

The joint project of five major movie studios (MGM, Paramount, Universal, Sony, and Warner Brothers), the Movielink site (*www.movielink.com*) has been renting films as downloads since 2002. In the spring of 2006, the site began to *sell* video downloads of popular movies, including many of the year's Oscar-nominated flicks. The prices, though, were up there with what you'd pay for the DVD—or higher.

In addition to the usual Hollywood blockbusters, you can find date movies, action boomfests, documentaries, cult classics, cartoons, and even filmed

Shakespeare productions from the BBC. Prices vary, but most films can be downloaded for less than $5. There's even a bargain section of $2 rentals, mostly of undistinguished films that appeal primarily to certain narrow slivers of the populace.

To use Movielink, you need a PC with at least Windows 2000 and Internet Explorer 5.0 or later. You can use either RealPlayer or Windows Media Player to watch your downloads, and you can view them in a mini-player size (Figure 12-1) or full-screen mode across your monitor. If you have the right video cables, you can also output the movie to your TV screen and watch it just like anything else from the comfort of the couch. (There's more on linking PC to TV in the box on page 217.)

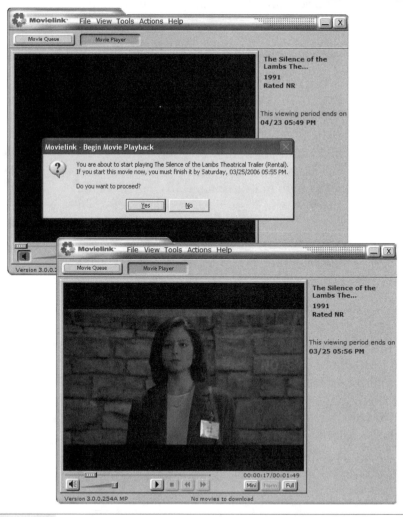

Figure 12-1:
When you rent a download from Movielink, the software tells you what you have and how long you have to play it (top). Once you click the Play button, the show begins. You can watch your movie in the mini-window (bottom) or click to expand the picture to the full width of your computer screen.

When you sign up for Movielink, the site gives you a free download (usually a movie trailer) to test your connection and system requirements before you hand over your credit card digits. Along the way, you may be prompted to upgrade your RealPlayer software and fiddle with your firewall program (when, for example, it tries to block the Movielink program from sending signals from your computer to the Internet; for more on firewalls, see Chapter 21).

You are also prompted to install the Movielink Manager software, which is your inbox for downloaded files. The files themselves take up their temporary residence in your My Videos or Shared Videos folder.

Once you sign up, renting a movie is just like any sort of online shopping: point, click, pay. You can store your rental on your PC for 30 days before it expires. The file works for 24 hours from your first click of the Play button. You can rewind it, fast-forward it, and watch it again and again. But when those 24 hours are up, the rental's over.

You don't have to wait for your movie to fully download before you can start the show; you can start playing the movie as soon as the Play button lights up. You can also pause the download process if you need to, like when a storm's rolling in and you need to shut down the PC before the lightning starts.

Movielink recommends you have at least one full gigabyte of free space on your drive to download a movie. A typical movie weighs in at about 550 megabytes.

You can't burn your rentals to a DVD. If you *buy* a movie download from Movielink, though, you can play it on up to three PCs and keep it forever to watch over and over.

Note: Most online rental places require you to be online only during the downloading of your rental. You can therefore watch a movie on, say, a plane without an Internet connection.

CinemaNow

CinemaNow (*www.cinemanow.com*) is another online rental site with hundreds of titles on its virtual shelves. It works quite similarly to Movielink: no membership fee, you have 24 hours to watch the movie, and you can even buy selected films to keep forever on your hard drive. Mainstream Hollywood fare like *Flightplan*, *The Constant Gardener*, and *The Legend of Zorro* are among the films available for download.

To use the service, you need Windows 2000 or later, Internet Explorer 6 or later, and Windows Media Player 10 or later. Once you sign up and create an account, you can rent downloaded movies for about $4 for a hot new flick or $3 for an older film. Depending on the download, there may also be choice of picture quality: Standard or DVD Quality. The latter has the better picture, but takes twice as long to download.

If you have a Windows Mobile Portable Media Center gadget, CinemaNow has more than 800 miniaturized movies you can buy outright for about $10 and transfer to your PMC player. Sports and travel documentaries are plentiful, as well as old popcorn pictures like *Short Circuit*.

Vongo

Vongo, backed by the Starz Entertainment group, brings a library of more than 1,000 movies and videos to your virtual doorstep, including extreme sports, concerts, and IMAX movies, along with mainstream Tinseltown titles. The service, at *www.vongo.com*, lets you play your rentals on computers or transfer them to Windows-based Portable Media Center gadgets.

To use Vongo, you need to download its own special Vongo software and install it on your PC. As for the PC itself: Windows 2000 or XP, Windows Media Player 9 or later, and at least a gigabyte of free hard drive space are required.

The monthly membership plan offers unlimited movie downloads for $10 a month (you can play them on up to three different computers or portable devices). The amount of time you can keep a Vongo download on your machine varies by film, but the preview box on each title's page lets you know the expiration date. You also get a free feed of the Starz cable channel pumping through your Vongo player software.

If you don't like monthly fees or don't want the Starz cable channel coming anywhere near your computer, you can go à la carte with the Vongo Pay Per View plan. Like television Pay Per View, you buy what you want to watch when you find it—and then watch it within 24 hours after you first start the film. (Thereafter, the file deletes itself from your computer.)

Watching TV Shows Online

Thanks to BitTorrent and the other file-sharing services, digitized mini-versions of popular TV shows like *Buffy the Vampire Slayer* and *The Sopranos* have been wafting around the Web for years.

Play on the PC, Watch on the TV

The convenience of downloading your rental to your PC is great, but you don't have to gather the whole family around the Dell Dimension to watch the show. Using inexpensive audio-video cables, you can connect the computer to your home entertainment system and present the downloaded motion picture on the big screen: your TV.

You can also connect a laptop to the TV; most have video-out connections. The portability of a laptop may make it easier to get close to the TV.

The type of cable you need depends on the ports on both your PC and your TV; prices range from about $15 to $75. You can find AV cables at stores like Radio Shack or CompUSA, or Web sites like Monster Cable (*www.monstercable.com*).

Some desktops can use *composite* video cables—those triple-connector RCA plugs with red, white, and yellow ends—for both the back of the computer and the TV. You may need a separate miniplug-to-RCA cable for the audio signal on the PC, depending on your model.

Many laptops and some desktops include an S-Video jack, as do most televisions. If so, all you need is an S-Video cable for the picture signal and a Y-shaped miniplug-to-RCA audio cable (red and

white plugs on one end) to carry the sound from PC to TV. Connect the two machines with the S-Video cable, and then connect the miniplug to the computer's audio-out port and the red and white RCA plugs to the red and white inputs on the TV or entertainment receiver.

Some televisions have a VGA jack, the same connector as you find on older computer monitors. In that case, you can unplug the monitor and plug in the TV with a VGA cable for the picture, and get your sound from a Y-shaped miniplug-to-RCA audio cable as described above.

Newer computers designed for multimedia use may even have a DVI jack to carry *high-definition* video signals. If both your computer and your television have one of these, you can cable them together DVI-style. (DVI carries only video, though, so you'll still need to string your audio in with the aforementioned Y-shaped audio cable—or a digital audio cable if your equipment offers a digital audio option.)

Once you get PC wired to TV, you can relax, sit back, and enjoy the show—without having to worry that someone will spill a cherry Slurpee all over the keyboard.

But the notion of *legal* TV show downloads really got a jump-start in 2005 when Apple whipped the veil off its video iPod. At the same time, the company also announced that iPod-optimized episodes of *Desperate Housewives, Lost,* and a whole bunch of music videos were for sale in the iTunes Music Store for $2 a pop. The files never expire because, like Apple's music downloads, you *own* them.

This announcement set off a couple of mad stampedes: one by eager iPodders to get the absolute latest version of the player (and then to get videos to play on it), and the other by companies rushing to create their own online video stores.

iTunes Music Store

Apple sells over 3,000 music videos, television shows, short animated flicks, sports broadcasts, and more in its iTunes Music Store. To get there, fire up your copy of iTunes 6 or later and click the icon for the Music Store in the left-side list.

Now, for less than $2 apiece, you can download that episode of *The Office* you missed the other night, or finally have your own copy of Madonna's "Vogue" video. There's also a multi-pass (bulk purchase) option for nightly programs like *The Daily Show*: 16 episodes for $10. Although the picture quality isn't spectacular when viewed on a TV screen or full-size computer monitor, iTunes Store videos look simply smashing when viewed on an iPod. And as a cherry on the icing on the Cake of Joy: no commercials!

To buy such videos, click the link on the Store's main page for the type you want—music video, Pixar cartoon, or TV show (Figure 12-2). Apple's still building its video library, but dozens of old and new TV classics are already available, including episodes from *Lost, The Tonight Show, Alfred Hitchcock Presents, Battlestar Galactica, Saturday Night Live,* and *Law & Order* (just in case you're away from the TV, where all the permutations of *L&O* play constantly in a continual loop).

You buy a video just like you buy a song: browse, preview a sample, and click the Buy button for the title if you want it. Video files are much heftier than music files, though (one 45-minute episode of *Battlestar Galactica*, for instance, is close to 200 megabytes), so make sure you have enough time and hard drive space to accommodate your shopping spree.

Once you buy and download the files from the iTunes Store, they land in your Library and on your Purchased list, just like songs do. You can watch them on your computer or move them over to the iPod to watch on the go; unless you've fiddled with the settings, iTunes comes set to transfer your videos to a video-capable iPod automatically the next time the iPod is connected to the computer.

If you have a computer with ultra-zippy USB 2.0 connectors, copying videos over to the iPod usually doesn't take much time. The transfer time over a USB 1.1 connection can be tedious, however. You may even want to go watch TV in the living room while your shows for your iPod TV copy over from the computer.

Tip: Trapped at your desk on game days while the Boys of Summer swing for the bleachers? For $80 a season (or $15 a month), you can stream Major League Baseball games live through your Web browser at *www.mlb.com*. As with television, live games in your local market are blacked out, but MLB.TV works on both Windows and Macintosh systems with either RealPlayer or Windows Media Player. Just to be on the safe side, you may want to have a large, full-screen spreadsheet right behind your browser window to click in case the boss comes around and you need to sacrifice bunt.

Figure 12-2:
You can buy just one episode of a television show or click a button to download an entire season. Short descriptions give you an idea of that episode's events; you can double-click the title for a short preview of the show.

Google Video

Google doesn't call its video store a video store; it prefers the phrase, "the world's first open online video marketplace" (*http://video.google.com*). The big idea here is that anyone, from the biggest TV network to the family man with a camcorder, can post videos for all the world to see—and even buy. Who needs a movie studio to distribute your digital film when you've got Google?

The commercial offerings include TV shows, music videos, movies, NBA basketball games, and *Rocky and Bullwinkle* cartoons, all for a few bucks.

There's a lot of free, searchable stuff to see, too, from Super Bowl commercials to videos by future rock stars.

Google's marketplace isn't nearly as simple as the iTunes video store, where every TV show costs $2 and has the same copy-protection limit (play on five computers or an unlimited number of iPods).

On Google, some videos are copy protected, others aren't. Some can be downloaded, others viewed online only. Some have ads, some don't. Some videos are free, some cost money. Some can be transferred to a Sony PlayStation Portable or video iPod, others can't.

Once you land in Google's video emporium, you see a screen full of thumbnail images, each representing a particular clip or show. Videos with the familiar tape-deck Play triangle button in the corner can be played online; click the link to go to the video's page, where you see it play (or a short clip from it, if it's for sale), or even download it for a portable player, as shown in Figure 12-3.

Figure 12-3:
After you click a video's thumbnail, Google takes you to a larger version that you can play onscreen, and, in some cases, download to a computer or portable video player. Information about the video is listed on the right side of the screen, and the ubiquitous search box is up top to help you find what you're looking for.

Some videos, though, must be downloaded and played through the Google Video Player (see below), a free piece of Windows software ((a Mac version is also available).

Each video's page gives you information about where it came from, when it was made, and the run time. Buttons (Figure 12-3) tell you what exactly you can do with this video:

• **Download** means the video is free. You can pipe your own copy of it down to your computer to play with the Google Video Player, or, in some cases, to your Mac, your video iPod, or your Sony PSP.

• **Day Pass** means that the video is time-limited. Your download fee lets you watch it with the Google Video Player anytime within 24 hours of your purchase. After that, the file stops working, like a Blockbuster rental that evaporates into thin air.

• **Buy** means you can pay for it, download it, and keep it around on your PC to play forever.

Prices to buy a show or get a day pass vary widely. Most TV reruns cost about $2 to buy, while some sporting events can cost around $15; day passes average about a buck or three. You need Windows and a Google Account (page 99) to buy videos.

Note: One thing about copy-protected shows you may buy from the Google Video Store is that you have to be *online* to play them, so Google can check the playback and make sure everything's Copyright Kosher. While it's fine if you're in a hotel with Internet access, this little sticking point really stinks if you wanted to watch your purchases off the grid on a plane, train, or bus.

Watching free Google Video on the Web is the simplest option for most people. You need Windows 2000 or later, or Mac OS X 10.3 or later; Google Video requires Internet Explorer 5.0, Safari 1.0, Firefox 1.1, or later versions of these browsers. You also need to add the Adobe/Macromedia Flash player plug-in, free at *www.adobe.com*. Finally, for smooth playback that won't have you reaching for the Dramamine, you need a broadband Internet connection.

As mentioned previously, some of the Google videos play only in the Google Video Player software. You may be prompted to download the player when you try to get a video; you can also download it from a link at the top of the main Google Video page.

The Video Player can display your vids in full-screen mode, skip over the boring stuff to get to the good parts, and browse the different scenes in the video with the built-in thumbnail pictures (much like DVD chapters).

Some of the Google videos can be downloaded to your computer and then shuttled over to an Apple video iPod or Sony PSP for watching on the go. Look for a pop-up menu next to a video's Download button. If there's a portable version available, there'll be a "Sony PSP" or "Video iPod" option to select in the list (Figure 12-3).

Once you download the file to your computer, you can copy it to your portable player just like any other video clip you've added:

- **iPod.** Add the file to the iTunes library, which automatically sends it to the iPod.

- **Sony PSP.** Rename the video file to MAQ*XXXX*.MP4 (where the *X*s are random numbers you make up from 0 to 9), and then copy the renamed file to the \MP_ROOT\101ANV01 folder on the PSP's Memory Stick. (Nobody said this was going to be easy.)

If you're having trouble finding portable video in the first place, use the Search bar at the top of the page to seek out *video iPod* or *Sony PSP*.

Tip: For further details on Google's Video Store, visit *http://video.google.com/support*.

AOL In2TV and Hi-Q

America Online joins the video club with its own broadband TV network populated with hundreds of TV shows—*old* TV shows. Episodes of *F-Troop, Wonder Woman, Maverick,* and *Welcome Back, Kotter* stream through 14 different themed channels in the Television area of the AOL service (Keyword: TV), or on the Web at *http://television.aol.com/in2tv*. (This service requires Windows XP and a recent browser.)

AOL's Hi-Q feature lets you download high-quality versions of many programs to your computer. To do so, you need to install the Hi-Q software (*http://television.aol.com/in2tv/high_quality_video* or the more memorable *www.missingmanuals.com*); Internet Explorer 6 or later is required. After you install the software and select a show to download, AOL proceeds to send you a very large, high-resolution video file. The Hi-Q video player can be a little clunky and will probably set off your firewall and spyware detectors, but that's life in the rerun lane.

Free video sites

Google Video has an ever-growing collection of quirky video clips and home movies uploaded by its members that you can watch for free, but it's not the only online warehouse for such things. A few other free-to-watch video sites include:

- **YouTube.** This site encourages you to "Broadcast Yourself"—to post your own mini-movies and videos for all to see and play right in their Web browsers. You can search for videos by keyword or topic, but the Most Popular links are a good way to find the funny stuff right off the bat. As a creator of YouTube videos, you can create your own profile page to display your cinematic efforts. YouTube is a community-oriented site where people who love to chat about videos can meet other people with the same interests. (*www.youtube.com*)

- **iFilm.** This site is a long-time Web bonanza of movie clips, music videos, commercials, bits of TV shows, and other snippets of video that people love to e-mail around. It can play videos in standard formats like QuickTime, RealPlayer, or Windows Media Player. Registration is free and you can add your own clips to the mix, tag others as your favorites, and discuss video on the iFilm forums. (*www.ifilm.com*)

- **Veoh.** Once you sign up and install the free Veoh software for your Mac or PC, you can download and watch vintage Superman and Popeye cartoons, old Bruce Lee flicks, and classically bad movies like *Little Shop of Horrors*. Many of the site's videos can also be transferred to a video iPod or Sony PSP. (*www.veoh.com*)

If you have young children, by the way, be aware that many sites also host a fair amount of adults-only material and have no automatic parental controls built into the interface. This means, of course, that the control has to come *manually* from the parent.

Tip: Trapped in a hotel room in Tokyo when you know your TiVo at home has the latest cliff-hanging episode of *24* just sitting there with no one to watch it? The Slingbox ($250 at *www.slingmedia.com*) lets you watch live or recorded shows from your own TV, video recorder, or cable box—all the way across the Internet—on your PC screen or even Windows Mobile cellphone. It works like this: You connect the Slingbox to your TV and your home computer network, and install the SlingPlayer software on your PC. Using the software's onscreen remote controls, you can change the channel and watch live TV, call up a recorded show, navigate your TiVo, or even set your TiVo to record something in the future.

DVDs by Mail

Downloading movies from the Internet may be cutting-edge and very quick, but it's not a moviephile's dream by any means. You have to figure out a way to connect your PC to your TV (or else watch movies on your computer, like a total nerd). The quality is fairly low. The selection is poor. The 24-hour window for watching is draconian. And you don't get any DVD extras (director narration, omitted scenes, and so on).

For millions of people, online DVD rental shops are a much better bet. Granted, it takes longer for the DVD to arrive in the mailbox than for *Mr. & Mrs. Smith* to download to your hard drive off the Net, but you still don't have to dig up your car keys.

Netflix

With 55,000 DVD movies in stock and high-speed shipping that can deliver a DVD to your door in about one business day, Netflix (*www.netflix.com*) gets as close to instant gratification as you can expect from activities that involve the post office. When you rent a movie, it shows up in your mailbox in a bright red envelope; after you've watched it, you mail it back to Netflix in a bright red *return* envelope with prepaid postage. The next DVD on your wish list gets mailed to you automatically.

The beauty of Netflix (and its rival Blockbuster, described next) is that there are no late fees—ever. You can keep your DVDs as long as you like, and watch as many as you like; your monthly fee's the same either way. Of course, it's in your interest to mail them back when you're finished (because, otherwise, you're paying that monthly fee for nothing).

Netflix's monthly fee depends on how many movies you like to have "checked out" at a time. For example, you can check out one DVD at a time ($10 monthly), two ($15), or three ($18). Free two-week trials of each plan are often available.

The flat-fee system means that you can help yourself to more movies per month (the average subscriber rents about six). It also makes you a more adventurous renter, leading you to explore movies you wouldn't have felt like spending money on before.

Once you sign up, you can browse Netflix's well-structured catalog and build a list of movies you want to rent. That way, as soon as you return each movie, the next one is automatically shipped out.

Netflix may not be as zippy as a download service, but you don't have to worry about filling up your hard drive or wrestling the PC close enough to the TV to watch your films without hunching over a computer monitor. And the movies are, literally, DVD-quality.

Books and Games Get the Netflix Formula

The Netflix formula—pay a monthly fee, check out as many titles as you like—works so well, the Web's entrepreneurs have applied it to other borrowable goodies, too.

For example, if you have time left over after watching your movies, Blockbuster's online service also rents out video games for Sony's PlayStation 2 and PSP consoles and Microsoft's Xbox game station.

Similarly, with 3,500 titles in stock, GameFly (*www.gamefly.com*) rents video games; its pricing starts at $15 a month for one game at a time with no late fees.

But why stop there? If there's even more time to kill, you may as well rent audio books, too. These are all the bestsellers, read by professional actors and recorded on CDs that get sent to you in exactly the same way Netflix sends you movies.

SimplyAudioBooks.com and *Jiggerbug.com*, for example, let you check out two audio books at a time for $25 a month. (Jiggerbug also lets you download one *electronic* audio book for that price. It plays on a Windows computer or a non-iPod portable player.) As usual, when you return one set of CDs, the next set gets shipped to you automatically. If you want to keep your audiobook downloads and play them on your iPod or other portable, visit the huge selection of titles at Audible.com.

But why stop at books on tape? What about books *on paper*?

This, too, is a blossoming business on the Web. *Booksfree.com*, for example, will happily mail you books on the Netflix plan. Read 'em, send 'em back, read the next ones, all for a fixed monthly fee. (Works best for people with no public library nearby, of course.)

Blockbuster

Retail rental giant Blockbuster (*www.blockbuster.com*) has obviously felt the heat from Netflix; it opened its own online rental service that works almost identically.

Just like Netflix, Blockbluster stocks more than 50,000 movies to mail back and forth, imposes no late fees, charges $18 a month for unlimited three-at-a-time rentals or $10 for one DVD at a time, and so on. (In fact, Netflix thought that Blockbuster's service looked so familiar, it filed a patent-infringement lawsuit against Blockbuster in April 2006.)

There are a couple of key differences, though. Blockbuster also has physical video stores all over the States, which it uses to its advantage. For example, Blockbuster's online membership includes coupons for two free in-store rentals each month, which is handy when you can't wait for the mail.

Note, however, that even if you live next door to a Blockbuster store, you still have to mail the rented movies back. The physical shops don't handle the virtual store's stock.

Tip: Netflix and Blockbuster aren't the only online DVD rental outfits. GreenCine (pronounced GreenScene; *www.greencine.com*) is a third one. It specializes in art-house films, film noir, documentaries, Japanese anime, and cult movies. And true movie nuts swear by it.

Watching Webcams

Wondering what the pandas in the National Zoo are up to right now? Curious about what it's like outside in Anchorage? Open your browser window and take a look with a *Webcam*. As you may have gathered from the name, a Webcam is a camera that's hooked up to the Web and transmits live pictures of whatever it's pointed at.

You may see either live video or a series of still shots updated every few seconds. Some cameras may require the Java plug-in (page 176) for your browser to display the images properly.

Thousands of Webcams are set up all around the world, often pointing at city streets for traffic conditions or public beaches so you can check the surfing conditions at any moment. With an inexpensive camera-and-software package like those from Veo or Logitech, you can even set up your own Webcam. From across the Internet, you can keep an eye on, say, the kids' room or your vacation house in another state.

Note: Tons of Webcams are focused on, ahem, steamier subjects than the downtown area of Banner Elk, North Carolina, if you get the drift. You'll have no problem finding such things if that's what you're looking for.

Just finding Webcams can be the hardest part. The Web sites of local TV stations and newspapers often have them for traffic reports, as do the sites of tourist destinations like ski lodges and resorts. Luckily, there are also people who take the time to hunt down Webcams and post directories full of links for the rest of us:

- **Cincy Street.** This site has a giant collection of 2,000 Webcam links, with sections devoted to City Cams, Travel Cams, and Live Cams (meaning anything from oral surgery in a dentist's office to a library in Evansville, Indiana, where a lady ghost is said to roam the stacks). Each includes a thumbnail image so you can get some idea of where each camera is aimed. (*www.cincystreet.com*)

- **EarthCam.** Beaming in images from Times Square to Red Square and many points in between, the cameras on the EarthCam network literally bring you a global perspective. Don't miss the site's World Map page, where you can click the image of a country or continent and see a list of all the cities hosting Webcams. For example, you can find a camera on the lookout for leprechauns in a field in Tipperary, Ireland and one at the base of the Osorno Volcano in Puerto Varas, Chile. (*www.earthcam.com*)

- **BBC England Webcams.** Anglophiles can see dozens of sights around England, from pastoral scenes in the country to the surf at Watergate Bay in Cornwall. Traffic conditions around London, feeding time for the slender-tailed meerkats at the Marwell Zoo, and a lovely view of Durham Cathedral are also available (*www.bbc.co.uk/england/webcams*; there's also a list of non-BBC Webcams at *www.bbc.co.uk/webcams/wwwcams.shtml*).

Webcams got a huge boost in popularity in 2005, as two black-and-white baby bears were born in U.S. zoos under the watchful eye of zookeepers and Webcams. If you need a panda break in your day, check out the National Zoo's pandacam at *http://nationalzoo.si.edu/Animals/GiantPandas* (Figure 12-4) or the San Diego Zoo's feed at *http://www.sandiegozoo.org/zoo/ex_panda_station.html*.

Figure 12-4:
Spend your morning coffee break with the pandas at the National Zoo in Washington, courtesy of a Webcam. The Zoo has about a dozen Webcams in operation, so when you get tired of pandas, you can move on to see how the tigers, elephants, and naked mole rats are doing. There's a list of the zoo's Webcam offerings at http://nationalzoo. si.edu/Animals/.

Photos

It's no wonder digital cameras are so popular: You don't need film, you don't need processing, and you don't need extra shoeboxes to store the pictures until you get around to buying photo albums. And digital cameras are *everywhere:* in cellphones, on the ends of keychains, peeping out of PDAs, nestled in shirt pockets, and even hanging around the necks of tourists in Oahu. With all these cameras out there—and the human urge to communicate visually and share experiences—there's bound to be a whole lot of digital photographs to see.

And there are. The Internet is brimming with pictures, from Web-based vacation photo albums to electronic snapshots of newborn babies. The Web's vast archive of images is at your service for research purposes, too—with a few simple searches, you can go back in time and see the celebration in Trafalgar Square on VE Day in 1945, or Dr. Martin Luther King Jr. on the steps of the Lincoln Memorial during the March on Washington in 1963. Photographs have been documenting life on earth since the 1830s, but finding and sharing them has never been as easy as it is now.

Finding Photos

Locating pictures on the Web isn't difficult at all, but finding pictures you actually *want* to see can take some search time. Using a site specifically designed to look for image files can speed things up.

Once you find a photo you want, you can drag a copy right out of your browser window to your desktop, where you can turn it into wallpaper, a screensaver, or some other decorative object.

You can use photos to illustrate personal newsletters, personal book reports, and personal whatever. Just don't use them on posters, brochures, or other copyrighted material, because copyright laws come into play here. You need the copyright holder's permission if you want to publicly reproduce the work for your own purposes. If there's no photographer or photo agency name on the image file, try contacting the owner or Webmaster of the site where you originally found the image.

There are two types of sites where you can find photographs:

- **Photo-sharing sites** like Flickr (*www.flickr.com*) combine millions of images with an online community where members can browse each other's work and post messages next to the photos. These sites are great for snaps of the Zeitgeist and modern daily life frozen in pixels.

- **Photo search sites** like Google Images (*http://images.google.com*) can round up photos by analyzing whatever keywords were assigned to them. They're even better at finding historical and commercial images.

Here's what Flickr and Google have to show *you*.

Flickr

Flickr is a great big photo-sharing site (*www.flickr.com*) that lets its members upload and organize their own personal pictures. Both amateur and professional photographers use the service, which is free. And, since Flickr's owned by (can you guess?) Yahoo, you can use your existing Yahoo ID.

You don't need a Flickr account to browse or search the collections. But if you want to post a comment or download the full-resolution original of the photo (if it's been made available), you need to sign up for a free account. (This section focuses on *finding* pictures; if you want to know more about uploading your own images to Flickr, flip to page 237.)

Searching for photos on Flickr

Flickr encourages its members to tag their photos with keywords—text labels—to make them easier to find. (For more about tagging your own pictures, see page 240.) For example, if you're looking for photos of Paris, type *paris* in the box on the Flickr home page. Flickr puts tagged photos from a broad category into *clusters*, or subsets of the larger set (see Figure 13-1).

Figure 13-1:
Flickr helps you dig through your search results by further grouping images into clusters, or subsets.

So when you get hundreds of Paris photos back from your search, look for a link for "Paris clusters" on the side of the page, which leads you to a page of more specific shots, like *sacre coeur* or *louvre* or *seine,* to drill down further. Click a photo thumbnail to see a larger version of it with more information, like the date it was taken, how many times it's been viewed, and any comments people have left.

Each photo thumbnail on a search results page has a link to its photographer underneath as well, so you can go right to the person's own Flickr collection (called a *photostream*) to see more. Each photostream can be divided up into *sets* by its owner, so you can hone in on a roundup of similar pictures like "airborne cats" or shots of fancy club chairs.

Flickr members can also see and join groups, which collaborate on *pools* of photos on a certain theme—say, Altered Signs (creative graffiti) or Rural Decay (rusting barns). Group members can upload contributions and post messages on public forums.

Tip: A picture's worth a thousand words, but you can add a few more words by embedding notes in photos to point out certain elements or comment on parts of the picture. Point to a photo without clicking it. If there are notes attached, the text appears in a floaty yellow balloon. Both the photographer and the viewer can leave notes, and all the text within is searchable.

Flickr is especially great for finding photos of extremely current or offbeat events, because people can snap photos with their cellphone cameras and send them directly to their Flickr pages without having to stop and use a computer. Its freshness, along with its freeness and tagging features, make it easy to find quirky collections devoted to say, street art or underground events like New York's annual Idiotarod race (where, instead of dogs and sleds, costumed teams of people push decorative, "borrowed" shopping carts along in a madcap race through Brooklyn and Manhattan). (To see some hysterical race-day coverage, search Flickr for *idiotarod*, as shown in Figure 13-1.)

Other Flickr features

If you have a Flickr membership, you can tag certain photos as favorites and send messages to other members with Flickr Mail. The Flickr staff itself helps round up the most interesting photos it can find each month and posts them on the Explore Flickr page, which is sort of a snapshot of all the different kinds of snapshots it's added in the last 30 days.

Flickr may not be your best choice if you need a picture of Henry Ford for your school report on American industry, but it's a great place to go to see a slice of life—even if it's not your own.

Google Images

If you can search for it, Google can probably find it, and images are no exception. You don't even have to remember or bookmark a new URL, either: Go to *www.google.com* and click the word Images above the search box. (But if that extra mouse click bugs you, just go to *http://images.google.com*.)

Searching for images on Google

To find pictures of something specific, type into the search box—*Tom Cruise*, say, or *Sony HC3*. Even Google can't "see" a photo, recognizing what's in it; it can only search the names of photos on the Web and whatever text *keywords* their creators have associated with them. (Google also takes a peek at text surrounding an image, deducing, for example, that a page with an unlabeled picture and a line of text that says "Look at my beautiful panda" probably contains an image of a panda.)

After you click Search, Google Images brings back a results page full of little thumbnail images, as shown in Figure 13-2.

Figure 13-2:
Type your keywords into Google Image Search and the little search engine that could goes out and finds all sorts of pictures for you. Each image in your search results comes with a bit of information like the size of the file and where Google found it.

Note: You can filter your results based on image size—small, medium, or large—which can make it easier to find, say, a photograph of a turkey that's big enough to print clearly on your Thanksgiving dinner invitations. That's important because Web graphics usually wind up blurry and pixilated when printed out. Turns out that a photo with enough pixels (resolution) to look good onscreen may not have nearly enough resolution for a printer. So the bigger the image file, the better chance you usually have of a decent print. In fact, you should probably avoid printing any photos Google designates as Small or Medium, unless you print them at very small sizes.

Each thumbnail tells you something about the picture, like the file name, how big the file is, and where it originally came from. Click the thumbnail to go to the original page, where you can see the image at its full size and in its intended context. Getting linked back to the original page is quite useful if you're doing both photo and text research on a topic because the links often lead back to articles on the subject of your image search.

Google Images knows about photo files in the .JPG, .GIF, and .PNG formats (see the box on page 235 for more about file formats). In addition to photographs, search results may include maps, charts, diagrams, and graphics. Search for *pantheon*, for example, and you get thousands of pictures of the old Roman temple, plus floor plans, cross sections, and virtual 3-D models of the building.

Fine-tuning a Google Image search

Getting so many results for general topics is more of a bad thing than a good one because you may have to wade through page after page looking for what you had in mind. To narrow things down a bit, here are a few tricks of the image-search trade:

- **Stick to short but specific keywords.** Searching for *kermit* brings up thousands of pictures of a certain green cloth frog, but if you were actually looking for screenshots of the eponymous computer program or a photo of the 26th president's son, specify *kermit software* or *kermit roosevelt*.

- **Fiddle around.** Experiment with your keywords. Google can sometimes be inconsistent with its keywords for images, so what makes sense to you may not have occurred to Google. If you don't like your results for *1974 volkswagen microbus*, try *volkswagen van* or *1974 volkswagen bus*.

- **Use the Advanced Image Search page.** Similar to the Advanced Search page for text queries (page 74), Google Images has its own full-page form to fill out. Click the Advanced Image Search link next to the search box to get to it. There you can specify file type, file size, or color mode (full color, grayscale, black-and-white) of the images you want to find. You also get some guidance on your choice of keywords and can instruct Google to look only within a certain domain.

Google generally tries to weed out pornographic images, but a few may occasionally slip through, depending on how you worded your search. You can use settings on the Advanced Search page to up the filtering to "strict" (in an attempt to screen out more of Those Types of Images) or turn filtering off entirely (if adult material is, in fact, what you're looking for).

Tip: The search pages for Yahoo and MSN mentioned back in Chapter 3 have similar image search functions. If Google doesn't goggle your eyes, try *http://images.search.yahoo.com* or *http://search.msn.com/images*.

Figuring out Photo Formats

Graphics come in dozens of file formats. Some formats, like TIFF and EPS, are common primarily in the printing industry; others, like DXF and STEP, are used in architectural or 3-D rendering programs. On the Web, the three file formats you're likely to encounter most often bear the sonorous names JPEG, GIF, and PNG.

JPG or JPEG images (created by the Joint Experts Photographic Group—get it?) are the most common for Web and digital photography. Just about every digital camera saves photos as JPEG files; browsers can readily display them within Web pages.

GIF files (Graphics Interchange Format) are also common in Web pages because their files are relatively small, which makes the images appear quickly. GIFs can't display as many colors as JPG files

(256 vs. 16,777,216) and are therefore better used for graphics, logos, cartoons, and other images where a real-world rainbow of colors is not required.

PNG files (Portable Network Graphic) are the new kids on the format block, but they're catching on fast. The format was designed specifically for Web pages. These files can represent a full range of color at relatively small sizes; like JPEG files, you can even embed short amounts of text into a PNG file's data so that image-search engines can find them more easily.

Programs like Adobe Photoshop Elements, Corel Photo-Paint, and GraphicConverter X (for the Mac) can convert images from one format to another.

Sharing Photos Online

If you have a digital camera, you no longer have to order multiple copies of photos and mail them to share with friends. Of course, you *can* still order prints for your friends who don't have Internet access. Most drugstores and photo-processing places can give you a CD of your images even if you took the pictures with a film-based camera, so there are still many ways to share digital photos. But one of the most common ways is through a photo-sharing site, like the previously discussed Flickr.

Photo-sharing sites let you display pictures in an online album for friends and family to see. This means you don't have to attach 15 pictures to an email message addressed to 30 people and clog up their inboxes; your buddies come *to* the photos instead. If the images are deeply personal, like pictures of a newborn baby that you want to share only with a close circle of family and friends, you can even password-protect your photo pages to keep strangers from wandering through.

Most photo-sharing sites let you turn your pictures into prints or novelty items like calendars, greeting cards, stickers, and mugs. Many of the bigger companies have a photo-book service where you can arrange to have a select group of images printed and bound in a paperback or hardcover album delivered by mail.

Uploading Your Images

How you get your pictures up online varies slightly depending on which photo-sharing service you decide to use, but the rough outline goes like this:

1. **Find a photo-sharing site you like and sign up for an account.**

   Not surprisingly, a few of the big sites are owned by companies that sell digital cameras; you may get coupons, onscreen hints, or brochures inviting you to sign up when you install your camera's software. Hewlett-Packard owns Snapfish, and Kodak owns EasyShare Gallery (both described in a moment). Depending on the site you choose, you may also need to install special software to do things like upload a bunch of images all at once.

2. **Once you're signed in, look for a link or button that says something like Upload Photos.**

   The site takes you to a screen and asks you to locate the pictures you want to put online. In some cases, you can just drag the pictures you want to use into the browser window. Other sites may require you to use a dialog box to navigate to the folder where the images are stored. (If you pulled them off the camera with Windows, check your My Pictures folder. Mac OS X fans, click your Pictures icon in the Finder window.)

3. **Select the images from their location on the hard drive and upload.**

   Some services let you do minor image editing (like removing red eye or rotating a horizontal shot to a vertical one) before anyone else can see the pictures.

   Along the way, you're given the chance to tag your pictures (page 240), arrange them in sequence, add captions, and perform other organizational tasks. You can also add a password to your photo page to keep it private.

4. **Tell your friends where to look for your photos.**

   Some sites let you email a URL out to friends and family right there, or you can paste the new album's link into an email message yourself and send it around. If you put a password on your pictures, be sure to give it.

That's it. You've just created an online photo album—no glue stick or plastic sheets necessary.

Choosing a Photo-Sharing Site

The big photo-sharing sites all give you a place to publicly post your pictures and offer optional services like photo prints. Some may only give you a certain amount of space to store pictures online, especially if you have a free basic account with the site. If you're a prolific photographer (or have a brand new photogenic kitten/baby/antique car), you may quickly max out the amount of space you're allotted, but you can get more room to show off your handiwork with an upgraded account or additional fee.

Flickr

As mentioned earlier in the chapter, Flickr (*www.flickr.com*) is a great place to find photos, but you can also use it to share your own. With a Flickr account, you can upload photos from your computer, send photos straight onto your page by emailing them, or send them directly from your camera-equipped cellphone; Flickr supplies you with the email address needed to post the images. You can order prints from a Flickr partner and, if you have your own blog (page 357), you can also send copies of your pix right to your Web journal as well.

A free Flickr account lets you upload 20 megabytes' worth of pictures a month. Flickr doesn't measure that 20 megabytes by the amount of space your pictures take up on a hard drive, though, but by how much *bandwidth* you take up to get them online. Bandwidth is the amount of data you can transfer over a network from one computer to another.

Tip: High-resolution photos can weigh in at about one or two megabytes apiece, which quickly eats up your Flickr limit. Lots of pixels are great for quality prints, but a photo needs far fewer dots to look good on a computer screen. Reducing copies of your pictures to Web-friendly sizes, therefore, lets you upload more of them to Flickr; programs like iPhoto or Photoshop Elements can shrink a 2 MB picture down to a mere 300 kilobytes and still have it look fine online.

So why should you care about the bandwidth limit? Because the site's keeping tabs on your bandwidth usage—and not the amount of hard drive space you're occupying—deleting photos you've already uploaded doesn't give you the ability to add more pictures if you've already hit your monthly bandwidth allowance. You either have to wait until the bandwidth meter is reset the first day of each month or give Flickr some money for an upgraded account.

If you choose a *paid* Flickr account for $25 a year, you get two gigabytes of uploads, unlimited photo sets (Flickr's version of the "album" feature in most photo organizer programs), ad-free pages, and permanent storage for archiving your high-resolution shots. (Free accounts get only three photo sets and can display only the 200 most recent photos.)

Once you're signed in to Flickr, you're ready to upload photos. Click the Upload link at the top of the page. The site gives you two ways to upload your pictures. You can use the Web form on the Upload page to manually select and tag six pictures at a time, as shown in Figure 13-3, or you can download the free Flickr Uploadr program that lets you put up a pile of pictures all at once. There's a link for the Flickr Uploadr on the main Upload page, and the software works with most versions of Windows and Mac OS X 10.3 or later.

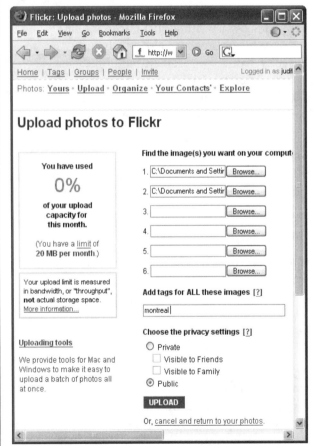

Figure 13-3:
Flickr gives you a Web form to upload six pictures at a time from your computer to the site. To add a photo, click the Browse button and navigate to the place it lives on your hard drive. Once you select the image and tell Flickr to upload it, a copy of the picture is added to your photostream (page 231).

Tip: Industrious Mac/Flickr fans have also created their own Mac-friendly upload programs (available right on Flickr.com), including a plug-in that lets you send photos right from iPhoto to Flickr—an incredibly convenient feature.

Using Flickr's privacy settings, you can restrict pictures to just people you designate as Family, just Friends (in case you don't want your Family to see those shots of you with the lampshade on your head), or both.

Once you've got your photos uploaded, you can use the Flickr Organizr to arrange them in sets or *pools* (page 231). There's a lot more fun on Flickr, so the best way to see it all is to sign up and dive in.

Shutterfly

If you want to make things with your photos (including prints) as well as share them online, Shutterfly (*www.shutterfly.com*) has plenty of projects for you. Like Flickr, you can either upload photos through Shutterfly's Web page or with free utility software provided by the site after you've signed up and created a Shutterfly account. You can do basic photo editing with the site's free tools, like crop images, apply color effects and borders, reduce red eye, and add captions to your images.

When you upload your pictures, the site guides you through sending out email invitations for people to come see the photos at your own Web page address, with optional password protection. People on your list have the opportunity to order prints of your work from Shutterfly, so Grandma can take matters into her own hands if she feels she's not getting enough action shots of the grandkids to suit her.

You can make all sorts of things out of your uploaded photos and order the finished products: photo books, calendars, coffee mugs, T-shirts, tote bags, playing cards, mouse pads, coasters, jigsaw puzzles, and more. All kinds of photo albums and brag books are available, too; you can even reproduce a photo on canvas with fade-resistant inks. For about $150, that shot of the two of you at the Left Bank café on your honeymoon can become a 24×36-inch framed portrait hanging over the couch.

Snapfish

Snapfish (*www.snapfish.com*) doesn't care if you don't have a digital camera. It politely offers to process your 35mm and APS film rolls, send you prints and negatives, and put all the pictures online—all for $3 and mailing costs.

If you do have a digital camera, you can upload your images right from your computer, email them from a computer or cameraphone, and order prints.

A Snapfish account is free and lets you store as many pictures as you'd like. You can let your friends and family see your online albums in the usual way: sending them an email invitation with a Web link and a password. Like Shutterfly, you have basic image-editing tools at your disposal to crop, rotate, and adjust colors in your pictures.

Along with film processing, Snapfish makes its cash by selling you all sorts of objects adorned with your images—mini-soccer balls, shirt-wearing teddy bears, golf towels, candy tins, boxer shorts, baby bibs, pillowcases, and more—to show off your photographic efforts on a variety of surfaces.

FREQUENTLY ASKED QUSTION

Tag! You're a Hit!

What's all this noise about "tagging" photos? Why would I want to do that?

Before tagging came in vogue with people who like to organize things, most photos on the computer were stored in folders, which were often stored in *other* folders. Unless all these folders and subfolders were clearly labeled and meticulously filed, finding the exact image you were looking for could take some time, especially if it was buried two or three folders deep—or even stuck in the wrong folder.

Tagging changes the way you find photos because it lets you search for pictures based on their content rather than where you stored them. Many photo-sharing Web sites and most photo-organizer programs (including Photoshop Elements, iPhoto, and Picasa) let you apply keywords (tags) to your photos, which help to identify their subjects.

For example, you can use the keywords *Ralph, birthday,* and *2006* for that set of pictures from Ralph's birthday party in 2006. Later, when you search the site or your software for any of the terms, you're rewarded with all the pictures that contain those keywords—without having to dig around through folders or albums for them.

As you can see on Flickr, tags are essential for finding photo in any decent amount of time, especially when there are millions to look through. But even if you don't share pictures online, keeping them organized with tags can spare you hours of stomping through picture folders looking for that one perfect shot you want to use for your New Year's card.

Kodak EasyShare Gallery

Kodak's online gallery (the sharing site formerly known as Ofoto) adds a sense of history to the notion of Web-based picture pages. Kodak, after all, has been in the consumer photography business since 1888, which is plenty of time to figure out how people like to take and share pictures. It even offers famous archival images from *Life* magazine for sale in its gallery pages, including the photograph of Margaret Bourke-White snapping pictures atop the Chrysler Building, an astronaut walking on the moon, and a cow wearing a cowboy hat (Figure 13-4).

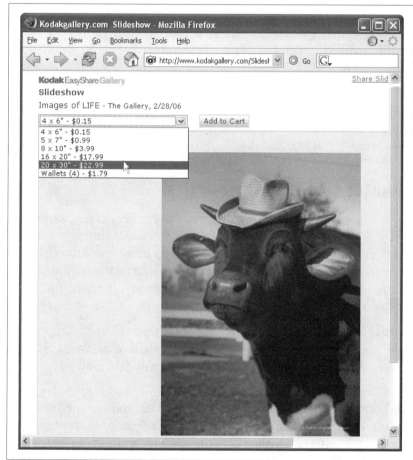

Figure 13-4:
In addition to giving your photos an online home, Kodak offers to sell you vintage Life magazine reproductions in a variety of sizes. Of course, you can also order prints of your own pictures, too.

To get started on the personal part of the Kodak Gallery, sign up for a free account at *www.kodakgallery.com*. (If you have a Kodak digital camera, the EasyShare software that came with it makes it easy to upload your pictures to your EasyShare Gallery page.)

With your free account all set up, you can upload images one at a time at the Web site, or in batches with special Mac or Windows software. Like Snapfish, Kodak also accepts and processes film rolls by mail for a few bucks; it will automatically park digital copies of the resulting prints on your EasyShare page for you.

You can send out invitations to select viewers, enhance your images with basic editing tools, and create online slideshows from your pictures. If you like one of your pictures so much you want to carry it around with you like a wallet photo, you can transfer your photos to your cellphone with the Kodak Mobile Service for $3 a month.

This being Kodak, you can order all sizes and kinds of prints right from the site, plus photo-decorated tchotchkes like mugs, tote bags, and calendars. Paid "Premier" Gallery accounts, starting at $25 a year, give you more flexibility in what your home page looks like and discounts on prints.

Sending Photos to a Printing Service

All four of the big photo-sharing sites offer printing services, should you decide you want some hard copies of your pictures. True, printing photos at home on an inkjet photo printer has an appeal all its own—namely, that you get the pictures *right now*. But, the truth is, when you factor in the special photo paper and all the ink those printers guzzle down, you might find that, economically speaking, ordering prints online is actually a better deal.

Flickr, Shutterfly, Snapfish, and Kodak let you order prints in all shapes and sizes and have them mailed right to you. The Web is also crawling with services that do nothing but create prints (and de-emphasize all the photo-sharing stuff):

- **Winkflash.** You can upload your photos to Winkflash and use the site's free organizing and editing program (Windows only) before ordering prints. If you connect to the Internet with a dial-up modem and don't particularly relish the thought of spending the entire weekend uploading photos, Winkflash will mail you a CD; you burn your photos to it and mail it back to them with your print order form. (*www.winkflash.com*)

- **dotPhoto.** With free software for Windows folks called dotPhotoGo, you can crop, adjust, and upload your digital images to the site. Basic membership is free, provides Web space to show off pictures, and lets you order 3×5-inch prints for 15 cents each. Monthly plans ($5 and up) give you a certain allotment of prints per month. (*www.dotphoto.com*)

- **Walgreens.** The venerable Main Street drugstore chain has gone high tech. You can upload your pictures to Walgreens' photo site or email them in (even by cameraphone) to place your print order. If you live near a Walgreens store, you can pick them up in person an hour later; alternatively, the service can mail you the goods. The digital pictures you upload for printing stay on the site—no charge—and can be viewed by your pals. (*http://photo.walgreens.com*)

Wal-Mart stores (*www.walmart.com/photo-center*) have jumped into online photo-processing with in-store pickup as well, so check with your area stores to see if that's an option.

Greeting Cards the Online Way

You don't have to spend two hours and a trip to the mall just to give someone a Hallmark moment. Like everyone else, Hallmark has moved online (*www.hallmark.com*); among other perks, it lets you send free electronic greeting cards to people's email boxes.

To send an e-card, sign up for a free Hallmark account, pick out a style and personalize it with your own greeting, fill in your recipient's email address, and send it on its way.

For a few dollars, you can also choose a physical greeting card, direct Hallmark to print your personal greeting on it, address the card to your recipient, add your return address, and mail the whole thing off. (Emily Post Alert: If it's a sympathy card, paper cards are still probably a better way to go than an e-greeting.)

American Greetings (*www.americangreetings.com*) offers e-cards as well, and you can download and print your own cards and other projects. They offer several monthly membership plans based on the types of things you want to do, as does its subsidiary, BlueMountain (*www.bluemountain.com*).

If you're looking for personalized cards, say for a college graduation announcement, don't forget the photo-sharing and printing sites, which will only be too happy to whip up 50 custom greeting cards or postcards from one of your own pictures.

Tip: Mac OS X fans can order and buy prints, cards, calendars, and photo-books right from the iPhoto program that comes free on new Macs. Those with .Mac accounts ($100 a year at *www. apple.com/dotmac*) get a gigabyte of online storage to use for email accounts and displaying photos.

If you, your friends, and family use iPhoto 6 (or have an *RSS reader*—see page 113), you can even publish *photocasts*. These are sets of pictures that you've broadcast to selected friends and family, which they can view online at no charge. What's cool is that every time you update your set of "published" photos, your subscribers can see the changes, too.

Sending Photos via Email

If you just have a few photos you want to share—or would prefer to keep Web sites out of it for whatever reason—sending pictures as email attachments (page 274) is still a perfectly fine way to send them around to your friends.

There are several ways to attach a picture (or pictures) to an email message, including:

- In Windows, right-click a photo file or selected group of files (on your Desktop or in your My Pictures folder or wherever) and choose Send to → Mail Recipient from the shortcut menu. Your email program opens a new outgoing message, with the photo already attached; just address and send.

- On the Mac, drag photo files from your desktop onto the *Dock icon* of your email program (Mail, Entourage, or whatever). Once again, the program is smart enough to get the hint; it creates an outgoing message and attaches the files, ready to send. (You can also drag photos into the *body* of an out-going message you've already created.)

    If you keep your pictures in iPhoto, it's equally easy: Select a photo (or several) and then click the Email button at the bottom of the window. The beauty of this approach is that iPhoto offers to resize the photos to screen resolution before sending them (read on).

- If an outgoing message is already open and addressed in your email program, click the Attach File button. The standard Open File dialog box appears; navigate to the place on your hard drive where the picture you want to send lives.

Before you try any of these techniques, however, steel yourself for the Email Resolution Nightmare.

The Email Resolution Nightmare

The most important thing to know about emailing photos is this: *full-size photos are usually too big to email.*

Suppose, for example, that you want to send three photos to some friends—terrific shots you captured with your 5-megapixel camera.

First, a little math: A typical 5-megapixel shot might consume two megabytes of disk space. So, sending along just three shots would make at least a 6-megabyte package.

Why is that bad? First, it will take forever to send (and for your recipients to download). Dial-up email accounts gag and crash as they attempt to retrieve a message with a huge photo attachment.

Second, the average high-resolution shot is much too big for the screen. It does you no good to email somebody a 5-megapixel photo (3008×2000 pixels) when his monitor's maximum resolution is only 1024×768. If you're lucky, his graphics software will intelligently shrink the image to fit his screen; otherwise, he'll see only a gigantic nostril filling his screen. But you'll still have to contend with his irritation at having waited 24 minutes for so much superfluous resolution.

Finally, the typical Internet account has a limited mailbox size. If the mail collection exceeds 5 MB or so, that mailbox is automatically shut down until it's emptied. Your 6-megabyte photo package will push your hapless recipients' mailboxes over their limits. They'll miss out on important messages that bounce as a result.

For years, this business of emailing photos has baffled beginners and enraged experts—and, for many people, the confusion continues.

So, how do you avoid the too-big photo problem?

- **On the Mac.** iPhoto offers to shrink your big photo files into mail-friendly sizes, like 640×480 pixels.

- **In Windows.** As shown in Figure 13-5, Windows XP offers to resize your photos for email when you attach them from the desktop, so take it up on its kind offer. Most consumer-oriented photo programs—Photoshop Elements and Google's free Picasa program, for example (*http://picasa.google.com*)—make this offer, too.

Reducing the image size not only makes it easier to email, it makes the photo easier to see as an email attachment on the recipient's end.

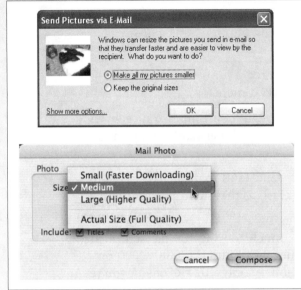

Figure 13-5:
Top: Windows XP can take a load off your email by reducing the size of the photo attachment so that it still looks good but is much smaller and easier to send.

Bottom: Mac OS X offers similar assistance in iPhoto, which can send picture attachments in several sizes.

File Formats

The JPG format is the lingua franca of photos on the Internet; both Web sites and email programs can display them. Conveniently, that's exactly the same format produced by most digital cameras.

There are a couple of cases when an emailed photo might show up blank in your audience's inboxes:

- **It wasn't actually a JPEG file.** Fancier cameras can take pictures in something called RAW format, which professionals like because it offers fantastic editing flexibility in Photoshop (but which consumes appalling amounts of disk space). Email programs (and Web browsers) generally can't display RAW files.

- **It wasn't in RGB mode.** Most cameras describe the colors in a photo using a scheme called *RGB* (in which each pixel has a specified amount of Red, Green, and Blue). It's possible, however, that you've sent a photo that somehow got converted to the CMYK mode used in the printing/publishing industry. (It stands for Cyan, Magenta, Yellow, and *Key*, better known as Black.) CMYK photos generally don't show up in email programs, either.

So, if you're mailing out digital images, here's a checklist to make sure your recipients have the best shot at opening the files:

- Use the JPEG format, in RGB mode.

- Reduce the size of large files to make them easier to handle. Most photo programs have a pre-set resolution of 640×480 pixels for emailed images, which is a decent size to see and send photos.

- Don't send too many images at once, so as not to overwhelm your recipient's mail program—or senses.

If you have other questions about sending files by email, getting and organizing email, or even how to set up your email account, you don't have to go far for answers. In fact, just flip to the next chapter.

5

Part Five: Communicating with Others

Email

Email has long been considered the Internet's first *killer app* (killer application)—a software program so desirable and useful that people will go out and buy a computer just to run it. People were emailing each other even before the Web became world wide. Today, it's become a vital tool for business, education, and haranguing elected officials.

And no wonder. Like telephone calls, you can initiate a transaction anytime you like—but unlike phone calls, the recipient doesn't have to interrupt dinner to get the message. Like postal mail, email offers a handy printed record of the "conversation" so far; but unlike postal mail, email is essentially free.

There are some choices to be made along the way, though, including what kind of email program to use and how to set it up. This chapter explains what your options are.

As wonderful as email can be for keeping up with faraway friends, you're probably familiar with its dark side—the spam, viruses, and identity-theft scams that come along with it. That stuff's covered here, too, and you'll learn how to protect yourself so that your killer app doesn't kill your computer.

Email Program vs. Web-Based Email

There are two basic ways to check your email: using a special, separate email program or on a Web page. Both have their pros and cons, and both have gotten much more flexible over the years about how and where you can pick up your mail.

How Computer-Based Mail Works

Many people use a dedicated mail program to download messages—programs like Outlook, Outlook Express, Entourage, Mail, Thunderbird, or Eudora. These programs download your mail, display it for you, and let you send messages of your own. These email programs—sometimes called email *clients*—live on your computer. They generally store all your messages on your hard drive, not on the Internet; the advantage here is that you can work on your email even when you're in a plane, train, automobile, or otherwise not online. (There are exceptions to this, covered later in the chapter.)

When you choose a program to use, you have to configure the software to work with your Internet service provider's *mail server*. A mail server is a computer that serves as an electronic post office. Like the post office, it has mailboxes for all the people who have email accounts with the ISP; it stores your incoming mail until you "pick it up."

When you use your email program to check for new messages, it knocks on the mail server's door with your password and asks for the mail addressed to your account. The mail server hands it over to your mail program, which downloads and deposits the new messages in the inbox on your own computer.

Here are some points to consider if you're on the fence about getting a computer-based mail account.

- **Pros.** Because they're full-fledged software programs, dedicated mail applications have more built-in features to make mail easier to use and organize. You often get more robust spell checkers and the power to set up mailboxes for multiple accounts—like your work and personal email.

  Most programs provide simulated folders, so you can organize all the messages from certain people or concerning certain topics. You also get customizable toolbars and can do fun things like pick your own audio alerts for incoming messages.

  You can also set up an unlimited amount of *mail rules,* or conditions and instructions that tell your mail program what to do with certain types of messages. For example, if you've created a special folder called Mom in your mail program, you can make a mail rule that tells the program to look at the return address of each new message and send all messages from *mom@younevercall.com* right into your Mom folder so they don't get lost in the jumble of your inbox.

  Junk mail filters, which use elaborate mail rules to screen incoming messages for the scent of spam, are included with most mail programs (Outlook

Express 6 is a notable exception). Junk mail filters, which you can fine-tune if you find they're tagging your friends as spammers, can be set to route unwanted mail into a Junk folder or right into the Trash.

Note, too, that a separate email program keeps your old mail right there on your hard drive, which means that you always have access to it in case you need to look up a previous conversation.

Finally, a dedicated email program doesn't slap ads on your outgoing messages. (Web-based email services, described next, often do stamp your emails with commercial messages.)

- **Cons.** It takes a few minutes to configure your mail program's settings so it knows how to find your mail server. (The steps are explained in detail on page 267.)

As noted previously, your downloaded mail lives on your computer's hard drive where you can always get to your old messages. There's a downside to this, though: If something goes wrong with your hard drive or your mail program crashes and corrupts your mailbox files, those messages are gone forever (unless you've backed up your computer).

Many ISPs scan incoming messages for viruses; some mail programs, including Outlook Express and Thunderbird, have security features built-in to help stop viruses from spreading. But, even so, if you use Windows, you may want to invest in antivirus software that scans your incoming messages for infection because these programs usually catch newer viruses faster. (All the antivirus programs covered in Chapter 21 do this.)

How Web-Based Email Works

Some people prefer to work on their email on a Web page (instead of a special email program), using what's known as a *Web-based email* service. Hotmail, Gmail, and Yahoo are the Big Three.

Most Web-based email systems work like this: you sign up for an account. Whenever you want to go postal, you log into your account on the Web site and work right in your browser window.

- **Pros.** The best part about Web-based email is that you can check your mail and send messages from any Internet-connected computer. Even if you use a Mac at home in Cleveland, you can check your Web-based email from the PC in the hotel lobby in Dublin and not miss a message. Your email address book is online, too. You're not even giving up the ability to save messages on your hard drive at home; you can save online messages at any point.

Another big plus: Your email address never changes (unless you want it to). When people move or switch ISPs, they typically have to give up their old email addresses (for example, *guitarman@aol.com* has to tell everyone that he's now *guitarman@@earthlink.net*). A Web-based email address, in contrast, never changes. You can move to a new city, state, or even a different country, or you can fire AOL as your ISP and hire Earthlink; the point is, it doesn't matter *who* provides your Internet connection. With a Web-based email account, you never have to change your address.

Web-based mail also may work better when sending mail from certain WiFi hotspots (page 32). That's because an increasing number of WiFi providers block traditional, PC-based mail services to keep spammers from parking down the street and flooding the network with spam. That doesn't effect Web-based email, which handles mail differently.

Some people find Web-based mail easier to set up because they're spared the chore of configuring those annoying settings called SMTP, POP3, and/or IMAP (see the box on page 262). Most Web-based email sites offer ways to send copies of your mail to a dedicated email program like Outlook Express, if you wish, giving you the best of both worlds: You can read and respond to email while on the road, and have that same mail waiting for you in your computer's inbox when you return home. That lets you store a master record of all your mail on your computer for reference.

Many Web-based mail services now screen messages for viruses ahead of time, so you have much less chance of getting your own computer infected with a wormy file attachment. Many services give you a basic junk mail or spam filter, too, that automatically routes offers for herbal remedies and fine jewelry right into a holding pen and away from your real mail.

Many Web-based mail services can handle HTML messages just fine and offer their own tools for jazzing up your text if you want to stand out from the plain-text crowd. Spell checkers are a standard now, too.

Best of all, the three Web-based email services described on page 261 are free.

- **Cons.** The biggest problem with Web-based services is that you have to go online to work with your email. You can't work on a plane or a train (unless you've set up your mail program to grab a copy of all your Web-based mail, too).

Furthermore, some people think it's creepy—and possibly a security risk— to store their email on any computer other than their own. But this shouldn't be particularly frightening; after all, your PC-based email travels through dozens of other computers (each with its own potential security problems) before safely arriving in your Outlook Express inbox. There's nothing inherently insecure about Web-based email.

Space may be an issue, too. Most free services limit the amount of mail you can keep in your account (those are *their* servers, after all). You may also have limitations on the size of the file attachments you can send and receive. And if you don't log in for a few months, your service may think you've bailed on them and delete your waiting mail.

Free Web-based mail services don't give you as much freedom to customize your mailbox as computer-based mail programs do, either. For instance, Gmail doesn't let you make your own mail folders. Yahoo Mail limits you to 15 mail rules (automated message filing).

Note: This chapter describes the two ways people check their email: in a Mac or PC program, or on the Web. But other people find *both* systems attractive. They'll sign up for a Web-based service to keep in touch while traveling, and keep their standard, PC-based email program for use at home or work. There's nothing wrong with having several email addresses from different types of email systems.

	Yahoo Mail	Gmail	Hotmail	Outlook Express	Outlook	Thunder-bird	Eudora	Apple Mail
Storage limits	1 GB	2.5 GB	250 MB	Depends on your computer	Depends on your computer	Depends on your computer	Depends on your computer	Depends on your computer
Junk mail filters	Yes	Yes	Yes	No	Yes	Yes	Yes	Yes
HTML mail	Yes	No (Rich text only)	Yes	Yes	Yes	Yes	Yes	Display only
Spell checker	Yes	Yes	Yes	No	Yes	Yes	Yes	Yes
Multiple Mail Accounts	Yes	Yes[a]	No	Yes	Yes	Yes	Yes	Yes
Extra Folders	Yes	No	No	Yes	Yes	Yes	Yes	Yes
Mail Rules/ Filters	Yes	Yes	Yes	Yes	Yes	Yes	Yes	Yes

[a] The Gmail Manager extension for the Firefox and Mozilla browsers lets you keep an eye on new messages in all your Gmail accounts, if you happen to have more than one. Download it for free from the "Missing CD" page at *www.missingmanuals.com*.

Email = Postcards

As noted previously, the typical email message may fly through dozens of computers on its way to its destination. An evildoer at any one of these locations could, in theory, have a look at what you wrote.

Now, that's pretty unlikely, and actual stories of this happening are virtually nonexistent. (Sure, newspaper headlines sometimes describe bad guys who were busted based on their email, but those messages are generally brought to light the more traditional way: the recipient turned it in to the police.)

Still, a good rule of thumb for email safety is to never put anything into a plain email message that you wouldn't put on the back of a postcard. Be especially careful with personal info like credit card numbers or your Social Security digits.

The truly paranoid, and those who work in industries where corporate secrecy is key, should consider programs that protect your messages from random eyes. PGP, which stands for Pretty Good Privacy, is a well-known program that encrypts your message into undecipherable gibberish; your recipient requires a serial number to unlock and read the message's true text.

The PGP software is available in a commercial version at *www.pgp.com*; an older freeware edition and instructions for using the program are at *www.pgpi.org*. Encrypting your mail can keep it more secure, but it may be a bit too much for messages like, "Don't forget to bring home Pampers."

Dedicated Email Programs

Most Internet service providers don't care what program you use as long as you configure it properly. All Windows-based PCs come with Outlook Express, and all Mac OS X systems come with Mail, so, if anything, you've already got *one* program you can use for email. And if you don't like what you've got, you can switch to something else.

Outlook Express

Many people look no further than Windows' Outlook Express (Start → All Programs → Outlook Express) to take care of their email. Legions have grown up with this freebie, tossed into every edition of Windows since 1996.

Outlook Express (see Figure 14-1) isn't particularly fancy, but it handles the basics very well. It can send, receive, delete, print, forward, sort, and file your email; manage your address book; send and receive files; and even block email from people you've marked as spammers, enemies, or just plain annoying.

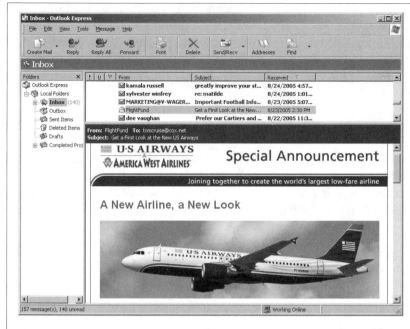

Figure 14-1:
Outlook Express lives on the Start menu of nearly every PC sold today. Like most email programs, Outlook Express stores your mail in folders along its left edge. Incoming mail moves straight into your inbox for you to read; your currently selected message appears in the Preview window. Your sent mail heads for the outbox, ready for Outlook Express to send. After sending the mail, Outlook Express places a copy of the message in your Sent Items folder for reference. Deleted mail goes into your Deleted Items folder. And Drafts contains mail you've started, but haven't yet finished.

Note: A Mac version of Outlook Express once existed, but it never made the leap to OS X. Microsoft still makes a very good email program for the Mac—called Entourage—but you have to buy it. It's part of Microsoft Office.

- **Pros.** Outlook Express is fairly easy to use, free, and already on your PC. Many people fire it up and never turn back. Still, if you ever upgrade to a more powerful email program, your old email isn't trapped: Nearly every email program can import Outlook Express's messages and contacts. iPods can even carry your contacts from Outlook Express or Outlook.

- **Cons.** Because it's used so widely, Outlook Express is a big target for viruses, worms, spammers, spyware, and other dark forces. The program shares Internet Explorer's vulnerabilities, as well, because it borrows Internet Explorer's code for displaying messages. And many viruses peek into Outlook Express's address book, emailing a disguised copy of themselves to everyone listed there.

You can minimize these threats by making sure Windows Update is set to Automatic, which lets Microsoft automatically patch newly discovered security problems. (To do so, choose Start → Control Panel → System and click the Automatic Updates tab.) Add an antivirus program (page 405), and Outlook Express stays reasonably safe from viruses.

The biggest gripe about Outlook Express boils down to its lack of a spell checker. That's Microsoft's subtle way of prodding you to buy Outlook, the full-featured email program included with the pricey Microsoft Office. It's also a way to push you into buying Microsoft Word. (When you install Word, Outlook relies on Word's spell checker, giving you an easy way to proofread your outgoing email.)

Outlook

Outlook (*www.microsoft.com/outlook*) is Outlook Express's bigger, cooler, more talented older brother. You can buy it for around $100, or pay even more money and get it as part of Microsoft Office, the suite that brings Word, Excel, and PowerPoint to the party.

Outlook does more than just fetch your mail. It's a full-on *personal information manager* for Windows, meaning that it also has a calendar program and to-do list. Although it won't pick up your dry cleaning, it can send you little alerts to nag you into remembering to pick it up yourself.

- **Pros.** Outlook mail is vast and versatile, allowing you to check messages from multiple email accounts and store them in folders and subfolders so you can keep track of all the correspondence on a project or with a particular group of people. There's a built-in dictionary, plus a thesaurus and links to research sites if you're working on long, complex messages. Outlook also has a built-in spam filter, although it's not much of a match for today's flood of junk mail.

- **Cons.** Outlook has been plagued with many of the truck-sized security holes that have swallowed Internet Explorer and Outlook Express. The program is so feature-packed, it might be overkill if all you want to do is send and collect messages. And it costs a lot.

Thunderbird

Thunderbird (*www.mozilla.org/thunderbird*) is a free, very good email program for Mac or Windows.

Note: It's brought to you by the Mozilla Foundation, the nonprofit organization that also unleashed the popular Firefox Web browser (page 58). Both Thunderbird and Firefox are *open source,* meaning the programs' code is freely available for any programmer to inspect or modify. With everything on the drawing board, some miscreants can look for weak spots to unleash viruses. But this open approach also lets other programmers find potential flaws and fix them before the attacks occur.

So far, Thunderbird contains far fewer security problems than Outlook Express.

- **Pros.** Thunderbird's open source underpinnings let programmers offer small add-on programs called *extensions*—spam killers, address book enhancers, duplicate message removers, and so on. By downloading only the extensions you need from inside the program (Tools → Extensions → Get More Extensions), you can keep the program small, speedy, and free of long menus with unused features.

  Like most competing email programs, Thunderbird automatically imports your information from Outlook Express (as well as from Outlook or Eudora), keeping your originals safe inside Outlook Express. Thunderbird looks and feels like Outlook Express, but with a few more features: A built-in RSS reader (page 111), for instance, alerts you to updates on your favorite Web sites. New features appear almost daily as programmers release more extensions.

- **Cons.** Although Mozilla's Web site is well written, with Frequently Asked Questions areas and a searchable support database, there's no phone number to call for free tech support. Instead, you have to seek help on the community forums (*www.mozilla.org/support/* and, under the Thunderbird header, click Community Support Forums). Or, you can call a company called InfoSpan (1-888-586-4539) and pay $40 per tech-support problem.

Eudora

Eudora (*www.eudora.com*) was named after the esteemed Southern writer Eudora Welty, author of the classic short story "Why I Live at the P.O." It's been around for years and has a devoted following, most of whom are determined to cut down on the number of Microsoft products on their computers.

If that quest appeals to you, your biggest challenge is deciding which version is for you:

- **Paid Mode.** The $50 version, used mainly by businesses, includes 12 months of free upgrades, six free calls to tech support (within the first year), and a spam filter.

- **Sponsored Mode.** This free version lacks the spam filter and the free tech support. It also displays a small ad in the screen's bottom corner, as well as two ad buttons on the top menu.

- **Light Mode.** If you find ads so offensive that you're willing to sacrifice the program's spell checker to rid yourself of them, choose this option.

All three versions of Eudora handle the same email basics as Outlook Express. Installation is easy, too: The program visits Outlook Express to import your email account settings as well as your previously received messages. (It only *copies* your messages; your originals remain safe with Outlook Express.) When the program finishes installing itself, it appears on the screen with all your old email waiting for you.

- **Pros.** Eudora comes in both PC and Mac versions, a plus if you find yourself computing on both types of computers. To help keep your different email conversations separate, you can assign different colors to different "conversations" (chains of related email back-and-forths).

  The program also makes extensive use of *tabs*—buttons that resemble filing-folder tabs. Click a tab on your Mailboxes window, for instance, and the window switches from a row of in- and outboxes to a file browser, a handy way to drag a file into an outgoing email. Click the Mailboxes tab to bring back your inbox, outbox, and other mailboxes.

- **Cons.** Many people find Eudora to be overkill, yet, frustratingly, it lacks some of the details of Outlook Express. For example, it doesn't show how many unread messages are waiting in each folder, nor does it let you create and nestle subfolders inside your inbox to track different projects. And although the ads try to be unobtrusive, it's annoying when a misplaced click on your part interrupts your workflow with a word from the sponsor.

Apple Mail

This freebie mail program that comes with Mac OS X has an elegant look and meshes well with the system's other staples, including the iChat instant messaging program and the Mac OS X Address Book.

For example, if you're logged into iChat while you're catching up on your correspondence, Mail displays a green dot next to the names of people in your Mac OS X Address Book who are also online. If you want to contact the person directly instead of sending off a whole email, just click the name in the mailbox window and press ⌘-Shift-I to open an iChat message neatly addressed to your pal.

Mail is smartly designed, thanks to Apple's attention to visual detail (subtle colors and sleek icons, as shown in Figure 14-2). A software assistant guides you through setting up Mail for the first time and can import old messages from Eudora, Entourage, Outlook Express for Mac, Netscape mail, and Claris Emailer. You can send and receive mail from multiple accounts, all in the same window.

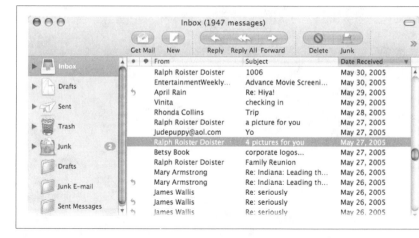

Figure 14-2:
Apple Mail, which comes free with the Mac OS X operating system, is Apple's counterpart to Microsoft's Outlook Express for Windows. The program handles all the standard mail chores and includes a Junk Filter that shovels spam into its own mailbox so you don't have to worry about it touching your real messages.

Apple Mail has its own spell checker and junk mail filter. Using the Spotlight file-finding feature of Mac OS X 10.4 and later, Mail can quickly search through thousands of messages for that one note you need with the directions to the wedding on Saturday—without even having to switch to the Mail program first. When someone sends you several picture attachments, click the Slideshow button in the top part of the message window, and Mail plays the photos one at a time as a full-screen slideshow. It also syncs up great with .Mac mail on the Web (page 267).

The program has a few bugs, and it sometimes breaks long URLs pasted into messages so the links won't work when clicked. But, overall, Apple Mail can easily handle most standard mail chores and look good doing it.

Tip: If you want to really learn the ups and downs of Mail inside and out, visit the Hawk Wings blog at *www.hawkwings.net*. Tips, tricks, and workarounds for using Mail are plentiful. For example, to keep Mail from stomping on your long URLs, the site suggests going to TinyURL (*http://tinyurl.com*) and pasting your big unwieldy Web address into the form on the main page. Once you click the Make TinyURL! button, the site converts your lengthy Web address into something like *http://tinyurl.com/okum2*, which is short enough to survive without the Mail program breaking it.

Web-Based Email Services

In the B.G. era (Before Google), most Web-based mail services offered only a couple of megabytes of mail storage—10 megs if you were lucky. For some people, that was enough, although 10 megabytes can fill up awfully quickly thanks to the Internet's spam plague.

Alphabet Soup: IMAP, POP3, and SMTP

When it comes to actually setting up an email account for the first time, the onslaught of acronyms can seem overwhelming. POP3? IMAP? SMTP? *Whaaaaaa?*

All three terms refer to email *protocols:* ways of sending, storing, and retrieving messages so every computer along the delivery chain knows what to expect. Your ISP decides which one of these you use, so check the account information and setup instructions you got from them when you signed up. Here's what it all means.

POP3 (Post Office Protocol, Version 3). This is still the most common way of receiving email; most ISPs still use POP mail, as it's casually known.

In a POP mail system, your computer picks up your email from a centrally located mail-server computer. Think of this server as a post office that holds your mail until you and your computer come get it.

When you turn on your email program and ask it to check your mail, your POP program (Eudora, Outlook Express, Mail, or whatever) presents your account password to the mail server and asks if there are any new messages. If so, the server sends any new messages and then deletes its own copies of those files so it doesn't fill up with old mail.

Most POP3 mail servers can hold around 10 megabytes of messages for each person. To prevent the dreaded *bounce* (messages returned to sender), check your mail frequently.

Some Web-based mail services, including Gmail, can forward messages to your POP3 program at no charge (page 266); others, like Hotmail, want you to pay for the privilege.

IMAP (Internet Message Access Protocol). This offers a newer way of getting your email; it's gaining some acceptance among providers like AOL and .Mac.

Unlike POP3 mail, where you download messages to your computer from a mail server, your IMAP mail stays on the server. You can move from computer to computer, or from computer to Black-Berry—the messages are always there, organized in folders just the way you left them. Large corporations, university mail systems, and other large networks typically use IMAP.

If you don't know whether your ISP uses POP or IMAP, call its customer service department and ask, or check its Web site for the email settings and mail server addresses you need. You'll need that information when you set up your email program for the first time and it asks you what to use for your *incoming* mail server.

As for your *outgoing* mail server, choose SMTP (Simple Mail Transfer Protocol) and enter any other information your ISP has provided for security or authentication purposes—which varies by ISP. (SMTP refers to the system Outlook Express and many other mail programs use to send out your messages.)

But then Gmail arrived with a mighty *whomp* in 2004, offering each person a whole *gigabyte* of space to store mail (that's more than 1,000 megabytes).

Suddenly, the rest of the Webmail companies had to play catch-up. Yahoo and Apple's .Mac service now offer a gigabyte of space, too; Hotmail upped its allowance to 250 megabytes. Meanwhile, Gmail has quietly continued to raise its total; it's now nearly 3 gigabytes per person.

Yahoo Mail

Yahoo Mail (*http://mail.yahoo.com*) offers a one-gigabyte mail limit, plus virus scanning and spam filtering. If a virus is discovered in one of your incoming messages, Yahoo cleans it for you with Norton Antivirus (page 407), disarming its evil payload before it reaches your computer. The site also looks for mass-produced junk mail and reroutes the offers for Rolexes and questionable pharmaceuticals into a Bulk mail folder.

As for mail handling, Yahoo lets you set up to 15 *filters* (sorting rules) to help compartmentalize your mail; for example, it can autofile all the messages from people in your book club into a single folder (page 280). To keep annoying people out of your hair, you can block up to 500 addresses from sending mail to you. Yahoo Mail accepts incoming and outgoing file attachments of up to 10 megabytes, which is usually enough for several photos or a PowerPoint presentation file.

The QuickBuilder feature checks the return addresses of the people who've mailed you and lets you add them to your Yahoo Address Book with a mouse click.

And if you travel a lot, Yahoo Mail collects messages from other mail servers (like your work mail or your ISP mail) so you can read it all on your Yahoo account page.

Note: While other Web-based email services just give you the one email address with your account, Yahoo gives you two. Once you sign up and set up your primary account, you can make up a secondary email address. Mail from both accounts show up on the same screen; a menu lets you specify which account to use when you're composing a new message. Having a second email address can be extremely useful, as described on page 255.

Like most free mail services, Yahoo sticks little advertisements at the bottom of your outgoing messages. If you find the ads cheesy and annoying, you can pay Yahoo $20 a year for a Mail Plus account, which gives you ad-free messages, two gigabytes of mail storage, a better spam filter, and the ability to download

Yahoo messages with an email client like Outlook. Paying for a Plus account also ensures that Yahoo won't discard all the messages in your account if you don't log in for four months—another risk of free accounts.

Gmail

With nearly three gigabytes of storage, text-formatting tools, a spell checker, sortable labels, and the super-searchability you'd expect from a Google product, Gmail (*http://gmail.google.com*) is the Webmail service the other guys wish they'd thought of first.

Note: At the time of this writing, you can receive a Gmail account in only one of two ways: through an invitation from an existing account holder or by visiting the Web site with your PC and entering your cellphone number. Google then sends your cellphone a text message with an *invitation code* that you enter at the Gmail site to complete the sign-up process. The cellphone-number business is Google's clever way of ensuring that each person can sign up for only one or maybe two Gmail accounts per person. The point is to thwart spammers and commercial entities who might otherwise abuse the Gmail privilege by snagging up hundreds of gigabytes of free online space.

Once you get a Gmail account, you don't have to worry about hitting your mail limit for quite awhile. You get a spam filter to help block junk, and Google scans for and blocks viruses in attachments; in fact, Google blocks *anything* that's an *executable* file (that is, a program). (While games and shareware programs are executable files, so are viruses.)

You can't make your own folders in Gmail, but you can set up labels for messages from certain people and then sort your mail by label. Click the Edit Labels link on the side of the Gmail window to create a label. In the Gmail Setting area, you can set up filters to tag messages from certain people with one of your custom labels by choosing Filters → Create New Filter. When messages are filtered and labeled, the label name appears next to the subject line. You can sort mail by label when you click a label name on the left side of the Gmail window.

All messages with the same subject line are merged into one big thread Gmail calls a *conversation* (Figure 14-3) that saves you the trouble of digging through your inbox looking for the first few exchanges in your 39-message thread about who's bringing the Chex Mix to the Oscar party next Sunday.

Nor do you have to scroll through all of these messages to see the back-and-forth; Gmail collapses all the message headers into one line until you click a particular one to open it.

Figure 14-3:
Gmail neatly stacks messages in the same thread into "conversations," so you never have to dig around your mailbox looking for the message that started the topic. Click one of the message headers in the conversation to see what it said.

Gmail generates money for Google Inc. in an ingenious and controversial way: It places ads on your screen—clearly labeled and off to the right—when you're reading your *incoming* messages or looking at old messages in your Sent folder. And they're *targeted* ads—that is, ads that pertain to what you're reading. For example, if a friend writes to ask when you get back from your trip to the Napa Valley, you may see ads for California tourism or wine merchants beside the message.

(The controversial part: It makes privacy advocates get all wiggy to know that something is *reading* their messages to find out what they're about. Of course, the truth is, Gmail's inanimate software robots are doing the reading, not actual people.)

Google's text-scanning powers can be used for good, too, especially if you use Google Calendar (page 395). When someone sends you a message about going out to dinner at 8:00 on Saturday night, Gmail recognizes a date and time; you can schedule the event by clicking the Google Calendar link in the Gmail window. Google automatically pops the info into your schedule without you having to type a thing.

One of the coolest things about Gmail is that Google doesn't charge you if you want to download the mail from your account using a standalone email program like Outlook Express or Mail. You just have to pop into your Gmail settings, click the "Forwarding and POP" tab, and tell Gmail to allow POP downloads. (For the poop on POP, check out page 262.) You then have to set up a Gmail account within your email client (page 267).

MSN Hotmail

Microsoft offers several different flavors of Web-based mail: regular free MSN Hotmail, $20-a-year MSN Hotmail Plus, or $10-a-*month* MSN Premium. When you cruise over to *www.hotmail.com* and click the Sign Up button for the free account, Microsoft slyly plants you on an up-sell page with all three of its plans laid out so you can see how many features you get if you cough up the cash.

Note: For $35 a year, Microsoft will sell you a Hotmail account with your *own* name on it, as in *bruce@brucewayne.com*. The company calls the service MSN Personal Address. (You can check to see if your name's available at *http://join.msn.com/en-us/personaladdress/overview*.) People with peculiar names may have more luck than those with more common family names—you're definitely not going to get *john@johnsmith.com* at this point—but it never hurts to check.

As you might expect, the free account gives you the bare minimum. But for many people, it's enough to get by: a 250-megabyte mailbox, junk-mail and phish filters (page 412), virus-scanning, and the ability to swap attachments up to 10 megabytes each. The low-budget Hotmail includes some nice touches, though, including fancy backgrounds, fonts, and layout styles for your messages, plus an online calendar for keeping track of your schedule. You need to check your account at least once every 30 days, or Microsoft will empty out your box.

MSN Hotmail Plus gets you a two-gigabyte mailbox, ad-free messages, and the ability to download and manage your mail with the Outlook Express email client. You can also send attachments up to 20 MB, and you don't have to worry about your account getting whacked if you go backpacking through Europe for a month.

If you aim for the top and get the MSN Premium account, you get special Windows-only software: MSN Internet, which is like Microsoft's version of America Online, sort of a gated Internet community with some members-only material and services like Chat (page 306). MSN Premium includes firewall (page 414) and parental controls, plus free access to the Encarta online encyclopedia (page 94) and online photo-sharing tools.

Note: As part of its Office Live system of online software (page 392), Microsoft has another Web-based mail plan called Outlook Live. When you sign up for $60 a year, you get email and a Web-based version of Microsoft Outlook (page 258) to keep all your contacts and calendars within reach from a Web browser.

.Mac

Apple Computer's $100-a-year .Mac service gives you a Webmail account along with a spiffy *@mac.com* email address. Although it's not really an ISP, .Mac is a suite of useful tools and programs that benefit Mac OS X fans—like online file storage, a slick backup program, free Mac software, tutorials and free book chapters, online photo-sharing and Web-page creation, and more. (You can sign up at *www.mac.com*.)

You can read your .Mac messages either on the .Mac Web site or using a regular email program like Entourage or Apple's Mail program (page 260).

The .Mac service uses the IMAP protocol (page 262), which means that messages you see on the .Mac Web site are also copied to your desktop email program. These messages don't show up as new mail, however, because .Mac knows you've already looked at them. Instead, they're marked as already read.

You can also manually synchronize your .Mac mail on all the computers you use, so each machine is up to date with the latest mail.

Setting Up Your Email Program

If you use a Web-based email program (page 261), there's no setup to speak of. Signing up for a name and password is all you need to do to set up your mail account.

If you use a desktop email program, though, you may have to slog through a bevy of geeky abbreviations and acronyms to set up your account. During the process, you'll supply a few pieces of information so that the mail program knows how to find your ISP's mail server so it can collect your mail for you.

Since Outlook Express is the most common email program on the planet, it's a good one to use as an example. (If, later, you install Thunderbird or some other mail program, it will import all your Outlook Express settings anyway to save you the time and trouble of re-entering them.)

Putting Your Address Book Online

Palmtops and cellphones are great for carrying your electronic address book around—but in case you lose 'em, it's good to have a backup. Want a backup device you know you won't lose? Consider the Internet. Several programs can now store all of your contact and address information online so your data's only a Web browser away.

Webmail users always have their address books waiting for them when they log into their accounts, but ISP mail people can keep their contacts close at hand, too, even when away from their own computers.

WhitePages.com (*www.whitepages.com*) offers a free service called MyInfo Address Book, which lets you import, store, print, and sort your contacts. You can store and retrieve all your addresses and other info when you log into your MyInfo account

on the Web site; the company also has a free ContactsManager program that syncs the contacts in your Outlook folder with your online address book.

If you have a .Mac account (page 267), you can sync your Mac OS X Address Book with the .Mac Web site by choosing System Preferences → .Mac → Sync and turning on the Contacts checkbox (along with any other items you'd like synced). When you click the Sync button, all the contacts from your home Mac are shuttled to the Web. The beauty of this system is that you can then sync them to *other* Macs, so that every machine is always up to date.

As the old saying goes, "You can't take it with you," but you can always store it online.

To get rolling, open your Windows Start menu. If Outlook Express isn't listed there, choose Start → All Programs → Outlook Express.

If you've never opened the program before, the Internet Connection Wizard barges in to help you along. If the wizard doesn't show up or you've already set up one Outlook Express account and want to add another, you can summon the Wizard by choosing Tools → Accounts → Add → Mail.

After you answer each question the wizard asks (see below), click the Next button.

1. **Your Name.**

   Type in your *real* name here, or at least the name you want to appear in your "*From:*" field. This is the name other people will see when you write to them (and how you'll be known in their address books), so don't call yourself Pangalactic Gargle Blaster unless you want to be remembered that way in all your friends' contact files.

2. **Internet Email Address.**

Your Internet service provider either let you pick an account name or assigned you a variation on your real name when you signed up. Your email address is your user name, followed by the @ sign, and then the ISP's domain name, so it'll look something like *starbuck@galactica.com* or *john.smith726@comcast.net*. Whatever it is, fill it in here.

3. **Email Server Names.**

Here's where you tell Outlook Express what kind of mail server your ISP uses, plus the addresses of the mail servers it uses to send (outgoing) and receive (incoming) mail.

Type: If your ISP uses a POP3 sever (most do), you don't have to specify the Type; the "My incoming mail server" menu, as shown at the top of Figure 14-4, already says POP3. If your ISP uses IMAP, though, choose IMAP from the drop-down menu.

Server name: Your incoming mail server is probably named something like *mail.comcast.net*, and your outgoing mail server is likely named something like *smtp.comcast.net*. (Of course, substitute your ISP's name for *comcast* in this example.)

But double-check with your ISP. Some ISPs call their mail servers things like *pop.central.coxt.net* or *pop-server.fish.net*, so get it right. Otherwise, you won't be able to send and receive email, which will put something of a damper on your email activities.

If you can't find your paperwork from the ISP, check its Web site and look for a Technical Support or Frequently Asked Questions area. Look for pages on "Mail setup," "POP Access," or "Server names."

4. **Internet Mail Logon (Figure 14-4).**

In the Account Name box, type your account name—the part of your email address before the @ sign. So if your email address is *starbuck@galactica.com*, just enter *starbuck*.

Your password is the one you chose—or that the ISP assigned you when you signed up. Despite the fact that you're typing in your password here, don't turn on "Log on using Secure Password Authentication (SPA)" unless the setup instructions from your ISP specifically tell you to do so.

When you're finished, the wizard deposits you on the Outlook Express mail screen, which shows your mailboxes and folders.

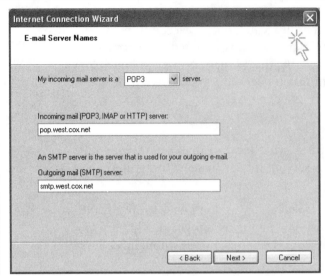

Figure 14-4:
*You encounter these two windows on the
road to Outlook Express account
configuration.*

*Top: Tell Outlook Express whether your ISP
uses the POP3 or IMAP protocol (check out
the box on page 262 if none of this makes
sense to you). Then, carefully type in the
addresses of your ISP's incoming and
outgoing mail servers. If you make a typo,
you won't get your mail.*

*Bottom: Type in your account name and
password in the Internet Mail Logon box.
Turn on "Remember password"—unless you
want to type your password every few
minutes when Outlook Express wants to
check your mail.*

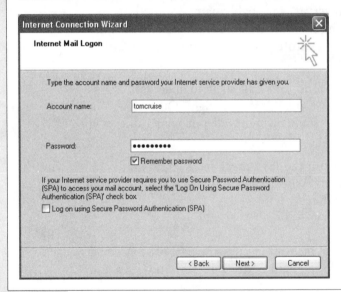

To test your handiwork, click the Create Mail button to make a new message.
Then address it to yourself. Type in a nice note congratulating yourself on getting through the mail setup, and then click the Send/Receive button to fire it
off. You've just sent your first message.

Now click Send/Receive again a few seconds later to *get* your first email message—the one you just sent yourself. If nothing happens, recheck your settings in Tools → Accounts → Mail → Properties.

Note: You set up an email account in Apple's Mail program pretty much the same way. The first time you open it, Mail offers to walk you through the setup. If it doesn't, choose Mail → Preferences → Accounts, and click the + button on the bottom-left corner of the box. A fresh set of blank boxes appears, which you should fill in with all your mail settings.

Writing and Sending Messages

Once you've gone to all the trouble to set up and configure your email account, odds are you're going to want to tell everyone you know to drop you a line. Here's how to create and send a message of your own.

1. **Open your email program or go to the Web site of the Webmail company you use. Log in and create a new outgoing message (see Figure 14-5).**

   You do that by clicking a New or Create Mail button, or by choosing File → New Message (or however your program phrases it).

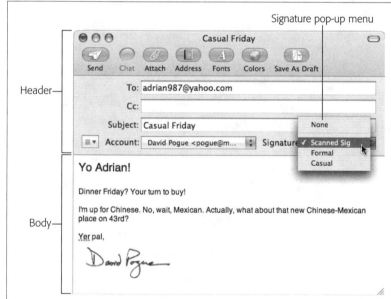

Signature pop-up menu

Figure 14-5:
A message has two sections: the header, which holds information about the message; and the body, the big empty white area that contains the message itself. In addition, the mail window has a toolbar, which you can use to access other features for composing and sending messages. The signature pop-up menu doesn't exist until you create a signature (page 273).

2. **Type an email address into the "To:" box.**

   If somebody's name is in your address book, just type the first couple letters of the name; most email programs automatically complete the address. (If the first guess is wrong, just type another letter or two until the program revises its guess.)

If you're typing in the address manually, remember that there are no spaces in email addresses; everything's squished together on either side of the @ symbol.

As in most dialog boxes, you can jump from blank to blank (from the "To:" field to the "CC:" field, for example) by pressing the Tab key.

To send this message to more than one person, separate their addresses with commas: *bob@earthlink.net, billg@microsoft.com, steve@apple.com.*

3. **If you want to send a "carbon copy" to other people, add their addresses in the "CC:" or "BCC:" fields in the message header.**

CC stands for *carbon copy*. Getting an email message where your name's in the CC line implies: "I sent you a copy because I thought you'd want to know about this correspondence, but I'm not expecting you to reply."

UP TO SPEED

Blind Carbon Copies

A *blind carbon copy* is a secret copy. This feature lets you send a copy of a message to somebody without any of the other recipients knowing that you did so. To view this field when composing a message, choose the BCC option, which is usually in your email program's View menu.

You can use the BCC field to quietly signal to a third party that a message has been sent. For example, if you send your co-worker a message that says, "Chris, it bothers me that you've been cheating the customers," you could BCC your supervisor to clue her in without getting into trouble with Chris.

The BCC box is useful in other ways, too. Many people send email messages (containing corny jokes, for example) to a long list of recipients. You, the recipient, have to scroll through a very long list of names the sender placed in the "To:" or "CC:" field. But if the sender used the "BCC:" field to hold all the recipients' email addresses, you, the recipient, won't see any names but your own at the top of the email. (Unfortunately, spammers have also learned this trick.)

---

4. **Title the message with a few short words in the subject line.**

It's courteous to put some thought into the subject line (use "Change in plans for next week" instead of "Yo"). Don't leave it blank; you'll just annoy your recipient.

Another justification for good subject lines: Spammers often resort to crafty tactics to get their junk messages read by using subject lines like "Did you get my photos?", "About last night," or "Account update information." You can make sure your message gets read by being more specific.

5. **Choose an email format.**

There are two kinds of email: *plain text* and *formatted.* Plain text messages are faster to send and open, are universally compatible with the world's email programs, and are greatly preferred by many veteran computer fans. And even though the message is plain, you can still attach pictures and other files.

(Resourceful geeks have even learned how to *fake* some formatting in plain messages: They use capitals instead of italics [GO HOME], "smileys" instead of pictures [:-)], and asterisks for emphasis [I *love* Swiss cheese!].)

By contrast, formatted messages sometimes open slowly, and, in some email programs, the formatting doesn't come through at all.

You can control which kind of mail you send on a message-by-message basis (look for a Format menu), or you can change the factory setting for new outgoing messages (check the program's Options or Preferences dialog box).

By the way: If you plan to send formatted mail, remember that your recipients won't see the fonts you use unless their machines have the same ones installed.

The bottom line: HTML works best for party flyers or casual email between friends. If you're sending the email to somebody at work, stick with plain text; some corporate email programs strip HTML messages of their formatting, turning your colorful stationery back into plain text.

6. **Type your message into the message body box.**

Click into the message body below the header and start typing. You can also copy and paste in Web links or chunks of text from other documents.

If your mail program has a spell checker, you can use it to weed out embarrassing typos.

7. **Add a signature (optional).**

Signatures are bits of text that get stamped at the bottom of your outgoing email messages. A signature may contain a name, postal address, a pithy quote, or even a scan of your *real* signature.

You can set up a signature (or a choice of several) in your email program's preferences. You generally have the choice of adding a signature manually to each message or, to save yourself the trouble, having it auto-stamped at the bottom of every message you fire off.

8. **Attach a file, if you like.**

You can paper-clip business cards, photos, spreadsheets, and other documents to paper-based memos or mail, so why not with email?

To attach a file from your hard drive to a message, you just—attach it. The procedure varies from mail program to mail program, but an Attach button (bearing a paper-clip icon) is usually involved. A Choose dialog box then appears, so that you can navigate to the desired file.

Most email programs also let you drag file icons into the waiting message window directly from your desktop (see Figure 14-6).

Figure 14-6:
As demonstrated in Thunderbird here, you can attach files by dragging them from the desktop and dropping them on the open message window. If the file you want to attach is buried six folders deep on your computer, though, clicking the email program's Attach button and navigating through your hard drive to the file's location may be quicker.

Tip: On the Mac, you can drag file attachments directly from any desktop window onto the *icon* of your email program (on the Dock). The program is smart enough to know what you mean: "Attach these files to the message I'm working on."

After you attach a file, you see its icon and file name on your email message. If you grabbed the wrong file and need to *detach* it, right-click its name and choose Remove from the shortcut menu, or click the icon and press Delete on the keyboard. You're not deleting the original file from your computer; you're just deleting the copy from the message.

Tip: It's not a sure thing that your recipient will be able to open the file you're sending. Most people can open common formats like photos, text files, and Microsoft Office (Word/Excel/PowerPoint) files. But if you send a file that requires a less common program to open—a sheet-music program, for example—the recipient probably won't be able to open it. Even movie files aren't a sure thing because there are so many different formats, each of which requires a special program to open. There's more on working with photos, sharing them online, and sending them as file attachments on page 244.

9. **Send your message.**

Click the Send or Send/Receive button to shoot your message across the Net and into the inbox of your recipient.

Tip: If you connect to the Internet via dial-up modem, you can address and compose a bunch of messages before you go online; the emails collect in your outbox. After you go online, the messages in your outbox actually go *out*.

Email Etiquette

Because email is a written form of communication, it's less expressive than *spoken* communication; you lose subtle aspects like nuance, emphasis, inflection, facial expressions, and body language. If you're naturally and good-naturedly sarcastic when you speak, you may come off as caustic and negative in email. Many huffy exchanges and flame wars (page 277) arise when people misunderstand each other's tone as expressed by email.

If you know your recipients quite well, sarcasm is fine and probably expected. Otherwise, you may want to stick with a more straightforward approach when emailing people you don't know that well.

Other Miss Mail Manners tips to keep in mind:

• **Keep your messages short.** Not many people want to scroll through 11 screens of message text waiting for you to stumble upon your point. Keeping your messages brief and direct makes them more memorable. Reading text onscreen is tiring for some people, who may take a gander and file your message away for later (or never) reading.

• **TURN OFF THE CAPS LOCK!** In cyberspace, everyone can hear you scream—and that's what USING ALL CAPS HAS COME TO SIGNIFY ONLINE. It's harsh, hard to read, unnecessary in most cases, and it looks like a telegram from the 1930s.

- **Reply to an existing message instead of making a new one.** Replying to a message keeps the same subject line and usually includes the previous text, which makes it easier to track ongoing conversations and sort mail. (If you've been sending and responding to the same message for 20 or 30 passes, though, deleting the most ancient text from the body is fine—and often appreciated by your recipient because it keeps message size and length smaller.)

  Once you break the message thread by continuing the conversation with a new subject line, the conversation can splinter. Web-based email services like Gmail (page 264) depend on having the same subject line in order to group your messages together properly.

- **Don't forward chain messages or hoaxes.** Email has become overrun not just by spam, but also by ridiculous hoaxes and chain letters.

  Some of these bogus messages—about PC-destroying viruses, bootlegging the Mrs. Field's cookie recipe, or getting free money from Microsoft—have been circulating for decades, but that doesn't make them true. These messages urge you for forward copies to all your friends; a telltale sign of a hoax is hundreds of addresses in the header from all that forwarding.

  If you're curious that a warning message *may* be real, check the urban legend debunkers and Internet hoax stompers over at Snopes (*www.snopes. com*), a site that collects the most popular missives and properly deflates them.

- **Don't send too many attachments.** Just as rambling on and on makes your message longer than it probably needs to be, attaching a ton of photos or other files can annoy your recipients, who may have slow Internet connections, mailboxes stuffed to the max, or no interest in 17 pictures of your gerbil running on its wheel.

Reading and Organizing Email

Even though it may just be a form-letter welcome note from your ISP, getting your first real email message is a thrill because someone *out there* knows your email address.

Each time your mail program collects your mail, it deposits the fresh batch of new messages into your mail program's inbox. Until you delete or move the message, it stays there. To help you tell the old from the new, most mail programs highlight the new mail's subject lines with bold text or colored dots.

Mailing Lists

Before the Web caught on, many people shared common interests by creating email *mailing lists* (that is, an email discussion group)—and many still do.

Such lists can be on any subject: Welsh corgis, the works of Mark Twain, swine health, flatpicking guitar, and so on. A mailing list is made up of subscribers who sign up with someone called the *list master* to receive all the messages sent around by other members of the mailing list.

Many colleges have their own mailing lists for faculty and alumni, as do professional groups and corporations. You can even create your own mailing lists, thanks to special features of Google and Yahoo groups (page 323).

Once you sign up for a mailing list, the list master provides you with instructions on posting messages to the list, as well as how to unsubscribe if you decide the list isn't for you. You're supplied with a single email address to send your messages to; the mailing list's software automatically distributes your e-note to everyone on the list. Unlike public forums, where anyone can post, only the members of the mailing list get the messages.

Depending on how prolific the members are, you may get a trickle or an avalanche of mail every day. Some people use message rules or filters (page 282) to route messages from a mailing list into a special mailbox to keep it from getting mixed in with regular mail.

People can get passionate about their feelings on mailing lists (and anywhere else online), and *flame wars* of overheated, flying insults can break out when two or more people disagree. Some lists are *moderated*, meaning that the human manager may step in and tell all parties to chill out. But on unmediated lists, the war can rage on for days.

If you decide you want to join in on the fun, you can find directories of mailing lists—where else?—on the Web. Some sites dedicated to a specialized topic may have links that take you through signing up for the email list, like the RootsWeb genealogy list at *www.rootsweb.com*. LISTSERV, one of the most popular list-manager programs, has a searchable directory of groups to join at *www.lsoft.com/catalist.html*.

Outlook Express, Apple Mail, Thunderbird, and some other mail programs divide their main windows into multiple sections called *panes*. The preview pane is the horizontal section below the list of messages in your inbox. When you click a message's subject line in the inbox, the body of the message appears in the preview pane, as shown back in Figure 14-1. If you want more room to see the message preview and less for your inbox, drag the divider bar between the two up or down.

If you double-click a message's name in the inbox list, it opens into a window of its own so that you can see all of it (or scroll down to the bottom if it's a really long one). You can resize the window by dragging the lower-right corner, move it around your desktop, or open more messages in their own windows to compare their contents side by side.

Opening a message in this way makes it easier to see all the *header* information, which is the "To:", "From:", subject line, and other address stuff at the top. The part of the message with the text is the *body*.

If you have a stack of mail to plow through, you can blast through it quickly in the preview mode by tapping the up and down arrows on your keyboard. If you've opened a message into its own window, you can use the Previous and Next buttons (in most email programs) to move through the messages.

Note: As handy as the preview pane can be, some security experts warn against using it on Windows computers. Because it opens each message automatically, the preview pane can, in theory, open a virus or worm that's attached to a piece of mail. Of course, if you have an up-to-date anti-virus program (page 405) on your computer, this syndrome shouldn't affect you.

How to Deal with Email

Sooner or later, you'll have to *do* something about every piece of email that reaches you. Apart from just helplessly letting it sit there in your inbox forever, these are your options:

- **Reply to it.** To answer a message, click the Reply button on the message toolbar. If the message was originally addressed to multiple recipients, you can send your reply to everyone simultaneously by clicking the Reply All button instead.

  A new message window opens, already addressed. The letters *Re:* (short for "regarding") preface the message's original subject line, so your friend knows you're responding to that particular message. As a courtesy to your correspondent, your email program places the original message at the bottom of the window, denoted by brackets or a vertical bar, as shown in Figure 14-7.

Tip: In most programs, if you highlight some text before clicking Reply, only that portion of the original message gets pasted into your reply. That's a great convenience to your correspondent, who now knows exactly which part of the message you're responding to.

Figure 14-7:
A reply includes the original message, marked in a special color, by vertical rules, or by >brackets >like >this. The original sender's name is automatically placed in the "To:" field. The subject is the same as the original subject with the addition of Re: (shorthand for "regarding"). You're ready to type your response.

At this point, you can add or delete recipients, edit the subject line or the original message, attach a file, and so on. When you're finished, click Send.

Tip: Use the Return key to create blank lines in the original message. Using this method, you can splice your own comments into the paragraphs of the original message, replying point by point. The brackets preceding each line of the original message help your correspondent keep straight what's yours and what's hers.

- **Forward it.** Instead of replying to the person who sent you a message, you may want to pass the note on to a third person.

  To do that, click the Forward toolbar button. A new message opens, looking a lot like the one that appears when you reply. You may wish to preface the original message with a comment of your own, along the lines of: "Frank: I thought you'd enjoy this joke about Congress." (Many people forward jokes around the Internet this way, but many bosses like the Forward command to delegate requests to their employees.)

  Finally, address it as you would any outgoing piece of mail.

- **Print it.** Sometimes there's no substitute for a printout. You can use the standard print keyboard commands (Ctrl+P for Windows; ⌘-P for Mac) or choose File → Print in most mail programs.

On the printout, most programs include the sender's name, subject, and time stamp.

Note: Messages formatted in HTML (page 273) may be too wide to fit on standard paper; you might have to do some tinkering in your print preferences—like rotating the paper orientation from Portrait to Landscape or shrinking the message—to make it fit on one page.

- **File it.** You can create little onscreen folders to organize your saved messages, as described in the next section. You might create one for important messages, another for all order confirmations from Web shopping, still another for friends and family, and so on.

- **Find it.** You can sort the columns in your main email list just by clicking the headings (From, Subject, Date & Time, and so on).

But what if you're trying to find a message according to what's *in* it, rather than just its subject line or sender name? That's the purpose of the Find command, which is available in every email program; take a tour of the program's menus to find it. You may not have to look very far: Outlook Express gives you a big ol' Find button in the program's toolbar that pops up a Find box, as shown at the top of Figure 14-8. Apple Mail has a search box at the top of the window, which you can jump right into by pressing Option-⌘-F on the keyboard. As shown in the bottom of Figure 14-8, such a command triggers a search of all text in all messages in the current folder, resulting in a tidy list of matches.

Tip: You can also search for specific text *within* a single message that's open on your screen, too. Here again, a Find command is at your disposal.

- **Delete it.** Sometimes it's junk mail. Sometimes you're just done with it. Either way, it's a snap to delete a selected message, several selected messages, or a message that's currently on the screen. You can press the Delete key, click the Delete button on the toolbar, or drag messages out of the list window and into your Trash mailbox.

All of these commands move the messages to the Deleted Items/Trash folder, described below. If you like, you can click its icon to view a list of the messages you've deleted. You can even rescue messages by dragging them into any other mailbox (right back into the inbox, if you want).

Figure 14-8:
*Top: The Find box in
Outlook Express also lets
you seek out messages
from specific people or
messages that contain
certain words.*

*Bottom: Using the search
box in Apple Mail rounds
up a whole list of messages
containing your search
words.*

The Parts of Your Mailbox

The inbox isn't the only "folder" in your email program. Outlook Express, for example, has five folders in the vertical pane in the mail program's main window:

- **Inbox.** This box holds all the messages you've received, both read and unread—at least until you delete or move them.

- **Outbox.** Like an outbox on your desk—the one holding a stack of inter-office memos waiting to be picked up—the outbox holds messages that you've written but haven't sent yet. Click the Send/Receive button (or its equivalent in the program you use) to shoot the message out to the Internet and on its way.

- **Sent Items.** Once you send a message, your copy of it moves to the Sent folder. (Some mail programs don't save outgoing messages until you fiddle with their Options or Preferences settings.)

- **Deleted Items or Trash.** When you delete a message (by pressing the Delete or Backspace key), it goes here. Like the desktop Recycle Bin (Windows) or Trash can (Mac OS X), the contents stay in this "folder" until you manually empty it. The point is to provide a safety net for messages you delete by accident.

  To empty the Deleted Items folder (Windows), right-click it and choose "Empty 'Deleted Items' Folder" from the shortcut menu. In Apple's Mail program, choose Mailbox → Erase Deleted Message.

Tip: Better yet, get to know your email program well enough that you can find its auto-emptying feature. You can set the program to empty its Deleted Items/Trash folder automatically every six months, every week, every time you quit the program, or whatever.

- **Drafts.** This folder holds messages you started but haven't yet completed, either because it was time for dinner or because it's a *really* angry letter to somebody and you're smart enough to wait until you cool down before sending it. To go back and finish, click the Drafts folder and then the message you were writing.

- **Junk** (optional). Mail programs like Thunderbird, Eudora, Outlook, and Apple Mail automatically route obvious spam into its own festering holding pen. Every once in a while, you're supposed to click this folder, glance through its contents to make sure some good mail didn't get filed away with the bad, and then delete the whole mess.

  Conversely, if spam lands in your regular inbox, teach your mail program to identify it as junk by clicking the This Is Junk button (or command).

You can create and name your own folders, too, using the New Folder or New Mailbox command.

Filters and Message Rules

Once you know how to create folders, the next step in managing your email is to set up a series of *message rules* (also known as mail rules or filters) that file, answer, or delete incoming messages *automatically* based on their contents (such as their subject, address, and/or size). Message rules require you to think like the distant relative of a programmer, but the mental effort can reward you many times over; message rules turn your email program into a surprisingly smart and efficient secretary.

To set up filters or rules for incoming messages, go into your mail program's preferences area or menus and look for a command called New Rule or New Filter.

Once you've begun the process, you'll be asked to supply some information:

• **How to spot the messages you want processed.** For example, if you'd like the program to watch out for messages from a particular person, you would set up the dialog box so that it watches for messages from somebody whose email address you specify (Figure 14-9).

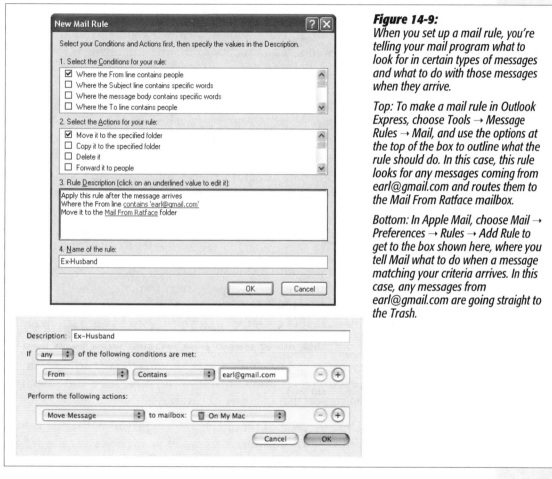

Figure 14-9:
When you set up a mail rule, you're telling your mail program what to look for in certain types of messages and what to do with those messages when they arrive.

Top: To make a mail rule in Outlook Express, choose Tools → Message Rules → Mail, and use the options at the top of the box to outline what the rule should do. In this case, this rule looks for any messages coming from earl@gmail.com and routes them to the Mail From Ratface mailbox.

Bottom: In Apple Mail, choose Mail → Preferences → Rules → Add Rule to get to the box shown here, where you tell Mail what to do when a message matching your criteria arrives. In this case, any messages from earl@gmail.com are going straight to the Trash.

To flag messages containing *loan, $$$$, XXXX, !!!!,* and so on, you want to tell the program what the *subject* line should include.

In fact, you can set up *multiple* criteria, so that you flag messages whose subjects contain any one of those common spam triggers.

• **What you want done with messages that match the criteria.** For example, if you've told your rule to watch for junk mail containing *$$$$* in the subject line, you now tell the program to delete it or move it into, say, a junk folder.

With a little imagination, you'll see how these rules can do absolutely amazing things with your incoming email. A good email program can colorize, delete, move, redirect, or forward messages—or even play a sound when you get a certain message.

Finally, you generally name and save your new rule. If you've set up more than one rule, you can usually choose a sequence for them by dragging them up and down.

Tip: Rules are generally executed in order, from top to bottom. If a rule doesn't seem to be working properly, it may be that an earlier rule is intercepting and processing the message before the "broken" rule even sees it. To fix this, try dragging the rule up or down in the list.

From now on, when your mail program checks for new mail, it consults its rulebook to see if any messages match your conditions and routes them accordingly.

Opening Attachments

You can tell if someone has sent you a file attachment before you even open the message: a telltale paper-clip icon appears next to the message's name on the inbox list. When you double-click to open the message, the attachment appears under the message text or in the Attachments box at the bottom of the message window (Figure 14-10).

In some mail programs, you just double-click the attachment to open it. In others, you have to peel the attachment off the email message and save it to your hard drive. You can do that in either of two ways:

• **Drag and drop.** Drag the icon of the attached file right out of the email window and onto your desktop (or onto a folder of your choice). If the sender went nuts with the attaching and sent a bunch of files at once, first click one and then press Ctrl+A (on the Mac, ⌘-A) to select them all. Now you can do a group-drag out of the message.

• **Click and save.** Right-click the attached file (on the Mac, Control-click) and choose Save As from the resulting shortcut menu. When the Save As box opens, navigate to the folder where you want to put the attachment and click Save to dump it in. (Here again, you can also select all of the attachments first to deal with them en masse.)

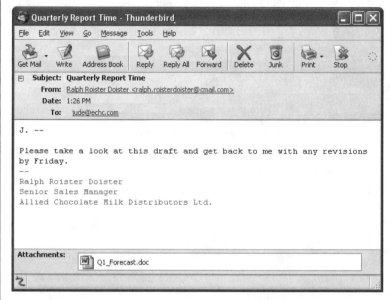

Figure 14-10:
The message shown here has a Microsoft Word file attached to it. In most mail programs, right-clicking on the attachment icon opens up a world of options, including opening the file or saving it to a folder on your hard drive. You can also drag the attachment icon off the bottom of the message and drop it on your desktop.

If you have Windows XP Service Pack 2, Outlook Express may block your attempt to see, open, or save an attachment. That's a somewhat brute-force method of pursuing a worthy goal: preventing your PC from getting infected by viruses that came along for the ride. (You'll know when this attachment blocking is happening because the file's name appears in gray, or a warning banner appears when you try to save the attachment.)

Of course, most attachments are perfectly innocuous, and it's frustrating when Outlook Express butts in between you and that file you really need to open. If you have an antivirus program installed on your computer, you can safely tell Outlook Express to back off. Choose Tools → Options → Security; on the Security tab, turn off the option called "Do not allow attachments to be saved or opened that could potentially be a virus." Click OK. (If Outlook Express still refuses to let you see the attachment, quit the program and reopen it.)

Fighting Email Pests

As helpful and convenient as the Internet can be, it's also a fairly lawless land. Email has become a tool of sleazy, shady individuals, so treat all messages from strangers with a skeptical eye and a cautious mouse. Many of the programs mentioned in Chapter 21 can help protect you and your computer from two of the Internet's biggest infectious parasites: spam and viruses.

Who Moved My Graphics?

Hey, what's the deal? My incoming messages in Outlook Express have big white gaps in them, with a red X where a picture ought to be.

Like any good email program, Outlook Express lets you see photos and graphics mixed in with the message text. Sometimes, though, you'll just see a blank frame with a red X instead of the image.

Turns out Outlook Express is sanitizing your email for your protection.

A common spammer tactic is to send you a message that seems to contain a graphic—but, in fact, contains only a *reference* to a graphic that's actually retrieved from a Web site somewhere. Your email program fetches the graphic *at the moment you open the message*. The request for the image is a signal that lets the spammers know that their message has fallen on fertile ground—a live sucker who actually looks at these messages.

Activating a so-called *Web bug* in this way is an open invitation for even more spam.

Outlook Express, in other words, is *not* showing you the image that's supposed to appear because it's trying *not* to transmit that "Hey, this sucker just opened your message" signal.

That's why the message at the top of the window says, "Some pictures have been blocked to help prevent the sender from identifying your computer."

If you know the sender, and that she was just emailing you some photos, click the banner to reveal the images. But if you've never heard of the sender and see that it's spam, delete the message. And take pleasure in the fact that you've just ruined some spammer's day.

Spam

Because it's inexpensive and efficient, email is a great communication tool for people to keep in touch with each other, but those qualities also attract people trying to make a buck. Unsolicited email ads have increased exponentially since email first began to gain traction in the 1990s. Junk mail—better known as *spam*—now constitutes 80 percent of the messages sent around the Internet.

Note: The term *spam* comes from a famous Monty Python sketch about a café menu that features spam in just about every dish (*"Lobster thermidor aux crevettes with a Mornay sauce served in the Provençale manner with shallots and aubergines, garnished with truffle paté, brandy and with a fried egg on top and spam"*) and Vikings who nonsensically sing the word over and over. (Get it? They *drown out* the legitimate conversations going on around them.)

Most spam messages are designed to hawk products of questionable legality (bootleg software, pharmaceuticals, and so on), and come in such volume that your mailbox can easily get flooded in a single day. Other forms of junk mail may be from sites or services you've used on the Web, but forgot to uncheck the box next to the "Send me information about special offers" when you signed up to download that free media player or program update.

You may even get junk mail the first day you open your email account. Spammers use programs that crunch through millions of potential variations of email addresses, and then spew messages to those addresses whether they're real working addresses or not. (Why not? It's free.)

Even though laws have been passed against sending spam, tracking down the perpetrators is difficult because most return addresses are forged (also referred to as *spoofed*). Worse, many messages begin, or are routed through, other countries, where U.S. laws have no leverage.

Spam can also contain viruses sent by people who would love nothing more than to plant a program on your computer that lets them control your machine from afar. Once spammers plant a control program on your PC, they can turn your machine into a relay station that secretly shovels out even *more* spam—right over your own Internet connection. You don't even notice except perhaps for the fact that your PC seems to be getting slower in its old age.

Here are some ways to cut spam out of your mailbox's diet:

- **Don't ask for it.** When filling out forms on the Web, turn off the checkboxes that say, "Yes, send me exciting offers and news from our partners."

- **Don't reply to spam.** Don't click the "Remove Me" link on a junk message; it's usually a trick. Doing this tells the spammer he's got a live one on the hook. You'll get even more junk in your mail trunk.

- **Get a spam filter.** Most email programs and ISPs already use spam filters that are supposed to block junk before it even gets to your inbox.

  But if they're not doing the trick, you can supplement them with add-on antispam programs that you buy yourself. Internet security programs like Trend Micro can snag, tag, and dump spam right to the Trash. Granted, you still have to download the messages and let the filter weed out the junk, but junk filters make it faster to see all the garbage at once and dump it with one click.

- **Rules.** Set up some message rules, as described on page 282, that auto-flag messages as spam that have subject lines containing trigger words like "Viagra," "Herbal," "Mortgage," "Refinance," "Enlarge Your," and so on.

• **Create a private account.** If you're overrun by spam, consider sacrificing an email address to the public areas of the Internet, like chat rooms, online shopping, Web site and software registration, and newsgroup posting. Spammers use automated software robots that scour every public Internet message and Web page, recording email addresses they find. That's how they got your address in the first place. Using this technique, at least you've restricted the junk mail to one, secondary email account.

When spammers find your disposable address and your mailbox starts overflowing again, dump the account and make another free one to use as your disposable mail pickup window.

Meanwhile, your principal, separate, private email account—which you *only* give out to friends, family, and business associates—stays out of sight and off the grid because you *never* use it when filling out a Web form, posting on a message board, or other public forum.

Viruses

Email viruses have found a friend in spam, and some criminals are using the *blended threat* of unsolicited mass mail with a virus payload tucked inside the message. Email viruses, like Melissa in 1999 and ILOVEYOU in 2000, used infected attachments to propagate themselves to every email recipient in a computer's address book, destroyed files, and shut down entire office networks. New Windows viruses are turned loose every day.

Many viruses appear to be coming from people you know (they snatch addresses from your address book), so the old advice to open attachments only from acquaintances isn't entirely foolproof.

The best way to stay safe is to be alert and keep your Windows antivirus program up to date. Many of the Internet security suites mentioned in Chapter 21 include spam filters along with antivirus and antispyware components. They're designed to separate the wheat from the spam-encrusted viruses—and catch them if they happen to escape onto your computer.

If you use the Internet frequently, installing protective software is becoming almost mandatory for safe online computing in general. The ones that smack down spam make life online a little bit better.

Instant Messages and Chat

If you think email is a fast way to communicate, wait until you get a look at *instant messaging* (or IMing, in the lingo). As anyone under the age of 21 can tell you, instant messages whip back and forth without any delay, gloriously free of email's administrative overhead. No longer do you have to go through all that bother of creating a message, entering the address and subject header, writing your note and, finally, sending it. As an IMer, your exchange is much more like the conversations everyone *used to have* when they weren't sitting in front of computers. So forget about waiting 5 or 10 minutes for an email acquaintance to lob back a response; with an IM, you get an answer as quickly as your pal on the other end can type.

Chatting is similar to instant messaging, except that several people can join the conversation. They might join a chat room to pick a movie, rant about their favorite shooting guard's foul trouble, or meet new people.

These two forms of online communication may take a little getting used to. But once you find programs you like and people to talk to, you might discover a whole new reason to reach out and touch someone.

Instant Messaging: An Introduction

Instant messaging programs, shown in Figure 15-1, work like email, but *instantly*. You type a short message in your IM program, click a button, and your words pop up on your friend's screen, whether he lives in Paris or the cubicle next to yours.

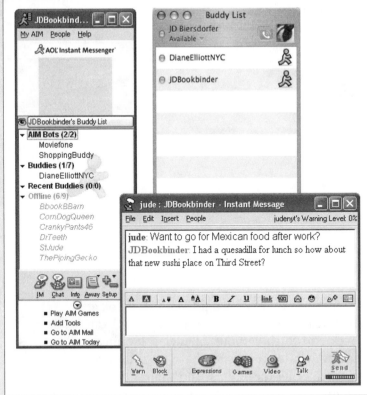

Figure 15-1:
AOL Instant Messenger (top left) and iChat (top right) are two popular IM programs. In either program, you add your friends' screen names to your Buddy List. When a pal is online, his screen name is displayed in bold; the names of absent friends are dimmed or listed in the Offline area of the Buddy List. When you see buddies online, you can send them a message that pops up right on their screens. Thus begins the conversation.

Bottom: A discussion in progress inside the AIM window.

Some people love instant messaging; others find it too casual and intrusive. Love it or hate it, instant messaging has attracted more than 400 million people for several reasons.

First, it's free, which is always a plus. Also, it lets you know at a glance who among your friends is currently sitting at their PC, letting you fire off a quick message and avoid telephone tag. It's a multitasker's dream; you can simultaneously hold several instant message conversations *while* talking on the phone *and* motioning to coworkers not to drink all the coffee.

Although instant messaging programs started as a way to swap text messages, they've expanded their powers considerably. Now these programs let you swap files as well (page 303). If your computer has a microphone (page 341)—or if your head has a headset—you can *talk* with your friends, too (in the traditional vocal-cords sense).

And if you're up for connecting a small Web cam or camcorder, you can even create the videophone (page 301) that comic books have promised us for years.

IM Services: The Catalog

Unfortunately, the simple concept of instant messaging and easy communication now resembles a certain tower in Babel: Different companies have released mutually incompatible instant messaging programs. Microsoft's got one that doesn't communicate with America Online's; Yahoo's IM program doesn't work with Microsoft's, and so on.

So which program should you use? That depends entirely upon on who you want to chat with: You and your friend both need the same messaging program to communicate.

The simplest solution is for you and your pals to agree on the same program. But if you agree to disagree, you can always run several IM programs simultaneously on your PC; that way, you can talk to everybody. With all that in mind, the next section gives you an introduction to the biggest instant messaging programs.

Tip: If you're a fanatic about instant messaging but can't get all your friends onto one service (and don't want all the clutter of three IM programs on your desktop), try Trillian (*http://www.trillian.cc*). Trillian lets you talk to folks who use AIM, ICQ (a play on the words, "I seek you"), MSN Messenger, Windows Messenger, *and* Yahoo IM—all in the same window. For other multi-service IM solutions, see the box on page 300.

AIM

If people tend to pick their IM programs based on what their friends use, then America Online Instant Messenger (AIM) is a very friendly place indeed. By early 2006, AIM had amassed 42 million members in the U.S. alone, busily sending 1.6 *billion* instant messages a day.

You can use AIM on Windows, Mac, or Linux computers—even on cellphones or palmtops. If you're not already one of the 42 million, you can get your own copy of the software on the AIM download page at *www.aim.com*.

AIM provides lots of big, well-labeled icons and plenty of ways to customize your online look with fonts, colors, and personal buddy icons (the icons your friends see next to your name in the IM window). You can also play AIM games like poker or transfer files back and forth (page 303). One small annoyance: Ads appear above the IM chat window.

Note: The Mac version of the software inevitably lags a version or three behind the PC version. Then again, Mac fans have their own, far superior chat program right on their hard drives: Apple's iChat program (page 294). It's fully compatible with the AIM service and its 42 million acolytes.

The AIM software installer for Windows sprays a lot of desktop shortcuts and other stuff in your PC's Startup folder. For example, it wedges the AOL Explorer browser into your Programs menu. (AOL Explorer serves as sort of a portal page for your screen name and features links to AIM Mail, new buddy icons, and lots of news about the entertainment world, in which AOL's parent company, Time Warner, has quite a large stake.)

On the AIM software download page, you can download the latest AIM version for Windows, nicknamed Triton. Like plain AIM, AIM Triton lets you send instant messages—but it also has its own Web-based mail service called AIM Mail, and it combines your Buddy List with contact information from Outlook, Outlook Express, Hotmail, or Yahoo Mail. You wind up with one Big Giant Online Address Book.

Although it seems to be intended as a one-stop communications console for all your messaging needs, early versions of Triton were buggy as all get-out, and the whole concept comes perilously close to overkill. If you just want an uncomplicated IM program, stick with regular AIM.

Tip: Want to find out if a new movie's playing in your area? Just send an instant message to the AIM Moviefone Megabot (its address is already in your Buddy List), consisting of nothing but the movie's name. (See page 297 for details on how to send an IM.) The automated Moviefone bot instantly responds with links to movie information and theater schedules.

Several such AIMBots are online 24/7, including the ShoppingBuddy that points you in the direction of objects you might like to purchase. Type in what you want to buy, like *gas grill* or *chenille bathrobe,* and press Enter. The ShoppingBuddy takes your request and presents you with a list of links to merchant Web sites right in your IM window.

There's a list of bots at *http://aimtoday.aim.com/aimbots.*

Yahoo Messenger

Yahoo has its own IM program—all you need is a free Yahoo ID to use it. You can get the Yahoo Messenger software for Windows, Macintosh, and Linux systems at *http://messenger.yahoo.com.*

By clicking buttons in the Messenger window, you can add themed backgrounds to your messages and choose stylized avatars (character icons) to represent yourself online. As in AIM, you can stream radio or play games like chess and checkers with your IM cronies.

Thanks to a thawing in the IM diplomatic relations department, Yahoo Messenger and MSN Messenger (described next) have agreed to join forces (and gang up on AIM). By mid-2006, Yahoo and MSN chatters will be able to communicate with each other, bridging that network divide for the first time.

GEM IN THE ROUGH

Google Talk

Not to be left out of anything Yahoo and MSN are doing, Google now has its own text and voice chat program. It's called Google Talk; you can download it at *www.google.com/talk*.

Google Talk requires Windows 2000, XP, or Vista—and a Gmail address (page 264). Mac fans can join Google Talk's network using iChat or GAIM (see pages 294 and 300).

Gmail automatically saves a transcript of every IM session in the Chats area of your mailbox. If you'd rather not have your comments on the record, you can tell it *not* to save the chats. To do so, log into your Gmail account, click the Settings link, and click the Chat tab to get to the settings for Chat History.

MSN Messenger

Don't confuse MSN Messenger, the IM program, with Windows Messenger, a program that Microsoft built into Windows. MSN Messenger is a separate piece of IMware that you can download at *http://join.msn.com/messenger*. It works with Windows 98 and later.

Note: Even though most Mac people use AIM or iChat, there's even a Mac version, called Microsoft Messenger, waiting at *www.microsoft.com/mac*. It has many business-oriented IM features built into it, like the ability to have secure chats behind a corporate firewall, and integration with Microsoft's Office suite for Mac.

MSN Messenger gives you the standard text-chat and file-transfer powers that you find in most other IM programs. You can also play Minesweeper and other games with people on your Messenger contact list.

If the spirit moves you and you've installed the mobile version of MSN Messenger on your phone (*http://mobile.msn.com*), you can even exchange text messages with people when you're on the go (or in a library or other public place where talking loudly might be shushed, or at least sternly frowned upon). Note, though, that MSN isn't the only portable IM program in town—AIM and Yahoo have cellphone editions available on their sites as well.

Tip: If you play music as you work, you can broadcast the name of whatever song you're currently playing so that your online cohorts can admire your taste. Go to the Tools menu on the Messenger window and choose Options; in the Personal area, turn on "Show song information from Windows Media Player as a personal message."

FUTURE WATCH

Windows Live Messenger

As Microsoft brings its followers into the age of Windows Vista, it has big plans for MSN Messenger. In fact, it's replacing the program with a more powerful version called Windows Live Messenger. A beta, or test version, of the software was released to the public in spring 2006 and you can get it at *http://ideas.live.com* if you feel daring enough to try unfinished software.

Along with traditional IM chat, WLM offers PC-to-phone-number voice calls (for a fee, of course). To use this feature, you need to sign up for the MCI Web Calling service. (See Chapter 18 for more on Internet phone calls; see page 301 for more on IM audio chat.)

Once you buy a block of minutes, you can use Windows Live Messenger to place calls to physical telephones. However, you still have to talk through your computer's microphone.

Windows Live Messenger has another new feature called Sharing Folders. Instead of emailing photos and files to friends, you can drag the files onto a name in your Contacts list to create a Sharing Folder that appears on both desktops (yours and your buddy's). Every time you add, delete, or modify a file in the Sharing Folder, your friend's folder gets updated, too.

---

iChat

iChat comes preinstalled on every Macintosh. It can hook you up with fellow chat partners on four different networks:

- **The AIM network.** You can chat with anyone in the 42-million-member AIM universe.

- **The .Mac network.** You can chat with anyone else who has a .Mac email address (page 267). (And you can get a .Mac email address yourself—for free—by choosing iChat → Preferences, and then clicking the Accounts button, the + button, and then Create New .Mac Account. That takes you to an Apple Web page where you can sign up for a free iChat account name. You'll also get 60 free days of the more complete .Mac treatment—usually $100 a year—described on page 267. When your trial period ends, you'll lose all of the other stuff that .Mac provides, but you'll get to keep your iChat name.)

Note: When the chatter is between .Mac people, you get the bonus of an encrypted, secure connection for the chatstream, which few other services offer.

- **The Jabber network.** Jabber is another chat network whose key virtue is its *open source* origins. In other words, it wasn't masterminded by some corporate media behemoth; it's an all-volunteer effort, joined by thousands of programmers all over the world. There's no one Jabber chat program (like AOL Instant Messenger); in fact, there are dozens, available for Mac OS X, Windows, Linux, Unix, Palm and PocketPC organizers, and so on. All of them can chat with each other across the Internet in one glorious frenzy of typing.

  And now there's one more program that can join the party: iChat.

- **Your own local network.** Thanks to *Bonjour,* an automatic, no-effort-on-your-part, network-recognition technology, you can communicate with other Macs on your own office network without signing up for anything at all—and without actually being on the Internet. This is a terrific feature when you're sitting around a conference table, idly chatting with colleagues using your wireless laptop (and the boss thinks you're taking notes).

These chat networks operate in parallel. Each network (AIM/.Mac, Jabber, and Bonjour) has its own separate buddy list window and its own chat window. You log into each network separately; otherwise, chatting and videoconferencing work identically on all three networks.

Tip: As you accumulate buddies, your iChat Buddy List may become crowded. But if you choose View → Show Offline Buddies to turn off the checkmark, you'll only see your *currently online* buddies in the Buddy List—a much more meaningful list for the temporarily lonely.

Phase 1: Build Your Buddy List

In any IM program, you start by adding your pals' names (IM addresses) to the buddy list. (This list may be called Contacts or Friends, but it's still a buddy list.)

- **AIM.** Adding friends to your Buddy List—the folks you've anointed *people I want to IM with*—is as simple as typing in their screen names: choose My AIM → Setup Buddy List. Click the Add Buddy icon at the bottom of the Setup window (shown on the left in Figure 15-2) and type your pal's screen name in the highlighted *New Buddy* line.

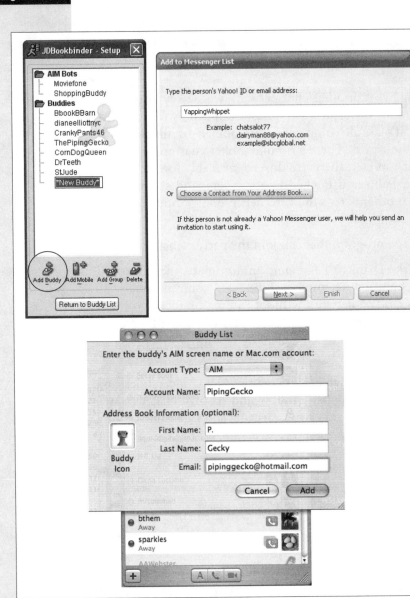

Figure 15-2:
Making friends is the hard part—adding them to your buddy/contacts/friends list is easy no matter which IM program you use.

Left: In AOL Instant Messenger, click the Setup icon at the bottom of your Buddy List window (or choose My AIM → Setup Buddy List). Then click the Add Buddy icon (circled) and type your pal's screen name to replace the *New Buddy* text shown here.

Right: Once you click the yellow plus sign to add a new contact in Yahoo Messenger, this "Add to Messenger List" box pops up so you can enter the screen name.

Bottom: When you add a New Person to your iChat buddy list, you get a box to fill in the screen name and account type, plus optional info like real name and email address to keep on file in your Mac OS X Address Book.

Tip: There are 42 million people on AIM's network, and that's 42 million potential typos. Because there are so many AIM names, get the precise spelling. You also might want to send a test message to your pal before you add the name to your Buddy List to make sure you don't wind up complaining about your love life to a total stranger.

- **Yahoo Messenger.** If you've signed up for one of the company's many other services (like a Yahoo Mail account), you already have a Yahoo ID. If that's the case, just type in the chunk of your email address before the *@yahoo.com* part. Then use your regular password to sign in and get started. To add pals already using Yahoo Messenger, click the yellow plus (+) sign next to "Add a Contact" in the top part of the Messenger window to get the "Add to Messenger List" box shown on the right in Figure 15-2.

- **MSN Messenger.** Fill up its buddy list (Contacts window) by clicking the "Add a contact" link at the bottom of the window.

- **iChat.** Click the plus (+) sign in the bottom-left corner of the iChat window. Out slides a window into your Mac's Address Book program. If your chat companion is already in Address Book, find and click his name, and then click Select Buddy.

  If not, click New Person and enter the buddy's AIM address, .Mac address, or (if you're in the Jabber list) Jabber address, as shown in Figure 15-2. You're adding this person to both your Buddy List and Address Book.

Phase 2: Start the Chat

Once you have your cast of characters in place, you can see who's online and who's not with a quick glance at your buddy list, which shows you who's also logged on. Most services give their members the options of placing little status messages next to their names like Available, Away, or Out to Lunch; the names of offline folks are typically dimmed.

When you see that one of your pals is online (boldface type is usually the indicator), you send an instant message by double-clicking that person's name. A new message window opens (Figure 15-3); type your greeting, and hit the Enter key or click Send.

On your friend's screen, a message window pops up, displaying your message. Some services give the person the chance to accept or decline your message; if he clicks Accept, the conversation gets rolling. Your friend writes back, you write back to that, and it goes on from there until one of you says goodbye, signs off, or crashes.

Security check

In some cases, people you don't know may send you a message. It may be a long-lost friend, or it could be someone trying to sell you something or otherwise harass you. This is where the Decline button comes in handy if you know right off you don't want to talk to this person.

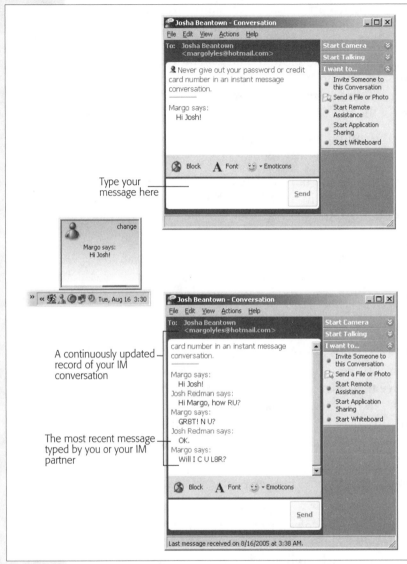

Figure 15-3:
*Top: To start up a
conversation, double-click
one of the names in your IM
program's buddy list to
summon the message box
window shown here. When
you start typing you see your
text in the bottom part of the
window so you can look it
over before you send it.*

*Middle: Here, in MSN
Messenger, when you click
the Send button (or hit the
Enter key) your friend gets a
little toaster alert box
popping up from the bottom
corner of the screen. When
your pal clicks the alert, his
or her IM window opens,
ready for a response.*

*Bottom: As you and your
friend type away, your
conversation scrolls by in the
top part of the window. As
you can see on the right side
of the IM window, MSN
Messenger lets you do audio
and video chats as well over
an instant message session;
more on page 301.*

If someone starts hassling you, you can add her to your Block list, which bans
future messages from that screen name until you unblock it. The Block command is, for example, on the People menu in AIM and the Buddies menu in
iChat.

Most IM programs give you some say in who can contact you out of the blue.
If you don't want to be pestered by strangers, you can limit your future conversations only to people who have already earned buddy-list status from you.

Parents often use this feature because it lets them control who can strike up an online conversation with their kids. Check your program's preferences for the privacy settings; Figure 15-4 shows the ones for the Windows version of AIM.

Note: Spam, which no email account seems to be without these days, has made the leap to IM. If you get a message trying to sell you something, well, you've got *spim*.

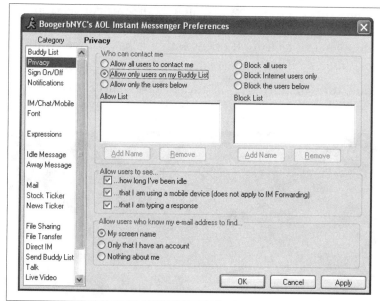

Figure 15-4:
If you don't want strangers IMing you out of the blue, you can adjust your program's privacy settings to allow only people on your buddy list to contact you. In case of a squabble, you can also block certain people.

The chat transcript

Every now and then, you'll wish you could *preserve* a chat for all time: a particularly meaningful conversation with a friend, lover, or customer service agent. Fortunately, it's easy:

- **AIM.** With your message window still open, choose File → Save. You can save your transcript in AOL Rich Text Format (which saves the fonts, icons, and other visual spice used in your conversation) or Text Only (which just saves the text).

- **Yahoo Messenger.** In the Messenger IM window, choose Conversation → Save As, and then type a file name and choose where you want to save it. To save your chat text by default, choose Messenger → Preferences → Archive and click the button next to "Yes, save all of my messages." To see your collection at a later date, return to this dialog box and click the View Archive button.

• **MSN Messenger.** Choose File → Save As from the message window and then pick a place to save the resulting file. You can set MSN Messenger to automatically save all your conversations in Tools → Options. Click Messages in the left pane, and then in the Message History section, turn on the checkbox next to "Automatically keep a history of my conversations." Here, you can also choose what folder to store your chats in, too.

• **iChat.** On the iChat → Preferences → Messages panel, turn on "Automatically save chat transcripts." From now on, the text of your conversations is automatically saved in your Home → Documents → iChats folder. To view a chat later, just double-click its icon. It opens within iChat, compete with all colors and formatting.

Even if you don't turn on this "Automatically save" checkbox, you can always save individual chats in progress by choosing File → Save a Copy As.

POWER USERS' CLINIC

Multi-Service Chat: IM What I Am

Some people love instant messaging. They take every chance they can to chat. They even download *every* IM program they can find and keep them all open simultaneously, so they never miss their friends online.

While this approach certainly works, there's an easier way to keep up your end of the conservation with friends who use different IM programs: a *multi-service program* that can connect to all the major IM services at once. This way, you only have one buddy list to keep an eye on.

These programs work by hooking up with the services of the major IM players, including AIM and Yahoo, but the ride has not always been smooth.

In the past, AIM has been known to block and boot the multi-service programs off its server. A patch war escalated: The smaller companies figured out how to get back on, and then AIM blocked them again, and then they figured out how to get back on...and so on.

AOL has now opened its AIM service to programmers who want to develop their own versions or plug-ins for the program, but the company still pooh-poohs software that can connect to multiple services, citing security risks among its objections.

Still, the multi-service programs persist and continue to make IM life easier for people with pals scattered across Yahoo, AIM, and MSN. They include Gaim (*http://gaim.sourceforge.net*) for Mac, Windows, and Linux; Trillian (*www.trillian.cc*) for Windows; and Adium (*www.adiumx.com*) for Mac OS X.

Along with plugging you into a bunch of IM servers at once, most multi-service clients pack in some clever features of their own—like *tabbed conversations*, which let you have several different chats going on in the same window.

Beyond Text Chat

You can now send a lot more than typed greetings over most instant messaging systems. You can make phone calls, start up videoconferences, shoot files back and forth, play games, and otherwise blow onlookers' minds.

Voice calls

If your computer has a microphone and a good set of speakers (or better yet, a headset), you can ditch the typing and click over to actual spoken communications. The "call" is free, as long as you're both using the same IM service.

Some IM programs also let you use your computer to call people on their *telephones*. It costs extra and can be a little echo-laden as your voice bounces through the Internet, but it's still a heck of a lot cheaper than making the call over conventional landlines (as low as 9 cents a minute to São Paulo or 6 cents to Seoul). For more on calling people over the Internet—with or without a computer—see Chapter 18.

- **AIM.** Select your friend's name and then choose People → Connect to Talk at the top of the Buddy List window. When your pal accepts the invite to gab and you get a box onscreen confirming it, click the "Push to Talk" button and start talking.

- **Yahoo Messenger.** Yahoo also offers PC-to-PC voice calls and Webcam videoconferences. To call someone through the PC, choose Actions → Call Computer, and select the person from your Contact list. And in case you're fretting about missing something when you're away from your computer, you can Yahoo yap on certain cellphone models, too. Visit *http://mobile. yahoo.com* for instructions.

- **MSN Messenger.** Click the "Start a voice conversation" link at the bottom of the Messenger window.

- **iChat.** Buddies with iChat audio powers have a green telephone icon next to their names. Click the telephone icon to ring up that pal for an audio chat.

Video calls

Plug a $30 Webcam (or camcorder) into your computer and fire up your IM program, and you're ready to broadcast live video images to your similarly equipped friends.

A broadband connection is vital for this, and some programs may require specific types of cameras, so check your program's Help guide. Depending on

Internet traffic congestion, your video feed might be a little skippy and not as smooth as it always was on *Star Trek*.

Nothing, however, melts the miles away like being able to see and say goodnight to your loved ones when they're home in Boston and you're on a business trip in Berlin.

Note: If your firewall's smothering all of your advanced IM fun by not letting you connect to your friends with audio-video chat or file transfers, check your IM program's Help guide to find out which ports on your computer need to be open. For example, Apple recommends opening ports 5060, 5190, 5297, 5298, 5678, and 16384 through 16403 when trying to use iChat through firewalls in Mac OS X. Flip ahead to page 415 for the details on how to open firewall ports.

- **AIM.** Start an IM session with the buddy on your list you want to chat with, and then click the Video button at the bottom of the instant message window. Once you confirm that you want to connect, the Live Video IM panel slides open on the right side of your message window.

- **Yahoo Messenger.** Yahoo's video options are more convoluted than other IM programs, but you can see a pal over a Webcam by clicking the View My Webcam link next to the name in your Contacts list. (You can find Yahoo Messenger's settings for using Webcams at Messenger → Preferences → Webcam.)

- **MSN Messenger.** MSN Messenger also offers video chat if all connected parties have compatible Webcams. Microsoft recommends Logitech's QuickCam Pro 4000 or the QuickCam Communicate STX, which has several models that work well with MSN Messenger.

- **iChat.** Up to four people can videoconference at once with iChat; everyone needs a FireWire-based camera (digital camcorders or Apple's iSight video camera do nicely). Video-enabled pals have a green movie-camera icon next to their names in the Buddy List; click it to open the video chat window and get rolling.

Insert a smiley

Online, no one can see you smile. And that's too bad; in person, your facial expression can make all the difference between a friendly response and a nasty one. There's a world of difference between "I hate it when you do that" (said sternly) and "I hate it when you do that" (said with a grin and a wink).

That's why people still use little smiley faces in email and in chats. These symbols—also known as *emoticons*—are cutesy and a little clichéd, but they do the job: they soften or spin your typed remark very effectively.

When you choose a face from the smiley pop-up menu (like Undecided, Angry, or Frown), your IM program inserts it as a graphic into your response.

- **AIM.** In the IM window, click the smiley face in the toolbar above the text-input window to see a whole slew of yellow heads sporting a range of expressions.

- **Yahoo Messenger.** Click the smiley face on the left side of the Yahoo Messenger window to see more than 50 emoticons to choose from.

- **MSN Messenger.** Like the other programs above, just click the happy face above the text-input box in the MSN Messenger window and pick an expression that suits you.

- **iChat.** Choose a smiley from the pop-up menu at the right end of the text-input box.

Or, if you know the correct symbols to produce smileys—where :) means a smiling face, for example—you can save time by typing them instead of using the pop-up menu. Your IM program converts them into smiley icons on the fly, as soon as you send your reply.

Swapping Files

Just about every IM program lets you trade digital pictures, text documents, and other files from computer to computer. Your intended recipient must choose to accept the file—and then a direct machine-to-machine transfer begins.

This is a fantastic way to transfer files that are too big to send by email. A chat window never gets "full," and no attachment is "too large" to send.

This method halves the time of transfer, too, since your recipients get the file *as* you upload it. They don't have to wait 20 minutes for you to send the file, and then *another* 20 minutes to download it, as they would with email or FTP.

- **AIM.** At the top of the message window, choose People → Send File, and then select the file or folder you want to deliver to your buddy's computer.

- **Yahoo Messenger.** Drag the desired file's icon right into the IM window, or choose Actions → Send a File.

- **MSN Messenger.** Click the Send Files icon at the top of your IM window and select the file you want to send from wherever you have it stored on your hard drive, or just drag the photo or file into the message input box.

- **iChat.** Drag the file's icon from the Finder into the box where you normally type. (This trick works great with pictures because your conversation partner sees the graphic right in the iChat window.)

Note: Two things to remember about IM file transfers: First, firewalls with strict security settings can interfere with your ability to send files. Second, don't accept files from people you don't know; they're probably trying to get you to take a virus disguised as something else.

UP 2 SPEED

IM Teenspeak, FWIW

Thanks to the arrival of IM and text messaging, no longer do teenagers have to limit themselves to phone calls to recap the day at school (with the friends they just spent the day at school with). Kids can now IM each other all night, party in chat rooms, text message friends from the mall, and—on the rare occurrences when no one cool is online—even email each other.

With all this lame typing getting in the way of imparting important information, a new online text language has evolved. These text shortcuts are made up mostly of abbreviations for common phrases (FWIW means "for what it's worth," for example). These text shortcuts may look like license plate numbers, but they do save a lot of time—especially for people pecking out messages on cellphone keypads.

IM shortcuts condense many words into just a few letters: "by the way" becomes BTW, "as far as I know" shrinks down to AFAIK, and so on, giving the frantically typed missives something of a conversational flow. Other shortcuts like ".02" ("my two cents") and "<g>" (the speaker is grinning) add

other dimensions to the chat. One exceedingly popular abbreviation favored by chat room participants is "ASL?," which cuts to the chase and asks a newcomer's age, sex, and location.

Some of the abbreviations have been around since the early days of Usenet (page 312), the Internet's first major public bulletin board. Some, like SNAFU (Situation Normal: All F***ed Up) date back to World War II.

Several online dictionaries can help you decipher some of the more obscure abbreviations. A good one to start with is the Tech Dictionary's page at *www.techdictionary.com/chatsms.html*, which can help you figure out what the teens are typing these days. You can even pick up a few shortcuts yourself.

Don't feel like you have to use text-chat abbreviations in online conversation, though. Some people like them and some people don't; YMMV (your mileage may vary).

Games

Yahoo Messenger, AIM, and MSN Messenger all offer a selection of online games to play with your online pals.

- **Yahoo and MSN Messenger.** Click the Games button to strike up a round of chess.

- **AIM.** The AIM Buddy List window offers a Play AIM Games link that opens up a panel of game icons. Once you click an icon, you're taken to AOL's Games area (page 176), and you can send invites to buddies to join you.

Customize

Because they represent a virtual version of *you* hanging out on the Internet, instant messaging programs just beg for personalization. You can change the standard font to something more typographically funky, for example.

Even more fun: You can add your photo (or any image you fancy) to your IM name, so that people can identify you visually in their buddy lists. Most programs offer a selection of stock images for this stunt. But if you want to use your own photo, you'll probably have to crop it and shrink it to fit comfortably within the IM program window.

- **AIM.** In AIM, buddy icons can't be bigger than 50×50 pixels and 7 kilobytes in size. Use an image-editing program like Picasa or Photoshop Elements to do the cropping and resizing. Then you can add your photo by choosing My AIM → Edit Options → Edit Preferences → Expressions, and clicking the Browse PC button to navigate over and select your picture.

- **Yahoo Messenger.** Choose Messenger → My Display Image in the Contacts window. Click the button next to "Share my picture" if you want others to see it. Click Select, and if you don't like any of the sample images, click the Browse button to use one of your own; Yahoo handles the sizing for you.

- **MSN Messenger.** Click your own name at the top of the MSN Messenger Contacts window and choose Change My Display Picture from the drop-down menu. Using the My Display Picture box, you can pick an image from Microsoft's stock (soccer ball, chess pieces, orange flower) or click the Browse button to find one of your own. A preview window shows what your picture looks like after it's automatically squished down to IM size.

- **iChat.** Click the icon at the top of the iChat window and select Edit Picture or choose Buddies → Change My Picture from the iChat menu. Click the Choose button to select a photo on your hard drive (or just drag the desired image into the window), and then use the slider bar to adjust the cropping to the correct proportions.

Channel Surfing with IRC

Before there was IM, there was IRC, or *Internet Relay Chat*.

IRC is a method of instant typed communication that's still used today by Net-savvy people in special IRC chat rooms.

Developed in 1988 by a Finnish programmer named Jarkko Oikarinen, IRC went on to be an unstoppable form of communication. In fact, it got the news out to the world in the early 1990s even during the media blackouts that surrounded the attempted Soviet coup and the Kuwati perspective during the Iraqi invasion. (Read the logs of the unfolding events at *www.livinginternet.com/r/rp.htm*.)

IRC's lean, mean interface doesn't spackle your screen with ads and extra windows, but there's no denying that using IRC is far more technical and less graphic than a standard IM program.

For example, you're expected to find an IRC *server* to host your chat—and then choose an IRC *channel* (discussion topic) to join. Some people use IRC for sharing files (often copyrighted material).

If IRC intrigues you, you can get started with tutorials and links to IRC client programs at *http:// irchelp.org* and *www.ircbeginner.com*. The Windows program mIRC has some informative pages, too, at *www.mirc.com*.

Chat Rooms

If instant messaging is primarily a private conversation between two people, a chat room's like a big party full of people all jabbering away in a group discussion. A chat room window (Figure 15-5) even looks a bit like an IM conversation, except there might be a few dozen screen names all scrolling by as the conversation progresses.

Some chat rooms are hosted on Web sites (like *www.talkcity.com*). Some are sequestered behind the gates of online services like AOL or MSN. And some you can visit through Yahoo Messenger.

To participate in a chat, you generally need a screen name and a password from whoever's hosting the chat room.

For example, to join a chat room at Talk City, you first sign up for a free or paid membership plan. Once you have your user name and password, you can browse the chat room topics and click to join one that interests you.

When you first join a chat room, it's a good idea to read, not write, for the first few minutes, until you get a feel for the conversation. Basic rules of conversational etiquette apply in virtual communications as they do in real-world ones: don't ramble, don't cuss, and don't insult people.

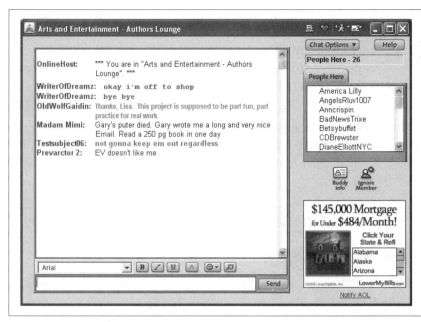

Figure 15-5:
*AOL members have a big
private hotel of chat rooms
to choose from, but you can
also talk in a Yahoo chat
room with a menu option in
Yahoo Messenger, as
explained on page 308.*

On the other hand, unlike those deadly cocktail parties where you get trapped
in the corner listening to someone wax rhapsodic about lawn chemicals,
online escape is just a click way. As in the real world, you'll probably find a
mix of personalities in the chat, with both thoughtful, well-written comments
and bigmouthed blowhards.

Chat rooms can be organized by topic, like Textiles or FIFA World Cup. Many
chat rooms are set up so people can meet and possibly date each other. You
can create a profile that tells anyone who's looking a little bit about you, but
do yourself a favor and keep it vague.

Online, people can represent themselves any way they like. Therefore, if you're
looking for love in chat rooms, be extremely cautious when setting up real-life
encounters. Don't reveal too much information about yourself at first. Kids
should *never* give out *any* personal information online. And if you do agree to
meet someone in person after talking on the phone for a few weeks, choose a
busy public place. Read Chapter 17 for more on online dating and socializing.

A simple Google search for *chat room* should bring you a lot of hits. Several of
the big online services have chat options, too:

• **AOL Chat.** If you're an AOL subscriber, you have full access to the service's
huge complex of chat rooms. When you're logged into AOL, choose Community → Chat Room Listings for a current list of rooms created by both
America Online's staff and AOL members themselves.

You can start a conversation by clicking Start Your Own Chat on the AOL Chat Room Listings window. There's also an option there to start or join a *private* chat, but unless you're starting one yourself, you need to know the name of a private chat before you can enter the room—which means somebody else on AOL needs to tell you about it first.

You use your AOL screen name for chatting, but if you want to protect your privacy, don't log into AOL with your main account name. You can create another screen name just for the chat rooms; AOL lets you create six other screen identities after your first one (visit the Account Settings area).

Some chat rooms are quite polite; others can be completely filthy. You can set your AOL privacy settings to block anyone who's harassing you online (use the AOL Keyword: *Privacy Settings*). There's also a Notify AOL button in the bottom corner of the chat window that lets you file a formal complaint against the person who's harassing you (AOL Keyword: *Chat*).

• **Yahoo Chat.** Yahoo's chat rooms used to be free and open to the public at the company's Web site. But those freewheeling days are long gone, thanks to an overwhelming wave of bad behavior and predatory activity.

The Yahoo chat rooms haven't completely closed their doors, though. You just need the latest version of Yahoo Messenger for Windows (page 292) to gain entry.

Once you sign up for an account with Yahoo (if you don't have one already), you can download and install the Messenger software. Log in with your Yahoo ID and password. Click the Chat icon on the Yahoo Messenger window and select a screen name for your chat session.

Select a Category, or topic of conversation, from the left side of the window, and a specific room from the right. Double-click the name of the room you want to join; a chat window pops up on your screen, giving you a place to type your comments and revealing the names of everyone else already in the room. (*http://chat.yahoo.com*)

• **MSN Chat.** In an effort to shield its clients from unsavory behavior and the Spam Invasion, Microsoft has moved its formerly public chat rooms inside its MSN subscription services: MSN Hotmail Plus (page 266), MSN Radio Plus, MSN Premium, MSN Dial-up (page 19), MSN Radio Plus, and MSN TV.

If you don't have any of these but still want to talk, you can sign up for MSN Chat by itself for $20 a year (*http://getchat.msn.com*). You must be over 18 to join in the chats, which include the typical romance-entertainment-sports topics you'd expect.

On the main MSN Chat page, you can click to join featured and popular chat rooms; have your MSN user name and password ready to go.

If you don't want to take out an MSN membership, you can still find some live chat options sequestered in the online discussion rooms inside its MSN Groups areas described in the next chapter. (*http://chat.msn.com*)

If you don't want to wander through public chat rooms, most IM programs let you form quick temporary chat rooms with people on your buddy list; look for a Chat Invitation command in your program's menus. When the chat window opens, click the names on your buddy list to invite them.

GEM IN THE ROUGH

IM-to-Cellphone

If you know somebody whose cellphone can get SMS (Short Message Service) notes, you can shoot them short text messages right from your chat window. It's a great way to send a "Call me!" or "Running late—see you tonight!" or "Turn on channel 4 right now!!!" message to someone's phone.

AIM. Click the Setup button at the bottom of the Buddy List window and then click the Add Mobile icon in the Setup window. Type in your bud's mobile number, give it a name ("HerbertMobile" or something), and click OK. When you want to send 'em a text message, click that name in the list and fire off a message just as you would with any IM session.

Yahoo Messenger. On your Contacts List window, choose Actions → Send an SMS Message. If you don't have the cellphone number of the recipient in the My Contacts list, click the Other Contacts tab and type in the phone number, like *2125551212* and enter your note in the message window.

MSN Messenger. To set up mobile messaging with MSN, right-click a contact's name in your list and choose the "Add a Mobile Number for This Contact" option. Then type in your friend's mobile number. When you want to send a message to the person, right-click the name in the contacts list and choose Send Other → Send a Message to a Mobile Device. Type your message in the window and click Send.

iChat. Choose File → New Chat with Person. In the address box that pops up, type +1 and the full cellphone number. For (212) 555-1212, you'd type this: *+12125551212*. Press Enter to return to the chat window. Type a very short message (a couple of sentences, tops) and then press Enter.

Discussion Groups

The chat rooms and instant messages described in the previous chapter are great for real-time mingling. But like conversations around the water cooler, they're not very long-lasting. Enter the *discussion group,* a thriving corner of the Internet where folks gather to post their opinions and expertise on every conceivable topic. Anyone reading along can chime in and post a message to contribute to the discussion—or read the whole thing from start to finish, because it stays on the Web site or server hosting the group.

A discussion group is like a chat room in *extremely* slow motion. And thanks to the permanence, it can be a treasure trove of useful information on everything from computer repair to the proper care of the viola da gamba.

Online discussion groups have been around since 1980, but they've gotten a lot easier to use in the past few years. Thanks to some of the same tools that make Web searching efficient, you can find the answers you seek in older discussion groups more quickly than ever before. Seek and ye shall find discussion groups on your favorite topics where you can jump right in with posts of your own. And if you don't find a group that you like anywhere on the Internet's vast frontier, you can play pioneer and start your own.

Finding and Searching Groups

Google Groups is the biggest and most famous community of discussions; it tends to hog a lot of attention due to its Usenet pedigree. But it's not the only discussion game in town.

A Brief History of Newsgroups

All the big portal players (Yahoo, MSN, AOL, and Google) host their own discussion groups. But their origins were far humbler.

These Web-based groups morphed out of a bulletin board system called *Usenet,* which was started in 1979 by two graduate students at Duke University. Like the Internet, Usenet was a decentralized global network of computers. But unlike the Internet, Usenet was designed solely to carry the traffic of a massive collection of typed discussions—*newsgroups.*

These groups were organized by topic; anyone could jump in with a comment (also called *posts, articles,* or *postings*) at any time. The system caught on; soon, hundreds of thousands of people participated in newsgroups—on topics ranging from aviation to zoology—making Usenet one of the first popular systems for online communication.

Before the Web arrived, Internet service providers offered access to Usenet. People who participated in newsgroups read and sent messages using software programs called *newsreaders*, which were something like email programs. In fact, many email programs, including Outlook Express, Entourage, and Mozilla Thunderbird, can also read newsgroups; you can send and receive newsgroup messages just like email. You do have to configure your mail program to get the messages from your favorite newsgroups, so if you're just starting out, exploring newsgroups through the Web is easier.

Because it was sprawled over multiple servers and stuffed with data, Usenet was a hard network for the ISP's and other Usenet hosts to maintain. As a result, most ISPs eventually limited or even eliminated your access to newsgroups. On top of that limitation, the email-like interface of newsreaders was a convenient way for individuals to get messages, but it didn't provide a good way to *search* newsgroups. And if you participated in a lot of active groups, you could tie up your phone lines (not to mention your free time) forever.

Meanwhile, the Internet was turning into a better environment for online communication. In particular, people liked using this groovy new part of the Internet called the World Wide Web to read stuff.

In 1995, Deja News created a Web site that let people read and participate in the thousands of existing Usenet groups without requiring a newsreader. At DejaNews.com, you could search for keywords in articles and group titles, and read and join groups—all right on a Web page. It was a glorious development because you could actually find older stuff on Usenet without spending a month swimming through the reservoirs of old posts in your newsreader archives.

Deja was eventually, and perhaps inevitably, snapped up by Google. Today, you can go to Google.com, click Groups, and search and read newsgroups with amazing efficiency. You can find all the old newsgroups—the Deja archives and even the original Usenet groups dating back to 1981—in Google Groups.

Yahoo, America Online, and MSN offer similar groups. These groups are separate communities, though; if you post about your 1971 Dodge Dart in the vintage cars group on AOL, nobody in Yahoo or MSN's car groups can see it.

You may have to browse until you find a group that feels like home, but you can find or make a group on anything and everything. To give you some idea of what's out there (and what to expect once you get there), the next few pages take you on a tour of the bigger players in the discussion groups game: Google, Yahoo, MSN, and AOL.

Tip: In addition to groups hosted by the big guys, there are thousands upon thousands of other discussion forums around the Web, including those hosted by gaming and music sites. While posts from many forums show up in standard search engine results, a search engine dedicated to tracking down all the ongoing conversations can help you zero in on topics you'd like to join. If you're bored with the boards you're on already or haven't found a good one yet, try searching for new conversations with specialized search sites like BoardTracker (*www.boardtracker.com*) or Board-Reader (*www.boardreader.com*).

Google Groups

Google has hosted Usenet newsgroups under the name Google Groups since 2001. You can see it at *http://groups.google.com.*

The Big G recently gave the whole enterprise a speed boost; new postings to the boards now appear online in about 10 seconds. (In that time, they also become available for searching when you use the Search Groups box described on page 318.) Google Groups now includes thousands of very active groups, plus the Usenet archives—all of which total about a *billion* messages and counting.

The biggest advantage of being part of the Google family is that the groups and their archives now appear as Web pages, with the power of the Google search system built right in. You can look up information by keyword, by date, even by author, and you're bound to find something juicy every time you dive in.

To create, join in, and post messages in Google Groups, you need to sign up for a free Google Account. A Google Account isn't the same thing as a Gmail account (page 264); but if you already have a Gmail user name and password, you can use it for Groups. There's a Sign Up link on the front page of Google Groups, shown in Figure 16-1.

As you click through the screens during the account-creation process, you can pick an online nickname that will appear on your messages. If so inclined, you can also fill out a biographical profile: your geographic location, blog address (if you have one), and favorite inspirational quote.

Figure 16-1:
Listing every single Google Group on the main page might make your eyeballs melt, so Google gives you a "Find a group" search box right up front so you can search for topics that interest you instead of staggering through a list the size of the Shanghai phone book. The Search box at the top of the page lets you search for keywords within Group postings. Google lists some of the popular groups on the page as well, and gives you the opportunity to start your very own group at the bottom. Of course, to do that, you need a Google Account, and you can either sign up or sign in to one on the right side of the page.

Using Google Groups

There are two ways of finding discussion groups to join on Google. This *is* Google, after all, so *searching* for groups by keyword or topic is one option. Using the "Find a group" box on the main Groups page, you can seek out topics you're interested in, like ferret care or dulcimer playing.

If you prefer to just poke around, click the "Browse group categories" link. On the resulting Group Directory page, Google neatly clumps all its groups into categories arranged by:

- **Topic.** Broad categories like Arts and Entertainment, Computers, and Recreation are listed, as well as how many groups are nestled under this topic. Click the topic that interests you to see the subtopics, and keep clicking until you arrive at the group concerning your specific area of interest. If you click through Recreation to Antiques, you can see a list of all the groups discussing various collectibles, from Fiestaware to ancient Roman coins.

- **Region.** International groups are divided up by geographic location, from Asia to the United States. Once again, you can click from region to country, narrowing your search all the way to groups devoted to traditional Irish step-dancing. As you might expect, many groups in the Region area are in other languages, but you can focus on the ones in English by clicking the English link at the top of the page.

- **Language.** To find *only* groups with postings in other languages, click the tongue of your choice in the Language category to find groups. That's how you find people discussing photography in German or the nuances of Outlook Express in Japanese.

- **Activity.** The posts fly fast and furious in some groups—and show up once in a blue moon in others. To focus on groups where there's lots of discussion, click the links under Activity: High, Medium, or Low message traffic.

- **Members.** You can see groups sorted according to membership size with the options under the Members area.

Note: There may be some variation in the wording, but the corresponding group home pages on Yahoo Groups and the other portals break out major topics almost exactly the same way as Google. All the sites may have group discussions devoted to sailboating, so if you don't like the personality mix or info offered on Google, try one of the other group gatherings.

There's also a "Browse all of Usenet" link that lets you drive by all the groups created by Google Groups members and takes you to all the old-school Usenet newsgroups (page 312), many of which are still very lively.

When you click a category link on the Group Directory page, all the groups that fall under it are displayed in a list, along with a brief *TV Guide*–style capsule description for each ("Shortwave radio enthusiasts" or "A group for Grateful Dead-heads"). You also see how many members are in the group and how active it is. Click a group's name to go to its page.

Note: Some groups require formal membership before you can participate in the discussion. Members-only groups are labeled as "restricted" in the description. To join a restricted group, click "Apply for membership" to send a message to the group's owner or moderator for approval. Some restricted groups are also listed as "invitation only"; click "Send email to owner" to compose and send your humble request.

If the group belongs to Usenet or has an open membership, you see all the recent posts and topics under discussion by its members. Each topic title is a link; click to see all the responses to the original message (Figure 16-2).

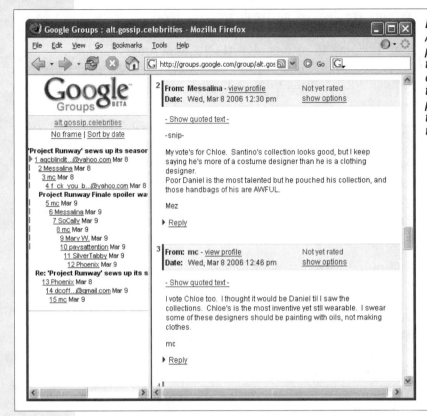

Figure 16-2:
As you read through the posts on the right side of the screen, you can see the discussion thread on the left that shows who participated. Click a link in the thread to jump directly to that person's post.

To respond to someone's comment, click Reply, and type your message in the resulting text box. Once you finish, click Preview to proofread your message or Post to add it to the ongoing discussion.

If you want to take the conversational lead, click "Start a new topic," found at the top of each Google Group's home page.

> **Note:** Each Google Group's page offers a link that lets you *subscribe* to a group, but that's not the same as becoming a member. Instead, this link adds the group to your My Groups list: a clickable list of all the groups you've joined. The idea is to keep your favorites all in one tidy list, so you don't have to search or browse to find the groups you like to track.

Usenet groups on Google

The old-school Usenet groups are organized by categories, subcategories, sub-subcategories, and so on, until you hit a specific topic. Each topic has many discussions (also known as *threads*) associated with it, and each discussion is made up of one or more posts.

Just to make sure you know you're in geekland, Usenet groups have a peculiar naming system. Top-level categories, like those listed in Figure 16-3, are called *hierarchies*. All newsgroups fit into a hierarchy, as indicated by the first part of a group's name (*aol*, for example, for discussions related to America Online). Subsequent parts of a name consist of subcategories and then, finally, specific topics.

Figure 16-3:
Usenet used to take center stage in Google Groups. Even though the company has changed things up a bit on the Groups home page, you can still find all your quirky Usenet faves in their own sections.

Each part is separated by a period (or *dot*). For example, the *sci.* (science) hierarchy has a subcategory called Agriculture, which has four topics: *sci.agriculture.beekeeping, sci.agriculture.fruit, sci.agriculture.poultry,* and *sci.agriculture.rarites.* In the beekeeping topic, a recent thread was called "Swarm prevention by foundation in the brood nest," and it had 10 posts.

Note: Usenet group names always have at least two parts—a hierarchy and a category—and sometimes five or more subcategories (for example, *alt.collecting.beanie-babies.discussion.moderated*).

The Usenet area of Google Groups lists more than 1,000 hierarchies. Some of the most active are described in the following list.

- **Alt.** Stands for alternative, but might as well mean "anything goes." The topics—over 15,000—are sometimes very specific (*alt.minneapolis.the-other-minnesota*), and the conversations are often freewheeling.

- **Comp.** Short for computers: hardware, software, operating systems, theory, and more. You've just hit the Geekville city limits.

- **Misc.** Miscellaneous—which is odd, because *most* Usenet hierarchies carry pretty random groups. Notably, Misc. contains some employment and for-sale groups like *misc.jobs.fields.chemistry* and *misc.forsale-computers*, plus *misc.kids, misc.rural,* and *misc.metric-system*.

- **News.** Info about Usenet itself—*not* current events. (For current events, see the Talk. hierarchy.)

- **Rec.** Recreation and entertainment, including arts, aviation, food, games, hobbies, humor, knives, music, outdoors, sports, travel, and so on.

- **Sci.** Science of all kinds: aeronautics, cognition, cryonics, the environment, language, and physics, to name a few. And larger discussions of science, like *sci.skeptics.*

- **Soc.** Social issues. A few groups here get the most activity, including *soc.culture* (which covers countries, like *soc.culture.australia* or *soc.culture.cornish*); other active groups include *soc.geneology, soc.history,* and *soc.religion.*

- **Talk.** Current issues, especially those that lend themselves to controversy and debate. Politics and religions are hot. *Talk.meow*, however, appears to be floating facedown, drowned in a pool of spam.

Searching Google's archives

Many groups permit full searching through their *archives*—all the messages ever posted there. When browsing for a group, check its description to see whether it keeps a message archive for newer members to search or look through. Yahoo and Google, for example, let only members of a group search through past posts.

Since Google Groups contains the complete Usenet archive dating back to 1981, this is where you'll have the most luck searching; this material has been open to the public forever. You can search in all Google Groups (type your query into the search box on the main Groups page), or within a single hierarchy or any subcategory (page 317).

Figure 16-4 shows a Google Groups results page that looks a lot like a regular Google listing, with your results along the left and a few ads (a.k.a. sponsored links) along the right.

UP TO SPEED

Godwin's Law

The subculture of Usenet newsgroups has done its part to contribute to the English language. The terms *spam* and *FAQ* (Frequently Asked Questions) first appeared on Usenet, which also popularized *troll* (losers who purposely pick fights with other people in newsgroups) and *flame* (angry personal attacks).

And speaking of flames: long-running feuds between prolific posters are common. This tiresome tendency even inspired Godwin's Law (also known as Godwin's Rule of Nazi Analogies).

Godwin's Law, an Internet adage coined in 1990 by lawyer Mike Godwin states: *As an online discussion grows longer, the probability of a comparison involving Nazis or Hitler approaches one.*

Many Usenet newsgrouppers hold that once someone invokes the Nazi comparison, the discussion thread is over, and whoever brought Hitler into the debate has officially lost the argument.

Figure 16-4:
A roundup of all the newsgroups discussing "Project Runway." Usenet groups are still loud and proud, but there are plenty of newer discussion groups that have sprung up since Google gave Groups a facelift in December 2004. Like many Google services, a strip of sponsored links adorns the right side of the page.

Google normally shows group results listed by relevance—just like regular results. But, in many cases, sorting by *date*—which puts the most recent post at the top—gives you *much* more useful listings. In fact, sorting by date is often the way to go.

For example, if you're searching for a person or event that's been in the news lately, sorting by date (click the link in the upper-right corner) gives you the freshest messages. When you've found a snippet that intrigues you, and you want to read the whole message, click the title. You jump to the message in question, where your search terms are highlighted.

The Google Groups Advanced Search page (page 74) gives you a form that lets you specify what you're looking for with even more detail: messages posted within certain date ranges, by author or subject, or even containing exact phrases. It sure beats staggering through the millions of posts looking for that one nugget of information you seek, like how to install Linux on an iPod.

Yahoo Groups

Yahoo Groups has a few million discussions of its own going on at *http://groups.yahoo.com*, where members post up a storm of messages and pictures. Its main Groups page lists 16 general category links, like Music or Government & Politics, so that you can browse your way down through the listings.

You burrow down from categories to actual messages just as you do on Google Groups: by clicking your way from Hobbies & Crafts to Potato Guns, Juggling, and Pottery, to subcategories, to actual groups. You can search for groups by topic or keyword in the same way, too.

One cool thing about Yahoo's group effort is that, unlike Google, members are allowed to post photos along with text, which can really liven things up visually.

You can browse around without having to sign into the Yahoo mother ship. But if you want to post anywhere, the site asks you to sign in with your Yahoo ID. If you already have one for Yahoo Mail, Messenger, or whatever you may have signed up for before, you can use the same name and password here. If you don't have a Yahoo ID, you have the option to make one this very minute—free of charge, of course—on the Sign-in page.

Also, as with Google, you can create a little biographical profile for yourself; to preserve your privacy, it's best to leave out stuff like your address and phone number.

Groups Therapy

Online communities can be a pleasant distraction for some. But for other people, discussion groups are an oasis in times of trouble. People isolated by geography, culture, society, or health concerns can find solace, sympathy, and shared experiences among like-minded individuals. For people uncomfortable talking about sensitive topics in person or who are just plain shy, virtual reality can be a wonderful thing: You can express your thoughts and feelings from a safe spot—or even behind an alias, which can be a very liberating experience.

A good, thorough Web search (page 74) on your topic of interest will probably turn up a few results worth checking out, but here are a few sites with message boards or mailing lists designed to help people cope with life's most common big moments.

iVillage. This site is a sprawling Web portal aimed at women and their myriad interests. Its message boards permit members from all walks of life to gather together in text. The Relationships boards are especially active, with discussions about coping with divorce, dating military men, and online matchmaking among the topics. (*www.ivillage.com*)

About.com. This is a sprawling site packed with problem-solving practical advice written by the site's human and visible Guides. It offers online forums and blogs for many of the subjects it covers, including home-schooling, debt management, and health-related issues. (*www.about.com*)

HealthyPlace. With 100 message boards to discuss different issues related to mental health, HealthyPlace has plenty of places for members to share their feelings and experiences. (*www.healthyplace.com*)

The Wellness Community. This nonprofit site is devoted to supporting and educating anyone who's affected in one way or another by cancer. Links to online support groups appear right on its home page. (*www.thewellnesscommunity.org*)

GriefNet. This site, an online community for people dealing with death and grief, features 60 email support groups to help people cope with major loss. (*www.griefnet.org*)

Foundations and nonprofit organizations set up to deal with certain social issues may also have links to online support groups, so it's worth a check of the group's Web site for more information.

Yahoo's groups can be either Public or Membership Required. In Public groups, you see posts right away when you click the group's name, and you can post messages without formally joining (although you do have to sign into Yahoo). Members-only groups require that you click the Join This Group link and fill out a form to get in and see postings by other members.

One good thing about members-only groups is that the approval process prevents the random advertising invasion that has turned parts of Usenet into a vast wasteland of spam.

On a group's Yahoo home page, you'll find something called the Message History graphic, which shows how many posts people have generated since the group was formed. If you're a member, click a month to read all the posts generated during that time. Click the Members link on the left side of a group's page to see a list of everyone who belongs to the group along with their Yahoo profiles, if any.

Tip: You can participate in Yahoo discussions entirely by email, if you find that convenient. When you join the group, there's a place on the membership form for an email address of your choice. Furthermore, each group page lists all the email addresses you need to send posts to the group, subscribe, unsubscribe, and so on.

The panel on the left side of a Yahoo group's page gives you plenty of other things to share besides text messages. For instance, you can add pictures to the group's Web page by clicking the Photos link. You can share files like Word documents or PDF files, too, if you think they'd be helpful to the participants of a discussion (click the Files link). Click the Calendars link to create an online calendar for scheduling group activities.

Like Google Groups, ads and sponsored links surround each Groups page (though not the actual message area). These commercial links usually offer products and services related to the discussion topic on the page. They're a small price to pay for keeping in touch with your friends.

MSN Groups

MSN Groups are Microsoft's version of Web-based discussion boards. Each MSN group can be open to the public or entirely private and require an invitation to join. Your first stop on the way to joining one of MSN's Groups is *http:// groups.msn.com*.

To get into a group, you need a Microsoft ID, known as a .NET Passport, or a Hotmail address (page 266). There are thousands of groups available, all with their own Web sites; you can see the list by clicking Browse Groups on the main page.

Once again, you can click down through categories or perform a search for a discussion topic. MSN includes a graphic next to each group's description: an Activity Meter icon that resembles a speedometer to give you an indication of how busy this particular group is. If the needle's all the way to the right, this is a chatty group indeed.

Many groups let you snoop around without formally joining. Unless you sign up to be a member, though, you can't participate in the group discussion or interact with other members. Some groups, especially those that are women-only or men-only, don't even permit browsing by non-members.

When you have some memberships under your belt, you can check for new messages by clicking the My Groups tab on the main Groups page. Here again, you can read messages posted on the board's Web site or have them delivered to your email inbox.

Groups@AOL

Once the electronic equivalent of a gated community open only to paying subscribers, America Online has been opening up parts of its service to the general Web population for the past few years. For example, its online discussion circles are now available to the public at *http://groups.aol.com*.

Anyone with an AIM name (page 291) or AOL membership can join a group, although only paying AOL members can create new groups. Compared to some of the other services, AOL's Groups aren't as active or organized, and many groups listed on directory pages are obviously posts from spammers.

AOL Groups can be public or private and are run by group members. In contrast, AOL's discussion boards (*http://peopleconnection.aol.com/messageboards*) are all public and similar in size and scope to the old-school Usenet-style bulletin boards. Topics are set by AOL and some boards are moderated by AOL staffers to remove offensive posts and keep the peace. You can search and read posts without signing up, but you'll need an AOL account or at least a free AIM screen name to post replies. The best thing about the AOL discussion boards? You can choose to ignore messages by people you find obnoxious by clicking the "Ignore" link at the bottom of the offending party's post.

Creating New Groups

Thanks to the community-oriented efforts of Google, Yahoo, MSN, and AOL, you can create your own discussion groups. Your group can be joined by whomever you want to hang out with, and you can talk about whatever you want. Class reunion committees, vintage car enthusiasts, and gecko owners have all found uses for online groups as a way to organize events, trade tips, and participate in a discussion where everyone doesn't have to be online at the same time.

Once you've signed in, creating a group is as uncomplicated as clicking through a few Web pages and filling out some forms. To get started, look for the "Create a new group" link or button on the main Groups page.

Here are the basic steps you need to complete:

1. **Give your group a name.**

   As shown on Yahoo's "Start a group" page (see Figure 16-5), you need to give your group a name like "UTexas Alumni in LA" or "The Piping Gecko Owners" so people can find it when they search for keywords (like Texas or geckos), as well as a description. Your new group's name becomes part of the URL for its Web site, as in *http://launch.groups.yahoo.com/group/pipinggeckos*.

   The group-creation page automatically generates a similar email address (*pipinggeckos@yahoogroups.com*) that your members can use to post messages by mail.

2. **Rate your groups and set your membership policy.**

   Any group you create can be public or private. For public groups that anyone can join, you should indicate an age rating in the description, to tell people the intended audience level. In MSN Groups, for example, you can choose General, Mature (sort of a PG-13 to R rating, meaning "some content not suitable for children"), or Adult (explicit or graphic text or images within the group).

   As part of the group-creation process for most sites, you're asked to set the membership requirements for your group. In Google Groups, you can opt for Public (open to everyone to join and post); Announcement-only (anyone can join and read, but only the creator can post messages); and Restricted (invite-only to join and read, and your group's archived posts don't appear in Google search results). Click "Create my group" to continue.

   Yahoo and MSN Groups also offer members-only options. Additionally, both let you make your group Moderated (messages are screened by you before they appear in public) or Unmoderated (messages are automatically posted); you can also choose to have it listed in the public directory of groups—or not.

   During your group creation for most sites, you'll need to supply your contact email address and place your group in one of the general categories listed on the main page.

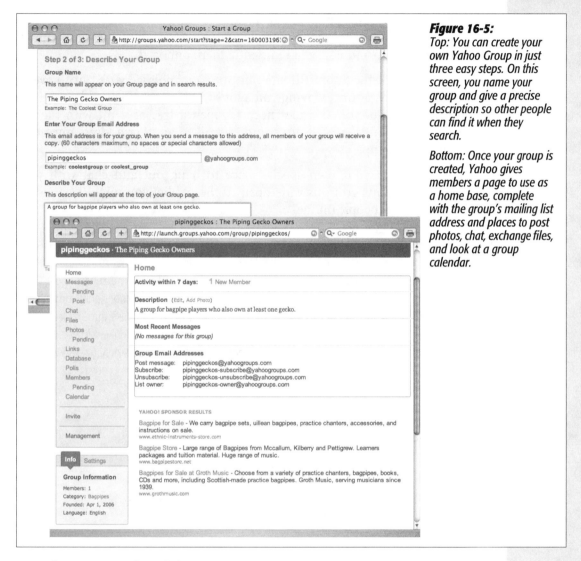

Figure 16-5:
Top: You can create your own Yahoo Group in just three easy steps. On this screen, you name your group and give a precise description so other people can find it when they search.

Bottom: Once your group is created, Yahoo gives members a page to use as a home base, complete with the group's mailing list address and places to post photos, chat, exchange files, and look at a group calendar.

3. **Invite some people to join your group.**

   Here, you can add the email addresses of friends and colleagues you would like to join your little social circle. With Google Groups, after you add their email addresses, you can decide how they can join (immediate membership from the get-go or only after responding to your initial invitation email) and in what form their messages initially appear (just on the Web site or by various email delivery options) before they join the group. Add a welcome message, and you're done!

Yahoo lets you enter up to 50 email addresses or Yahoo IDs of people you'd like to invite. Type up a short introductory message telling these folks about your new group and why you're inviting them onboard.

Once you click the Submit Invite button, your message goes out to everybody on the list at once, saving you a lot of individual email addressing. To join your group, your invitees need to open a free account with the site you're using, but they can direct group mail to another address once they log in and sign up.

At last, you have your own special place to hang out and chat with your friends. And if your group is wide open to the public, you might even get to know a few more people online.

Tip: Most Web-based discussion groups are free, but some long-standing online communities are full of paying members who have been on the Internet for quite a while. They're still going strong, discussing current culture, politics, news, and other daily events. Paying for a service that's freely available around the Web may seem extravagant, but these closed, subscriber-only communities are free of advertising and interference from traveling trolls who like to cruise through free public forums looking for cheap thrills. The Well (*www.well.com*) is one of the pioneers in this category; it's been online since 1985. Echo (*www.echonyc.com*) is another members-only board with a distinctly New York perspective on life. Its founder calls it "the crankiest group in cyberspace."

Social Networking

As you may have gathered from the previous three chapters, the Internet offers all sorts of ways to make contact with people. Email, chat rooms, and discussion boards all facilitate connections in the virtual world. But some folks want more than electronic pen pals—and that's where *social networking* sites come in.

Some are dating sites, which combine the old tradition of personal ads with some of the Internet's great strengths: the ability to post pictures, search for whatever you're looking for, and do it all whenever the mood strikes. Others are business networking sites, where professionals can get to know each other, share job tips and consultant contacts, and discuss business matters. Last, but not least, are the personal-profile sites, where people (mostly young ones) create highly personal autobiographical sites and link to their friends' sites, creating massive (and massively addictive) catacombs of people and their quirks.

Socializing and Dating Services

Millions of people use social sites every month. Some are just interested in making new friends, but the vast majority are looking for dates. Some people love the convenience and directness of online dating, where you can search exclusively for partners who share your interests. Others may find it a bit too conquest-oriented—too much like catalog shopping.

Either way, all the sites work pretty much the same way. You sign up for an account, create a profile that describes you and what you like, and post your profile on the site.

Other people can see your profile and send you a message in the hopes of getting acquainted. (All of this courtship business is conducted within the matchmaking service itself; your profile and messages are hidden from the outside world. This situation offers security on both sides—security for you, in the form of privacy protection, and security for the dating site's bank balance because you're sure to keep paying your subscription fees while looking for love.)

If both parties are interested, the personal contact moves from online interaction to live dates. Some people turn out to be exactly as they describe themselves. Others…not so much.

In any case, the date either works out and leads to a full-time relationship, or it doesn't, and you go back to browsing more profiles on dating sites.

Note: Most dating sites let you browse people's profiles for free, but if you want to actually contact anybody about a potential date, you have to pay a monthly fee. Prices vary, although there are a few free services, like Plenty of Fish (*www.plentyoffish.com*).

If you're curious to know how these services stack up against each other, try one of the comparison sites mentioned back in Chapter 7. ConsumerSearch, for example, delves into that very topic at *www.consumersearch.com/www/internet/online-dating/fullstory.html*.

Most sites offer checkboxes to narrow your search. Common categories include religion, age, sexual orientation, smoking status (cigarettes, not looks), and so on. It's not exactly like getting a mail-order bride (although there are sites for *that*, too), but some people go into these things with very precise expectations of what they want.

To avoid misunderstandings, be honest in your profile and your intentions. The relative anonymity and virtual reality of the Internet give people the chance to leave behind aspects of their lives and personalities they wish to hide. But these things can manifest themselves in ugly or awkward ways (*How could you not like my Sigmund—you said you love dogs!*), so make sure you're advertising a version of yourself that stays moderately close to the truth.

Finding the Right Site

Different sites take different approaches. Lavalife (*www.lavalife.com*) mainly caters to younger, tech-savvy people looking to date. SeniorFriendFinder (*www.seniorfriendfinder.com*) is aimed at older people looking for love and companionship. There are even sites that target people with special interests like owning horses or listening to Goth music (*www.equestriancupid.com* and *www.gothicmatch.com*, to be precise).

Tips for Online Dating

Online dating services let you meet, date, and even marry someone you might have never met in real life. It all starts with what you put in your profile and how you play things when the emailing begins.

Here are a couple of points to respect and protect the feelings of all involved:

- **Don't lie.** Trust is key in any relationship. If your profile claims you're a high-powered movie exec with a Ferrari and a house in the O.C., expect some harsh criticism from your dates if you turn out to be a middle manager at a paper-goods company who drives a 10-year-old Nissan. Similarly, if you're already hitched and trolling around the dating sites, at least be upfront about it.

- **Don't use ancient pictures.** It may still be you, but using an old snapshot from 20 years ago in your profile isn't accurately representing yourself.

Better yet, here are some tips to improve your chances of striking gold in the online dating world:

- **Don't send out form letters.** Take the time to read people's full profiles. Then compose personalized notes based on their interests.

People get enough spam in real life; they'll recognize a canned, three-line cut 'n' paste job if that's what you're sending out.

- **Don't write someone off after one message.** Some people take a little while to warm up, especially in online situations. Face it, some warm and wonderful folks just aren't great wordsmiths; give 'em a break if their prose isn't as polished as yours.

- **Don't hog the conversation.** If you meet someone and are in the email stage, ask questions about the other person's life. Make it a two-way exchange instead of sending long rambling messages all about yourself that suck the air out of the virtual room.

- **Don't use profanity or dirty jokes.** Until you find out more about the person, it's best to keep your communications courteous and G-rated.

When it comes down to it, dating is dating, and the online factor mainly facilitates the *meeting* part of the equation. Despite the electronics involved, you're still dealing with a human being with thoughts and feelings on the other end of your Internet connection.

Dating sites catering to people seeking marriage often refer to themselves as "online relationship sites." They attempt to approach the compatibility problem as scientifically as possible. For example, you fill out a lengthy personality profile and pay a fee ($21 to $60 a month, depending on how many months you sign up for in advance). At *www.eharmony.com*, for instance, you answer *436 questions* about all aspects of your personality, including sense of humor, intellect, and spiritual beliefs. The company's computers then attempt to match you up with somebody with a similar profile.

Speaking of spiritual beliefs: many sites are designed for those who want to date within their faith. Some of these include JDate (a site for Jewish singles at *www.jdate.com*); BigChurch (for Christian singles; *www.bigchurch.com*); and the Muslim Marriage Junction (*www.muslimmarriagejunction.com*). Other sites help people with similar ethnic backgrounds, sexual orientations, or interests (like pets) meet each other—the dating portal site TruDating has loads of links to these specialized matchmaking sites at *www.trudating.com*.

Online Dating Safety Tips

You've probably heard horror stories in the news about dates gone horribly, horribly wrong in one way or another. Like anything you do online, you need to use caution and common sense in your online dealings, and dating is no exception. For example:

- **Go slowly.** Take your time and get to know the other person through email and a photo exchange before you make the move to telephone calls or meeting in person. People who want to rush things along probably aren't a good match for you. Trust needs to be earned on the installment plan.

- **Guard your privacy.** Use the Internet's anonymity to your advantage. Don't put your whole life story in your profile—or your personal email address, your phone number, your mailing address, or where you work. You may even want to create a separate "dating-only" email account for your romantic expeditions.

- **Trust your instincts.** If anything raises nagging suspicions or makes you feel at all uneasy, don't hesitate to walk way. People who dodge direct questions, won't speak on the phone, or provide inconsistent background stories should get your Spidey Sense tingling.

- **Talk on the phone.** After you've emailed awhile, the next stage should be a phone conversation. You can tell a lot about someone from a simple voice chat (and also find out if you two can carry on a conversation that doesn't involve typing). But play it safe here, too—don't give out your home phone number and, if possible, call from a cellphone or one that can block Caller ID from displaying on the other end. Nowadays, you can even talk to someone by way of instant message audio chat (page 301).

- **Meet in a safe public place.** Before you shut down the PC and go running off to meet a date for the first time, tell a close friend where you're going and when you'll be back so someone knows your whereabouts. Meet in a public place with plenty of people around, like a coffee shop or in the café area of your favorite mega-bookstore. Don't let your date pick you up at home or make travel arrangements for you if it's a long-distance first meeting.

Needless to say, never do anything that makes you uncomfortable, no matter what the other person wants.

There's nothing wrong with a quick Web search on someone you're interested in, either. Sites like SafeDate (*www.safedate.com*) and True (*www.true.com*) even go as far as running criminal- and matrimonial-background checks on potential dates.

If you're new to the whole online dating scene and don't have any dead-set expectations about who you're looking for, Friendster and Match.com, described in the following sections, may be good places to begin your quest.

Friendster

With millions of members and the ability to find old classmates, co-workers, and that guy you used to skydive with, Friendster (*www.friendster.com*) fuses social networking with online dating. People in the real world meet other people through friends, and friends of friends. Friendster recreates social circles online by letting you create a profile page and then *tag* those folks who you've anointed as friends. Links to the profiles of all your friends appear on your profile page, making it easy to see who knows whom and where those social circles intersect.

You can tag people as friends in three different ways:

• Use Friendster's built-in invite tools and send them an email invitation to join Friendster, which automatically adds the person to your friends list if he or she accepts your invite.

• Use Friendster's search box to look up people who might already be members and invite them to be your friend through the site.

• When browsing other member's profile pages, click "Add person as your friend." This sends a message to the other member; if your intended pal accepts your invitation, you get a message back confirming that friendly fact.

When you sign up for Friendster (which is free but slathered with advertisements), you're invited to import your Yahoo Mail or Hotmail email address book and invite all your buddies to be your Friendster friends. As you work through your profile setup, you're prompted to upload a personal photo and fill out a form detailing your hometown, educational background, job, hobbies, and favorite books, movies, music, and TV shows. You also get a free-form box to describe yourself in 2,000 characters or less. Once you get your profile page rolling, you can add your own blog to it, post up to 50 personal photos, or share video clips with your pals.

You also get your own email inbox on the site, as shown in Figure 17-1, which you can use to send notes to other Friendsters. (This is a safer way to meet new people than passing out your email address to online strangers.) You can search profiles by name, location, college, or favorite TV shows.

Figure 17-1:
A Friendster account sets you up with your own well-sponsored mailbox. (Since it's free, be prepared to see lots of ads.) Click the Bulletin Board link to post messages (like group invitations) that you want all your Friendster pals to see.

Tip: If you enter friends' names in your Friend Tracker (located in the Connect With Friends box on your Friendster Home page), the site notifies you whenever those friends update their photos or profiles.

When you click the My Settings link at the top of any Friendster page, you can choose who has permission to see your full profile—friends, friends of friends, or anybody on Friendster. People who aren't on your approved list see only a very minimal profile, with just your first name, age, gender, location, and hometown listed.

The horizontal orange toolbar across the top of the Friendster page holds links to other corners of the site. Under Radio, for example, there's a streaming music service (powered by Pandora; page 200) where you can create personalized radio stations to share your taste in music with your Friendster pals.

And taking a cue from Craigslist (page 141), Friendster has a classifieds section where people can post details about anything from an open job to an open house. In the toolbar, click More and then Classifieds to see them.

Match.com

Match.com (*www.match.com*) has been around since 1995 and has more than eight million members; no wonder it claims to be the biggest online personals site.

Match.com doesn't waste any time getting you on the road to love: a form to create a Match.com account sits smack-dab in the middle of its home page (shown in Figure 17-2). Once you fill in a few essentials like your gender, location, age, and the gender and age range of the person you'd like to meet, click Find My Matches to see a few randomly selected people who match your criteria. To find really compatible people, though, you need to fill out an in-depth Match.com profile by clicking the My Profile link at the top of the page. You set up your profile by answering a multipage questionnaire, which includes questions like "How tall are you?" and "What's your sign?" Answer, "I don't believe in astrology" if you don't roll with the zodiac crowd.

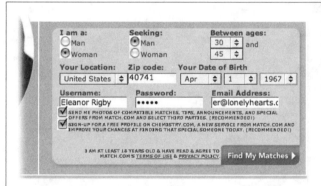

Figure 17-2:
Match.com doesn't waste any time booking you on the Love Train. The sign-up box on the home page, shown here, gathers basic information; you fill out a much more in-depth profile a few steps later.

Tip: You can update your profile at any time by clicking the My Profile link at the top of any Match.com page.

Posting a photo is optional, but consider this bit of dating research: Match.com says that men are 15 times more likely to look at a profile that includes a photo; women are 8.5 times more likely to look if there's a photo. (Insert your own wisecrack about gender-based approaches to dating here.)

After your profile is complete, you submit the whole thing to Match.com for approval. The site's customer service team checks it over (within 48 hours) to make sure you're not an ax murderer. Then your profile is available to people who are searching the site for someone like you.

Teen Dreams: MySpace and Facebook

If you've never heard of these sites, you're probably over the age of 21 or don't read the news. MySpace (*www.myspace.com*) and Facebook (*www.facebook.com*) cater to the teenage and young adult need for socializing and self-expression—and have zoomed up the popularity charts with the teen crowd. MySpace alone had more than 70 million members by early 2006 and dwarfs many of the dating sites aimed at adults. Facebook has around 10 million members. (An academic email address ending in *.edu* is required for admission.)

The idea is that you post your profile, photos, and personal essays onto free Web pages and create circles of friends culled from other members. Kids have taken to using the sites as tools to elevate and evaluate social status; sometimes they find new friends with shared interests. MySpace encourages all sorts of creativity, inviting its members to post their own movies and music videos; many up-and-coming bands and filmmakers use the site to display their projects and MP3 song samples (Figure 17-3).

Facebook is handy because you can find out more about that cute kid who sits in front of you in chemistry—like whether there's a relationship in progress already, or what extracurricular activities you could join to gain more access—before you have the courage to speak up in person.

But with that sort of unrestricted freedom come the inevitable risks. Some folks commit the big no-no of freely posting all their personal information—including email addresses, home addresses, IM screen names (page 290), and phone numbers—which can lead creeps and criminals right to your front door.

Some members have also posted indiscreet photos, which can come back to haunt them later in life. A good rule of thumb for anyone using either of these sites: If you don't want it to come back and bite you, don't put it online in the first place.

The Search button at the top of any Match.com page lets you search for people with similar interests, or based on self-described physical characteristics, location, lifestyle, age, and so on.

All the above activities are free. Once you find someone on the site you want to meet, however, contacting her requires getting out your credit card and *subscribing*. Prices for these plans are awfully hard to locate on the site, but currently go as follows: $30 for one month, $51 for three months, or $78 for six months. With your subscription in hand, you have your backstage pass to wander around and send messages or flirty little "winks" (instant message-type notes that express an interest in someone) to other members.

Figure 17-3:
MySpace has become an online hangout for millions of people, most of them teens and young adults, who all post their profiles, photos, and other personal details in order to make new friends. Emerging bands, artists, and filmmakers also use MySpace as a place to announce their projects, like the music festival shown here that includes MP3 song samples.

You can also sign up to have Match.com send you email messages featuring the profiles of people it thinks you'd match up with. Just click the Account Settings link at the top of the page and click the Match By Mail option. If you're frequently on the road, there's even a version of the site for cellphones at *http://mobile.match.com*.

Professional Networking

Sites that cater to *business* relationships can connect people, too. Part referral service, part virtual water cooler, part corporate headhunter, dozens of sites like LinkedIn and Jobster let professionals mingle online and do their networking over the Internet instead of—or alongside—conferences, conventions, and corporate retreats.

Tip: Recruiting Online, a company that offers Web-based courses for human-resource staffers and recruiters, has a list of social and professional networking sites at *www.recruiting-online.com/course53d.html*.

LinkedIn

This site (*www.linkedin.com*) has more than five million registered users who work in 130 industries. Using LinkedIn is not unlike using an online dating

site, except your profile lists your professional accomplishments and work history instead of your hair color and preference for chocolate chip ice cream.

Joining LinkedIn is free, but you can upgrade your account to a paid version
that offers more features (described below). During the initial sign-up process, the site asks you about your current job (if you have one) and where you
went to college. After you complete your registration, LinkedIn scans its database for other members who work at the same company or went to the same
school during the years you attended, giving you an instant set of potential
contacts, or *connections,* to use LinkedIn's lingo.

If someone already in LinkedIn sent you an invitation to join the site
(Figure 17-4), you come in as a "trusted friend" and are *connected* to that person and become part of his or her network. Once you're connected to other
people, you can see *their* list of personal connections on their profile pages.
When someone that you and another LinkedIn member know appears on
both your profile pages, that mutual friend is listed as a *shared connection.*
From the InMail and Introductions link on your home page, you can receive
and forward introductions from other LinkedIn members.

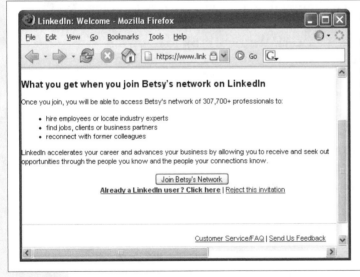

Figure 17-4:
*You don't have to go to conferences or
office parties to network anymore. Sites
like LinkedIn encourage its members to
invite their professional contacts to the
site and form their own overlapping
online networks.*

Even without joining the site, you can use the search box on the site's front
page to look people up by name. Once you sign up with the site, you can see
more details about people, including—if they've mentioned it in their profiles—whether they're looking for a *new* job. When you look at someone's
LinkedIn profile, you can see the person's entire educational and professional

history as they've listed it. If you've worked with the person, there's an Endorse link under each job entry that lets you write a public note about the experience.

Click the Services tab at the top of the LinkedIn site to get to a directory page—which can help if you're looking to hire, say, a corporate litigator or a branding consultant. Just click away until you find someone in the desired field who comes highly recommended. Clicking the People tab at the top of the page lets you search for folks by name and profession.

The free version of LinkedIn gives you plenty of electronic schmoozing tools, but the site also offers paid accounts that pile on extra features like the ability to make multiple introductions at one time, get technical support, and use a messaging system that keeps your email address private. Prices start at $60 a year for the Personal Plus account and go up to $2,000 for Pro accounts (designed for recruiters and other power users who need to communicate with large numbers of people each month). Click the Customer Service/FAQ link at the bottom of the LinkedIn page to get a full rundown of pricing plans and features.

Jobster

Combining the powers of a job-search site with the insider friendliness of a professional networking service, Jobster (*www.jobster.com*) lets you create a profile to highlight your talents to companies you'd really like to work for. American Express, Bose Electronics, and Bayer Healthcare—along with several marketing, insurance, and public relations firms—are among the companies that consult Jobster to find potential hires.

The whole thing's free and you don't have to create a profile to use the site (you can just search for openings, if you like), but a profile does give you a place to post your professional experience and education for those who may be looking.

Jobster regularly scans traditional job-listing Web sites (page 90) for fresh postings; you can sign up for email alerts to hear about these new positions. The site has two types of email alerts: Regular Job Alert messages give you the heads-up when a job that matches your stated interests is posted, and Insider Alerts. To get Insider Alerts, you have to be referred by an employee of a firm that already uses Jobster. But once you get that referral in your profile, you can ask those companies to contact you when other desired positions open up. In competitive fields, every little bit of inside information helps, and it sure beats scanning the tiny type in the classified job listings.

Skype & VoIP: Internet Phones

If you've got a microphone and an instant messaging program (Chapter 15), you can talk to friends and family around the world without paying the phone company a nickel. There's only one downside: these are *computer-to-computer* calls. You and your conversation partner are both chained to your computers and are required to use compatible IM programs.

But thanks to a technology called Voice over Internet Protocol, or *VoIP*, you can sidestep most of this geekery and still make free or cheap long-distance calls. It may sound like the noise a cartoon kangaroo makes hopping across the outback (*voip voip voip voip*), but this emerging technology lets you save tons of money. And you can make phone calls to people with regular ol' phone numbers and their quaint, old-fashioned telephone handsets—by picking up and dialing *your* quaint, old-fashioned telephone handset. The only difference is that the Internet, not the phone company's system, is carrying the call.

Before you dig in, however, it's important to understand that there are two ways to make such calls:

- **Computer-to-phone.** You sit at your computer wearing a headset, but you place calls to ordinary telephone numbers and ordinary telephones. The headset part's a bummer, but the calls are *incredibly* cheap.

- **Phone-to-phone.** These services let you place calls from any phone in your house *to* any phone, just as people have done for years. The only difference is behind the scenes: the phone company isn't involved. The price is around $25 a month for unlimited local and long-distance calling.

The following pages explore these two methods.

Skype: Computer-to-Phone Plans

Skype (*www.skype.com*) is *huge*. It's a free program for Mac, Windows, or Linux that *100 million people* around the world are using to make free phone calls across the Internet. (It's owned by eBay. Perhaps you've heard of it?)

Most of these fans are using Skype to make free *computer-to-computer* calls, just like the audio chats described in Chapter 15. That's when you and your chat partner each wear a headset, click a name in the Buddy list, and begin speaking normally. You enjoy astonishing, crystal-clear sound quality—and you pay *nothing*.

So what's Skype got to do with ordinary phones? It turns out that Skype actually does let you call actual telephone numbers, so your mother can pick up her actual telephone to answer. She never needs to know that you're sitting at your computer—and paying only 2.1 cents a minute, even though she's on another continent. That's the appeal of the SkypeOut service. (Skype increased its appeal even more in spring 2006 by announcing that calls to anyone in the U.S. and Canada on any phone would be free for the rest of the year.)

Here's a capsule description of SkypeOut's advantages and disadvantages:

- **Pros.** You get an actual phone number that people can call (something you don't get with instant message audio chats).

  Calls you make to other computers are free—and calls you make to telephone numbers are dirt-cheap.

  SkypeOut is especially nice if you travel with your laptop, particularly to other parts of the world where international calls are astronomically expensive and you can't use your cellphone. Anywhere you can get a broadband Internet connection for your laptop, you can VoIP (and not have to worry about finding someone online or using a compatible program for an IM audio chat).

- **Cons.** You're shackled to your computer if you need to make a call (but see page 342 for a way to free yourself to roam around). Depending on your computer's sound card, the audio quality might be noticeably worse than using a regular phone or a digital telephone service. (That said, many Skypesters report *better call quality, especially compared to cellphones.*) And VoIP through the computer may not be a natural fit for some people.

What You Need for Skype

To use Skype, your shopping list requires these items:

- **Skype, the program.** Download the software from Skype's Web site (*www. skype.com/download*). On the PC side, you need Windows 2000, XP, or Vista; Macintosh people need at least Mac OS X 10.3 or later. There's even Skype software on the download page for the Linux crowd and people who use Windows Mobile-enabled smartphones.

- **Some sort of speaker-and-microphone combo.** In addition to keeping your calls more private, a headset/mic combo can save you some back, shoulder, and voice strain, especially if you talk on the phone a lot. You can find headsets for less than $20 for a simple, lightweight model or pay as much as $300 for a futuristic version like the Plantronics CS50 USB VoIP Wireless Headset System. Plug the base station into your computer's USB port and you can meander up to 200 feet away while you talk. Wireless headsets, like the one shown in Figure 18-1, offer a great way to talk all day without getting a stiff neck.

Figure 18-1:
Wireless VoIP-ready headset-microphone combos like the GN Netcom 9120 take a load off your shoulder. With a base station that plugs into the computer, you can even get up and stretch your legs without getting tangled up in the phone cord.

If you want to go blue chip, you can invest in a fancy VoIP handset that looks just like a regular phone except that it plugs into a USB or Ethernet port instead of a phone jack. Several companies make phones just for the Skype service and software (click the Shop link on the Skype site to see phones, headsets, and more). Expect to pay anywhere from $40 for a standard handset to $150 for a cordless model.

Buying VoIP Gear

Skype has become so popular, it's spawned an entire industry of add-on gear. You can shop for VoIP hardware at online megastores like Amazon (*www.amazon.com*), office-supply sites like Staples (*www.staples.com*), or places that specialize in phone stuff like the Ahern Store (*www.ahernstore.com*).

Products like the $60 VoSky Call Center box (*www.vosky.com*) free you from having to sit at your computer; it routes your Skype calls to any phone, landline or cell. It also lets you call your Skype pals from your cellphone by dialing your home number, punching in your password, and then dialing your contact's Skype number. The box also forwards incoming Skype calls to any phone number you choose, so you don't have to sit home and wait by the screen for someone to call.

You might also consider buying a special phone handset that has VoIP built-in. You can plug it into *any* computer's USB port to listen to your mountain of voice messages or place calls. On airlines (like Lufthansa) that offer in-flight Internet access, you can even talk on a VoIP phone handset even when the captain requests that you turn off all cellphones in the cabin.

If you do pick out a VoIP handset, make sure it's compatible with your operating system (some are Windows-only).

Skype is also teaming up with Netgear (a company that specializes in home-networking hardware) to release a Skype-enabled WiFi phone in mid-2006. As long as it can pick up a signal from a nearby wireless network, the Netgear Skype SPH101 WiFi phone (shown in Figure 18-2) can make Skype calls just like using Skype from your computer. With a suggested list price of $300, though, going wireless with a Skype WiFi handset bites early adopters hard—right in the wallet.

Figure 18-2:
You can Skype in mobile style with the Netgear Skype WiFi SPH101 wireless phone. Anywhere you can get a wireless network signal, you can call your Skype buddies for free—or call regular phones at those low Skype rates (page 340). Like Skype on the desktop, Skype on a cellphone shows you who's online and available to chat.

On the low end, you can get a $20 headset that plugs into the computer's USB port and works fine with Skype, although you'll feel like Cindy at *Time* magazine, waiting to take someone's order.

And if you're on a bargain-basement budget, just use your computer's sound card, speakers, and built-in microphone, although you may sound like you're locked in a basement.

Starting Up with Skype

As part of Skype's installation process, you create an account, including a name and password, just as you do when setting up an email account, instant messaging account, or an account on a Web site. This is your *Skype name*, which your friends need to know in order to find you and call you on Skype's system.

Tip: As you create your Skype account, you're asked for your country, city, and email address—your own entry in the Skype telephone directory, as shown in Figure 18-3. Privacy-minded people (and those hassled by too many telemarketers during dinner) may be tempted to type in a fake name or leave everything blank. If you do this, however, your friends won't be able to look you up in the Skype directory. (Then again, you can always email them with your Skype name.)

Finally, you fill in your Skype address book with the Skype names of all your friends. If the Find command doesn't work, call or shoot them a message and ask them for their Skype names.

To add someone's name to your Skype address book, choose Tools → Add a Contact. Once you've got some friends listed in your address book, you're ready to take the plunge and call them up.

Making Calls

To call somebody you've added to your Contacts list, either right-click the name in the Contacts list and choose Call This Contact, shown at left in Figure 18-4, or click the name and then the green phone icon at the bottom of the screen.

You hear the phone ring either through your computer's speakers, your handset, or your headset. Then you hear your buddy say, "Hello?"

(If your friend isn't home at the time, you hear a Skype answering machine message [Figure 18-4, right].)

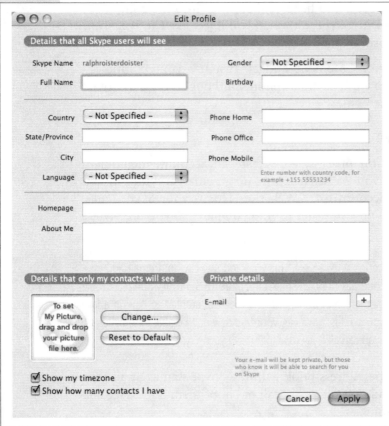

Figure 18-3:
As part of your Skype setup, you have the opportunity to provide both public and private details about yourself. People who don't want to get Skyped out of the blue (or who aren't using Skype as a de facto dating service) typically skip most of the blanks in this box.

To make calls to real telephone numbers, you have to set up a SkypeOut account and use your credit card to buy some SkypeCredit. Calls to numbers around the world are just a few cents a minute.

Tip: If you want to let the world know you're around to receive calls from other connected folks, Skype offers a Skype Me mode; it's a great way to test Skype's free service. To find people who want to be "Skyped," choose Tools → Search for Skype Users → Advanced, choose "Search for people who are in 'Skype Me' Mode," and click Search. Some "Skype Me" regulars are bound to be whopping nutbars. Some are normal people who want to connect internationally to sharpen their language skills. Others want to test their hardware, and some are just bored. To put yourself in Skype Me mode, choose File → Change Status → Skype Me.

Figure 18-4:
Left: To call a fellow Skyper, right-click the contact name in the list and choose Call This Contact. A phone rings through your speaker or headset as the call goes out, and you hear a voice when the person on the other end picks up the call.

Right: If the person on the other end isn't around or doesn't answer, your message may go right to Skype Voicemail (page 347).

Receiving Calls

Receiving a call from another Skype fan doesn't take a whole lot of effort. The Skype software must be running at the time, of course. In general, it loads automatically when you start your computer—an option you can turn off in the Tools → Options → Advanced dialog box (Windows), or Skype → Preferences → General (Mac).

Once loaded, the program waits patiently for incoming calls. You'll spot Skype's icon in your Windows taskbar or Mac OS X dock. (The little white checkmark inside the Windows icon, shown in the bottom corner of Figure 18-5 [bottom] lets you know you're online and able to receive calls.)

If you don't see the Skype icon, open the program manually (on a PC, choose Start → All Programs → Skype; Mac fans should choose Home → Applications → Skype). When someone calls you, a message pops up onscreen, as shown in Figure 18-5 (top). Click the phone icon to answer the call and start talking.

SkypeIn

If you call people on their telephones with SkypeOut, it only makes sense that people with regular telephones should be able to call *you* at your computer.

Figure 18-5:
Top: Skype alerts you with a message in the bottom right corner of your screen when somebody calls you on your Skypeline. Click the phone icon (circled) to answer the incoming call.

Bottom: To screen your calls and see who's ringing you, check the bottom of the Skype window. The caller's Skype name is listed, which may or may not have anything to do with the person's real name.

POWER USERS' CLINIC

Troubleshooting Skype

As simple as using Skype sounds, it can be complicated technically because it combines a lot of things: the Internet, hardware and software on your computer, and networking (which is a special brand of Jedi knowledge all its own).

If any one of these factors isn't working right, your fancy-free phone fun comes to a grinding halt.

Here's how to fix some of the more common hiccups you'll experience in Skype, which can make it so your friends can't see or hear you:

- **Sign off and on again to show your online availability.** Sometimes this action gives your software a swift kick and reconnects it with Skype's database so other Skype types see that you're online and accepting calls.

- **Make sure you appear as Online.** Nobody can call you directly if your Status isn't listed as Online. To confirm that you're actually seen as Online, choose File → Change Status → Online.

- **Check your sound levels.** Skype relies on your computer's hardware for both transmitting and playing back sound. If you and your friend are having trouble hearing each other, check your PC's sound control panel and make sure the Mute option isn't turned on for any of the following settings: Microphone, WAV/MP3, and Play Control. Also, slide their volume levels to the top of the bar to ensure full volume. Mac fans should check the Sound area in the System Preferences to make sure the Input and Output settings aren't muted or set too low.

- **Check your Internet connection.** Without a live Internet connection, you're an island unto yourself and isolated from the rest of the world. Make sure your computer has a working broadband connection. One way to test it: If you can download email or use your Web browser to visit Web sites, your Internet connection isn't the problem here.

They can, thanks to a similar service called SkypeIn. It gives you a phone number that non-Skype folks, using their ancient telephones, can use to call you up on your computer. And for that rare moment when you're offline or not around to be Skyped, the SkypeIn service (which costs around $40 a year) comes with free Skype Voicemail to collect the messages you miss.

Tip: Many serious Skypers expand their service by downloading and installing *plug-ins*, which add features like voice recording and integration with email programs. The Skype site offers browser and email-program toolbars for Windows, and even a Mac OS X widget to dial calls and look up country codes and calling rates. To check out extensions like these, read about VoIP phones, find lists of other Skype community sites, or chill with other Skype fans, drop by SummitCircle (*www. summitcircle.com*). And for thoughtful posts on big issues like the state of online communication, visit SkypeJournal (*www.skypejournal.com*).

Phone-to-Phone Plans

If having to make calls from the computer sounds limiting—and it is—paying a little more buys you more freedom. The increasingly popular phone-to-phone VoIP plans don't require a computer at all. You just pick up your telephone and dial normally, secure in the knowledge that you're going to save a lot of money by avoiding the phone company's wiring.

When you sign up for a phone-to-phone plan, you get a little box called an *analog telephone adapter* (ATA), like the one shown in Figure 18-6. You plug your cable modem or DSL box into one side, and your ordinary telephone into the other side. Then you're ready to make unlimited local and long-distance calls, all for a low fixed monthly fee.

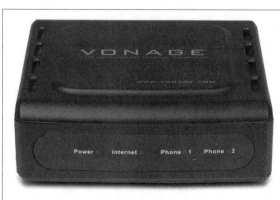

Figure 18-6:
An analog telephone adapter, like the D-Link VTA-VR shown here, links your telephones to your broadband network so you can use them with your VoIP service. This particular D-Link box works with the Vonage service (page 351).

- **Pros.** Calls may be free to other customers of the same service (depending on which one you've chosen). In general, you get to keep your existing phone number, too.

  The monthly fee includes every digital phone feature known to man: voice-mail, call waiting, caller ID, and three-way calling. It does *not* include any motley assortment of tacked-on fees, either; voice-over-Internet service is exempt from FCC line charges, state 911 surcharges, number-portability service charges, and so on.

  Many Internet phone services use the power of the Web to enhance the standard calling features. To listen to your voicemail, for example, you can dial a code on your phone, visit a Web page, or even receive the voice messages as sound attachments sent by email (which you can save forever).

  Once you get everything set up, it's just like using any old telephone you've ever used in terms of dialing, talking, and hanging up on telemarketers. Some companies offer *software phones* (programs you can install on your computer to use your same VoIP service from your PC), so you can use your computer *or* your handset at home.

  Wildest of all, your phone number no longer requires any relationship to your physical location. You can choose almost any area code as your phone number, even if it's not where you live.

  A related perk: you can travel with your little VoIP box. You can plug a telephone into it anywhere you find broadband Internet service. Your home phone number will make the phone ring whether you're in Thailand, Tibet, or Tallahassee—and there's no such thing as a roaming charge.

  Travelers also enjoy the freedom to stop at any Internet-connected computer to check their Web-based voicemail.

- **Cons.** You need broadband Internet service to use VoIP for high-quality audio. And if you have multiple phone jacks around the house, connecting them all to the VoIP adapter box can be a technically tricky prospect.

  Then there's the power issue. Traditional phones (not including cordless models) keep working during power outages and New York City blackouts because they aren't connected to the main power grid. VoIP hardware, however, needs power, so when you lose electricity, you lose your phone service as well. (Most people who have VoIP service also have cellphones for this very reason.)

Call quality can be an issue, too. VoIP relies on the Internet—part of which still uses a patchwork system of old wires, satellites, and cables—which isn't always reliable. That means the voice conversation occasionally becomes garbled or drops out, like a wireless phone sometimes does, especially when you're downloading big files on your computer simultaneously.

Finally, note that if you ditch the phone company, it will also ditch you. You'll no longer have access to the company's 411 and 911 services, though most VoIP companies now offer their own similar services. You may not be able to get a listing in the phone book, either. Also, because VoIP doesn't use a physical, wired connection in a permanent place like a phone jack, operators may have trouble pinpointing your location electronically.

Thanks to its price, convenience, and flexibility, VoIP is catching on fast. Millions of people already use the system, and millions more are looking into it each time they get a hefty phone bill for long-distance charges. If you think you want to make the jump to VoIP, it's time to find a company or service that fits your needs.

Questions to Ask About VoIP Service

When shopping for VoIP service, consult this checklist:

- **What do I get for my monthly fee?** Most big VoIP providers offer an array of plans catering to different calling habits. For example, BroadVoice (page 351) tiers its pricing: $10 a month for unlimited in-state calling, $20 a month for unlimited international calls to 21 countries (including most of Europe, China, Chile, and all around the U.S.), or $25 a month for unlimited international calls to all those countries *and* 14 more like Japan, South Korea, Brazil, Argentina, and New Zealand. Figure out where you call the most and look for a plan that fits your patterns.

- **What kind of VoIP number can I get?** Will this company offer a home phone number in your area code? Conversely, what if you don't want that? What if you live in Mississippi but your entire family's in Missouri—can you get a Missouri number so your folks can make "local calls" to you in Mississippi?

  Or, if you want to keep your existing telephone number, can you?

- **How much does it really cost?** The monthly bill may be $20, but what are the activation fees, hardware installation costs, or penalties for canceling the service before the end of the first year? A few companies actually charge more for calls to cellphones; ask before you sign up.

Choosing a VoIP Service

There are plenty of VoIPs in the sea, so finding a provider isn't hard. If you already have broadband service, your cable or DSL provider may have slipped a few colorful ads for their Internet phone service into your monthly bill. Several smaller companies have also started up; while they may not be able to offer you a big combo package of broadband access and 800 channels of digital TV programming, they can cost a lot less.

- **AT&T CallVantage.** AT&T's roots go back to 1875. Even though the company has switched its focus from telephones to global networking services, you can still reach out and touch someone with its CallVantage VoIP plan: $30 a month for unlimited calls around the U.S. and Canada, or $20 for unlimited local calls. International rates vary, but calls to France and Germany are 5 cents a minute. CallVantage offers some of the best features in the business, including a Web-based call log that shows not just the numbers you've called (or received calls from), but the actual names of the people. And you can just click the person's name to call someone back. As shown in Figure 18-7, you can even see your voicemail calls displayed in the log. (*www.att.com/voip*)

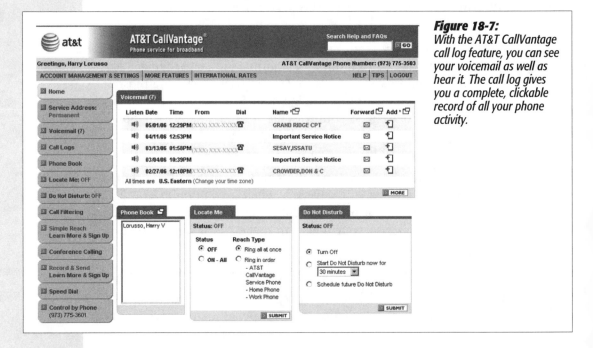

Figure 18-7:
With the AT&T CallVantage call log feature, you can see your voicemail as well as hear it. The call log gives you a complete, clickable record of all your phone activity.

- **Verizon VoiceWing.** If you already have Verizon's DSL service, you can probably get a small discount on your first year of VoiceWing VoIP; the unlimited monthly plan is $35 for calls to the U.S., Canada, and Puerto Rico. The package includes all the usual phone-plan features, plus email notification if you receive a voicemail, and address book integration with Outlook. If you aren't a big talker, you can get 500 minutes a month for $20. (*www.verizon.com/voicewing*)

- **Vonage.** Vonage was among the very first VoIP companies and is still one of the largest.

  With Vonage, you can check your voicemail on the phone, the Web, or by email. The Click-2-Call feature lets you click a phone number in your computer's address book or Outlook contact list to dial it, saving you time and possible misdials. Vonage offers phone software that lets you dial from your PC, too.

  There's a wide range of pricing plans. Unlimited calls to the U.S., Canada, and Puerto Rico are $25 a month. If you want to pay for a block of time, a 500-minute plan costs $15. International calls average about 5 cents a minute to London, Paris, and other major cities. (*www.vonage.com*)

- **Time Warner Digital Phone, Comcast, CableVision.** If you get cable TV, you may be able to add digital phone service to your TV and broadband packages, thereby cutting down on the amount of paper plugging up the mailbox each month.

  The phone service alone may seem expensive ($40 a month for unlimited Time Warner calling, for example). But combo packages for all the company's services can cost less than $100 a month. (*www.timewarnercable.com*, *www.comcast.com*, *www.cablevision.com*)

- **BroadVoice.** As mentioned in the previous section, BroadVoice offers four different calling plans. All plans include call waiting, caller ID, speed dial, voicemail, and more. (*www.broadvoice.com*)

- **Lingo.** Lingo, one of the newer companies, offers a $20-a-month plan for unlimited calls to numbers in the U.S., Canada, and Western Europe (not including cellphone numbers). You can keep your old phone number or get a new one, and you get the usual redial, speed dial, call waiting, and voicemail features. (*www.lingo.com*)

- **Packet 8.** With both Internet phone and Internet *video*phone plans available ($20 a month for unlimited calls to the U.S. and Canada), Packet8 provides an inexpensive option for those who'd like to see as well as hear the people they're chatting with. (The videophone option, however, works only with other Packet8 videophones; each videophone costs $100.) Its $50-a-month Freedom Global Unlimited Plan gives you unlimited calls to landlines in 40 countries spread out over Europe, Asia, and Latin America. (*www.packet8.net*)

- **Broadvox Direct.** You get unlimited local, regional, and national calling anywhere in the U.S. and Canada for $30 a month. International rates for calling landlines and cellphones range from pennies to quarters per minute. (*www.broadvoxdirect.com*)

Once you sign up with a service, you'll be told what equipment you need. In many cases, you can just use your old phone with the company's adapter box.

UP TO SPEED

VoIP Acronym Fun

When you're shopping for Internet phone services, VoIP isn't the only acronym you may encounter. Here's a glossary, for your clip-n-save pleasure:

SIP (session initiated protocol) is an Internet standard for establishing audio conferences and call forwarding over computer networks; some VoIP-enabled handsets are called SIP phones.

PSTN stands for *public switched telephone network*, the technology that carries traditional telephone calls.

Finally, if you just have ordinary copper phone wiring and no digital high-speed lines, you've got POTS (*plain old telephone service*). Cute, huh?

All together, now: POTS uses PSTN, and you can use a SIP phone to cheaply call a PSTN phone, and some VoIP services make SIP-to-SIP totally free.

Setting Up VoIP

Setting up VoIP phone-to-phone service entails plugging the adapter box into your cable modem or DSL, and then plugging your phone into *that*. (The big-name telecom companies may even send a technician to your house to do this for you.)

No matter how you use your digital telephone connection, it's certainly cheaper than most standard telephone plans. The costs for using VoIP range from "absolutely free" to "way cheaper than using my regular long-distance calling plan."

Using VOIP

Pick up your phone and dial a number. Think you can handle it?

More VoIP Gear

In general, a telephone is all you need to use a VoIP service. But adding additional gear offers more flexibility.

For example, Linksys (*www.linksys.com*) makes a wireless router (Figure 18-8) that has built-in VoIP ports for phones. (Models are also available for the Vonage and AT&T CallVantage services.) The advantage here is that you have only one box to plug into your cable modem instead of two (router and phone adapter box). Netgear also has a wireless router with an integrated VoIP phone adapter.

Many small offices looking to save big bucks are switching to VoIP systems like Linksys Voice System, which can support up to 16 phone lines and centers around a network device that performs more than 100 telephone-operator chores like automatically routing calls to the right person and piping in cheery music for people on hold.

Linksys also sells phones that go with its Voice System. VoIP business phones with programmable keys and big display screens are popping up from several other manufacturers, too, including Grandstream (*www.grandstream.com*) and Uniden (*www. uniden.com*); prices range from about $60 to $350.

New VoIP products and services are whizzing onto shelves faster than kangaroos bounding across open terrain. VoIP-News (*www.voip-news.com*) is a great place to keep up with new developments.

Figure 18-8:
If you're adding or upgrading a home wireless network, plenty of companies now make network routers that include ports to plug in VoIP phones. The memorably named Linksys WRT54GP2A-AT wireless broadband router here serves as an access point to beam your network signal all over the house—and gives you two ports to plug in VoIP phones for the AT&T CallVantage service (page 350).

6

Part Six:
Internet Power and Protection

Chapter 19: Your Own Blogs, Web Sites, and Podcasts

Chapter 20: Living on the Web

Chapter 21: Staying Safe

Your Own Blogs, Web Sites, and Podcasts

Back in Ye Olden Days of Mass Communications, you had to wait for the radio to play what you wanted to hear, wait for your newspaper to arrive, and wait until after supper for Walter Cronkite to come on the *CBS Evening News*. Thanks to the great Web Stampede of the 1990s, that all changed. No longer did you have to wait—and more importantly, no longer were regular folks restricted to watching *others* deliver their news and entertainment.

Problem was, though, Web sites could be a hassle to create and maintain. If for some odd reason you didn't want to master HTML, CSS, FTP, and a host of other techno-geekery, you were consigned, once again, to watching producers and broadcasters prance around on this new digital stage.

Not anymore. The three most popular forms of online self-expression—Web logs (blogs), Web pages, and podcasts (amateur radio shows)—are now about as technically complex as sending an email message.

Blogs

A *blog* is an online diary or journal. It looks like a series of short text blurbs that appear in descending chronological order on a Web page; links to monthly archives of older posts are on the page, too. (The term *blog* is a shortened version of *Web log,* so called because of its resemblance to a ship captain's log—a written record of daily activities and documentation that describes a journey.)

Each blog post can be three screens deep or three lines long. Blogs can be about anything at all, from world politics to life as a retail clerk; from popular culture to penguins (Figure 19-1).

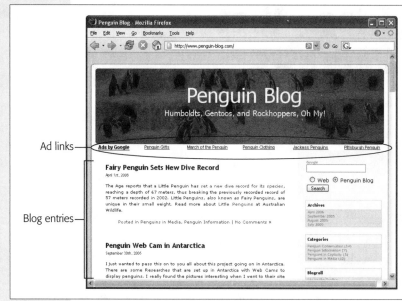

Ad links

Blog entries

Figure 19-1:
The main page of a typical blog. New entries appear in the main part of the window (the newest entry is at the top) and links to older posts are along the right side. Some blogs, like this one, have ad links displayed on the page; some free blogging sites put banner ads on your blog whether you want them or not. Upgrade to a paid account or host your blog on your own Web server (page 374) to banish the ads.

Some blogs have a commercial feel; they're well written, garner national attention, and are on par with the best reporting in the news media today. Other blogs are poorly spelled and have a total readership of two, but they still give their owners a public forum to complain about gas prices.

Whatever its intention, a blog reflects the personal and unique viewpoint of its creator. Chapter 5 has more on how to find existing blogs that match your interests.

With an Internet connection, the right software, and something to say, anyone can create a blog.

Creating a Blog

Blogs have been going like gangbusters for several years now, largely because of the many free and easy-to-use blog-creation tools to choose from. Forget about file transfers and arcane text-formatting commands—a blog's all typing, pointing, and clicking.

The precise steps for creating and running a blog vary depending on which blog-creation site you choose to use, but the process is roughly as follows:

1. **Pick out a site to host your blog.**

   If you already have your own Web site (page 369), you can buy blog software like Movable Type to use for composing your blog and posting your latest thoughts on your site.

   If you *don't* have your own Web site, free sites give you both software to make your blog *and* a place to put it on the Web. The big companies in this game—Blogger, Xanga, LiveJournal, and TypePad—are all discussed in this chapter.

   America Online's AOL Journals feature is available to AOL and AIM users; details on how to get started are at *http://hometown.aol.com*. Likewise, if you favor Microsoft's MSN network, you can sign up for free blogspace at *http://spaces.msn.com*.

   Social networking sites like Friendster, MySpace, and Facebook (Chapter 17) give their members room to blog, too. So, if you already belong to any of these sites, just do a quick search for *blog* and they'll let you know how to get started.

2. **Sign up for an account.**

   Opening a blog account is as easy as signing up for free Web-based email. Click the "Create an account" button or its equivalent on the site's home page and fill in the requested information. You pick out your blog's name here, too, which will later appear in its URL (Web address)—something like *http://pipinggecko.blogspot.com*, where *pipinggecko* is the name of your blog and *blogspot* is the name of the blogging service you're using.

3. **Choose a page template.**

   With the administrative stuff out of the way, you can move on to aesthetics. Most blog sites offer a handful of preformatted page designs to choose from. (Figure 19-2 shows some of the selections over at Blogger.com.) These templates explain why most blogs from these sites tend to look the same, but you can add little tweaks and photos here and there once you get rolling.

4. **Write some posts.**

   Now you just need to provide your readers with something to *read*. Click the New Post button (or find a similarly named tab on your blogscreen) to open the composition area. Here, you can type a message and do light formatting chores like adding bold and italics to the text, dropping in a photo, and sticking in a link to another Web site.

Figure 19-2:
Most free blogging sites give you a handful of page styles to choose from. Here, on Blogger, you can change the look of your blog even after it's up and running; just log into your blog account, click Change Settings on your Blogger Dashboard page, and click the Template tab. You can edit your current settings and change basic things like the color of your navigation bar—or change its entire look by clicking the Pick New link and selecting a whole new template from Blogger's stock.

Most blog sites now offer a spell checker, which helps prevent embarrassing public typos. You can get a sneak peek at your post-in-progress by clicking the Preview button to make sure everything looks good. When you're satisfied, click the Publish button to reveal your inner thoughts to any of the billions of people using the Web today.

The best blogs are the ones where their creators take the time to update them on a regular basis. (The most *popular* blogs tend to be the ones that are entertaining, snarky, and even mean-spirited, but that's not so much a requirement as a sign of the times.)

Once people get hooked on your prose, they're going to want steady doses of it. The Web's already too cluttered with abandoned blogs that have three ancient posts on them and nothing more.

Tip: On most blogs, readers can make comments following your posts. If you don't want to hear any sniping from the peanut gallery—or want to individually delete rude remarks in response to your postings—log into your blog account to disable the comments feature or delete specific comments. Blog sites that offer *moderated comments* allow you to screen the comments before they appear on your page and reject the ones that don't pass muster.

Free Blog Sites

Now that you know what to expect if you've never blogged before, the next few pages describe some popular blog sites.

Blogger

With a clean, clear site design that gently guides you through the steps of blog creation, Blogger (*www.blogger.com*) is a great place to start out. Its tagline is "Push-Button Publishing," and that about covers it (see Figure 19-3).

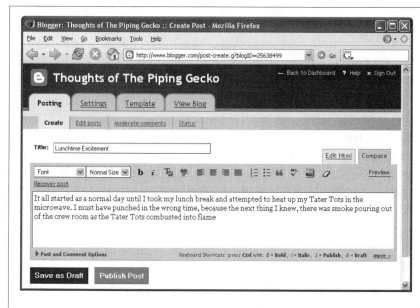

Figure 19-3:
When you log into your Blogger account, you land on the Dashboard page, where you can manage the look and contents of your blog. After you click the Create Post button on the Dashboard page, you land in this composition area where you can type away, check your spelling, and read things over before clicking the Publish Post button. The toolbar above the text window includes shortcuts for basic text formatting like adding boldface and italics, pasting in links to other Web sites, and adding pictures to your posts.

A click-through tour of the site shows off Blogger's main features: easy-as-pie blog configuration (it permits photos and reader comments) and a thorough explanation of how to add posts from a cellphone.

Your actual site is hosted on a *server* (an industrial-strength computer that dishes out Web pages) that uses the *blogspot* Web address. That means your blog's URL will be something like *http://yournamehere.blogspot.com*.

Tip: Blogger has a well-stocked Help section that can answer most common questions about using the site and service. Visit *http://help.blogger.com* to browse the Q&A section.

A small San Francisco company started Blogger in 1999, but Google bought the firm in 2002. Having the power of Google behind it gives Blogger a couple of nice perks. For one, you get great searching through the site and a link to the Google Blog Search site to find other blogs around town.

More importantly, though, you gain the ability to use Google's AdSense program on your blog. AdSense can put automatic ads on your blog, relevant to the topic (flip back to Figure 19-1 for a look at a blog with such ads). And why on earth would you want to put ads on your blog? Because every time a reader clicks one, *Google sends you money*.

For example, if you blog about your life as a ski instructor in Aspen, AdSense might insert ads from ski-equipment manufacturers and local restaurants; you earn a dash of money each time someone clicks one of the ads. You can sign up for an AdSense account within Blogger when you log into your account. (To find out more about AdSense, go to *http://help.blogger.com* and click the link for Add-Ons.)

The Blogger Mobile service, meanwhile, lets you post photos and text from your Internet-enabled cellphone directly to your blog. When you snap a photo the world must see right now, send it from your phone to *go@blogger.com*; the pic pops up on the Web a few minutes later. (Insiders have a name for this mobile blogging: *moblogging*.) You don't even need to download or install any extra software on your phone to use Blogger Mobile, but you do need a phone and a service plan that let you send text messages or picture mail.

If you don't already have a blog, sending text or photos to *go@blogger.com* automatically creates a new blog for your stuff. Blogger sends a message back to your phone with instructions for finding your new blog on the Web; details are at *www.blogger.com/mobile-start.g*.

You can also send text and images to your page by email, using a special email address Blogger provides.

Finally, there's AudioBlogger, which lets you call in audio commentary from your cellphone right to your blog—which could be really fun or really embarrassing, depending on your state of mind at the time. The number is +1 (415) 856-0205; long-distance charges may apply if you don't live in the San Francisco area.

Note: All of these services are free, although your cellphone carrier may charge for sending photos and text over the airwaves.

Xanga

Xanga (*www.xanga.com*) mixes online journals and diaries with social networking (Chapter 17). The result is a Weblog community that's heavily favored by high school and college students. It's a great place to post about anything and make new friends with other Xangans in the process.

Because blog posts can be deeply personal, the site offers a security feature that lets you "protect" journal entries by making a list of other Xanga members who have permission to read the posts.

As on other social networking sites, you can fill out a personal profile of yourself, and even add a link to your Xanga page from an AIM user profile to encourage instant message buddies to visit.

Accounts come in three flavors: Classic (free), Premium ($25 per year), and Plus ($45). Classic account holders get limited design-tweaking capabilities plus 200 megabytes worth of photo storage. A Premium account gets you two gigabytes of photo storage and complete control over the look of your Xanga page. The Plus version jacks that up to unlimited photo storage. If you're a paying member, you also get to ditch the banner ads that appear on the pages of the free account holders.

LiveJournal

LiveJournal (born in 1999) hosts millions of blogs from all corners of the globe. You can sign up for a free LiveJournal account at *www.livejournal.com*, which gives you basic templates where you can write your posts and add icons and small photos to express your current mood.

If you don't want to do your post-making in a Web browser, you can download free desktop software for Windows and Macintosh systems from the site so you can blog without browsing. (The blogging software option is good if you have a dial-up connection or work in a yurt; your LiveJournal software options are at *www.livejournal.com/download*.)

LiveJournal also offers paid accounts ($20 a year) that offer a gigabyte of storage for photos, the ability to submit posts via email, and the freedom to add voice clips sent from any phone to your page. Holders of paid accounts also get more control over the look of their page, and they can create custom mood icons using their own pictures to accompany their posts. (Free account holders must choose from a selection of stock characters.)

Some key social networking features are included with LiveJournal, which makes it comparable to sites like Friendster and MySpace (see Chapter 17). For instance, members can search for other members by email address, instant message screen name, or school. You can also join community groups within LiveJournal that are devoted to certain subjects. Finally, the site also lets you set up a page of "friends" and then read all the new journal entries from your acquaintances in one place.

Note: Blogs are an excellent forum for self-expression, but remember not to give out too much information about yourself on your pages. You never know who's reading. Vague generalities are fine (*"Here in the center of Houston, it's another 103-degree day..."*), but it's best to avoid specifics (*"Here in my gorgeous six-bedroom house at 400 Webster Street in beautiful downtown Houston, I realized my Mercedes-Benz really needed a good waxing..."*). When you create a blog, you potentially invite millions of people into your life, and you probably don't know every one of them.

TypePad

LiveJournal's parent company, Six Apart, also owns TypePad, a professional blog-creation and hosting service. (The same company sells the Movable Type blogging software, too.)

TypePad (*www.typepad.com*) is free—but only for 30 days. After that, you do have to pay, but for your money, you get slicker, more graphically pleasing page templates for your text, online photo-sharing, and cellphone blogging. You also get actual technical support from the site if you have a problem or a question. Still, if you want to try your hand at a blog, the free 30 days may be enough time to let you experiment and see if you want to stick with it.

TypePad offers three pricing plans. If you're your blog's sole author and you only want one Web log, TypePad's Basic account costs $50 a year. If it's just you and you want to have up to three different blogs because you have *a lot* to say, the price goes up to $90 a year for TypePad Plus.

The third option, TypePad Pro, is for big collaborative blogs with multiple folks posting—like DotMoms (*http://roughdraft.typepad.com/dotmoms*), in which 40 different mothers scattered all over the world contribute posts about their parenting experiences. Pro accounts, about $150 a year, also offer full-on HTML editing so you can really get in there and whip that page code into the shape you want. (HTML, short for HyperText Markup Language, is the underlying code used to design Web pages.)

Finding Vlogs, Phlogs, and Audioblogs

If words aren't your favorite way to express yourself, join the AV Club and see the online diaries of people who've opted for videos, photos, or audio files to report the events of the day.

The influx of affordable digital camcorders and video-enabled cameraphones have added moving pictures to the blogosphere, as young filmmakers document their lives using video clips instead of text posts. Video Web logs, naturally condensed to *vlogs,* are popping up all over. You can get a gander at some vlogs at *http://videoblogging-universe.com* and *www.vlogmap.org,* which round up the good ones for you.

Blogs don't have to be boring fields of plain text, either. As the photo-sharing site Flickr (page 230) has demonstrated, you can shout out to the world with pictures, too. Loosely referred to as *phlogs,* photo blogs are another popular sight around the blogosphere. If you don't use Flickr or one of the other online photo services, software like the $50 MyPhoto (*www.prosidio.com*) lets you publish your photos online to your own Web site or server.

MP3blogs or *audioblogs* can also be found around Blogville. Unlike podcast sites (page 205), these sites host the favorite audio files of their owners. Fluxblog (*www.fluxblog.org*) is a fine example of the audioblog form, and you can find plenty more at The Hype Machine's audio blog aggregator (that is, collector) at *http://hype.non-standard.net* or in the audioblog section at *www.podcastingnews.com.*

You generally can't post such hefty files at the free text-based blogging sites. But you can always create your own Web site (page 369) and put your audio, video, and photo goodies up there.

Super-Simple Web Pages

Sometimes, a blog isn't enough. If you really want to control the look and feel of your site, or if you want to do non-bloggy things like set up a shop that actually sells things online, you need to build your own Web site.

Creating your own Web pages and linking them together to form a site used to be a lot more work than dashing off a few pithy lines for a blog before breakfast. You had to do everything from writing the site's text to troubleshooting broken links to fixing pages that displayed weirdly in different Web browsers.

These days, though, creating a simple Web site can be every bit as easy—and free—as maintaining a blog. Granted, it won't be whiz-bang flashy or as sprawling as those monolithic Web beasts like Amazon.com or the BBC's extraordinary news site. But you have to start somewhere.

The following pages describe two different scenarios:

- **Simple sites** using automatic, free, or cheap, idiot-proof online Web-creation services.

- **More professional sites** that require a lot more knowledge, skills, software, and money to design and maintain.

Google Page Creator

In addition to its Blogger site, Google is tinkering with full-on Web site creation, design, management, and hosting for its Gmail members. Google Page Creator, which was still in the testing phase in early 2006, gives you 100 megabytes of server space and an editing program that lets you design your own customized pages without having to hack around in the underlying HTML code. If you have a Gmail account, you can sign up and start making Web pages at *http://pages.google.com.*

The Page Manager screen (Figure 19-4, top) that greets you when you log in is your starting point for making and managing your own Web pages. Click the "Create a new page" link to start constructing your first point-and-click Web page with Google.

As shown in Figure 19-4, bottom, Google Page Creator gives you a screen full of boxes to fill with text and a vertical panel of tools along the side of the page to style that text. You can add photographs, graphics, and links to other Web pages with toolbar buttons, too. Click the Preview button at the top of the Page Creator window to make sure your site looks good.

When you're ready to release your brand-new page into the wilds of the Web, click the Publish button on the Page Creator page. Your new Web site lives at an address that combines your Gmail account name with Google Pages, as in *http://yournamehere.googlepages.com.*

After you've whipped up a few Web pages, you see all of them listed in the Page Manager for easy access and further editing. Using the Page Manager, you can also delete pages from your site and send out a message from your Gmail account to announce the address of your new site.

Tip: Wherever you find Google, Microsoft is never far behind. Microsoft Office Live offers a huge collection of online tools including a site-building service that works just like Google Page Creator. And Microsoft's version comes with something you *won't* get from Google: free registration of your own domain name. See page 392 for more on Office Live.

Figure 19-4:
*Not only can Google help
you find Web pages, it can
help you make your own.
All you need is a Gmail
account and a little bit of
time.*

*Top: The Page Manager
screen greets you when you
log into your account, lets
you create new pages, and
lets you keep track of the
ones you've already made.*

*Bottom: When you click the
"Create a new page" link
and land on the Page
Creator screen, making a
Web page is as
straightforward as typing
into boxes and using the
tool panel on the left side of
the screen to style text, add
images, and properly
format links to other Web
pages.*

Homestead

Host to more than 12 million Web sites since 1998, Homestead (*www.
homestead.com*) is another company that can get your personal Web site up
and running with a minimum of complications. Homestead offers hosting,
plus tools and templates for do-it-yourself page design; monthly fees start at
about $10, which gets you a basic 10-page Web site and 25 megabytes of space
to store it on Homestead's servers.

Site packages for small business owners are available, too. These deals—priced
at $20 for the Gold package with 100 megabytes of disk space or $50 a month
for Platinum service with 300 megabytes of storage—include an unlimited
number of pages within your site, the ability to process PayPal transactions
(page 140), and site-matching email addresses. Click the Packages link on the
main Homestead page to see a comparison chart of all the plans.

All of Homestead's subscription plans offer full access to the company's QuickSite Design Gallery—2,000 prebuilt Web sites just waiting for you to pick one and pop in your own text and pictures, no HTML assembly required.

Once you select your site design, you can use the SiteBuilder tool to drag and drop your own content onto the pages. (The SiteBuilder software works only with Windows, but Mac folks can customize their sites with the online Site-Builder Lite tool that works with the Firefox browser; the Safari browser isn't supported by Homestead.)

Homestead walks you through the site creation and publishing process once you sign up. You can get a free 30-day trial of the service before you commit to a package to see if it suits your needs.

Yahoo GeoCities

If you just have a few pages in mind for your site, a free account at Yahoo's GeoCities (*http://geocities.yahoo.com*) might provide all the room you need. With the free option, you get 15 megabytes of server space for your pages. (That's an *enormous* amount of space for text-based Web pages. Graphics, movies, and other goodies fill it up much faster.) You also get PageWizard and PageBuilder tools to help you customize the provided page templates.

Of course, even free stuff has a price somewhere; in this case, it's banner ads that get slapped on your pages. And as noted previously, you don't have much choice when it comes to your domain name: your Web site address will look something like *www.geocities.com/yournamehere34245*.

If you want more room, more control, or want to add a shopping feature to sell your handcrafted Honda hubcaps, GeoCities has some more sophisticated options. For $5 or $9 a month, you can get an ad-free site with either 500 megabytes or 2 gigabytes of space.

As a separate service, Yahoo also has Web-hosting packages available for small businesses. They include a choice of your own domain name, 1,000 business email addresses for your army of salespeople and employees to use, product catalog templates, shopping cart software, and the ability to process credit card transactions or PayPal payments; hosting prices start at $40 a month. There's more information at *http://smallbusiness.yahoo.com/merchant*.

Tip: America Online gives its members space to make a Web page and tools to build it. When logged into the service, use AOL keyword: *Hometown* to get started.

.Mac and iWeb

If you have a Macintosh, a .Mac account (page 267), and the iLife software
that's included on every Mac, you can make your own Web sites in a flash.
The iLife suite (version '06 and later) comes with a program called iWeb,
which lets you build blogs and Web pages with startlingly few clicks.

As shown in Figure 19-5, you can turn iWeb's canned design templates to
make a multipage site containing your own text; drag and drop digital pictures, movies, and audio files onto the pages to spice them up with multimedia. Once you publish the site to the Web, the software shows you the Web
address for your new site.

Figure 19-5:
*With Apple's iWeb software
you can whip up a Web site
with multiple pages using
any of the preformatted
templates included with the
program. You can add
images, video clips, and
audio from your other iLife
programs like iMovie,
iPhoto, and iTunes. When
you're ready to release
your site onto the Internet,
just click the Publish button
in the lower-left corner to
upload your pages onto the
free Web space provided
with your .Mac account.*

Professional Web Sites

There are super-simple, Web-based services ideal for the casual Web designer
who just wants to publish the Little League schedule or present the minutes of
the latest PTA meeting. But if you want to make your site look professional,
you'll have to do a little more rooting around.

This process can get so technical, in fact, that many small business wind up
hiring a professional Web designer to do the job. If you're interested in creating a professional-looking site, here's what the job entails:

- **Figuring out what's on it.** If you're going to have a Web site, you need something to go on it: not just text, but also visual elements like pictures, graphics, and logos. You should also start thinking of a name for your site so you can figure out whether the Web address you want is available. (It probably comes as no surprise that virtually all the most popular one-word addresses—*cars.com*, *sports.com*, and *ragu.com*—are already taken.)

- **Web editing software.** You need a program that lets you create, design, and check each Web page before you hang it up online for all to see; such programs range in price from free to several hundred dollars. The cost factor is often inversely proportional to the amount of work you need to do yourself; if you go low budget, expect to get a little less handholding and a little more code-wrangling.

  If you want to learn HTML (page 371), you can make Web pages with programs that come preinstalled on your PC or Mac. But there are easier software tools to use. Nvu (*www.nvu.com*) is a good freebie Web page editor; Dreamweaver (*www.macromedia.com*) will set you back around $400, but you'll be using the same tool the pros use. Both programs work on PCs and Macs.

- **A Web host.** Every Web site resides on a *server* somewhere—a computer that's running 24 hours a day and connected to a superfast Internet connection, so that dozens or thousands of people can be viewing your Web site simultaneously.

- **Delivery system.** Once you've created your pages, you need a way to get them *off* your computer and *onto* the Web server. In most cases, you upload your pages using your Web browser or a file transfer protocol (*FTP*) program. FTP software is specially designed to heft files from one computer to another. Some popular Windows FTP programs include CuteFTP (*www.cuteftp.com*) and WS_FTP (*www.ipswitch.com*); Mac OS X folks have programs like Fetch (*http://fetchsoftworks.com*) and CaptainFTP (*http://captainftp.xdsnet.de*) at their disposal.

Phase 1: Design Your Web Site

When it comes to actually designing, coding, and creating the Web pages that will be part of your site, a wide selection of software awaits.

Professional Web designers work in code. They manipulate strings of computer programming gobbledygook in a Web-description language known as *HTML*. If you wandered by their desks, you'd never guess that all that typewritten text on their screens was actually supposed to look like the Wal-Mart home page.

Ordinary humans, however, are frequently better off using a program that lets you design a Web page by dragging text and graphics around the screen; the program generates the HTML code automatically, behind the scenes.

Text editors

It turns out that a Web page, when you get right down to it, is little more than a page of text. It's filled with codes that, as noted above, the pros type out by hand. (Graphics, movies, and other non-text items aren't actually part of the Web page. The text codes *tell* those things where to appear, but they're actually stored separately on the Web site.)

So, if you know the HTML language, you don't need any fancy software at all. If you're a do-it-yourself type, you can't get any more DIY than using Notepad (for Windows) or TextEdit (Mac). Just choose Start → All Programs → Accessories → Notepad on your PC, or Applications → TextEdit on your Mac.

Tip: And what if you don't know HTML but would like to? For a quick course in HTML 101, visit the ever-helpful Webmonkey site for free classes and cheat sheets (*www.webmonkey.com*). Once you've created the HTML document in a text editor, save your file with an *.htm* or *.html* extension. Believe it or not, you can then preview your work by opening the page in your Web browser.

HTML Makes the Web Go 'Round

The name *HyperText Markup Language* makes it sound a lot scarier than it actually is. HTML is just a system of *tags*—a simple programming language, actually—contained in a text file. When one of your fans summons your Web page, these coded tags tell their Web browsers how to display the document as you intended it.

To italicize text on an HTML page, for instance, you just need to type it between the tag to turn on italic, *<i>*, and the tag that turns off italic, *</i>*. If you put the HTML tag for bold type around a word, like this—"Here's the **BOLD** tag!"—all Web browsers know just what to do because they all speak HTML fluently.

To make a very bare-bones Web page, you can use programs like Notepad or TextEdit because HTML documents are just plain text files containing HTML tags.

Basic HTML itself isn't hard to learn if you want to take a crack at coding your own simple Web pages by hand. You can find interactive tutorials on the topic at sites like *www.w3schools.com/html* and *www.davesite.com/webstation/html*. With a little diligence, you'll be your own Web guru in no time.

> **Tip:** You can even design a Web page in Microsoft Word (or any other word-processing program). Just format and dress up the document as you like, complete with graphics, and then choose File → Save as Web Page. The results look OK for pages that are mostly text; things can start to look a little funky once you add graphic elements, charts, or tables, however.

WYSIWYG (drag-and-drop) programs

WYSIWYG stands for "what you see is what you get," which means that you design your Web page as though it's in a graphics program. You get easy-to-use design features and tools to manage your site's pages and get them up on the Web. The best part about these programs? They generate the HTML code *for* you.

- **Nvu.** Nvu, a free, open-source program (that is, written by volunteer collaborators via the Internet), combines some of the graphical goodness and ease of a Web-editing program like Dreamweaver with the freeness of Notepad and TextEdit. Not only does it provide buttons that quickly and correctly add photos, forms, links, and tables to your pages, it can upload your pages to your host server with a click (see page 376).

  You can preview your pages right in the program's window (Figure 19-6) and even run its built-in spell checker to help keep those embarrassing typos at home where they belong. Nvu is available for both Windows and Macintosh. (*www.nvu.com*)

- **HTML-Kit.** It won't win any beauty contests for best user interface, but the free HTML-Kit program for Windows makes up for any esthetic shortcomings by letting you customize it to the hilt. The program's Web site has tutorials to help you get started, and the software itself includes handy features like a live preview that shows you your developing Web page as you type away in the text editor window. (*www.html-kit.com*)

- **Microsoft FrontPage.** If you're already a wiz at Word, Excel, PowerPoint, or other Microsoft programs, FrontPage for Windows should have a shorter learning curve than other Web software. The program's graphics and layout tools let you push and pull elements around the page until you like the look. You can create master templates for all your site's pages, so when you change an element on the master page, all the other pages take the change, too. FrontPage costs $200 by itself, although it comes with some versions of Microsoft Office. (*www.microsoft.com/frontpage*)

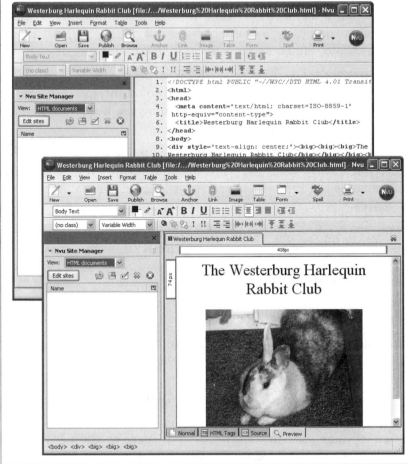

Figure 19-6:
The free Nvu (pronounced "new view") software takes much of the pain out of Web page creation. As shown in the foreground, you can use its toolbar to style text and add images by clicking, instead of having to type all that stuff shown in the background, which is what Web page code really looks like. The tabs at the bottom of the Nvu window let you see your page in its various stages.

- **Adobe GoLive.** Sure, it costs $400, but it's available for Windows and Macintosh and integrates well with Adobe's flagship graphics programs, like Photoshop and Illustrator. Using a palette full of visual tools, you can build complicated Web pages soaking in multimedia. A map displays all your site's pages and how they link to each other. (*www.adobe.com*)

Note: In 2005, Adobe acquired Macromedia. It now sells a software bundle that includes Dreamweaver, GoLive, and most of both companies' other programs for just under $2,000.

- **Dreamweaver.** Many Web-design professionals do their heavy lifting in Dreamweaver, which costs $400 for Windows and Macintosh. For new Web-site builders, Dreamweaver comes with a full suite of tutorials to help you understand how to construct your pages and add video or animation. If you want to do a lot of animation, you can also get Dreamweaver bundled with the Flash program (page 67) along with a few other Web-design tools in a $1,000 suite called Studio 8. (*www.macromedia.com*)

If you're not sure what kind of software you want to use, how many pages your site will have, or even how much server space you think you may need to rent from your Web host, a bit of advanced planning can help. That's where *wireframes* and *flow charts* come in.

A wireframe is a rough layout of your Web pages, with the places for text and images sketched in. A flow chart is an architectural map of your entire site, showing each separate page and where each page links, so you can see the big picture at a glance.

You don't have to get fancy software to make wireframes and flow charts—in fact, you can sketch them out on cocktail napkins if you want. They're just there to give you an idea of how much work you have ahead of you and help you decide what tools you need to get the job done.

Phase 2: Find a Web Host

Before you can put your Web site up on the Internet, you should line up a *host* for your future home on the Web—a company that will be responsible for keeping your site connected to the Internet at all times. The web host will park it on a high-speed computer (a *server*) that's fast enough to serve up your page to hundreds of visitors at once.

You have a few options here, including free Web space or extra space your Internet provider may have granted you as part of your monthly Internet subscription. Web hosting firms like Go Daddy (*www.godaddy.com*) and Network Solutions (*www.networksolutions.com*) specialize in renting Web server space for a monthly or annual fee.

You'll also need a *domain name,* which is the ".com" or ".org" part of the Web address—for example, *www.smithsonian.org* or *http://moisttowelettemuseum.com*. If you go with a Web hosting firm, its reps will usually help you pick out and pay for a domain name (more details on page 375).

On the other hand, if you've opted for free Web space on a super-simple service like the ones described back on page 365, you generally won't have to deal with getting a domain name; in fact, you couldn't choose one if you wanted to. Your Web site's address will incorporate the company that's providing the space. If it's Earthlink, for example, and your Web site is called SalsaFiend, your address will be *www.earthlink.com/~salsafiend*.

Using Web space from your ISP

Your Internet service provider may supply you with 10 or 20 megabytes of free space for your own personal Web pages. Check the paperwork you got when you signed up, or your ISP's Web site, to see if that was part of the deal. Most big providers, like Earthlink, Comcast, and Verizon, provide enough space for a small site.

Here again, you won't be allowed to choose your own domain name (like *www.picklepuss.com* or whatever). If you put up some pages through your Comcast account, you'll get a URL like *www.home.comcast.net/picklepuss*.

Using Web space from a hosting company

If you need more space or want more flexibility for your Web site, there's no shortage of companies out there that will gladly rent you some room on their servers for less than $10 a month. Once you buy space from them, such companies supply the information you need to upload your Web site to their servers, like passwords and directions.

If you don't have a domain name for your site yet, you can even buy an all-in-one domain name/hosting *package* from a company like Register.com (*www. register.com*), Go Daddy (*www.godaddy.com*), Dotster (*www.dotster.com*), and Network Solutions (*www.networksolutions.com*).

Each offers a selection of hosting plans for everything from personal sites to major e-commerce operations. Because you're buying a domain name to go with your site, you can also check its availability to see if it's in use. You can look up, say, *www.corndoghut.com*, to see if anyone has nabbed it yet.

When shopping for Web space, consider these factors:

- **Data transfer limit.** Also known as *bandwidth*, this is the amount of information your site is allowed to send each month—namely, copies of your Web pages into the browsers of your site's eager readers/fans/customers. Ask the hosting company what happens if your site gets really popular and you exceed your bandwidth limit; do they temporarily shut you down or just charge you more money? (If this happens to you, temporarily shutting down is the much less expensive option.)

- **Disk space.** If the 10 or 20 megabytes from your ISP isn't enough room to hold all your pages and graphics, how much space do you actually need? If you've already built all your site's pages and have them all in a folder, check the folder's size. In Windows, right-click the folder, choose Properties, and then look at the "Size on Disk" figure. On the Mac, Control-click (or right-click) a folder and then choose Get Info to see its size. Be sure to take into account any new pages or sections you may want to add to your site in the future.

- **Price.** You shouldn't pay more than $10 or $15 a month in hosting fees for a small site. If the price is higher, find out why; see if the company is tossing in tools and features you don't need.

Phase 3: Publish Your Web Site

Once you've designed your pages and lined up a service to host them, you have to transfer the former to the latter. This is where those FTP programs mentioned back on page 370 come into play.

File transfer programs are designed to deliver batches of files from one computer to another in one fell swoop. When you upload your Web site's files, you're basically telling the FTP program *where* you want to move your files (to your Web host's computer), and then pointing the program to the files or folders on your machine that you want to transfer.

Before you can upload your Web site's files to your host server, your FTP program will ask you for three data points that your chosen Web host company must supply:

- **The host address.** This is the address of the server that will harbor your site. The address usually looks something like *ftp.mywebhost.com*.

- **Your user name.** This is whatever you picked when you signed up for the account. If you're using free Web space from your ISP, it's often the part of your email address before the @ sign.

- **Your password.** If you're using your ISP's Web space, this is probably the same password you use for email. If not, it's whatever you picked when you signed up with your Web-hosting company. Passwords are important here because they keep strangers from changing your site's pages.

These three nuggets of info get you into your own assigned directory on your Web host's server. Then you just need to upload the HMTL files and images you created for your Web site to that directory.

The buttons and commands may vary slightly with the FTP program you use, but look for a Put File or Transfer File option. This command lets you select the files on your hard drive to be copied over to the Web server that you're now connected to through your FTP program.

Once you upload your pages to your rented space on the host's server, your brand new Web site is live for the world to see. When you need to make changes to pages or add new ones, upload the corrected or new files to the same folder on your Web server.

___

Tip: Even if you hire professional Web designers to create and upload your pages for your site, you don't have to drag them (and their invoices) back in for every little text update. Services like Edit.com let you fix your pages, add new text and images, update links, and more, right in your own Web browser. Service plans start at $25 for unlimited editing per month; if you don't change your site all that much, you can also pay a flat $25 for one-time, 24-hour window-site updates. You can get more information and a demonstration of how it works at *www.edit.com*.

___

POWER USERS' CLINIC
Advanced Web Work

This chapter is intended to give you an overview of whipping up your own Web site or blog. But if you want to make more sophisticated sites, containing all of today's bells and whistles (like Cascading Style Sheets, JavaScript, and other elements that really jazz up your pages and bring them to life), there's a lot more to learn.

If this little walk on the Web has you wanting more, you can get it with *Creating Web Sites: The Missing Manual*. The book guides you through all the steps needed to create snazzy sites on your own, while also covering topics like how to figure out who your audience is and how to make money with your site. There's also an in-depth look at making a blog, and tips for making your personal Web diary a well-respected member of the blogosphere.

Podcasts

Podcasts, as you may recall from Chapter 11, are radio-style audio shows, usually created by amateurs. Chapter 11 also reveals where to find podcasts and subscribe to them so you never miss your favorite shows.

But the real fun is making your *own* podcasts for the whole world to hear.

The best shows deliver regular doses of insightful commentary on a subject, whether it's about books, Macintosh computers, the Green Bay Packers, or movies. Average Joes and Janes, previously living in utter obscurity, have developed cult podcast followings who can't get enough of their quirky, funny, or just bizarre personalities. (There are also plenty of corporate, slickly produced podcasts, of course.)

You don't need a fancy recording studio, a sound-mixing board, or pricey professional programs to make your own podcast. You can make one with just a microphone, some inexpensive software, and something to say.

To answer the software question, you can pursue either of two avenues:

- **Use a special podcast-making program.** These programs handle the entire process, from recording and editing your podcast to posting it to the Internet. The downside: they cost money.

- **Do-it-yourself.** This approach can save you money but cost you in convenience. The point is that it's also possible to create and upload a podcast using the software that's already on your computer, although it requires more steps.

The following pages describe both approaches.

Tip: No matter which software you use to record your audio show, don't worry if you make a mistake, cuss, or flub a line during your time in front of the microphone; you can always go back and edit that stuff out before you post the thing. All the audio programs described in the next few pages let you go back and fix things. Besides, lots of podcasters leave in that good stuff, on the premise that podcasts are meant to be real, human, and imperfect.

All-in-One Podcast Programs

Becoming a podcaster involves two technological steps. First, you have to record and edit the actual audio show and save it as an audio file. Second, you have to attach something called an *RSS feed file*—a file that supplies information required by podcast receiver programs (page 205), like the name of the file, the date it was published, and where to download a copy.

If you're willing to invest in dedicated podcasting software, you can record, edit, and publish your podcast all in one program. Here are a couple of them:

- **ePodcast Creator.** This $90 program works with Windows 2000 and XP and helps you record and edit multiple audio tracks. Once the podcast is complete, the program creates the RSS feed and uploads the new podcast to your server. There's a free trial version and free podcasting tutorials at *www.industrialaudiosoftware.com*; a professional version called ePodcast Producer offers more audio-editing features and costs $250.

- **Podcast Factory.** M-Audio's Podcast Factory provides everything you need to get rolling, all in one box: desktop microphone; audio interface box for connecting the microphone, headphones, or musical instruments to the computer's USB port; and audio-mixing software that also supplies RSS feeds and publishes your podcasts. The Podcast Factory kit (shown in Figure 19-7) works with Windows XP and Mac OS X and costs about $180; there's more info at *www.m-audio.com*.

Figure 19-7:
The Podcast Factory kit from M-Audio gives the gung-ho podcaster everything she needs to pepper the Web with personal audio shows. A professional-quality desktop microphone is included, plus podcast recording and publishing software, and an audio-interface box that connects the mic and other sound-oriented hardware to the computer's USB port.

GarageBand

GarageBand, Apple's music studio program, comes on every new Mac; you can also buy it as part of Apple's iLife software suite (iMovie, iPhoto, and so on). GarageBand's enormous library of musical instrument sound clips and loops makes it easy to compose your own instrumental work—and you can even plug your own guitar or keyboard into your Mac and add yourself to the mix.

GarageBand 3 and later, in fact, is loaded with special features that are expressly tailored for podcast creation. You can easily add artwork (still images that pop up on the listeners' iPod screens at designated points in the audio), URLs (which listeners can click to visit relevant Web sites if they're listening at their computers), sound effects, background music, and even canned "studio audience" audio clips like laughter and applause.

Here's a quick guide to get you up and recording your very first podcast:

1. **Figure out what microphone you'll use.**

   Most Macintosh models, including the iMac, eMac, and all laptops, have microphones built into the screens. Power Macs can accommodate USB microphones (sold separately).

   If your Mac doesn't have a built-in microphone or even a sound-in port, an *audio-interface box* like Griffin Technology's iMic (*www.griffintechnology. com*) or M-Audio's Fast Track USB (*www.m-audio.com*) connect to your computer's USB port. These boxes provide ports for a microphone and headphones for use while recording.

Before you begin recording, open System Preferences. Click the Sound icon, click the Input tab, and make sure the proper sound source is selected ("Built-in Microphone" or "iMic," for example).

2. **Open GarageBand and choose File → New → New Podcast Episode.**

As shown in Figure 19-8, GarageBand offers a ready-made podcast playpen with basic vocal tracks and sound effects ready to go. (If you have an older version of GarageBand, choose New Track → Real Instrument → Vocals, where there are several presets that can alter your vocalizing. Turning on the checkboxes for Gate and Compressor can help cut down on background noise and smooth out the sound of your voice.)

3. **Check the recording levels.**

"Testing 1...2...3." Experiment with your microphone's sound levels and adjust the volume settings in GarageBand—and on your audio-interface box—until you sound as clear and undistorted as possible. The dancing level meters should approach the red-colored danger zone without crossing over at the loudest parts.

4. **Start talking.**

Keep your mouth close to the microphone for consistent sound and don't worry if you flub a word here and there. You can always rerecord the parts you messed up or edit them out.

5. **Dress up the recording.**

For example, you know how so many people listen to podcasts on their iPods, right? Well, most iPods these days have color screens. And the really cutting-edge podcasts give you something to *see* as you listen.

GarageBand, starting with version 3, lets you plant photos or other still images at specified points in the show; the iPod displays them on the screen when the audience plays back your podcast. (They'll also see this artwork when playing the show in iTunes, on their computers.)

To add artwork in GarageBand 3, choose Control → Media Browser to open the Media Browser window. It lists all the photos, movies, and, audio files you can add to your GarageBand projects, including songs from iTunes and pictures from iPhoto. Drag the photos you want to use to the Episode Artwork well in the GarageBand window, as shown at the bottom of Figure 19-8.

Figure 19-8:
Top: To get the tape rolling on your podcast, choose File → New and click the button to make a new podcast episode.

Bottom: As you create your podcast in GarageBand, you can jazz up your vocal track with sound effects, background music, and artwork by simply dragging and dropping things where you want them. When you're all done, choose Share → "Export Podcast to Disk" to send your finished file out of GarageBand and onto your computer so you can upload it to a Web site. The Share menu gives you other destinations for your podcast as well: You can send it right into your own copy of iTunes or send it to iWeb where you can prepare it for posting on your iWeb site.

Don't miss the radio show-style sound effects, either: crowds cheering, clapping, laughing, and chortling, plus musical "stingers" (quickie sounds often used on radio talk shows as audio punctuation indicating a transition between segments), and other sound effects. You get to them by choosing Control → Loop Browser (or pressing ⌘-L). Click the category (Stingers, Jingles, or whatever) to see the selection of audio clips, and double-click the name of the loop file (Cartoon Space Boing is a fun one) to hear it. If you decide you like the sound, add it to your audio tracks by dragging your chosen loop to the part of your podcast timeline where you want the sound effect to occur.

6. **Export your show.**

Once you've added your sound effects, fixed your slip-ups, and perfected your podcast, save your finished file. Now you're ready to take your podcast out of GarageBand and release it into the wilds of the Web. If you have iLife '06 with the iWeb program and a .Mac account (page 267), all you need to do is choose Share → Send Podcast to iWeb, as shown in the bottom of Figure 19-8. Once you put it on an iWeb page and click the Publish button, your show is beamed up to the Internet.

If you don't have iWeb or .Mac, you can export your podcast and put it up on the Web site of your choosing. To do so, choose Share → Export Podcast to Disk, pick your landing folder, and click Save. You now have a podcast file to send on its way. You can also export your podcast right into your own iTunes library and give it a spin; choose Share → Send Podcast to iTunes to make it so.

Tip: Apple has a whole Web page of tips and suggestions on making podcasts with GarageBand, and there's also a link to a free Chapter Tool, which lets you insert Web links, pictures, and chapter markers into your files: *http://www.apple.com/support/garageband/podcasts/recording*.

Do-It-Yourself Podcast Programs

The programs described on the previous pages handle both the audio recording *and* all that RSS/XML distribution business. But to save a little money and get a little more mileage out of your technical expertise, you can also assemble a low-cost podcast studio from off-the-shelf software "parts." That is, you'll use one program to record the audio, and a second one to dress it up as a podcast and upload it to the Web.

Note: If your computer didn't come with a microphone, you can usually find a selection of external mics at your local computer store or Radio Shack.

Recording the audio (Windows)

Believe it or not, you can use the Sound Recorder program that comes with Windows to record your show (choose Start → Programs → Accessories → Entertainment → Sound Recorder). But the shareware archives on the Web are bursting with more flexible and robust programs for recording your own MP3 files. Search software-download sites like *www.hitsquad.com*, *www.download.com*,

FREQUENTLY ASKED QUESTION

Your Podcast + iTMS = So Happy Together

Now that I'm up and running with my weekly podcast, how can I get the iTunes Music Store to list it in the Podcast Directory so iTunes shoppers can subscribe to it?

The iTunes Music Store is host to thousands upon thousands of podcasts, and not all of them are slick professional productions. Many shows listed in the iTMS Podcast Directory are made by regular folks who've discovered that podcasting gives them a public voice, too—with or without a radio studio and a morning drive-time slot.

Apple doesn't *host* podcast files on its Music Store servers, but the company freely invites podcasters everywhere to submit their shows for *listing* in its Podcast Directory. This listing links back to your own server or site where you store your podcast files, making it incredibly easy for people browsing the iTunes directory to find you.

Keep in mind that podcasts in the iTunes Music Store need to meet certain technical requirements;

Apple has the complete list posted at *www.apple. com/itunes/podcasts/techspecs.html.*

Once your podcast passes technical muster, all you need to do is hop into the Music Store, go to the Podcasts area from the link on the main page, and then click the link for Submit Podcast. Here, you type in the link for your podcast's RSS feed (page 111) and give some basic information about your show so people poking around know what it's about.

Your submission doesn't appear immediately after you complete the form; it may be reviewed before your show appears in the Podcast Directory. One thing to note: If your podcast contains any copyrighted audio material used without authorization and someone complains about it to the company, Apple reserves the right to zap your show right out of its listings.

or *www.tucows.com*, and you'll find plenty of audio-recording programs to sample.

FASoft's n-Track Studio, for example, is a versatile recording and mixing program that you can sample for free at *www.fasoft.com* and buy for about $50. Once you record yourself using the program, you can export the result in any of several audio-file formats, including WAV and MP3. (MP3 is the best option, though, because it's the standard format for podcast files. MP3 files are relatively small files, and they work on every pocket music player alive.)

Once you have your audio file the way you want it, you're ready to distribute it as a proper podcast. Jump to page 385 for instructions on posting your podcast.

Tip: Got a microphone but no sound port? If you don't have a sound-in port on your computer, you can do it the USB way with the iMic from Griffin Technology. The iMic works with both PCs and Macs through the USB port, as described on page 379. If you don't have the microphone either, consider the $40 MicFlex from MacMice (*www.macmice.ca*), a flexible microphone that plugs right into the USB port.

WORKAROUND WORKSHOP

WAV to MP3

Suppose that you, an impoverished computer fan who's stranded on a desert island with no Internet access and only the built-in Windows Sound Recorder program, have created a masterpiece of a podcast. But because it's Sound Recorder, it can create only WAV files, which aren't ideal for posting on the Internet as podcasts.

What to do?

Here's how you can convert them to MP3 files right in iTunes:

In iTunes, choose Edit → Preferences → Advanced → Importing and, from the Import Using pop-up menu, choose MP3 Encoder. Click OK.

Once the file is in your iTunes library (choose File → Add to Library, if necessary), select it and then choose Advanced → Convert Selection to MP3. iTunes spins out an MP3 version of the WAV file; you'll probably see them listed consecutively in iTunes.

Drag the new MP3 file out of the iTunes window and onto your desktop, ready for action.

Recording the audio (Macintosh)

If you have GarageBand—it's been included on every Mac since 2004—use that; later versions, in particular, are ideal for making podcasts, as described on page 379.

Otherwise, plenty of inexpensive Macintosh shareware programs for audio recording await you on the Web; visit *www.osxaudio.com*, for example, or *www.hitsquad.com/smm/mac/recording*. Two popular shareware programs for audio recording for Mac OS X are Amadeus II ($30) and Audiocorder ($20). (Both are available through links on this book's "Missing CD" page at *www.missingmanuals.com*.)

Publishing the podcast

Once you've created an MP3 file of your podcast episode, you have to upload it to your Web site, blog, or wherever you want your listeners to find your audio file. To do so, you need to publish it in a format that incorporates an *RSS feed*.

You can find many programs for Windows and Macintosh that automate the process of uploading your audio files all wrapped up in a nice RSS feed. For example, try Podifier (*www.podifier.com*) or FeedForAll (*www.feedforall.com*), shown in Figure 19-9. Each program walks you through the steps for publishing your podcast and RSS feed to your Web site or blog, where your adoring fans are clamoring.

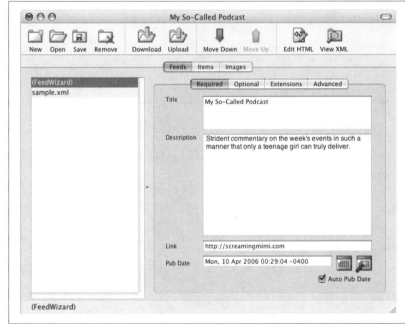

Figure 19-9:
FeedForAll gently guides you through the RSS-feed creation dance that keeps your podcast subscribers happy. Once you upload your feed file and podcast to your chosen server, other people's podcast programs take it from there and snag a copy of your latest episode.

The Podcasting News site, a wonderful place to learn all about podcasting, has a lengthy list of feed-publishing programs and services for both Windows and Mac pod-jockeys. If you're in search of even more software to make the whole getting-my-voice-heard-on-the-Web part of the podcast process easier, check out *www.podcastingnews.com/topics/Podcasting_Software.html*.

And, if you happen to blog with Blogger (page 361), Podcasting News has an illustrated tutorial showing how you can create your own RSS feed with services like FeedBurner's SmartCast service (*www.feedburner.com*); you can find it directly at *www.podcastingnews.com/articles/Make_Podcast_Blogger.html*.

Living on the Web

From bargain airfare to movie rentals, the Web is full of tools that are designed to make life easier. And thanks to its ability to link people and computers, the Web itself becomes a Swiss-Army-style apparatus at your disposal, especially when you're away from home—or away from your own computer.

Yes, the Web can be your personal radio station, newsstand, and gaming arcade, but it can be even more than that. It can be your backup drive. It can be a word processor when you're working at a computer that doesn't have Word or WordPerfect installed. It can be an electronic version of the family calendar that would otherwise be stuck to the refrigerator with Snoopy magnets. It can be a conference room, complete with whiteboard and slide presentation, for people in six different regional offices.

Yes, while this book's previous chapters describe how to live *with* the Web, this chapter shows you how to live *on* the Web—and the rent's way cheaper than your apartment.

Online Backup and Storage

Just about every book, magazine, or Web site about computers stresses the importance of backing up your computer files.

It's good advice, especially if you've moved important parts of your life—such as music, movies, photos, and other personal documents—into digital form on a hard drive. You may not care if that hard drive crashes and you lose your spreadsheet of business travel expenses. But if the machine goes south and takes the complete library of your kid's digital photos—from ultrasound to kindergarten graduation—odds are you're going to be mightily upset.

Yes, backing up is important and you should do it, by external hard drive, by DVD, by CD, by whatever it takes. But for truly vital data, there's another option to consider: *online* backup and storage. Under this kind of system, you copy your most important files to a secure server on the Internet that's owned and maintained by an online storage company.

Online storage frees your desk from an external drive or stacks of backup CDs. Better yet, your backup copy isn't in your home. So if something catastrophic happens, and your computer equipment gets stolen, damaged, or destroyed, *your files are still safe.* You can get to them from any Internet-connected computer, whether it's one of yours or somebody else's machine three states away.

In many cases, copying your files to an online storage facility is as easy as dragging a folder onto a disk, because that's exactly what you get when you sign up—a chunk of disk space for your stuff, albeit on somebody else's computer. It's sort of like renting a parking space in a big, heated, high security garage: You don't have to maintain the garage; you just drive in and out as you please.

How to Find Online Storage

Dozens of companies offer online file storage and backup for reasonable monthly fees. When shopping around, here are a few things to consider:

- **How much storage and how many features are included in the price?** Most companies can give you as much room as you need (for a price). Also, does the company offer services like remote file-sharing (the ability for you—or someone you authorize—to access files stored on the company's computers) and automatic backup?

- **How do you move your files to the offsite servers?** Do you use your Web browser or do you need special software? A Web browser is the more universal approach—and one that Mac fans can always use. But specialized software (which tends to be Windows-only) often provides shortcuts like drag-and-drop file storage and the ability to save documents from the program you're working in directly onto your remote server.

- **What are the company's system requirements?** Speaking of browsers and software, will this service work with your particular operating system and Web browser?

- **Are the file transfers and your data secure?** Just as you want to make sure your credit card digits are safe in Web transit, you don't want anybody intercepting your personal data files, so make sure the online storage company offers encryption and other security measures.

- **Do you have access to 24/7 tech support?** You don't want to end up desperately trying to download a backup copy of your financial records onto your old laptop at 3:00 a.m. on April 15th after your desktop PC took a power surge from a spring storm—and not have any tech help available if something isn't working right.

You may find a suitable company right off the bat with a quick Web search for *online storage*, *virtual storage*, or *off-site file backup*, but here are suggestions.

Xdrive

For about $10 a month, you can stash up to five gigabyte of files safely and securely on Xdrive's servers (*www.xdrive.com*; a free trial is available). Like any good data-storage service, the company even makes its own backups of *your* backups to make sure those files are always around when you need them.

You work with the service right in your Mac or Windows Web browser; a special Windows file-transfer program (called Xdrive Desktop) is also available.

Once you log in, storing or backing up your files is just a folder-drag from your computer to your Xdrive folder on the screen; if you use Xdrive Desktop, you can even schedule automatic backups. Xdrive uses secure 128-bit encryption to shield your data as it moves across the Internet from your computer to theirs.

Although you can share your files with others by making certain Xdrive folders public, you can't use the service as a Web host to store linkable files or your Web site. One neat treat: If you're waiting around for files to upload, you can browse the titles in the Xdrive Library, a public folder with more than 1,500 free eTexts from authors like Agatha Christie, Mark Twain, Sir Arthur Conan Doyle, and H.G. Wells.

FilesAnywhere

If you like what you see after the free trial of FilesAnywhere (*www.filesanywhere.com*), paid accounts start at $4 a month for 100 megabytes of file storage and sharing, and go up to $70 a month for 50 gigabytes. Plans that include both file storage and scheduled backups start at $9 a month for 2 GB. People collaborating on projects from different locations can sign up for a workgroup plan, which lets several people log into the same account.

The service works with Windows and Mac and most Web browsers. But if you use Internet Explorer 5.5 on Windows, you get a few extra features, like Advanced File Search through your online data vault.

You transfer your files to FilesAnywhere right in your Web browser. You can also set up a digital drop box that lets other people deposit files; all connections are wrapped up in 128-bit (hard to crack) encryption.

If you keep your digital picture collection on the site, you can put certain photos in something called a PhotoFolder, which turns FilesAnywhere into a photo-sharing site (page 235) so that you can share them with your friends.

IBackup

Browser-based file storage for Windows and Mac machines is also an option at IBackup, another company offering plenty of server space to park your data.

You can sign up for a free trial or full service at *www.ibackup.com*. Prices for a basic drag-and-drop storage folder range from $10 a month (5 gigabytes of space) to $50 (50 gigabytes); automated backup plans cost a bit more. Data transfers through your Web browser are encrypted for security, and you can also share your online files by granting others permission to access your files.

When you sign up for an IBackup account, you get a program that installs an IDrive—a virtual disk—on your computer. It shows up in Windows Explorer or on the Mac's desktop, just as though it were a really, really big USB flash (keychain) drive. You can drag files between desktop and this virtual drive, and even create new folders, to keep your invisible giant backup drive tidy.

.Mac

If you're a Mac fan, this business of a virtual hard drive icon on your desktop (whose storage is actually online) might sound familiar. This, of course, is precisely the idea behind the iDisk, a one-gigabyte virtual disk that's offered to anyone with a .Mac account (page 267).

When you've got your iDisk set up, it appears just like another drive icon on your desktop (Figure 20-1, left), and you can drag files on or off between your computer and Apple's; there's also an iDisk Utility tool that lets you tap into your online folders from a Windows computer.

All of this is made much simpler by the Backup program that's also part of .Mac membership. Backup can copy your most important folders to the iDisk—or any other drive—automatically (as shown in Figure 20-1, right).

Figure 20-1:
Left: Like other online file-storage options, Apple's iDisk service for .Mac members gives you another drive in your list to use for stashing copies of your important documents. If you need more than 1 GB, you can buy up to four gigabytes for $100 a year.

Right: The Backup program included with any .Mac subscription gives you plenty of choices about where, when, and what to back up—including data dumps to your iDisk online storage space

Online Word Processing Programs

Microsoft Word rules offices; Notepad and TextEdit are free on every Windows PC and Mac. So, for anybody who wants to process some words in a pinch, the idea of online word processing programs may seem redundant.

But having your word processor reside on the Internet, rather than your hard drive, has all kinds of payoffs:

- Most online word processors are free. Here's your chance to create, open, edit, spell check, and distribute Microsoft Word documents—without actually owning Microsoft Word.

- As with any Web-based program, you never have to worry about installing upgraded or bug-fixed versions; you're always using the very latest.

- You never have to worry about losing your work. If it's on the Internet, your hard drive can choke, gag, die, and keel over, but your document is safe. Some of these online programs, moreover, auto-save and auto-back up your work as often as every 10 seconds.

- Many online word processors are designed for collaboration, where two or more people can all work on the same documents. Say you and your old college buddies, now in far-flung locations, want to work on a screenplay together. Using an online word processor, one person could start the draft and the others could come along in turn and add their own material and comments—all without the hassle and version confusion of emailing individual files back and forth.

- The software works right in your Web browser, so compatibility with different operating systems is also a non-issue.

Some programs require the use of a specific browser like Firefox, but Firefox itself runs on most common operating systems like Windows, Mac OS X, and Linux.

Microsoft Office Live

Microsoft has acknowledged the benefits of putting software on communal servers for online collaboration. In the fall of 2005, the company announced Microsoft Office Live (*http://officelive.microsoft.com*), a suite of Web-based tools and programs for small business owners and others. They let you create your own Web site, set up your own corporate email accounts, and collaborate on documents and spreadsheets.

Three different plans are available. Live Basics gives you a Web site and a handful of email accounts, all for free. Live Collaboration and Live Essentials (both $30 a month) add a calendar, online file storage, and information-sharing. Subscribers also get To-Do Lists, asset trackers, inventory control programs, project-management tools, and more—all password-protected and locked up online.

Live Essentials customers also get server space and software tools to design a small Web site. Some features require Microsoft Office to be installed on each computer, but all the files added to the Live site can be shared among employees.

In short, if you have a small or medium-size business where your employees (wherever they may be) need to share information to keep the company running smoothly, Microsoft has an Office Live plan it hopes to sell you. If you *don't* have a small business, Office Live may seem too much to deal with, but there are plenty of free online word processors to play with for more casual collaboration.

Other Online Word Processors

But what if you have no need for the virtual office and company-records room that Office Live can provide? What if you just want to do things like open and edit a Microsoft Word file on a Word-free computer or work on a document with someone on the opposite coast? In those situations, there are much simpler options. Some of them are absolutely free.

- **ajaxWrite.** ajaxWrite is a zippy word processor that pops up, ready to go, in about five seconds. It can open documents in Word, Microsoft Works, and WordPerfect formats.

  It's free, but it requires the Firefox browser for Windows or Mac OS X. If you're so equipped, you can do such text-styling and formatting tricks as fancy font treatments (Figure 20-2) and numbered lists. You can start your own files and save them to your desktop.

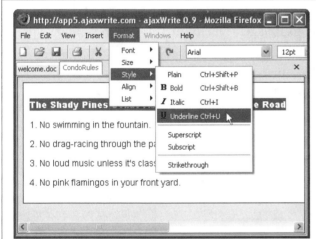

Figure 20-2:
With ajaxWrite, your word processing program is right in your Web browser. Once you create or open documents created in most common word processing programs, you can write or edit them, style the text, and save them to the desktop of the computer you happen to be using.

The program itself occupies less than 400 K, making it lean, mean, and free of the menu bloat that makes other word processors so lethargic.

You can't save an ajaxWrite file online to share with other people. Still, this program can be a real bacon-saver when, say, you're using a borrowed computer to read your Web-based email and need to open a Word attachment. A companion program, ajaxSketch, is also available for your drawing and diagramming needs. (*www.ajaxwrite.com*)

- **Writely.** Writely was snapped up by Google in early 2006, so you can expect it to gain new fans thanks to the reach and reputation of its new owner.

Writely lets you create, edit, spell check, and share documents online with other folks via emailed invitations—or even publish them (the documents, not the folks), blog-style. Writely saves the different revisions of your file, so if you want to toss out the edit you did when you were in the bad mood and flying high on cold medicine, you can roll back to a previous version of a document. You can send documents to or from the site in Word, Rich Text, HTML, PDF, or plain text formats.

The site is compatible with Firefox and Mozilla on Windows and Mac OS X, as well as Internet Explorers 5.5 and later for Windows—and, as with most Google services, it's free. (*www.writely.com*)

• **Zoho Writer.** Zoho Writer lets you create, edit, and share files online from any computer that meets its browser requirements—Internet Explorer 5.5 or later, Netscape 7, and Firefox work; Apple's Safari does not. Like Writely, Zoho Writer keeps multiple versions of a file so you don't have to clutter your desktop with backup copies. As shown in Figure 20-3, Zoho Writer's interface looks like any word processor you've ever used and you can even publish your documents to Blogger, LiveJournal, WordPress, and TypePad blogs. (*www.zohowriter.com*)

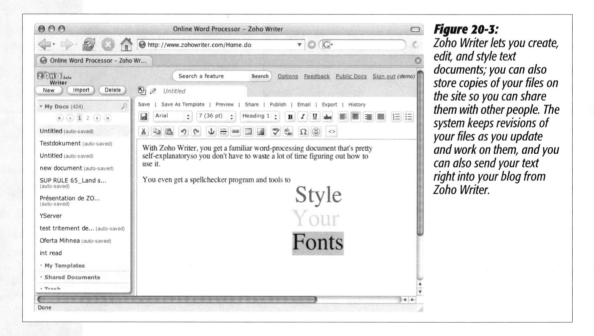

Figure 20-3:
Zoho Writer lets you create, edit, and style text documents; you can also store copies of your files on the site so you can share them with other people. The system keeps revisions of your files as you update and work on them, and you can also send your text right into your blog from Zoho Writer.

• **ThinkFree Office Online.** Sign up for a free basic account with ThinkFree, and you get 30 megabytes of server space to open, edit, and store files. You can open and edit Word, Excel, and PowerPoint documents here, and save finished files in the nearly universal PDF format.

The site uses Java (page 176) and works with most browsers for Windows and Macintosh. If you've already got a big chunk of your life online, you can post to your blog from ThinkFree and even add your Flickr photos to your documents. (*http://online.thinkfree.com*)

Project Planning and Group Calendars

Forget the tattered kitchen calendar. Forget the assorted Palm handhelds, on which everyone on the team wrote down a different time and day for the next meeting. With online planning and calendar software, you can keep everybody literally on the same page—a Web page, to be precise.

The modus operandi for using this sort of online service should be pretty familiar by now: find a site that you (or y'all) like, sign up for an account, and log in when you need to use it.

The beauty of an online calendar is that people all over the building—or country, or planet—can share the same calendar. And because they're online, Web-based calendars are cross-platform and networkable (so you and your spouse can see each other's calendars).

In some cases, the site can even send you little electronic shoulder-tap reminders of your looming appointments by email or instant messaging program.

Google Calendar

Google Calendar is beautiful, fast, and simple to use; it feels like a regular piece of desktop software, not like a Web page that blinks every time you make a change.

For example, if you already have a Gmail account (page 264) and you sign up for a calendar (*http://calendar.google.com*), Gmail recognizes messages that mention dates or events and offers to add such events to the calendar. You can import your life from other calendar programs like Microsoft Outlook or Apple's iCal program into your Gcalendar in just a few steps, too.

There are two ways to add events to your day: fast or by form.

- With the Quick Add option (Figure 20-4), you just click a one-line box and type your info ("Brunch with Julia at Mayrose Sunday at noon"). Google understands your plain-English notation and slaps a proper appointment into your online datebook in the right place. Then, Google being Google, you also get a link to a map of your restaurant's location based on its name, complete with address, phone number, link to its Web site, driving directions, and reviews posted by other diners.

Figure 20-4:
The Quick Add box in Google Calendar lets you dash off a note on the fly for an upcoming event in regular hasty English. Once you hit the Enter key, your appointment shows up on your calendar page on the proper day and the right time, making it a much speedier way to keep your schedule current than plodding around in drop-down menus to make a date.

- You can also add an event to your calendar the long way: by clicking the Create Event link and laboriously filling in the form for time, date, place, title of appointment, and all that.

You can view your life by the day, week, month, or the next four days, and there's also an Agenda tab on the main screen that shows you a vertical list of all upcoming events. In the Settings area, you can select your privacy options for sharing your calendars with others. That's also where you configure your options for getting reminders sent to your email (Gmail) account or your cellphone as a text message.

Yahoo Calendar

If you've already got Yahoo email, instant messenger, address book, or any other Yahoo services in your life, it makes sense to add Yahoo Calendar to your stable; you can find it at *http://calendar.yahoo.com*. It integrates nicely with the email and address book components (clickable tabs for both appear right on your main calendar window).

Scheduling an appointment is as easy as clicking the Add Event button and typing in your info on the resulting screen. Yahoo gives you more than a dozen labels to indicate exactly what type of event you're scheduling, including Meeting, Dinner, Bill Payment, Party, and—helpful for many—*Anniversary*. You can view your schedule by day, week, month, or year.

On the Options tab, you can share your day's view with other people, add personalized touches like photos and horoscopes, and import data from other calendar programs (like Palm Desktop). Even if you keep all your contacts and calendars in another program, you can sync it up with your Yahoo Calendar to give yourself an online backup, no matter where you are or how hard you bounced your PDA off the train platform this morning.

Tip: Calendar sites abound on the Web. If you don't want to add to the Yahoo/Google empire, Kiko (*www.kiko.com*) is another option.

Basecamp/Backpack/Ta-da List

If you love to be meticulously organized in both your life and your collaborative projects, check out Basecamp, Backpack, and Ta-da List—a related trio of services. All three are available at *www.37signals.com*, along with the company's own online word processor (Writeboard) and group chat (Campfire) applications.

- **Basecamp** is a big group project and planning service (Figure 20-5). Tossing out stodgy spreadsheets and charts, Basecamp lets you set up your own workspace online. You can communicate with others assigned to the same project by means of message boards, to-do lists, file sharing, and community calendars.

  A free account lets you manage communications and scheduling for one project at a time (no file sharing included). For $12 a month, you can have three projects going at once—with an unlimited number of people—and share up to 100 megabytes of files on the site.

  For $100 a month, you get a gigabyte of file-sharing space, time-tracking capabilities, and encrypted file transfers for your top-secret project.

- **Backpack** is also all about organizing, but it tends to be more of a personal thing. Once you sign up for an account, you can make individual idea or project pages in a topic ("My Summer Trip to Québec City" or "Plans to

---

Figure 20-5:
*A Basecamp project page
lets you visually organize a
plan or project and lets
everyone involved
communicate in the same
space, even if they're not all
online at the same time.
Members of the same team
can post messages,
updates, and other general
information to keep
everyone in the loop.*

convert the basement into a photo studio") and then add photos, files, and
text to the page to help you develop and flesh out your plans. You can also
share your pages with pals.

For your further organizational pleasure, Backpack can send you a
reminder by email or cellphone text message when one of your to-do items
comes due.

Monthly Backpack plans range from free to $14; more money means more
pages, reminders, and room to store your stuff online instead of in your
mind.

• **Ta-da List** is completely free and, if you're the type that gets through the
day by sheer will and a detailed to-do list, completely addictive. You can
make lists for yourself, friends, spouse, and co-workers. And to make sure
you don't miss an item, you can get an RSS feed (page 111) of your list to
keep you on track.

All three services work on Windows and Mac OS X with modern browsers like
Firefox, Internet Explorer 6 and later, and Safari. And since it's all Web-based,
you don't have to tangle with installation or worry about hard drive space—
just make sure JavaScript is turned on in your browser and you're ready to go.
Anywhere.

Wandering Laptops vs. Online Nomads

The ability to store all your documents online means that travelers now have a serious decision to make: should I even bother lugging my laptop along?

If you store all your stuff online, for example, there's much less point in hauling your laptop through airport security. Instead, you can tap into your archives, whip up documents, and show off your photos on any computer with an Internet connection. You can backpack through Europe with a much lighter bag and check your Web-based email and voicemail (page 348) in a local Internet café. The main drawback to productivity here is not being able to find a computer or Net connection.

The alternative, of course, is bringing the laptop with you; that way, you have everything on board. If

you just need to do a little word processing or want to sooth your nerves with a little chill-out music, you don't need an Internet connection.

There is, however, a way to combine both approaches: keep all your valuable files on a pocket hard drive or USB flash drive. That way, you've got your stuff with you at all times on any computer, whether it has an Internet connection or not.

Some pocket drives—like Lexar's JumpDrives with its PowerToGo software, Verbatim's tiny Store 'n' Go USB hard drives, or its U3 flash drives—actually let you install and run your own *programs* without first having to copy them to the computer you're borrowing. Prices vary with drive capacity, but you can pay anywhere from $50 to $200 for 1 to 8 gigabytes of space.

Note: Not sure whether your browser has its JavaScript revved up? In most cases, you just need to turn on the checkbox next to Enable JavaScript in the browser's preferences or options area and then restart the program to have the change take effect.

Of course, *finding* this JavaScript box is the hard part, but here's a quick guide for the most common browsers. In Internet Explorer for Windows, choose Tools → Internet Options → Security; click the Custom level tab and scroll down to Scripting so you can click the Enable button. For Firefox for Windows, choose Tools → Options → Content. In Firefox for Mac, choose Firefox → Preferences → Content; Safari fans can find the JavaScript option by going to Safari → Preferences → Security.

Online Meetings/Web Conferencing

As efficient as the Web can be at giving people in disparate locations a centralized spot to exchange memos, messages, and flowcharts, sometimes live communications are called for—especially for things like time-sensitive projects or sales presentations. In those cases, the Web can welcome everyone into the

---

same conference call or virtual room, so you can hammer out the details in real time. Conference-call setup on the Web can be less expensive than using an audio-conferencing service, and you can usually have at least 25 people on the line—far too many for an IM audio-video chat.

FreeConference.com

When the time comes to round up everyone in the project for a progress meeting, a conference call (by telephone) lets you cut right to the chase, especially if half the team is in San José, the other half is in New Jersey, and the client is in Indianapolis. When it comes time to set up the call for all involved, FreeConference.com (*www.freeconference.com*) gives you a gathering place. It provides a dial-in number for all your participants to use, as well as an access code to punch in so they can enter the digital conference room and talk to the others.

FreeConference.com has three levels of service:

- **Reservationless Standard.** This free service is fine for small, uncomplicated group chats. (Free, that is, except for the actual phone calls the participants make.) No registration is required. You pick out your own dial-in number from the site's directory—numbers from a few different area codes are available, but there's no guarantee they can handle your conference at your chosen time, and you may get a busy signal. You also need to make up your own access code to keep uninvited people from accidentally joining your call by mistake. Then up to 25 people can join in and gab away for up to three hours.

- **Web-Scheduled Standard.** You have to register for a free account and fill out a form online to set up your call, but FreeConference.com takes care of the secretarial work by picking out a phone number and access code for you—and making sure there's room for your conference at your chosen time. Furthermore, it sends out the info in email invites to all the people on your list. You can have up to 100 callers on the line for three hours.

- **Web-Scheduled Premium 800.** This plan costs 10 cents a minute per conference participant, but everyone gets a toll-free number, saving long-distance charges. Up to 150 callers can be on the line for five hours (although, truth to tell, a five-hour phone call with 150 people talking simultaneously sounds more punishing than productive).

For additional fees, you can get a downloadable MP3 recording or telephone playback of the call, or even have a transcription service produce a written text of the call.

WebEx

If you need to give a PowerPoint presentation or demonstrate a product for someone oceans away, WebEx (*www.webex.com*) brings the projector screen to the desktop.

Once your team members join you in your online, virtual WebEx meeting session (and install the necessary WebEx plug-in into their browsers), you can play your own presentation on everyone's computer screen. You narrate your slides over the phone, by streaming video, or by typed chat. You can transfer documents and spreadsheets directly to others in the Web-conference to keep everyone up to speed; when it's all over, you can cherish an automated recording of these meetings.

WebEx isn't free (except for the two-week trial). Prices start at $75 a month for unlimited gatherings in the WebEx Meeting Center, but for the budget-minded, there's also a pay-per-use plan that charges 33 cents a minute for each participant.

WebEx also offers traditional video and audio conferencing.

Breeze

Breeze blows in from Macromedia, the company that created the Flash software (page 67) for Web animations and interactivity. With Breeze (*www.breezecentral.com*), you can save the plane fare and show your PowerPoints online either in a live session or on demand for people to go find when they have the time to pay attention.

The system can do more than just play back a presentation, though. When you sign up for a Breeze meeting, your desktop can become a multimedia control room with live video windows, streaming audio, and online whiteboards for scribbling ideas—without getting dry-erase marker all over your shirt. You can narrate and control a full-screen presentation on everyone's screen, exchange files, and carry on Q&A sessions in a text-chat window.

Breeze is rather pricey—$375 a month for multimedia meetings with up to five people. But because it's powered by the same Flash software (page 67) used by just about every modern Web browser, you don't have to install extra plug-ins or fiddle with hardware. Plus, all the meetings take place on the Breeze servers. There is, however, a pay-per-use plan here, too: for 32 cents a minute per attendee, you can Breeze your way through that sales pitch or product demonstration from the comfort of your own computer.

Breeze and WebEx share many of the same Web-conferencing abilities, but Breeze's use of the Flash player may make it more compatible for use with a number of different operating systems. Its interface is a bit friendlier, too, and many companies have found Breeze's intuitive controls and ability to handle all kinds of audio and video great for online training courses.

Staying Safe

The Internet reveals humanity both at its most glorious heights of achievement and at its downright sleaziest. As you gaze at the new moons of Pluto (as seen from the Hubble Space Telescope at *http://hubble.nasa.gov*), your email inbox is filling up with viruses awaiting their chance to hop onto your hard drive. Mixed in with those messages are pitches from rip-off artists and identity thieves.

Threats from the Internet fall into four broad categories: programs designed to damage the information on your hard drive (viruses, worms, and the like), software that steals personal information from your computer (spyware), hackers who break into and run programs on your computer without your knowledge, and scammers who use the Internet to take advantage of unsuspecting victims (phishing).

This chapter shows you how to protect your computer using software that detects—and deletes—malicious software code or blocks unwelcome access. It also shows you how to use your computer's settings to control the information that flows in and out of your machine. And to help you keep your kids safe, the last section deals with parental controls.

Know Your Enemies

The steps to safeguarding your computer make more sense when you understand the nature of the threats you're dealing with. Here's the Internet's Seven Most Wanted:

- **Viruses.** A *virus* is a nasty little piece of code (that is, a small program) that invades your computer without your knowledge. Like a flu bug that spreads from person to person, a virus can replicate itself and jump from computer to computer by attaching itself to a host file. If you unwittingly open the infected host file—for example, a song you download illegally or a file called "Britney Bikini Pic.jpg"—the virus code leaps into action and starts doing its damage. Viruses can cause erratic computer behavior or even erase files on your hard drive.

- **Worms.** A member of the evil virus family, a *worm* also spreads by replicating itself over networked computers. But a worm doesn't need human involvement or even a host file to perform its nasty duty. Worms have caused entire office networks to crash, costing companies millions of dollars in damages and lost productivity.

- **Trojan horses.** Like the Greek myth it was named after, a *Trojan horse* is a deceptive file or program. It appears enticing—a game, perhaps—so you cheerfully install it on your hard drive. Once it's there, the software quietly gets down to business. Trojan horses can secretly transmit your passwords and account numbers to Internet criminals, or provide the means for someone to take over your computer.

- **Spyware.** Not as destructive as a virus but just as sneaky, *spyware* has become a huge problem around the Internet. A spyware program gathers information about you and your computing habits and then quietly transmits the information back to its spymaster—often an advertising or marketing company.

- **Third-party cookies.** Alongside the good cookies that let Web sites remember and automatically fill in your login information and other preferences, there are bad cookies. Called *third-party* or *tracking* cookies, they don't even originate from the Web sites you surf to. Instead, a company that advertises on that site slips its own cookies onto your computer to trace your movements as you roam the Web.

- **Phishing.** Those junk email messages clogging up your inbox are usually more of an annoyance than a threat. In the hands of sneaky identity thieves, though, email can be much more dangerous. *Phishing* refers to mass-emailed phony messages that trick people into handing over their passwords, credit card information, and even social security numbers. Just as the pronunciation implies, phishers sit back and wait for their victims to bite.

- **Hijacking.** You're the one who pays for the Internet connection and sits at the keyboard, so you're the only one who can control your computer, right? Wrong. That connection is a conduit both into and out of your machine. If you don't shield it properly with a firewall (page 414), anyone with a bit of programming skill (and a lack of moral fiber) can pipe in programs and commands that take over your computer.

Note: Most of these maladies affect only Windows PCs. The Macintosh is largely unaffected by viruses, worms, spyware, and so on, partly because its smaller market share makes it a smaller target for the virus writers, and partly because it's a more modern, much more secure operating system to begin with.

Fighting Internet Pests

Sadly, computers were a lot safer before people figured out how to link them into the giant network called the Internet. Although viruses dominate today's technology news, they first appeared on PCs in 1986. Back then, just about the only way a virus could travel from one desktop computer to another was on an infected floppy disk. So although viruses have been around for a couple of decades, it took the Internet to make them truly dangerous.

Nowadays, malicious programs can email themselves to everyone in your Windows computer's address book before you know it. They can secretly transmit information about your shopping and surfing habits back to unseen companies and pepper your screen with advertisements. A particularly virulent outbreak of nasty programming code can even crash Windows computers and grind the Internet to a halt.

Viruses, worms, and their ilk usually hitch rides on email messages sent from infected computers (whose owners probably have no idea they're infected). Or perhaps yet another angry, frustrated programmer launches a mass mailing of malicious code in a desperate cry for attention.

Fortunately, plenty of *antivirus programs* can swat down pestware before it has a chance to infest your PC. A good antivirus program also screens your mail for you. (A decent junk mail or *spam* filter on your email program can isolate messages emailed to a ton of people. See page 282 for more on how to activate the built-in spam filters you may already have in your email program.)

Many antivirus programs act like sentinels, performing real-time monitoring of your computer as you use it. These programs do things like check incoming email for infected attachments and screen CDs and other removable drives for evil code. You can also run periodic scans that sweep your entire system looking for viruses.

Every virus has its own telltale *signature* or pattern, sort of like the computer equivalent of a dirty fingerprint, that can be used to identify the malicious code. Antivirus programs keep a library of these virus patterns and use them to identify any viruses that may be lurking on, or about to enter, your computer. If the antivirus program finds a virus, it zaps it off your hard drive. To protect against the new viruses released into the wild every week, the antivirus program grabs updates from its manufacturer's virus patterns library. Figure 21-1 shows an automatic update in progress.

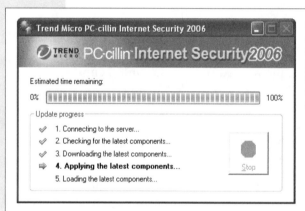

Figure 21-1:
As Trend Micro PC-cillin Internet Security suite updates itself with a fresh batch of virus definitions, you can watch its progress. Antivirus software usually checks for updates automatically, so you don't have to worry about downloading them manually.

These pattern updates are also called antivirus *subscriptions*. After a year of use, your antivirus program will likely start popping up alert boxes, reminding you to renew your subscription so you can keep getting updates. You may resent having to pony up $25 or $30 again, even though you paid $40 or $50 dollars for the software in the first place. But it costs the manufacturer money to update the pattern files as new viruses appear, and those files are what *keep* your PC virus-free throughout the year.

Depending on your PC manufacturer, you may be able to buy antivirus software separately or, for around $20 more, as part of an *Internet security suite*. These security suites, which range in price from about $50 to $70, offer protection from an assortment of Internet hazards. In addition to antivirus protection, you get firewall software (page 415) to shield your machine from Internet intruders, spam filters to weed out junk mail from real messages (page 286), spyware stompers to block sneaky programs from running around on your PC (page 408), and other components that turn your computer into a well-guarded fortress.

An unprotected Windows PC can be invaded and infected after less than 15 minutes on the Internet. Security software is an absolute necessity for safe computing. In fact, your new computer may have included a trial version of security software. But if you have to shop for your own software bodyguard, here are some popular options:

- **Trend Micro PC-cillin Internet Security.** This colorful, full-featured suite protects your PC from viruses, worms, and Trojan horses. It also guards against spyware, spam, wireless network squatters, and people or programs trying to infiltrate your machine. (*www.trendmicro.com*)

- **Norton Internet Security.** Symantec's Norton products have been fighting the good fight for years. The Windows suite includes Norton Antivirus, a robust firewall, spam and spyware protection, and a parental-control feature. (*www.symantec.com*)

Note: Norton AntiVirus is also available separately, in both Mac and Windows editions.

- **McAfee Internet Security Suite.** McAfee's package includes antivirus software, a firewall, spam filtering, spyware strangling, and privacy protection. It also combats phishing (page 412) and other forms of identity theft. (*www.mcafee.com*)

- **Panda Platinum Internet Security.** Panda Software's suite includes all the usual components—antivirus, firewall, spam, spyware, and other shields— as well as TruPrevent technology designed to isolate strange code even before it's recognized as a virus. (*www.pandasoftware.com*)

- **Intego Internet Security Barrier.** One of the rare security suites for the Macintosh, Intego's arsenal provides antivirus and firewall protection, encrypts iChat instant message conversations, filters spam, and filters out material that's inappropriate for children. It even has a backup program to save your bacon (along with your files) in case your Mac crashes hard and can't get up. (*www.intego.com*)

Tip: There are, believe it or not, *free* antivirus programs for Windows: AVG Anti Virus Free Edition from Grisoft (*www.grisoft.com*) and AntiVir PersonalEdition (*www.free-av.com*). Free programs don't get updated as frequently as programs you pay for, and you may not get much (or any) technical support. But if your software budget is $0, these programs afford your PC at least a basic booster shot against the raging virus plague.

In most cases, once you install your antivirus or security program, your work is done. Companies usually design antivirus software to start protecting your computer automatically, right out of the box. But you're free to adjust the program's settings if you feel the antivirus program is doing too much or too little. For example, if the automatic update window always seems to pop up while you're working, you can change the schedule to another time. Or if you're super paranoid, you can have it check for virus pattern updates more frequently.

Defeating Spyware

Spyware often arrives on your machine nestled inside the installer files for free software you download from the Internet—a game or file-sharing program, for example. Unfortunately for Windows fans, your operating system is spyware's prime target. Some spyware hogs your computer's processor, slowing it to a crawl and even causing other programs to crash. More belligerent types of spyware and overly aggressive adware give new meaning to the word nuisance—constantly changing your browser's home page, adding unwanted bookmarks, or pestering you with pop-up ads. And as it transfers information about you across the Internet, spyware can even create holes in your computer's security.

Sadly, it was probably you—yes, *you*—who let that spyware onto your computer in the first place. If you're like most people, you probably never read all the fine print on that dreary screen of legalese that you have to click through every time you install new software. But if you'd read the user agreement, you may have seen that you were agreeing to allow the software's maker to monitor and collect information about your computer or Web-surfing habits. (Some spyware is so sneaky, though, that it may not even come with a legal agreement; it will just slither onto your PC without announcing itself.)

Here's a representative bit of creepy fine-print legalese, whereby you install a program: "…in exchange for your agreement to also install ad-serving software, which will display pop-up, pop-under, and other types of ads on your computer based on the information we collect as stated in this Privacy Statement."

Needless to say, you don't need a Harvard law degree to see that this software is going to flood your screen with pop-up advertisements. Unless you want a screen full of ads, click the "I don't accept" box on the user-agreement screen or cancel the software installation (which probably happens anyway if you reject the user agreement).

Trying to pry spyware off your system if you've gone ahead and installed it can be an exercise in frustration. If you try to uninstall it with the Windows Add/ Remove control panel (Start → Control Panel → Add or Remove Programs), you'll find that it reappears the next time you start your PC. (Technically, that's because it's buried a backup copy of itself somewhere on your hard drive or added multiple entries for itself in your Windows registry file.)

Yanking out the spyware may also cause that free game or program you wanted in the first place to stop working, but you may not even care about that by then because you just want your computer back. Whatever your current relationship with spyware is, you may want to look into a rising new category of protective programs: *antispyware* software.

Most of the Internet security suites mentioned on page 407 include protection against spyware infestation. But if antispyware is all you need, here are a few to consider for your Windows PC:

- **Webroot Spy Sweeper.** One of the most comprehensive spyware shields available, Spy Sweeper rarely misses a trick. It ferrets out programs that hijack your browser, infest your Startup folder, and so on. The company's Web site also offers free PC spyware scans, so you can see whether you have a problem before you plunk down the bucks; you need to download an 8-megabyte program to your PC to run the scan, which may make some people feel a little spied-upon. (*www.webroot.com*)

- **Sunbelt CounterSpy.** This award-winning program makes short work of spyware. It also constantly monitors certain checkpoints around your PC to make sure no spies are loitering. (*www.sunbeltsoftware.com*)

- **Spybot Search & Destroy.** Free, feisty, and famous for its spywhacking, Spybot Search & Destroy has cleaned PCs the world over for years. If you try this software and like it, consider donating to this valiant effort. You'll find a PayPal link on the Download page. (*www.safer-networking.org*)

- **Lavasoft Ad-Aware.** Ad-Aware was one of the earliest antispyware programs, and it's still growing. You can download the free Ad-Aware Personal version, which removes spyware and similar infiltrators from your PC. Or for $27, you can bump up to Ad-Aware Plus and get scheduling and logging features, automatic updates, a continuous scanning option that blocks spyware that tries to install itself, and more. If you have an always-on broadband connection and spend a lot of time on the Web, the Plus option just might pay for itself in peace of mind. Its automatic features shoulder the burden of keeping spyware at bay. (*www.lavasoft.de*)

• **Windows Defender.** Microsoft is developing its own spyware stopper; you can download a free test version at *http://www.microsoft.com/athome/ security/spyware/default.mspx*.

Tip: It's OK to protect yourself with more than one antispyware program. If your chosen spyguard is letting in a few nuisances, beef up your defense by adding another program.

At this writing, "Macintosh spyware" is still an oxymoron. If you're worried that the Mac's freedom from spyware may one day change, though, anti-spyware software companies are only too happy to take your money.

For example, SecureMac (*www.securemac.com*) has the latest news on every known Mac security issue and how to deal with it. The news and information are free, but SecureMac also sells its own antispyware program—MacScan. For $25, it promises to remove Trojan horses, spyware, and other Mac attackers.

Note: Internet service providers like America Online, MSN, and Earthlink provide antivirus, spyware, and firewall protection to their members free of charge. Check with your provider to see what defenses they offer and make sure you're using the latest version of the software.

Controlling Cookies

The *cookies* that Web sites silently and invisibly deposit on your hard drive are usually as sweet and harmless as they sound. These tiny text files are preference-setting files for individual Web sites. When Amazon.com greets you with "Welcome, Casey!" (or whatever your name is), or when NYTimes.com gives you access to the special, fee-only articles you've paid for, you know they've stored a cookie on your hard drive so they can recognize you when you return.

But when an advertiser on a Web site gives your computer a cookie, it does you no good at all. Called *third-party* or *tracking* cookies, these text files benefit only the advertiser. As long as you carry that cookie, the advertiser can keep track of your surfing habits. When you visit one of its affiliated Web sites, the company can use that information to show you ads likely to tempt you into clicking. If you think tracking cookies are an invasion of your privacy, you're not alone.

Beware of Adware?

My brother says that the ads in my email pro-gram's window do the exact same thing as spy-ware. He says the program monitors my online activities and reports back to the company, which could use that information in any number of ways. Should I be worried?

Probably not.

Many useful programs happen to be adware. A company gives you the software gratis, but in return you have to look at a few advertisements each time you use it. It's a simple quid pro quo deal. For example, Eudora's email program (page 259) is free—if you don't mind seeing a few ads while you send and receive email. (The ads go away when you close the program.) The paid ver-sion doesn't show you the ads.

Like spyware, adware programs may run in the background of your PC and quietly transmit infor-mation about your online activities back to the mother ship, even if you don't actually have the program's window open onscreen. That's how it figures out what ads might interest you.

However, adware makers don't want spyware's bad reputation rubbing off on them, so they take pains to be more upfront about what information they gather and how they use it. For instance, some versions of WeatherBug, a popular program for displaying temperatures and weather forecasts, can pester you with pop-up ads and even install *other* programs on your PC. But that's only because you agreed to it.

The moral of the story: Read the fine print when-ever you install any software that connects to the Internet. Even if the user agreement is 16 pages long onscreen, scan the text for the area concern-ing Privacy, which is where you'll find details about the info an ad program collects. Especially if the program you've downloaded is adware, make sure you know what you're getting into before you click that Install button.

Fortunately, Web browsers have no trouble spotting—and refusing—third-party cookies. You simply set your browser to block cookies that come from sites *other than* the one you're visiting. To change your cookie settings, pro-ceed like this:

- **Internet Explorer for Windows.** Choose Tools → Internet Options → Pri-vacy, and then click the Advanced button. In the Advanced Privacy Settings window (Figure 21-2), turn on "Override automatic cookie handling" and then, under "Third-party Cookies", select Block.

Figure 21-2:
Internet Explorer's cookie controls are buried in the Advanced Privacy Settings dialog box. Go to the Tools → Internet Options → Privacy tab and click the Advanced button. Here, you can choose to have the browser block cookies from third-party sites that want to snoop on your surfing whereabouts.

- **Safari.** Choose Safari → Preferences, and go to the Security panel. Next to Accept Cookies, select "Only from sites you navigate to." This option even explains that it's going to block advertisers' cookies.

- **Firefox.** Choose Tools → Options → Privacy → Cookies. Put checkmarks in the boxes next to "Allow sites to set cookies" and "For the originating site only."

Tip: Somewhere in your browser's Options or Preferences you'll find an option to delete all cookies already on your computer. You can erase your tracks this way, although you'll also erase personalized settings for some Web sites.

Phishing Lures

Phishing is the 21st-century version of a tired old con. You get an email message from eBay (or PayPal, or your credit card company, ISP, or bank) urging you to update or correct your account information. There's even a link considerately offering to take you to the form you need to fill out. Should you do it? Well, would you let a stranger into your house just because he's carrying a clipboard and says the gas company needs to check your furnace?

In a word, no. Don't even think about it. Don't click any links in the email body. Don't reply to the message or attempt to contact the sender. Even if the email address or URL *looks* like it's from a legitimate company—PayPal, Visa Card Services, or whatever—it never is. These links redirect you to a different Web site, a phony one, set up by the perpetrators to rob you of your passwords, credit card numbers, and even your identity. The perpetrator is just *fishing* for your personal information (get it?). Unfortunately, these scams go on year after year because people keep falling for them.

As phishing has gotten more sophisticated, software to combat it has also stepped up. Some Internet security suites (like Trend Micro) now include phishing protection. Newer email programs like Mozilla Thunderbird even alert you to suspicious messages (Figure 21-3). The latest browsers, including Internet Explorer 7, also let you know, with all the subtlety of a sledge-hammer, when you've visited a Web site that's not what it pretends to be.

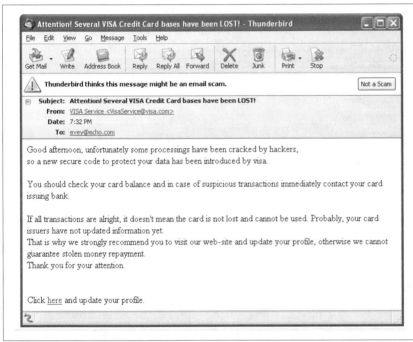

Figure 21-3:
Phishing lures are cast far and wide around the Internet. Fortunately, newer email programs like Thunderbird are equipped to help you spot scams. Look at the warning bar across the top of this phishy email message. For more tips on managing email, see Chapter 14.

There's a simple way to avoid phishing altogether: Never, ever give a Web site personal information like Social Security numbers, account numbers, or passwords unless *you* initiated the communication. Ignore any email that asks you to supply personal or financial information. If a legitimate company needs to contact you, it will send you a letter or wait until the next time you log into your account.

Tip: For more information about how to protect yourself from phishing threats, or if you want to file a complaint, visit the Federal Trade Commission's helpful site at *http://onguardonline.gov*.

Sealing Your Computer's Firewall

Believe it or not, there are even more bad things that can happen when you're online. Total strangers, next door or in Eastern Europe, can connect to your Windows PC, invisibly take control of it, and turn it into, for example, a relay station that helps them pump out millions of pieces of spam (junk email) every day. You might notice that your PC has slowed down, and you might not. But you've just become part of the problem.

How is this possible? To understand the technical underpinnings, you need to know about *ports*.

Ports are like TV channels. Your PC has a bunch of them, each one dedicated to letting certain kinds of Internet information pass through: surfing the Web, sending email, downloading files, playing videos, and so on. Trouble is, Internet intruders roaming around online know how to use these ports to their advantage. They use software that can slip into your PC through one of these ports.

Ready to yank your modem cable out of the wall yet? Relax. You can stop the baddies just by using a *firewall*, a security barrier that prevents people or programs from sneaking into your machine via your Internet connection. A firewall can be a software program or a physical piece of hardware.

Good firewalls can monitor both incoming and outgoing traffic. So, in addition to keeping out intruders, your firewall can detect—and stop—spyware or a virus trying to transmit information *from* your computer.

Hardware Firewalls

A hardware firewall is a physical box sitting squarely between your computer and the Internet outside so potential intruders can't see your machine. You may have one and not even know it. For example, if you've installed a *router* (page 17) so that more than one computer can share your cable modem, you may be delighted to learn that it's probably a hardware firewall. It constantly screens the traffic to and from your networked computers.

Even if you don't have a home network, a router with a built-in firewall is a good investment, especially if you have a broadband connection. When shopping, look for a router with a firewall that includes both SPI (Stateful Packet Inspection) and NAT (Network Address Translation). Security products like the AlphaShield (*www.alphashield.com*)—which plugs in between your computer and your broadband modem—also monitor all Internet traffic and block any suspicious activity.

Making Exceptions to the Firewall

Windows Firewall takes your security very seriously—sometimes *too* seriously. It may balk at letting you play online games or exchange instant messages. If you see a message like "Should AcroRD32.exe be allowed to connect to the Internet?", it means a program (Adobe Acrobat Reader, in this case) needs to go online and hunt for information or updates.

You can eliminate these annoying questions by making trusted programs (like Acrobat Reader) *exceptions* to the firewall's rules. Programs on the Exceptions list always pass through the firewall unhindered.

To add a program to the Windows Firewall Exceptions list, follow these steps:

First, Choose Start → Control Panel → Security Center → Windows Firewall. (Or, if you use the Control Panel's Classic view, just choose Start → Control Panel → Windows Firewall.) Now, in the Windows Firewall box, click the Exceptions tab and then click the Add Program button.

The firewall displays a list of programs it recognizes. If the program you want to add to the exceptions is listed, click its name and then click OK.

If you don't see the program in question, click Browse. In the dialog box that opens, navigate to and select the program's icon. Click OK. The program joins the Exceptions list, which means it can get past the firewall and talk to other computers or programs on the Internet.

Some programs, on the other hand, *ask* you for access. For example, the *World of Warcraft* online game requires you to open two of those Internet *ports:* TCP port 3724 and TCP port 6112. (If you're having trouble connecting your video game or any other program to the outside world, check its manual to see if it requires certain ports to be open on your computer.)

To do this advanced surgery, go back to the Windows Firewall Exceptions tab as described above. Then, in the lower part of the box, click Add Port. When the "Add a Port" dialog box opens, fill it in, as shown in Figure 21-4.

(If your firewall one day becomes so overloaded with exceptions that it feels about as secure as a piece of Swiss cheese, you can reset it back to the way it originally was by clicking the Advanced tab in the Windows Firewall box and clicking the Restore Defaults button.)

Software Firewalls

A software firewall is good protection, too. No wonder both Windows and Mac OS X come with such a feature built right in. (All the Internet security suites described on page 407 include firewall programs as well.)

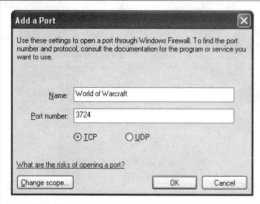

Add a Port

Use these settings to open a port through Windows Firewall. To find the port number and protocol, consult the documentation for the program or service you want to use.

Name: World of Warcraft

Port number: 3724

⦿ TCP   ◯ UDP

What are the risks of opening a port?

Change scope...   OK   Cancel

Figure 21-4:
Occasionally, to get a program through the firewall, you must open the port it wants to use. On the Windows Firewall Exceptions tab, click the Add Port button. In the "Add a Port" dialog box, type a name (so you'll remember why you're opening that particular port) and enter the port number, which you can usually find in the program's manual or Web site.

Tip: If you have a hardware firewall (like a router), you don't need to turn on a software firewall too.

The Windows XP Firewall

When Windows XP first appeared back in 2001, it came with a nifty new feature—built-in firewall software. Unfortunately, Microsoft left the firewall turned off, and few people could find it to turn it on. So, in the interest of greater security, Service Pack 2 (which Microsoft released a few years later) automatically flips the Windows Firewall on. In fact, once you install this update, Windows XP pesters you (by popping up yellow warning balloons from the taskbar) if you turn the firewall off.

If you do have Service Pack 2 installed—either because you installed it or because you bought your computer after October 2004—you can find the on/off switch for the firewall like this. Choose Start → Control Panel → Security Center → Windows Firewall. (If you use the Control Panel's Classic view, choose Start → Control Panel → Windows Firewall.) On the General tab of the Windows Firewall control panel, click the button next to "On (recommended)" and then click OK. The firewall's off button is here, too, if you need to shut it down for a minute to troubleshoot your Internet connection or something.

Note: If you like the sound of a sturdy, free firewall that's more powerful (because it blocks traffic coming *and* going through your computer) check out ZoneAlarm (*www.zonelabs.com*). With a friendlier interface, ZoneAlarm is often easier to use than the built-in Windows Firewall, which is set to block unauthorized traffic coming *to* your PC from the outside world, but it may not be much help against programs on your PC trying to sneak *out* to the Internet without your permission. ZoneAlarm works with systems as far back as Windows 98SE, so it gives you a firewall option if your PC is too old to run Windows XP. (And if you do have Windows XP, you can still use ZoneAlarm. The Windows Firewall is savvy enough to get out of the way when you install an alternative program.)

To try the software, scroll down to the bottom of ZoneLabs' home page and click "Free ZoneAlarm and Trials." You can get the free version here or buy the $50 full-featured edition with more controls and technical support. Once you download and install the program, ZoneAlarm makes your machine invisible to other computers nosing around on the Net.

Setting up the Mac OS X firewall

Apple's system security for its Mac OS X Tiger system is even stricter than Microsoft's: Out of the box, *all* communication ports and services on the Mac are closed to the outside. (That's one reason the Mac hasn't attracted hackers like Windows has.) The Mac also comes with its own built-in firewall that blocks all incoming Internet traffic *except* for the programs you allow through.

Its factory setting is Off, though, so you need to give it a little click-start.

To turn on the Mac OS X firewall, follow these steps:

1. **Go to → System Preferences → Sharing. Click the Firewall tab, and then click the Start button.**

   The Mac fires up its firewall software. Again, the firewall starts out blocking every sort of Internet communication, so you must *turn on* the ones you want to use.

2. **In the Allow list, select the programs or functions you want to let through the firewall.**

   As shown in Figure 21-5, turn on the checkboxes next to, say, iTunes Music Sharing and other network services you plan to use.

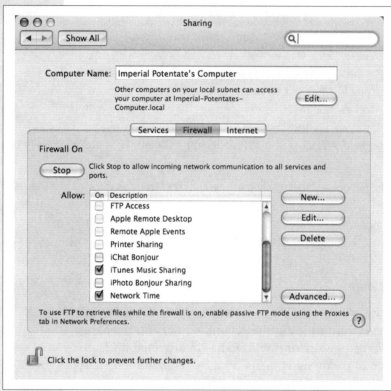

Figure 21-5:
*Mac OS X starts out fully
barricaded against Internet
intrusions. However, you can let
programs and services through
the firewall by simply selecting
them in the Firewall tab on the
Sharing preferences window.*

Tip: Want to make sure your computer's firewall is doing its job? Several online sites offer to knock on your computer's ports and see if there are any openings for intruders to slither through. Check out ShieldsUP (*www.grc.com*), Hackercheck (*www.hackercheck.com*), or Planet Security's firewall check (*www.planet-security.net*).

Protecting Your Kids

The Internet appeals to children's uninhibited, adventurous spirits. Kids find it rewarding to look up information themselves, explore online museum exhibits, and try their hand at interactive games. But the Internet isn't a babysitter, and it has millions of people prowling around on it. Some sites and services (and, quite frankly, some of the aforementioned *people*) just aren't suitable for children.

Tip: If you hear your kids talking about their online adventures and you have no idea *what* they're talking about—IM? Blogging? Podcasts?—check out Chapters 15 and 19. This book demystifies it all.

FREQUENTLY ASKED QUESTION

Private Info, Public Networks

Is it safe to connect to the Internet via the free wireless network at my local coffee shop?

If your favorite coffee joint has a WiFi hotspot (page 32), it's fine to browse the latest news and sports on your laptop while sipping a latte. However, be wary of doing online banking or any transactions that involve passwords, credit card numbers, or account information—even email, since it involves a password. It turns out that with the assistance of easily available free "sniffer" programs, strangers sitting nearby using their own laptops on the same wireless hotspot can, in theory, intercept text that gets sent from your computer.

Using a firewall can keep your laptop secure, and many firewalls have settings specifically for use on wireless networks. But your data is still flying around the airwaves.

Another WiFi hazard is the *evil twin*—a wireless hotspot that *looks* like the coffee shop's or hotel's network. In reality, someone with the nefarious intention of stealing your personal information has created this imposter hotspot.

So when you're out and about with your laptop or other wireless device, play it safe: stick to casual surfing and leave your passwords at home.

Ground Rules for Kids

If your children use the Internet, it's important to set up some ground rules to keep everyone safe and happy. For starters, keep the computer visible in a public location of your home, like the den or family room. Consider limiting the amount of time youngsters spend online, too.

But because you can't be looking over your kids' shoulders every minute, you can use protective software to filter out inappropriate material, as discussed in the box on page 421.

There are also some basic words of wisdom to give to any child or teenager surfing the Internet:

• Never give out your full name. Use a nickname or first name online.

• Never give out a telephone number or home address to someone you meet online.

• Never give out your passwords.

• Never agree to meet someone you met online in person.

• Never email or post photographs of yourself online.

• Never assume that everyone online tells the truth about who they are.

- Never hesitate to tell a parent if someone is harassing or bothering you online.

Advice for Parents

With the boom in chat rooms (page 306), personal blogs (page 357), message boards (page 311), and Web-based social networking sites like MySpace (page 334) that give plenty of opportunities for kids to express themselves online, getting youngsters to stick to the house rules can be difficult—but it's vitally important. Parents looking for more information on letting their kids use the Internet safely may want to do some further reading around the Web:

- **WiredSafety.** Perhaps the most all-inclusive Internet safety and help group on the Web, this site has sections of special interest for parents, law-enforcement officers, educators, women, and kids of all ages. WiredSafety keeps readers up to date on the latest issues affecting the online world. (*www.wiredsafety.com*)

- **SafeKids.** Jam-packed with safety tips and guidelines for the parents of children and teens using the Internet, this site also has a discussion forum and news updates on the latest viruses, spam, and scams going around. (*www. safekids.com*)

- **StaySafe.** This is an educational site funded by Microsoft that focuses on both the positive aspects of Internet life and secure navigation through the negative. (*www.staysafe.org*)

- **GetNetWise.** This frank, no-nonsense site for parents offers tips, tools, and plenty of practical advice for protecting the young ones online. (*http://kids. getnetwise.org*)

Tip: Want some great sites to keep your baby Web surfers educated and entertained? KidSites (*www.kidsites.com*) and the American Library Association's Great Web Sites for Kids page (*www. ala.org/greatsites*) are great places to start. Another option is FirstGov for Kids (*www.kids.gov*), which provides links to NASA's page for young space fans, national museum sites, and many states' Web pages among its varied offerings.

Software That Keeps Kids Safer

Your computer's operating system or your Internet provider may give you some tools that help make the Web a family-friendly experience. If you don't like what you already have, you can shop around for specialized programs that let you filter what your child can see on the Web and set preprogrammed time limits for Internet use.

Mac OS X 10.4 lets you set up user accounts (→ System Preferences → Accounts) for each child that limit his browsing to bookmarked sites. You can also set up a list of approved friends with whom the child can communicate by email and iChat; everybody else is off limits. If you're a Windows household, look for Microsoft's upcoming Family Safety Settings on the Windows Live site (*www.live. com*). This Web-based service can block specified sites and provide activity reports of where a child has been online. (Windows Vista, the 2007 version of Windows, has elaborate parental controls, too.)

ISPs like America Online and MSN also offer built-in controls that let you limit your offsprings' activities online. If you've purchased an Internet security suite (page 407), it probably includes basic parental control features that can block certain Web sites or prevent private information from being sent over the Internet.

If you're willing to spend $40 to $60, you can buy a separate parental-control program. Windows fans have their choice of software like CyberPatrol (*www.cyberpatrol.com*), Net Nanny (*www. netnanny.com*), CyberSieve (*www.softforyou.com*), and ContentProtect (*www.contentwatch.com*). CYBERsitter (*www.cybersitter.com*) and ContentBarrier (*www.intego.com*) help Mac-based parents do the same.

Remember, however, that no filtering software is perfect. Some overzealous programs block sites containing health information and other legitimate topics. And kids have a knack for stumbling onto things you'd rather they not see until they're about 40 and happily married. The ultimate defense against the ills of the Internet is an honest, forthright relationship with your kids in which they feel free to talk about what they've seen online.

Index

M

Colophon

Marlowe Shaeffer was the production editor and proofreader for *The Internet: The Missing Manual*. Sanders Kleinfeld and Genevieve d'Entremont provided quality control. Mary Brady provided production assistance. Michele Filshie wrote the index.

The cover of this book is based on a series design by David Freedman. Karen Montgomery produced the cover layout with Adobe InDesign CS using Adobe's Minion and Gill Sans fonts.

David Futato designed the interior layout, based on a series design by Phil Simpson. This book was converted by Abby Fox to FrameMaker 5.5.6. The text font is Adobe Minion; the heading font is Adobe Formata Condensed; and the code font is LucasFont's TheSans Mono Condensed. The illustrations that appear in the book were produced by Robert Romano and Jessamyn Read using Macromedia FreeHand MX and Adobe Photoshop CS.

Better than e-books

Buy *The Internet: The Missing Manual* and access the digital edition FREE on Safari for 45 days.

Go to www.oreilly.com/go/safarienabled
and type in coupon code 6FRG-VEGP-VTPH-YHPN-TQZ6

Search
over 2000 top
tech books

Download
whole chapters

Cut and Paste
code examples

Find
answers fast

Search Safari! The premier electronic reference
library for programmers and IT professionals

Related Titles from O'Reilly

Missing Manuals

Access 2003 for Starters:
The Missing Manual

AppleScript:
The Missing Manual

AppleWorks 6: The Missing
Manual

Creating Web Sites:
The Missing Manual

Dreamweaver 8: The Missing
Manual

Dreamweaver MX 2004:
The Missing Manual

eBay: The Missing Manual

Excel: The Missing Manual

Excel for Starters:
The Missing Manual

FileMaker Pro 8:
The Missing Manual

Flash 8: The Missing Manual

FrontPage 2003:
The Missing Manual

GarageBand 2:
The Missing Manual

Google: The Missing Manual,
2nd Edition

Home Networking:
The Missing Manual

iLife '05: The Missing Manual

iMovie 6 & iDVD:
The Missing Manual

iPhoto 6: The Missing Manual

iPod & iTunes: The Missing
Manual, *4th Edition*

iWork '05: The Missing
Manual

Mac OS X: The Missing
Manual, *Tiger Edition*

Office 2004 for Macintosh:
The Missing Manual

PCs: The Missing Manual

Photoshop Elements 4:
The Missing Manual

QuickBooks 2006:
The Missing Manual

Quicken 2006 for Starters:
The Missing Manual

Switching to the Mac:
The Missing Manual,
Tiger Edition

Windows 2000 Pro:
The Missing Manual

Windows XP for Starters:
The Missing Manual

Windows XP Pro: The Missing
Manual, *2nd Edition*

Windows XP Home Edition:
The Missing Manual,
2nd Edition